C000136074

12th Edition
WRECKS & RELICS

Compiled by Ken Ellis

MIDLAND COUNTIES PUBLICATIONS

Contents

Cover photographs:

Front: Imports from the Eastern bloc have been at the forefront of fashion since W&R11. Here we have former Hungarian Air Force MiG-21PF '503' alias G-BRAO with Aces High at North Weald (Alan Curry)

Back: Emphasising that *Wrecks & Relics* embraces rejuvenation as well as dereliction, former Belgian Air Force Spitfire LF.IXc SM-29/MK912 in the early stages of restoration at Ludham, August 1989 (Chris Michell)

Everybody's favourite Viscount G-APIM *Stephen Piercey* at Southend just prior to its move to a safe haven at the Brooklands Museum (Sebastian Zacharias)

Copyright 1990
Ken Ellis and Midland Counties Publications
ISBN 0 904597 82 2

This twelfth edition published by
Midland Counties Publications (Aerophile) Limited
24 The Hollow, Earl Shilton, Leicester, LE9 7NA

Printed in England
by BL & U Printing Limited, Wellingborough

Introduction

Another crowded two years have shot by and it is time for the 12th Edition. In between **W&R11** and **W&R12** the compiler and, more importantly, the publishers experimented with the introduction of a **Pocket Version** in May 1989. This was aimed at those readers who said the 'real' thing was too bulky (or even precious!) to take out and about and that two years was too long to wait for another fix! The **Pocket Edition** has been termed a 'mid-life update' by one reader but here and at Earl Shilton it is universally called **MiniWrecks** and this is how it has been referred to in the main text. If the existence of this work is new to you, it is still available – see the rear. Current plans have another one coming out in 1991 so stay tuned.

Much more significantly, we have invaded Europe! Well, more precisely Mike Bursell has extended the theme with the long awaited **European Wrecks & Relics**. More details appear at the rear of this book, but this is a major work that puts this version into the shade. Congratulations to Mike. **EuroWrecks** should be on your bookshelf now. If it isn't, go get it!

W&R11 suffered from the problems of integrating new technology with a decidedly old technology compiler. This time 'Deep Fraught II' has been introduced and it is hoped has improved the readability of the text no end. Other than that, the renaming of this the 'Introduction' and the more correct use of the 'Preface' to provide the oft-requested 'overview' and increased photographic coverage are the only major changes to format and presentation.

Now to the nice bit of thanking people for their many efforts to make this work a reality. More credits follow, but the following deserve singling out. Checking off the draft in its myriad forms were **John Coghill, Trevor Green** and **Dave Peel**, ably assisted by **Roy Bonser**. Much of the photographic coverage was supplied or overseen by **Alan Curry**; the mapwork is the domain of **Bev Risdon** and additional thanks go to **Duncan Cubitt** and **Kevin Chevis** of Key Publishing.

To all of the staff at **Midland Counties Publications** go my many thanks for their patience and skills, in particular to **Neil Lewis** and **Chris Salter**.

As ever, **Tom Poole** took on the bulk of the cross-checking and sleuthing work. Not content with working crazy hours with me on a day-to-day basis, **Dave Allport** has devoted large chunks of his 'spare' to making this work the definitive creature we believe it to be.

My thanks to all these people and to those given acknowledgement elsewhere and in the photo credits. Here's to the next one which can be termed **Edition 13** or **Edition 12A** depending on your sensibilities!

Deadline for material for the **2nd Pocket Edition** is scheduled for December 31, 1990 and for **Wrecks & Relics 13** December 31, 1991.

Ken Ellis
May 1990

Myddle Cottage, Welland Terrace, off Mill Lane, Barrowden, Oakham, Leicestershire LE15 8EH.

Preface

It has always been the intention of the compiler to make sure that **W&R** contained plenty of narrative so that readers get to know what is going on in the world of preservation, instead of just digesting a great wad of numbers. Several readers have asked that this be extended to a sort of 'overview' and to that end, herewith a very personal view of happenings and trends since **W&R11** raised its head. As with every other element of the book, your comments are always welcomed.

Armed Forces

With the **Royal Air Force** the wind-down of the Lightnings at Binbrook has caused the greatest ripples within the pages of **W&R**. Several dealers appear to have got their fingers burnt in the belief that there was a rich and limitless market out there! Phantoms from Leuchars are due to enter long term storage at Wattisham and the first Harrier GR.3s have begun to appear on dumps. At Abingdon the scrapping of the hapless Nimrod AEW.3 fleet is going on alongside the resurrection of the final stored VC-10s for use as tankers. The two remaining 60 Squadron Pembrokes will have gone by the time these words are read. As we closed for press, the tragic loss of the 8 Squadron Shackleton with ten souls on board on 30/4/90 was a shattering blow to an impeccable safety record in the definite twilight hours of the breed.

An era ended during 1989 with the closure of the fire school at Catterick and Manston fully taking on the mantle. Over at St Athan, the various craft schools have again rejoiced in the label of 4 School of Technical Training.

With the new policy towards gate guardians (see below) Ministry of Defence tender documents winged their way the world over to interested parties. As well as this form of disposal, the notion of the auction raised its head again. (Last used for the dissolution of the Colerne collection.) The sale held on 9/3/90 in London set new records for airframes and may well point the way to a future dominated by dealers.

With the **Fleet Air Arm** the Sea Devon and the Heron fleet went to auction and the Canberra T.22s at St Athan cannot be far off release. The **Army Air Corps** said goodbye to that lovely noisy stationary airborne object, the Beaver, and the type was snapped up by overseas operators. With the **United States Air Force**, Kemble came back into its own, with a cache of F-5E Tigers to rework and move on. At Midlenhall an early C-130 Hercules arrived for BDR training.

Fortunes have been mixed for the various historic flights. The **Fleet Air Arm Historic Aircraft Flight** lost the Sea Fury FB.11 on 10/6/89 (thankfully without loss of life) but regained the Sea Hawk. **Vintage Pair** lost another Meteor and its pilot on 30/5/88. Since then they have been grounded, although both a Vampire and Meteor have been found from other sources. **Battle of Britain Memorial Flight** reflew their own long-term restoration of a Spitfire XIX and have a Mk IX being 'eyed' for them at Abingdon. Their Visitor Centre goes from strength to strength. At Benson, the painstaking restoration of the **Bf 109** continues and it will be the subject of an historic melding of the RAF and the Imperial War Museum in operation. While there is cause for optimism, the operation of the mighty Vulcan by the **Vulcan Display Flight** is under review and we must atune ourselves that one day she will fly no more. Over in Eire, the **Irish Army Air Corps** have established an unofficial historic flight with the reflying of a Chipmunk T.20.

British Aviation Preservation Council

Largest change with the Council has been the adoption of the word 'Aviation' instead of 'Aircraft' within its title. This is to reflect the wide variety of interests and activities going in within its fold. Much of what is talked of below is direct BAPC activity, but the section devoted to the Council can be found in the rear as usual.

Classics

Some may argue with this title, but the compiler dislikes the Vintage/Veteran label
and needing to split warbirds away, this seemed a workable term. Much of the
activity in the classic 'department' is beyond the scope of **W&R** and has been
dominated with the mass import of aircraft from the USA - with the Luscombe taking
the numerical honours. It is difficult to pick out highlights from the realms of
W&R coverage, but several long-term inmates of the book have taken to flight. At
Hatch, Tim Moore's **Skysport** rebuilt Bleriot XI G-AVXV and it made a valiant attempt
to fly the Channel on 25/7/89, only to ditch just short of the achievement. From
the same stable came a magnificent reconstruction of the former Nigel Ponsford
Bristol F.2b frame into a museum exhibit for Belgium - bringing a Spitfire back to
the UK. Further south, Ron Souch's **Antique Aircraft Company** reflew DH.90 Dragonfly
G-AEDT in 1988 and Hawk Speed Six G-ADGP the following year. Over at **Breighton**
Aeronca 100 G-AEVS took to the air again in 1989. On a more depressing note, the
East Anglian Aviation Society's painstaking restoration of Dragon Rapide G-AJHO was
burnt out in a forced-landing 5/2/89. At Redhill, the **Tiger Club** have left as they
do not operate Lear Jets. Thankfully the lovely people at Headcorn have welcomed
them.

Gate Guardians

Most significant decision from the Historic Aircraft Committee (HAC) for many a
long year was the now-famous solution to the vexed question of the continued
presence on gates of precious Spitfires. HAC came up with two policy decisions.
First was that the expense of keeping gate guardians was to be closely controlled
in future by the application of the one gate-one aircraft policy. The chosen
aircraft was ideally to be relevant to the history of the base in question. All
other guardians were to be offered for tender. Secondly, the Spitfires were to be
replaced by plastic full-size replicas and that the bulk of the Spitfires released
from gate duty would be used in trades by the RAF Museum. There followed a series
of 'culls' at gates that is to a lesser extent still continuing and a rash plastic
Spitfires and Hurricanes have appeared.
    Funding the plastic Spitfires fell to the enterprise of Tim Routsis of Historic
Flying Ltd (HFL) who had entered into negotiations to this end. In return for some
of the Spitfires from the gates, HFL have supplied the plastic replicas and will
oversee the delivery of a Bristol Beaufort and Curtiss P-40 in museum display
condition from the USA for the RAF Museum. It may seem that HFL have made a
killing here, but the expense of building, supplying and maintaining the plastic
replicas, plus the not inconsiderable cost involved in acquiring and delivering
the Beaufort and P-40 will not leave much leeway after the value of the real
Spitfires in the deal is taken into account. It remains to be seen just what the
RAF Museum will be allowed to achieve with the 'barter' Spitfires no lying at St
Athan.

Groups

Much activity, as ever, with the many amateur aviation groups across the country.
Bill Miles, main mover behind the **North Weald Aircraft Restoration Flight** (NWARF)
died in late 1988 and the Flight stopped operations shortly afterwards. Ironically
named, the **Phoenix Aviation Museum**, formed out of the ruins of the Loughborough
Leicester group before it, folded in 1989 and its Vampire went to the Newark Air
Museum. Also closing its operations has been the **Scottish Aircraft Collection
Trust**, outliving the Strathallan Collection that it was initially designed to
'rescue' by only a matter of months. (See below.) With only the Fa 330 on show at
Manchester to its name in terms of airframes, the **Merseyside Aviation Society** has
also been wound up. Their major contribution to preservation lies in being the
original publishers of **W&R**, but their magazine and book policy leaves a void in the
world of amateur publishing.
    With the move of John May and family to Scotland and the loss of their operating
base, the **Wessex Aviation Society** have turned their attentions to acting in support
of the Southampton Hall of Aviation, with their airframes admirably filling gaps in
that Museum's terms of reference. **Berkshire Aviation Group** are making good

progress towards the establishment of a museum on the site of the former Woodley aerodrome. Also making good progress in the same direction is the **Gloucestershire Aircraft Collection**, with hopes of premises at Gloucester/Cheltenham Airport and the **Staffordshire Aviation Museum** who are starting to assemble aircraft at the former Seighford airfield. Chris Brydges and friends have managed to establish the **Grimsby Aircraft Preservation Group** and are striving towards the establishment of the **Museum of Weapons Technology** in Grimsby.

Established with a very different aim from other groups in recent times is the Bruntingthorpe-based **Lightning Preservation Group**. They have set themselves the sensible aim of preserving and cherishing a single example of the breed, but to keep life pouring through it by staging regular engine and taxi runs. These events have aroused considerable interest and their membership accordingly shows little reliance on geography, 'pulling' its volunteers from long distance.

The work of the **Cotswold Aircraft Restoration Group** should be familiar with most readers. Their unselfish list of 'supply missions' to other groups and worthy operations continues to swell. During 1989 they were honoured with a well deserved Scania Transport Trust award. Another group operating along similar lines recently has been the **South Yorkshire Aircraft Preservation Society** who have been instrumental in moving and storing airframes until new owners could be found for them - they helped considerable in the wind-down of the NWARF for instance.

Museums

Here we deal with museums open to the public on a very regular basis and hope no offence is caused to those organisations dealt with under 'Groups' above. The closure of the **Strathallan Collection** in late 1988 cannot have come as too much as surprise to most people, but it was the only major closure to talk of since **W&R11** which is something in the current economic climate. There may well be others to talk of by the time **W&R13** comes about. Keith Fordyce auctioned the majority of airframes held at the **Torbay Aircraft Museum**, but has plans to come back a-fighting in due course.

Opening up have been several new ventures, large and small : Elfan ap Rees saw his patience rewarded with achievement of the **International Helicopter Museum**; Dave Brett likewise, with the re-opening of the **Rebel Air Museum** and the transformation of the **Bomber County Aviation Museum** from Cleethorpes to Hemswell. Much needed in museum-starved Wales was the **Caernarfon Aviation Museum** which opened in 5/89. Also up and running by then where the collection at **RNAY Fleetlands** and **Fenland Aircraft Preservation Society**'s splendid venture at Wisbech. 1990 has seen Dave Cotton's collection gel together as the **Stratford Aircraft Collection** with an impressive list of hardware. **Lashenden Air Warfare Museum** announced plans early in 1990 for major expansion and **Newark Air Museum** opened their impressive hangar.

Dominating much of the headlines since the publication of **W&R11** has been the **Royal Air Force Museum** now under the command of Dr Michael Fopp. Grasping the nettle of a long period of inertia and not a little losing track of its terms of reference, Dr Fopp has brought a large number of airframes into Hendon and considerably enhanced the pace and style of the Museum. The breaking up of the Beverley caused many to throw their hands up in horror as the 'Battle of Britain Experience' made demands on space and finance. Poor management back when the 'Bev' touched down for the last time at Hendon, actually killed the noble beast, not recently decisions. Loss of the storage hangar at Henlow and the decision by the Ministry of Defence Historic Aircraft Committee (beyond the influence of RAFM) to close the fabulous St Athan collection put more airframes in auction, across to Hendon or over to swelling **Cosford**. This has also allowed some airframes to move elsewhere, including the Avro 504 to go to the **Manchester Museum of Science and Industry** for restoration under Basil Carlin and team.

Warbirds

Britain's warbird community has continued to expand and mature. Many of the operators and owners do not come within the scope of **W&R** as they are not part of a collection or museum. Importing from the USA has continued unabated, although there is a trade in the opposite direction. Inbounds have included two Avengers, four Corsairs, a Kingcobra, a Lightning and a Tigercat.

At Duxford, **The Fighter Collection** have established a top-class hangar and workshop facility that would be the envy of many US operations. Crowning this has come the first flight of the immaculate Hurricane restoration - true testament to their capabilities. Also at Duxford, the British Aerial Museum has been renamed **The Aeroplane Restoration Company** to properly reflect its skills and aims. While the rebuild of the Blenheim is central to its purpose, TARC has restored several airframes for the Imperial War Museum and has been involved in several restoration and recovery jobs.

The death of **Charles Church** in his 'series prototype' Mk V Spitfire on 1/7/89 was a severe blow to an ambitious warbird restoration and operation scheme. The Spitfire workshop is now **Dick Melton Aviation** and Dick and team continue to work their magic on the fleet and for other customers. The story of the Lancaster restoration and the aftermath of the Woodford hangar collapse looks set to grind on and on.

As with the USA and Australia, so with the UK. Jet warbirds are blossoming considerably. **Arnold Glass'** acquisition of a large slice of the 'Binbrook Air Force' led to hopes that this pioneering operator would put a Lightning on the show circuit, but this was not to be. Down at Plymouth another operator is trying to put a Lightning T.5 in the air. We shall await developments. Over at Bournemouth Adrian Gjertson and Eric Haywood have established the specialist **Jet Heritage Ltd** operating, buying, selling and maintaining, classic jets. Long-term jewel in their restoration crown is the former Connah's Quay Swift. More power to their elbow!

Acknowledgements

Wrecks & Relics is produced with the help of a large number of people and the compiler would like to thank the following specialists for their varied help with this edition :-

Alan Allen, Vampire sleuth and restorer; Peter R Arnold Spitfire historian and restorer; John G Chree for northern Scotland; Paul Crellin for constant up-dating and researching 'chestnuts'; Malcolm Fillmore for UK register observations; Alan Johnson for the latest news on the UK civil register; Maurice Morgan for handling the Scottish entries; Dave Pope for his extensive notes, particularly on all things Chipmunk and ATC; Paddy Porter - the answer to many a question!; Lloyd P Robinson for up-dates from his extensive travels; Robert Rudhall for monitoring museums and 'warbirds'; Bill Taylor for all things Eastern Counties and agricultural; Dave Wise for coverage of the 'Home Counties'.

Many people within the UK preservation movement have helped and my thanks are recorded below. Every museum and group receives a questionnaire before the assembly of each **W&R**. Names that don't appear here either can't read, can't write or have problems getting their act together!

Airborne Forces Museum; Colin Allen, Down-Bird UK; Museum of Army Transport; John Bagley, now retired from the Science Museum; Philip Baldock, Robertsbridge Aviation Society; Sandy Benzies, Aircraft Preservation Society of Scotland; Bomber County Aviation Museum; Dave Brett Rebel Air Museum; Bristol Museum and Art Gallery; Paul Brown, Avon Aviation Museum; David Buchanan, Kent Battle of Britain Museum; Paul Cannon, Newbury District Museum; Steve Challis British Classic Aircraft Restorations; Bob Coles Second World War Aircraft Preservation Society; Graham Cooper, RNAY Fleetlands Museum; A E Cormack, Royal Air Force Museum; David Cotton, Stratford Aircraft Collection; Major John Cross, Museum of Army Flying; D Davidson, Strathallan Estate; Lewis Deal, Medway Aircraft Preservation Society; Mike Dean Historical Radar Archive; N Devenish, Flambards Triple Theme Park; Peter Douthwaite, Yorkshire Air Museum; Huby Fairhead, Norfolk & Suffolk Aviation Museum; Ken Fern, The Helicopter Collection; Laurence Fitzgerald, Manchester Museum of Science and Industry; Peter Fitzgerald, Science Museum; Keith Fordyce, Torbay Aircraft Museum; Jean Fostekew, Berkshire Aviation Group; Martyn Hall, Midland Air Museum; Howard Heeley, Newark Air Museum; Tony Hewitt, Staffordshire Aviation Heritage Group; Eric Hayward, Jet Heritage Ltd; Harry Holmes, British Aerospace Avro Aircraft Restoration Society; Graham Jackson, Lightning Preservation Group; Andy King, Bristol Industrial Museum; David King, Booker Aircraft Museum; Peter Kirk, British Aviation Preservation Council; Les Lane, Battle of Britain Memorial Flight Visitor Centre; David Lee, Imperial War Museum, Duxford; Lincolnshire Aviation Heritage Centre; Ray Mackenzie-Blythe, Snowdon Mountain Aviation; Bob Major, Museum of Flight; Phil Maloney, Military Aircraft Preservation Group; A J Moor, Brenzett Museum; John Moore, Ulster Folk & Transport Museum; Tony Nuttall, Solway Aviation Society; Jeremy Parkin, Alpha Helicopters; M H Phipp, Wessex Aviation Society; Nigel Ponsford and Anne Lindsay, Ponsford Collection; Norman Pritchard, British Balloon Museum and Library; Neil Purvis, North East Aircraft Museum; Caroline Reed, Royal Engineers Museum; Elfan ap Rees, International Helicopter Museum; David Reid, Dumfries & Galloway Aviation Museum; P Robinson, City of Birmingham Musuem and Art Gallery; Mike Russell, Russavia Collection; Jim Rutland, North East Aircraft Museum; Elly Sallingboe, B-17 Preservation Ltd; Andy Saunders, Tangmere Military Aviation Museum; Chris Scivyer, Mosquito Aircraft Museum; Kelvin Sloper, City of Norwich Aviation Museum; Peter Smith, Friends of Biggin Hill; Graham Sparkes, The Aeroplane Collection; Carl Speddings, South Yorkshire Aircraft Preservation Society; David Stansfield, Pennine Aviation Museum; Peter Stoddart, Leicestershire Museums; Peter Symes, Shuttleworth Collection; Julian Temple, Brooklands Museum; Steve Thompson, Cotswold Aircraft Restoration

Group; <u>Graham Warner</u>, The Aeroplane Restoration Company; <u>Dave Westacott</u>, Newark Air Museum; <u>Kevin Whittaker</u>, Macclesfield Historical Aviation Society; <u>Graham Wickens</u>, Cirencester Air Group; <u>Nicola Wicksteed</u>, Fleet Air Arm Museum; <u>R J Willatt</u>, Fenland Aircraft Preservation Society; <u>Len Woodgate</u>, Aerospace Museum, Cosford; <u>Mike Woodley</u>, Aces High Flying Museum.

And to the many readers who have written in with snippets and observations since W&R11, such reports are the life-blood of the book. I look forward to hearing from you again in the next year and a bit. Many thanks to :-

Greg Baddeley; Tim R Badham; Frank Barnett-Jones; Martin Barsley; Darrel Bayley; Roger and Heater Brooks; Dave Burke; Graeme Carrott; Richard Cawsey; Dave Cheerless; Duncan Curtis; Eric Demi-Bee; Michael Drake; Bryn Elliott; Carrie Fisher; Julia Fordham; Wal Gandy; Ian Grierson; Ian Griffiths; Mikhail Sergevich Gorbachev; Steve Harris; Phil and Lynne Hewitt; D Higgins; Tim Hills; Steve Hird; Gawayne Hodgkiss; Dave Houghton; Scott Innes; Paul A Jackson; Wendy James; Alf Jenks; Nigel Kemp; John Winston Lennon; Steve Lister; Kevin MacDonald; Tony McCarthy; A Marsh; Chris Michell; Simon Murdoch; Dave Murray; Sid Nanson; Ian Oliver; Bob Parnell; Alan Partington; Clive Pattle; Col Pope; A G Preece; Francois Prins; R J Prichard; Chris Rea; Paul Regan; Steve Reglar; C Rooke; Steve Smith; Peter Spooner; Philip Stevens; Graham Taylor; TEAM 65; Keith Thompson; E J Thribb; Hugh Trevor; Michael Westwood; John Uncles; David Underwood; Evan Wylie; Sebastian Zacharias. And to those who I'm bound to have missed out!

Notes

Scope
Wrecks & Relics serves to outline, in as much detail as possible, the status and whereabouts of all known **PRESERVED** (ie in museum or other collections, under restoration etc); **INSTRUCTIONAL** (ie static airframes in use for training); and **DERELICT** (ie out of use for a long period of time, fire dump aircraft, scrapped or damaged etc) aircraft in the United Kingdom and Eire and Forces aircraft based on Crown Territory. Where information permits, all aircraft that fall into these categories are included, with the following exceptions :-
1] airworthy aircraft not part of a specific collection. 2] aircraft that fall into any of the above categories for only a short period of time. 3] aircraft without provision for a human pilot (unless registered in the BAPC system). 4] in general, aircraft will only be considered if they are at least a cockpit/nose section.

Entries
Generally, entries are all dealt with in a standard manner. As **W&R** covers a two year period, in this case 1988-1990, beyond the location header there is a narrative explaining the current status of the entry and outlining any airframes that have moved since the last edition. Airframes moving on are given <u>underlined</u> forwarding references. Thus, if the reader wishes, it is possible to <u>follow the</u> more energetic examples around the book. Any aircraft which fall out of any of the four categories above, or are exported, will not have forwarding references and their entry should be considered closed. The **LOST!** section acts as a 'safety net' for aircraft that have no determined fate. Entries new to a heading in this edition are marked + after the registration/serial.

Where possible, brief historical details of the aircraft listed are given, in a necessarily abbreviated form. This information varies slightly in presentation, but can mostly be found in column three in the tabulated entries or, rarely, in brackets behind an entry in the narrative. In each case units etc are listed in reverse order, ie first use of an aircraft is listed last. Readers should have little trouble with these potted histories, especially with continued reference to the Abbreviations section.

Following favourable comment on the serial layout in the **Pocket Edition,** from this version, the aircraft tables have been given a four-column format. The first column gives the primary identifier for the airframe, most often worn on the airframe. Column two gives a secondary identifier, with military airframes most likely an 'M' number or similar, or with an aircraft wearing a military serial, but also having a current civil identity, that is given. Again, it is felt readers will have little difficulty with this presentation.

Locations

Directions to the town or village in question are given after each place name. Readers should note that these directions are to the town or village mentioned and not necessarily to the actual site of the aircraft in question. Directions are not given in the following instances :- 1] where specific directions to the site are not fully known. 2] where the location is a large city or town. 3] where the location is an airfield. It is felt that for the last two points, readers will be able to find their own way around! At the request of several aircraft owners, who have every right to preserve their peace and quiet as well as their aircraft, some locations have been 'generalised'.

Access

Unless otherwise stated, all locations in this work are **PRIVATE** and access to them is strictly by prior permission, if at all. Museum opening times are given as a guide only and readers are advised to contact the museum in question before setting out on a journey.

Serial and Registration Presentation

Aircraft are listed alpha-numerically, using the following rubric. British civil first (except in Eire where EI- comes first), followed by BGA and 'B Condition' markings then overseas civil registrations in alpha-numeric order. British military serials follow (with reversal again in Eire) followed by overseas military serials listed by country - ie France before Netherlands before USA. Finally, come BAPC identities as these can take in both civil or military airframes. Anonymous airframes are inserted where it is thought most logical! Incorrect or fictitious registrations and serials are marked ", eg VZ999" or G-BKEN".

Wrecks & Relics is put together using the best information available to the compiler. Every effort is made to be as accurate as possible. However, neither the compiler nor the publishers can be held responsible for any errors or changes that may occur in the location or status of aircraft or places listed.

ENGLAND

Avon

BADMINTON

(East of the A46, east of Chipping Sodbury) First-time ever entry for this delightful airfield/estate and annual host to two exceptional airshows. The parachute club here have a Cessna fuselage to help simulate their unnatural acts. It has been here since at least 1982.

G-BBJD+ Cessna 172M ex Sywell, N20537. Crashed 30/6/78. Para-trainer.

BATH

Jet Heritage bought the **Sea Hawk Restoration Group**'s FGA.6 WV795 and it moved to Bournemouth 10/89. Status of the FB.5 spares ship and the Swift nose is not known.

WM993 A2522 Sea Hawk FB.5 ex Corsham, Culdrose, SAH, FRU, 806, 811, 800. See notes.
XF113 Swift F.7 ex Frome, Farnborough, ETPS, A&AEE, HS. Nose. See notes.

BRISTOL

A whole series of entries are to be found around the city. At the **City Museum and Art Gallery**, the Bristol Boxkite replica continues to 'fly' within the main lobby. Open every day including Sundays, 1000 to 1700. Address : Queen's Road, Clifton, Bristol, BS8 1RL. Tel 0272 299771.

BAPC 40 Boxkite replica ex Old Warden, built by Miles at Ford. c/no BM.7281.

Bristol Industrial Museum Open Saturday to Wednesday 1000 to 1300 and 1400 to 1700. The Museum has a wide array of aero engines on show and a Sycamore. Address : Prince's Wharf, Bristol BS1 4RN. Tel 0272 299771.

XL829 Sycamore HR.14 ex 32, MCS, Khormaksar SAR Flight.

Jim Buckingham's well-known 'Miles Duo' operates from a strip in the area. The **Bristol Plane Preservation Unit**'s spares ship Messenger 2A G-AKBM is best deleted, being only a small collection of airframe spares now. Visits to the strip are not possible, but the Gemini and Messenger can be seen regularly at displays.

G-AKKB Gemini 1A SAC logos, airworthy.
RG333" G-AIEK Messenger 2A ex Miles 'B' Condition U-9, airworthy.

Located on Ashley Down, off the A38 north of the city centre, is **Brunel Technical College**. Airframes held here are unchanged - see also Bristol Airport.

G-ATHA Apache 235 ex Aviation West, Bristol Airport. CoA exp 7/6/86.
G-AWBW Cessna F.172H ex Bristol Airport, Compton Abbas. Damaged 20/5/73.
G-AWUK Cessna F.150H ex Biggin Hill. Crashed 4/9/71.

Visits to the **Winbolt Collection** of aviation electronics and radio equipment are strictly by prior permission. A Sea Vixen nose is held. Contact : Dr G E Winbolt, The Cottage, Castle Road, Pucklechurch, near Bristol, Avon.

XN651 A2616 Sea Vixen FAW.2 ex Culdrose, SAH, 766, FAW.1, 893. Nose section only.

Scattered around are three restoration projects.

G-ADPJ BAC Drone II ex Benson, Thetford, accident Leicester 3/4/55. Under restoration by Phil Dunnington using parts from G-AEKU.
F-BFUT J/1N Alpha ex Fiskerton, Boston, Bodmin, fuselage frame, with wings of J/1N G-AJEL. Under restoration by Tim Cox.
MV154 G-BKMI Spitfire VIII ex Huntingdon, Duxford, Australia, RAAF A58-671, 82 MU, 6 MU. Under restoration for Robs Lamplough.

BRISTOL AIRPORT

(Also known as Lulsgate) At the Airport, the remains of Varsity T.1 WF376 had perished by 7/86. By early 1988 the hulk of Commander 112A G-BIUO on the dump had also given up the ghost. The Brunel Technical College airframes are unchanged - see also under Bristol.

G-ANAP Dove 6 ex CAFU Stansted. CoA expired 6/9/73. Brunel.
G-ARJW Apache 160 ex Biggin Hill. CoA expired 9/1/82. Spares.

G-AVFM	Trident 2E	ex BA and BEA. CoA expired 2/6/84. Brunel.
G-AVHN	Cessna F.150G	damaged 28/1/85. Stored.
G-AVVW	Cessna F.150H	CoA expired 31/5/82. Brunel.
WF410	Varsity T.1	ex 6 FTS, 2 ANS, 5 FTS, 2 ANS, RAFC, CNCS, 201 AFS. Brunel.

FILTON

At the **Airfield** the Concorde continues its deep storage. Canberra T.4 WT483 arrived from Samlesbury for the dump in 7/88. It was removed to Long Marston 1/10/88 in a swop with WH665. A former Argentine MB.339AA is with Rolls-Royce for trial installation of the RB582 engine - could this be the example from Yeovilton?

G-BBDG		Concorde 100-002	CoA expired 1/3/82. BA spares, stored.
WH665+	8736M	Canberra T.17	ex Samlesbury, Cosford, 360, RNZAF, 45, 10. Arrived 30/9/88. Dump.
+		MB.339AA	ex FAA Argentina. See notes above.

Across from the Airfield is the **Rolls-Royce Technical School** with its Provost.

| XF603 | Provost T.1 | ex Bristol, 27 MU, CAW, RAFC. |

KEYNSHAM

(On the A4 south east of Bristol). Construction/restoration of the Pup continues by Mr K Baker here.

| G-EAVX | B1807 Sopwith Pup | ex Dorset. Crashed 21/7/21. PFA project 101-10523. |

LOCKING

(On the A371 east of Weston-super-Mare) This RAF base was bound to suffer from the one aircraft-one gate policy introduced by the MoD. Canberra T.4 WH840/8350M was put up for tender in 11/89 and is reported to be bound for Seighford. Either the Gnat or the Meteor will also being going.

WH840	8350M	Canberra T.4	ex 19 MU, Geilenkirchen SF, A&AEE, 97, 151, 245, 88, 231 OCU, CFS. See notes above.
WL360	7920M	Meteor T.7	ex 229 OCU, 1, Wattisham SF, 211 AFS, 210 AFS, 215 AFS.
XM708	8573M	Gnat T.1	ex Halton, 4 FTS, CFS, HS. Red Arrows colours.

WESTON-SUPER-MARE

Cougar G-BAPS left the Woodspring Museum for Weston-super-Mare Airport by 12/89.

WESTON-SUPER-MARE AIRPORT

After many, many years of pioneering work the **International Helicopter Museum** was opened fully to the public in 1989. Born the British Rotorcraft Museum, the name change takes in the remit of the Museum to portray all rotary winged achievement, not just that of the British variety. Indeed, a Sikorsky S-56 is due to arrive from Tucson, Arizona, before too long. As well as a staggering array of rotorcraft, the Museum boasts a very well laid out interior display. Plans for Phase Two include a hangar for some of the exhibits - indeed the gales of 25/1/90 caused a lot of damage, all of which can be put to rights. There is a large open store of airframes, some of which will join the restoration 'line', others will be used for exchanges. Scout AH.1 XP165 was temporarily with 3 CBAS at Yeovilton for restoration as **W&R12** closed for press. IHM machines can also be found at Crawley and Wroughton. The Museum is open April to October daily 1000 to 1800 and Wednesdays, Thursdays, Saturdays and Sundays 1030 to 1600 November to March. Contact : Weston Airport, Locking Moor Road, Weston-super-Mare, Avon BS22 8PP. Telephone 0934 635227, FAX 0934 822400.

G-ACWM	Cierva C.30A	ex Staverton, AP506, 529, 1448 Flt, 74 Wing, 5 RSS, G-ACWM. Frame.
G-ANFH	Whirlwind Srs 1	ex Redhill, Great Yarmouth, Bristow, BEAH. CoA exp 17/7/71.
G-ANJV	Whirlwind Srs 3	ex Redhill, Bristow and VR-BET.
G-AOUJ	Fairey Ultra-Light	ex 'Essex', White Waltham, XJ928. CoA exp 29/3/59. Stored.
G-ARVN	Grasshopper 1	ex Shoreham and Redhill. CoA exp 18/5/63. Stored.
G-ASHD	Brantly B.2B	ex Oxford Airport and area. Crashed 15/2/67. Stored.
G-ASTP+	Hiller UH-12C	ex Biggin Hill, Thornicombe, 'Wales', Thornicombe, Redhill, N9750C. CoA expired 3/7/82. Arrived 12/10/89.

G-ATBZ+	G-17-4 Wessex 60 Srs 1	ex Bournemouth, Sykes, Weston-super-Mare, Bristows. CoA exp 15/12/81. First noted 7/88.
G-ATKV	Whirlwind Srs 3	ex Redhill, Bristow, VR-BEU, G-ATKV, EP-HAN, G-ATKV.
G-AVKE	Gadfly HDW-1	ex Southend, Thruxton. wfu 1971.
G-AVNE	G-17-3 Wessex 60 Srs 1	ex Bournemouth, Sykes Av, Weston-super-Mare, Bristows, 5N-AJL, G-AVNE, 9M-ASS, VH-BHC, PK-HBQ, G-AVNE. CoA expired 7/2/83.
G-AWOX+	G-17-2 Wessex 60 Srs 1	ex Bournemouth, Sykes, Weston-super-Mare, Bristows, G-AWOX, 5N-AJO, G-AWOX, 9Y-TFB, G-AWOX, VH-BHE, G-AWOX, VR-BCV, G-AWOX, G-17-1. CoA expired 13/1/83. First noted 7/88.
G-AZBY+	G-17-5 Wessex 60 Srs 1	ex Bournemouth, Weston-super-Mare, 'Full Metal Jacket' 'EM-16', Sykes, Bristows, G-AZBY, 5N-ALR, G-AZBY. CoA exp 14/12/82. Arrived by 9/88.
G-AZBZ+	G-17-7 Wessex 60 Srs 1	ex Bournemouth, Weston-super-Mare, 'Full Metal Jacket' 'EM-11', Sykes, Bristows, 5N-AJI, G-AZBZ. CoA exp 9/6/83. Arr by 9/88.
G-AZYB	Bell 47H-1	ex Thruxton, LN-OQG, SE-HBE, OO-SHW. Crashed 21/4/84.
G-BAPS+	Campbell Cougar	ex Weston-super-Mare. CoA exp 20/5/74. Arr by 12/89.
G-BGHF+	WG.30 Srs 100	ex Yeovil, Westlands. CoA exp 1/8/86. Handed over 22/12/88.
G-OAPR+	Brantly B.2B	ex N2280U. Airworthy, operates from the Airport. Reg'd 4/89.
G-48/1	G-ALSX Sycamore 3	ex Duxford, Staverton, G-ALSX, VR-TBS ntu, G-ALSX.
5N-ABW	Widgeon 2	ex Cuckfield, Shoreham, Bristow, G-AOZE.
VZ962	Dragonfly HR,1	ex Helston, BRNC Dartmouth. Spares.
WG719	G-BRMA Dragonfly HR.5	ex Shawbury, Weston, Yeovilton, Yeovilton SF, 705.
XE521	Rotodyne Type Y	ex Cranfield, White Waltham. Large components.
XG452	G-BRMB Belvedere HC.1	ex Ternhill, 2 SoTT 7997M, Westlands.
XG462+	Belvedere HC.1	ex Henlow, Weston-super-Mare, 72, 66. Cr 5/10/63. Nose. Arr 1989.
XG547	G-HAPR Sycamore HR.14	ex CCAS St Athan 8010M, 5 MU Apprentices, CFS.
XG596	A2651 Whirlwind HAS.7	ex Wroughton, 705, 829, 771, 705, 737.
XM556	G-HELI Skeeter AOP.12	ex Connah's Quay, Middle Wallop 7870M. Boom of XM529/7979M.
XP165	Scout AH.1	ex HAM Southend, RAE. See notes above.
XS149	Wessex HAS.3	ex Templecombe, Wroughton, 737.
XS463"	XT431 Wasp HAS.1	ex Fleetlands, Lee-on-Solent. Parts from XS463/A2647.
XT472	Wessex HU.5	ex Hullavington, Netheravon, Wroughton, 845.
ZE477+	Lynx 3	ex Yeovil, Westlands. Arrived 1989.
BAPC 128	Watkinson CG-4-IV	ex Bexhill. Man powered rotorcraft.
BAPC 153	Westland WG-33	ex Yeovil. Mock-up ultra-light helicopter/drone. Stored.

Bedfordshire

BEDFORD

Dick Hadlow sold off his restoration of Tiger Moth G-APMM during 1989, destination unknown. Kite I BGA.400 moved to Eaton Bray. This leaves the Cessna at **Manders Technical College** as the principal focus of interest in the town.

G-AVCC+	Cessna F.172H	CoA expired 6/11/88. First noted early 1988. Inst.

BEDFORD AIRFIELD

(Or Thurleigh) Much to talk of at the **Royal Aerospace Establishment Bedford**, with several additions to discuss. Turning first to the silent flight department, neither of the two Blaniks noted in **W&R11** can be found at the Establishment. BGA.1301/BWV moved during 1987 to 'Yorkshire' in not the best of condition. Of BGA.1459/CDL nothing is known, except that it is not at Bedford. Definitely stored here is the Blanik Syndicate's L-13. Previous issues of **W&R** have had more than a little difficulty with the split personality of Fournier RF-3s G-BCWK and G-BFZA.

Whatever it may comprise, an RF-3 calling itself F-BLEL/G-BFZA is nearing the completion of its restoration here. The sections of Canberra T.17 WH872 here had become so small by 1988 that it no longer merited the attention of this tome – please delete. Buccaneer S.2 XK530 was burnt during an exercise in 12/89 and suffered somewhat for the experience. Its days are numbered. The Charles Church Lancaster/Lincoln rebuild project could be listed here, but is more properly to be found under the Cranfield heading – which see. **W&R11** noted Canberra B.2(mod) WG789 as having moved to 'Sussex'. This can now be tied down to Burgess Hill and please take up the story from there!

G-BBSO+	Cherokee 140F	Crashed 28/5/82. First noted with Apprentices 6/88.
G-BCSY+	Taylor Titch	Unflown, but completed. Stored. First noted 11/89.
BGA.1831+	CVB L-13 Blanik	ex Twinwood Farm.
F-BLEL+ G-BFZA	Alpavia RF-3	ex Twinwood Farm. Nearing end of restoration. See notes.
XG210	Hunter F.6	ex BAe Hatfield, CFE, 19, 14. Apprentices.
XK530	Buccaneer S.2	ex RAE catapult trials and S.1. Dump – see notes.
XM694	Gnat T.1	ex Filton, Dunsfold, A&AEE.
XW241+	SA.330E Puma	ex RAE, Westlands, F-ZJUX. Withdrawn 11/88. Stored.
XW626	Comet AEW	ex A&AEE, MinTech, G-APDS, BOAC. Open store.

CARDINGTON

The workshops of the **Royal Air Force Museum Restoration and Storage Centre** continue to produce work of the highest calibre, with the Southampton I restoration project making staggering progress – a classic wooden-hulled biplane flying boat from a waterlogged houseboat. The close-down of the Henlow storage facility has brought two refugees here, perhaps a sign that they are next in the restoration and conservation queue. John McKenzie's excellent BE 2b has been under assembly on site since early 1988. Departures from here have been as follows : Wright Flyer BAPC.28 was disposed of and moved to Eccleston; Bristol M.1C 'C4912'/G-BLWM was completed as 'C494' and moved to Hendon by 12/89; the sections of Horsa known as 8596M moved to Middle Wallop. Dolphin D5329, long listed here, is described as a "box of bits" and is best disregarded – although exhibits have grown from less of a start in life. By 11/88 a V-1 was under restoration here (just which one is unconfirmed – but likely BAPC.92 ex St Athan) in readiness for the 'Battle of Britain Experience' at Hendon. It moved to Hendon by 3/90. Tempest II HA457 arrived from Chichester by 11/88. It and the rear half of 'KB418:MN' from Manadon moved to Duxford by 12/89 for restoration to static condition by The Fighter Collection.

G-AHED	Dragon Rapide	ex Henlow, RL962, DH Witney. Stored.
F-HMFI	Farman F.40	ex Henlow and Nash Collection. Stored.
687"	BAPC 181 BE.2b replica	Nearing completion – see notes above.
K4972	1764M Hart Trainer	ex Hendon, St Athan, Carlisle, 2 FTS. Restoration.
N5419	N5419 Bristol Scout D	ex Leo Opdyke, USA. US civil registration = 'serial'. Stored.
N9899	Southampton I	ex Henlow and Felixstowe. Fuselage only, under restoration.
FE905	Harvard IIB	ex Royston, London Bridge, Southend, LN-BNM, Danish AF 31-329, RCAF, 41 SFTS, FE905, 42-12392. Under restoration.
MP425	Oxford I	ex G-AITB, Shawbury, Perth, MP425. Restoration complete.
VX275	8884M Sedbergh TX.1	ex St Athan, BGA.572. On charge here.
WE982+	8781M Prefect TX.1	ex Henlow, Syerston. First noted 1/90.
XE946	7473M Vampire T.11	Ex Henlow, Habbaniya SF, Nicosia SF. Pod only. Stored.
	FE.2b	cockpit nacelle. Stored.
	Hawker Demon	believed ex Cloughjordan, Eire. Fuselage frame.
8417/18	Fokker D.VII/OAW	ex Hendon, Cardington, Hendon, Cardington. Under restoration.
15195+	PT-19A Cornell	ex Henlow, Canada. Arrived by 1/90. Stored.
13064	P-47D-40-R A	ex Bitteswell, Yugoslavia, USAAF 45-49295. Restoration.
BAPC 180	Silver Dart rep	ex Farnborough and Canada. Stored.

Across at the giant airship sheds, the news that **Airship Industries** are to give up their segment of hangar will put a question mark over the hulk of the Skyship 500 stored therein. On the positive side, there are moves afoot to establish an Airship Museum within these historic buildings. The other hangar is now used for smokehood/water barrage tests and a Boeing 707 fuselage arrived 5/89 for this work.

G-APFG+	Boeing 707-436	ex Stansted, BAAT, BOAC. Arrived 9/5/89. Fuselage.
G-BIHN	Skyship 500	wrecked in gale 27/4/87.

CLAPHAM
Skeeter AOP.12 G-BLIX/XL809 moved to Sywell by 10/88 and was flying.

CRANFIELD
Another airfield where industrial developments are set to change the entire vista, but in this case those runways and hangars are very much part of the deal - they stay! The **Cranfield Institute of Technology**'s fleet of instructional airframes has seen little change. More properly located under this heading is the Trident 3B listed in **W&R11** under 'Others'. Sea Vixen FAW.2 XJ604/8222M left by road 15/4/88. Rumoured destination was Otterburn, but as yet this is unconfirmed. Harrier T.4 nose XW272/8783M moved on to BAe at Kingston-upon-Thames. Prior to his death in Spitfire 'EE606'/G-MKVC, Charles Church had arranged for the CIT to undertake the rebuild of his Lancaster KB976/G-BCOH, following the hangar collapse at Woodford. Some sections are stored locally and at RAE Bedford, while parts of the damaged G-BCOH are also held at Tattershall Thorpe for insurance purposes. Also involved are sections from former Canadian example KB994 and the former Aces High Lincoln RF342/G-29-1. While what look set to be long term legalities are sorted, they remain in store and are listed here for ease of reference.

G-AWZN	Trident 3B-101	ex BA, BEA. CoA expired 16/1/86. Rescue instruction.
G-AZZT	Cherokee 180D	ex N5302L. Crashed 10/2/80.
G-BBOJ	Aztec 250E	ex 5Y-AOK, N14130. Crashed 3/12/80.
G-BGGY	AB JetRanger III	Crashed 13/9/84.
G-29-1+ RF342	Lincoln 2	ex North Weald, Bitteswell, Blackbushe, Southend, Cranfield G-APRJ/G-36-3, Napiers G-29-1, G-APRJ, RF342. Arrived 6/12/88. See notes above.
KB976+ G-BCOH	Lancaster B.X	ex Woodford, Strathallan, CF-TQC, St Albert, Calgary, Rockcliffe, RCAF, 405. Damaged 12/8/87. See notes above.
KB994+	Lancaster B.X	ex Exeter, Edmonton, RCAF. Sections - see notes above.
XN979	Buccaneer S.2	ex 801. Ditched 9/6/66. Nose section.
XT439	Wasp HAS.1	ex Wroughton, 829 HQ Flight. Crashed 25/3/86.

Using a series of canvas hangars and workshops in their own compound on the airfield, the **Vintage Aircraft Team** and **Militair** continue to busy themselves in acquisitions and restorations. (See also under Bushey.) By 11/88 the VAT Jet Provost T.3 XN637/G-BKOU was airworthy, joining the well-known Vampire T.11 WZ507/G-VTII and Venom FB.54 'WR410'/G-BLKA. Lightning T.5 XS451 moved by road to Plymouth in 9/89 for an ambitious restoration to flying condition. Harvard 1513/'FT323' left in late 1988 for rebuild in Exeter. Of the additions, Beech 18 G-BKRN is technically not so, having been noted as leaving Perth in **W&R11** but not being included under this heading! Ed Stead's Hunter T.7 ET-271/G-BNFT arrived here from Wycombe Air Park 11/1/87 for packing and shipped to the States. This was finally achieved in late 1988 and the aircraft became N10271. Two former Senegalese C-47 noses transitted through her from Le Bourget before settling upon Kew - which see.

G-AIBR	J/1 Autocrat	ex Bushey, Duxford, Sywell, Gamston. Crashed 5/9/70. Frame only.
G-AKJU+	J/1N Alpha	ex Southend, TW513 A&AEE. Damaged 16/10/87. Arrived by 7/88.
G-AMIK	Tiger Moth	ex Bushey, Rochester, Croydon, N6709, 2 GS, 6 EFTS, 1 EFTS, 34 ERFTS. CoA expired 27/5/66.
G-ANEH	Tiger Moth	ex Leighton Buzzard, Bushey, Didcot, N6797, 11 RFS, 1 RFS, 1 EFTS, 12 RS, 9 EFTS, 9 ERFTS. Damaged 7/5/73. Possibly moved on.
G-ARSL	Terrier 2	ex VF581, 664. CoA expired 30/9/85.
G-AVCS	Terrier 1	ex Bushey, Cranfield, Finmere, WJ363, Odiham SF, AAC, 1900F. Crashed 18/10/81. Under restoration.
G-AYUA XK416	Auster AOP.9	ex Bushey, Luton area, Sibson, Middle Wallop, 7855M, 651, 19 MU.

G-BKRN+	Beech D.18S	ex Perth, Prestwick, CF-DTN, Capitol Air Surveys, RCAF inst A675, RCAF 1500. See notes above.
G-BMSG	SAAB 32A Lansen	ex Swedish AF, Malmslatt, Fv32028. Stored.
G-MIOO	Student 2	ex Duxford, G-APLK, Glasgow, Shoreham, XS941, G-35-4. Crashed 24/8/85. Stored.
G-SHOW	MS.733 Alcyon	ex Booker, F-BMQJ, FAF 125. CoA expired 24/5/83. Under rebuild.
G27-239 G-BNCA	Lightning F.2A	ex Warton, 8346M, Saudi Support Unit, XN734, Rolls-Royce, A&AEEE, BAC. Stored.
NL985	7015M Tiger Moth	ex Leighton Buzzard, Bushey, Leamington Spa, Finningley. Frame.
TW467	G-ANIE Auster 5	airworthy, lodges with VAT.
WE402"	G-VIDI Venom FB.50	ex Swiss AF J-1601. Under restoration.
WR410"	G-BLKA Venom FB.54	ex Swiss AF J-1790. Airworthy.
WS760	7964M Meteor NF.14	ex 'Z-14', Bushey, Duxford, Brampton, Upwood, 1 ANS, 64, 237 OCU. Under restoration by The Meteor WS760 Group.
WV686	G-BLFT Provost T.1	ex Camberley, Blackbushe, Ascot, Halton 7621M, 2 FTS, CS(A), 8 FTS, 2 FTS. Under restoration.
WZ507	G-VTII Vampire T.11	ex Carlisle, 60 MU, CATCS, 3/4 CAACU, 5 FTS, 8 FTS, 229 OCU, 22 MU. Airworthy.
XF914	Provost T.1	ex Bushey, East Midlands, Barton, Connah's Quay, 27 MU, FTCCF, CFS, G&S UAS, Lon UAS.
XH328	Vampire T.11	ex Hemel Hempstead, Croxley Green, Bushey, Keevil, Exeter, 3 CAACU, 60. Under restoration.
XN637	G-BKOU Jet Provost T.3	ex Bushey, Duxford, Winterbourne Gunner, 1 FTS, RAFC. See above.
XP248	7822M Auster AOP.9	ex Wroughton, Marlborough, Old Sarum, Middle Wallop, 651.
XP283	7859M Auster AOP.9	ex Shoreham, Middle Wallop, 654. Frame.
MT-11+	G-BRFU CM-170 Magister	ex USA N219DM, IAI Israel, Belgian AF. Arrived by 7/89.
E-407 G-9-435	Hunter F.51	ex Lutterworth, Bruntingthorpe, East Midlands, Dunsfold, Aalborg, Danish AF, ESK.724. Arrived 1989.
J-1523	G-VENI Venom FB.50	ex Swiss AF. Stored.
J-1632	G-VNOM Venom FB.50	ex Swiss AF. Stored.
91007"	G-TJET T-33A-1-LO	ex Danish AF DT-566, USAF 51-8566. CoA expired 7/5/87.

By far and away the most prominent items of note in the **Others** section is the mass arrival of Lightnings for well-known jet collector Arnold Glass (AG). One of the T.5s has been put on the UK civil register but it would appear that the chances of one being flown in such markings are remote. Recently the fleet has been offered for sale. Along with these have been several Gnats, all of which departed here after only a short stay : XP514/8635M arrived from Cosford 11/88 and was roaded out 2/8/89 bound for Felixstowe and the USA; XP535/G-BOXP arrived from Leavesden by 11/88 and was sold in the USA as N1CW 8/89; XR987/8641M arrived from Cosford 11/88 and was roaded out 2/8/89 for Felixstowe and the USA; XR991/G-BOXO arrived by road from Leavesden during 1989 and left by road, bound ultimately for the USA 30/7/89 as N1CL; XS104/8604M arrived from Cosford by 11/88 but was acquired by Butane Buzzard Aviation and moved to <u>North Weald</u> to become G-FRCE. Finally, the hulk of Cessna F.150G G-AVGU moved to <u>Little Staughton</u> by 6/89. That makes the current situation is as follows :

G-AJIW	Auster J/1N Alpha	ex Panshanger. CoA expired 16/10/82. Restoration.
G-BDUX	T.31B Motor Cadet	ex BGA.1146. CoA expired 23/2/84. Stored in trailer.
XS101	G-GNAT Gnat T.1	ex Cranwell 8638M, Red Arrows, CFS. Airworthy. AG.
XS452+	G-BPFE Lightning T.5	ex Binbrook, 11, 5, 11, LTF, 11, 5, 11, LTF, 5, LTF, 11, 56, 111, 29, 111, 29, 111, 226 OCU. Flew in 1/7/88. AG.
XS458+	Lightning T.5	ex Binbrook, LTF, 11, LTF, 5-11 pool, LTF, 5, 226 OCU. Flew in 29/6/88. AG.
XS898+	Lightning F.6	ex Binbrook, 11, 5. Flew in 30/6/88. AG.
XS899+	Lightning F.6	ex Binbrook, 11, 5-11 pool, 23, 5. Flew in 29/6/88. AG.
XS923+	Lightning F.6	ex Binbrook, 11, LTF, 5-11 pool. Flew in 30/6/88. AG.
XV328+	Lightning F.6	ex Binbrook, 11, LTF, 5, LTF, 5, 29. Flew in 29/6/88. AG.

DUNSTABLE
This delightful gliding site still hosts the defunct Pawnee and stored Weihe.

	Pawnee	frame only. Stored, Farmair titles.
BGA 448	AKC DFS 108-68 Weihe	ex G-ALJW, BGA.448. Stored, damaged.

EATON BRAY

(3 miles west of Dunstable) Peter Underwood's glider workshop continues to be busy.
The Kite is being worked on for Dick Hadlow of the Russavia Collection.

BGA	400+	AHC Kite 1	ex Bedford, Bishops Stortford, VD165. See notes above.
BGA	493	ALZ Hawkridge Dagling	ex Dunstable, Duxford, Warton. BAPC.81. Restoration.
BGA	833	BBG T.8 Tutor	ex Lytham St Annes and VW535. Stored.
BGA	1754	CRU Grunau Baby III	ex RAFGSA. Stored.

HATCH

(Off the B658, south west of Sandy) The home of Tim Moore's **Skysport Engineering**
undertook the rebuild of Bleriot XI G-AVXV (ex Duxford) in readiness for a recreation of Bleriot's cross-Channel flight of 1909. G-AVXV made its first test
flights from nearby Old Warden on 16/6/89 with Gloria Pullan at the controls. On
25/7/89 Gloria set off from France to recreate the original flight - sadly the
little craft had to ditch not far from the English coast. Gloria was picked up and
the wreck was subsequently salvaged for rebuild. It is owned by Bleriot's
grandson. Skysport also took on the frame of Bristol F.2b BAPC.19 from Guy Black
at St Leonards-on-Sea and used it to create a stunning F.2b replica in Belgian
markings for the Brussels Museum. In exchange for a Belgian Spitfire (see under
Ludham), the completed 'Brisfit' was flown to Belgium in a BAF C-130H on 22/6/89.
The wreckage of Pup replica G-BIAT/N6160 (see **W&R11**) was sold in Australia 8/89,
possibly for rebuild. Otherwise the three projects listed in the last edition
continue their restorations.

G-AGOY	Messenger 3	ex Southill, Castletown, EI-AGE, HB-EIP, G-AGOY, U-0247. Restn.
	Wallace	replica, under construction.
	Beaufighter TF.X	ex Henlow, Halton. Long term project.

HENLOW

The poor state of repair of the hangar used by the **Royal Air Force Museum** for long
term storage forced the Museum to re-appraise its collection here and all of the
airframe stock has moved on, either to other museums and RAFM sites or disposed of.
All of this has helped to 'refind' several airframes previously thought 'lost' and
consequently many of the questions in **W&R11** have now been answered. Disposals from
here have been as follows : G-AIZE Argus II to Cosford; H2311/G-ABAA Avro 504K to
Manchester 2/89; DG590/8379M Hawk Major to Middle Wallop 1988; HS503/BAPC.108
Swordfish IV to Cosford; RH377/G-ALAH Messenger IVA to Lymm; Vampire FB.5
VX461/7646M to Cosford; Dragonfly HR.1 VX595 to Fleetlands 9/2/90; WE982/8781M
Prefect TX.1 to Cardington (not listed in **W&R11**); WV783/7841M Sycamore HR.12 to
Fleetlands 9/2/90; Venom NF.3 WX905/7458M was put up for tender 2/89 and moved to
Winthorpe; XD816 Valiant B.1 nose to Brooklands by 9/88; XF785/7648M Bristol 173 to
Cosford; XG462 Belvedere HC.1 nose to Weston-super-Mare; 8469M Fa 330A-1 to
Cosford; 8599M Cadet TX.1 was put up for tender 2/89, new owner/location unknown;
an anonymous Cadet stored here moved to Cosford; the P.1121 fuselage sections
thankfully survived, also to go to Cosford; 6130/AJ469 Ventura II to Cosford and
15195 Cornell to Cardington. Doubtless, there will be some amendments to this in
W&R13, but otherwise we should mark the passing of a significant **W&R** venue.
Not that Henlow will fade entirely from the realms of **W&R**... It is still a busy
base with the Hunter at the main gate, the Vampire displayed and the local ATC
keep their EoN Primary on base.

BGA	580	AQQ EoN Primary	ex Twinwood Farm, G-ALPS. Stored in VGS hangar.
WT612		7496M Hunter F.1	ex Halton, Credenhill, Hawkers, A&AEE. Gate guardian.
XH278		8595M Vampire T.11	ex Upwood 7866M, 27 MU, RAFC. On display on a plinth.

In the **local area** Lee Mullins sold off his Terrier 2 G-ASDK for continued rebuild
in 'Essex'. The Pup fuselage should still be with the town-based ATC (a different
mob from the lot on the airfield), but has not been seen for some time.

| HB-NAV | Pup 150 | ex Redhill, G-AZCM. Fuselage, ATC. |

LUTON

Derek Hunt's J/1 Autocrat G-AJDW was sold and moved, destination unknown, 5/88.

LUTON AIRPORT

Wide-bodied aloominum toobs dominate now. For the first time in many an edition, there are no tabled entries here. Building work on the ever-expanding and soon to be privatised airport brought about the scrapping in 8/88 of the fuselage of Britannia G-AOVS and Turbo Navajo G-TAXY. End of an era....

OLD WARDEN

Located at one of the most delightful airfields in the UK, the **Shuttleworth Collection** continues to host a regular series of flying displays (including their unique 'twilight' shows which are enchanting) as well as being open to viewing throughout the year. (Please note, there are higher admission fees for flying days.) Maintaining such a flying fleet is a costly affair and the Collection has managed to attract sponsorship for several of its 'flyers'. This has been achieved in a highly tasteful way with not so much as a sticker on the airframes themselves. Instead, the sponsors are happy to be mentioned in placards, programmes and, to return the favour, we shall list them here as well.   The Collection is open daily throughout the year, but is closed for one week during the Christmas period. Open 1000 to 1600 except for November-March when the times are 1000 to 1500. Contact : The Shuttleworth Collection, Old Warden Aerodrome, Biggleswade, Beds, SG18 9ER. Tel 076 727 288. A large SAE will bring details of flying days and other events planned for the year ahead.   Supporting the activities of the Collection is the **Shuttleworth Veteran Aeroplane Society** who are currently hard at work on the restoration of the Blake Bluetit. Details of membership from David Reader, SVAS, 151 Marshalswick Lane, St Albans, Herts, AL1 4UX.

Percival Gull G-ADPR did not go entirely to Salisbury, as recorded in **W&R11**. The wings went there for attention by Cliff Lovell, but all is now back in the workshop at Old Warden. Hawk Speed Six G-ADGP flew in 24/9/89 having completed a wonderful restoration at the hands of Ron Souch. It should be resident, on loan, during 1990, but may be based elsewhere. Shuttleworth Collection aircraft can also be found under the following locations : Dewsbury (Triplane - nearing completion); Duxford (Sea Hurricane); Flixton (Provost); Hatfield (DH.88); Loughborough (Jet Provost); Yeovilton (Sea Gladiator).

G-EACN		BAT Bantam I	ex Watton, Old Warden, K-123, F1654. Components, stored.
G-EBHX		Humming Bird	ex Lympne No 8. 'L'Oiseau Mouche'. CoA exp 11/6/81.
G-EBIR		DH.51	ex VP-KAA, G-KAA, G-EBIR. 'Miss Kenya'. Airworthy.
G-EBJO		ANEC II	ex Lympne No 7. Dismantled, stored.
G-EBWD		DH.60X Moth	airworthy. Sponsored by Tradition (UK) Group.
G-AAIN		Parnall Elf II	airworthy.
G-AANG	No 14	Bleriot XI	ex Ampthill, Hendon. BAPC.3.
G-AANH	No 43	Deperdussin	ex Ampthill. BAPC.4.
G-AANI	No 9	Blackburn Mono D	ex Wittering. BAPC.5. Airworthy.
G-AAPZ		Desoutter I	ex Higher Blagdon, Old Warden. CoA exp 3/3/39. Restn.
G-AAYX		Southern Martlet	ex Woodford. CoA expired 12/4/49. Under restoration.
G-ABAG		DH.60 Moth	airworthy.
G-ABVE		Arrow Active II	airworthy. On loan from Desmond Penrose.
G-ABXL		Archaeopteryx	ex Chillwell. CoA expired 22/9/82.
G-ADGP+		Hawk Speed Six	ex Hamble, Florida. Flew in 24/9/89 - see notes above.
G-ADND		Hornet Moth	ex Hawarden, W9385, St Athan SF, 3 CPF, G-ADND. Sponsored by Manchester International Airport. Airworthy.
G-ADPR		Gull Six	ex Old Warden, Ampthill, Old Warden, AX866, G-ADPR. CoA expired 31/12/69. See notes above. Under restoration. Sponsored by Hunting Associated Industries.
G-AEBB		HM.14 Pou du Ciel	ex Southampton. Taxiable.
G-AEOA		Puss Moth	ex ES921, G-AEOA, YU-PAX, UN-PAX. Loan from P & A Wood. Airworthy.
G-AEXF		Mew Gull replica	ex Hatch, Redhill, ZS-AHM. Loan from Desmond Penrose. Airworthy.
G-AFCL		BA Swallow II	airworthy. On loan from A Dowson.
G-ARSG		Roe Triplane rep	Hampshire Aero Club built. BAPC.1. Airworthy.
G-ASPP		Boxkite replica	Miles built. BAPC.2. Airworthy.
D8096	G-AEPH	Bristol F.2b	ex Filton, Watford, D8096, 208. Airworthy. Sponsored by Rolls-Royce.

H5199	G-ADEV Avro 504K	ex G-ACNB, 'E3404' and Avro 504N. Airworthy.
F904	G-EBIA SE.5A	ex 'D7000', Farnborough. Airworthy.
K1786	G-AFTA Tomtit	ex 5 GCF, 23 GCF, 3 FTS. Under restoration. CoA expired 16/8/86.
K3215	G-AHSA Tutor	ex HSA, RAFC. Airworthy.
K4235	G-AHMJ Cierva C.30A	ex Middle Wallop, 529, 1448 Flt, SAC. Static. CoA exp 10/4/47.
K5414"	G-AENP Hind (Afghan)	ex 'K5457', Kabul. BAPC.78. Airworthy. Sponsored by Aero Vintage.
N5180	G-EBKY Sopwith Pup	ex Sopwith Dove. Airworthy.
N5648"	G-AMRK Gladiator I	ex L8032, 'K8032', Glosters, Hamble, 8 MU, 61 OTU, 1624F, 2 AACU. Sponsored by Luton International Airport. 247 Sqn colours and camouflage for Battle of Britain 50th. Airworthy.
P6382	G-AJRS Magister I	complex composite airframe. Airworthy.
T6818	G-ANKT Tiger Moth II	ex Aston Down, 21 EFTS. Airworthy.
Z7258"	G-AHGD Dragon Rapide	ex NR786. On loan from Mike Astor. 'Women of the Empire'. A/w.
AR501	G-AWII Spitfire V	ex Duxford, Henlow, Loughborough, CGS, 61 OTU, 1 TEU, 58 OTU, 422, 312, 504, 310. Sponsored by Westland (= Yeovil built). A/w.
WB588	G-AOTD Chipmunk T.10	ex Chessington, 22 RFS. Airworthy.
7198/18	G-AANJ LVG C.VI	ex Stanmore, Colerne, Fulbeck. Airworthy.
BAPC 8	Dixon Ornithopter	Stored.
BAPC 11	EE Wren	No 4, Composite with G-EBNV. Airworthy.
BAPC 37	Blake Bluetit	ex Winchester. Under restoration by SVAS.

STANBRIDGE
(3 miles south of Leighton Buzzard) The **RAF Staff College** is loyally guarded.

WP190	8473M Hunter F.5	ex Upwood, Finningley, Bircham Newton 7582M, Nicosia, 1, 41.

Berkshire

ARBORFIELD
(On the A327 south of Reading) Having re-instated the Jet Provost fuselages in **W&R11** something was bound to give, and the Beaver was dropped out! Below is what is thought to be the current situation at the Army's **Princess Marina College** although reports on the inmates here are always thin on the ground.

XM379	Jet Provost T.3	ex Shawbury, 3 FTS, 6 FTS, 2 FTS. Fuselage.
XM413	Jet Provost T.3	ex Shawbury, 2 FTS, 7 FTS, CFS. Fuselage.
XP244	7864M Auster AOP.9	ex St Athan. Fuselage, engine test bed. 'M7922'.
XP806+	Beaver AL.1	ex Middle Wallop. Composite, based on XP806 Cat 4 16/9/70.
XP886	Scout AH.1	ex Wroughton.
XP899	Scout AH.1	ex Middle Wallop. Crashed 1/11/79.
XR601	Scout AH.1	ex 657.
XT827	Sioux AH.1	ex 654 'D'.
XV139	Scout AH.1	ex Wroughton.
XV141	Scout AH.1	ex Wroughton.
	Gazelle TAD	Possibly TAU.3/WA.67 which was here during 1985.

ASCOT
To travel back to **W&R9**, Hunter F.51 E-420 left the now defunct Staravia yard here for the Staravia yard at Marlow.

BINFIELD
(North of the B3034, north west of Bracknell) There being no reports to the contrary, the compiler assumes that there has been no change in the store of flightless choppers here.

G-ASXF	Brantly 305	ex Thruxton, Biggin Hill. CoA expired 16/2/79.

G-AYNS   Airmaster H2/B1   ex Blackbushe, Redhill. CoA expired 13/2/73.
G-BKXH   Robinson R-22   ex Luton, Stapleford, SE-HOF. Crashed 23/7/85. For rebuild.
G-BLMD   Robinson R-22   ex Luton, N90623. Crashed 8/4/85.

BRACKNELL

At RAF Bracknell the **RAF Staff College** is still guarded by its Hunter.   **John** and
Maureen Woods keep their Harvard restoration project in the area.
EZ259   G-BMJW Harvard III   ex Tattershall, Oxford, Sandhurst, 766, SAAF, EZ259, 42-84182.
XG196   8702M Hunter F.6A   ex Kemble, 1 TWU, TWU, 229 OCU, 19.

FINCHAMPSTEAD RIDGES

(On the B3016 south of Wokingham)   Another location thought to be maintaining the
status quo, the **Staravia** yard here is much the same as it ever was.
XH362   Vampire T.11   ex Shawbury, CATCS, CNCS, 8 FTS, 7 FTS, 1 FTS, DH.
XP586   Jet Provost T.4   ex Lasham, Shawbury, RAFC. Fuselage.
XP642   Jet Provost T.4   ex Lasham, Shawbury, 2 FTS, CFS. Fuselage.
XP669   Jet Provost T.4   ex Lasham, Shawbury, 2 FTS. Fuselage.
XP685   Jet Provost T.4   ex Lasham, Shawbury, 2 FTS, 7 FTS.

HAMPSTEAD MARSHALL

(Off the B4009, south of the M4)   The former Irish Tiger is thought still here.
G-ANEM   Tiger Moth   ex Bristol, EI-AGN, Weston, G-ANEM, R5042, 14 RFS, 3 RFS, 6 EFTS.
                                 UK CoA expired 13/11/54. Stored.

HUNGERFORD

At the **Newbury Aeroplane Company** Ben Cooper still works his restorative magic and
has attracted several new inmates since **W&R11**.   There are two departures to record
: BA Swallow G-ADPS moved to <u>Dorchester</u> in 1988 to join the Brian Woodford
collection; Tiger Moth G-AOIM first flew on 15/8/88 and moved to pastures new at
Shobdon.   Current situation is as follows :
G-AAWO+   DH.60G Moth   ex Swanton Morley, composite with G-AAHI. Crashed 26/7/88. Under
                                 rebuild, arrived by 2/89.
G-ACEJ   Fox Moth   ex Old Warden. Remains only, written off 17/7/82.
G-ADNE+   Hornet Moth   ex Biggin Hill, 77 Wing, 1448F, 5 RSS, 1 PRU, X9325, G-ADNE. Under
                                 restoration, first noted 2/89.
G-ADRH+   Hornet Moth   ex Wokingham, F-AQBY, HB-OBE. Under restoration. First noted 2/89.
G-AFAX VH-ACN BA Eagle   ex VH-ACN. Arrived 20/2/88. For restoration.
G-AFGH+   Chilton DW.1   ex Billingshurst. CoA exp 7/7/83. Restoration. First noted 2/89.
G-ANTS   Tiger Moth   ex Lower Upham, Strathallan, Mintlaw, N6532, BCCF, Wyton CF, 22 RFS,
                                 22 EFTS, 30 ERFTS. Under restoration.
G-AZGC+   SNCAN SV-4C   ex Booker, F-BCGE, French military. For Restoration following
                                 accident in Italy, 1988.

MEMBURY

Southern Sailplanes continues their fascination with Tiger Moths and Super Cubs and
the Jodel DR.400 has reared its head again.   Restoration of the Dragon Rapide as a
long term project also continues.   Adding to the notes in **W&R11**, the rebuild of
Robin DR.400/160 G-BJUD/PH-SRM used a new fuselage, and the discarded one remained
junked here until about 11/88.   Last noted here as a set of wings only in 9/81,
DR.400 G-BAMT 'surfaced' as a hulk here again during 1989.
G-AHAG   Dragon Rapide   ex Blandford Forum, Ford, Whitney, RL944. CoA exp 15/7/73.
G-AHVV   Tiger Moth   ex Lympne, EM929. Crashed 12/12/71.
G-AJHU   Tiger Moth   ex T7471, 83 GSU, 132, 65, 116. Crashed 4/6/86.
G-ALWW+   Tiger Moth   ex NL923. Arrived by 9/89 for restoration following damage. CoA
                                 expired 20/1/88.
G-AMIU   Tiger Moth   ex Booker, T5495, 16 EFTS, 54 OTU, Church Fenton SF. Crashed
                                 15/10/69.
G-APZJ   Super Cub 150   crashed 12/6/83. Original fuselage frame - G-APZJ still flying!
G-BAVA   Super Cub 150   ex D-EFKC, ALAT 18-5391. Crashed 20/11/77. Frame.
G-BAMT+   DR.400 Knight 160   crashed 8/1/78. Smashed wreck, noted 9/89 - see above.

NEWBURY

British Balloon Museum and Library continues to flourish with its main display
being inside Newbury District Library. The balloons it holds are in the majority
stored at various locations in and around Newbury and accordingly are not available
for inspection. Occasionally (such as the Icicle Meets), there are inflations of
various 'goodies' from the collection. **Newbury District Museum** is located at The
Wharf in Newbury and is open April 1 to September 1000 to 1800 Monday to Saturday
and 1400 to 1800 Sundays and Bank Holidays. October 1 to March 31 from 1000 to
1600 Mondays to Saturdays and closed Sundays and Bank Holidays. The Museum is
closed every Wednesday. Contact : The Wharf, Newbury, Berks RG14 5AS. Telephone
0635 30511. BBML exhibits on show at the Museum at the time of writing are noted
in the list below. There have been several additions to the ranks of the BBML and
three subtractions : G-AYAL Omega 56 envelope and basket and G-BCFZ Cameron D-500
basket have gone and G-ICES Thunder Ax6-56SS has returned to its operators.
Enquiries relating to BBML can be made to : N Pritchard, Secretary, BBML, 75 Albany
Road, Old Windsor, Berkshire, SL4 2QD. For this entry only, Column Two of the
table is used to define just how much of each balloon the Museum has :

B Basket; **E** Envelope; **G** Gondola or Car and combinations thereof.

G-ATGN	E Thorn Coal Gas	'Eccles'. See below for basket.
G-AVIL	E HAG Free HAB	'Bristol Belle'.
G-AWOK	E Sussex Free Gas	'Sardine'. Never flew.
G-AXVU	E Omega 84 HAB	'Henry VIII'.
G-AXXP	E/B Bradshaw Free HAB	'Ignis Volens'.
G-AZSP	E Cameron O-84 HAB	'Esso'.
G-AZUV	E/B Cameron O-65 HAB	'Icarus'.
G-BAMK	G Cameron D-96 HAB	'Isibidbi'. Original airship control car.
G-BBGZ	B Cambridge HAB	'Phlogiston'. At Newbury Museum.
G-BBLL+	E Cameron O-84	'Boadicea'. First noted 1/90.
G-BCAR	E Thunder Ax7-77	'Marie Antoinette'.
G-BCFD	E West HAB	'Hellfire'.
G-BETF	E Cameron SS HAB	'Champion'. Spark-plug shape.
G-BETH	E Thunder Ax6-56 HAB	'Debenhams I'.
G-BHKN+	E Colt 14A HAB	'Green Ice 2'. Includes harness/burner. First noted 1/90.
G-BHKR	E Colt 14A HAB	'Green Ice 5'. Includes harness/burner. At Newbury Museum.
G-BIAZ+	E Cameron AT-165	'Zanussi'. Inner gas cell, Atlantic attempt balloon.
G-BIGT	E Colt 77A	'Big T'. Fire damaged.
G-BKES+	E Cameron Bottle 57	'Robinsons Barley Water'. Bottle shaped. First noted 1/90.
G-PERR+	E Cameron Bottle 60	'Perrier'. First noted 1/90.
G-PNUT	E Cameron SS HAB	'Mr Peanut'. Peanut-man shaped.
EI-BAY	E Cameron Ax8 HAB	'Godolphin'. Original envelope. ex G-AYJZ.
HB-BOU+	B Brighton Gas	'Verdi'. First noted 1/90.
5Y-SIL+	E Cameron A-140 HAB	'Cumulonimbus'. Ex F-BTVO, F-WTVO, G-AZUW. Identity amended from **W&R11**.
+	B Gas balloon	circa 1949. First noted 1/90.
+	G Cameron DG28 Gas	airship car. First noted 1/90.
+	B Military Gas	circa 1941. First noted 1/90.
+	B Military Gas	circa 1941. Was used on G-ATGN - see above. At Newbury Museum.

READING

In and around Reading can be found a varied collection of **W&R**-type machines. Of
Ben Borsberry's collection of Tiger Moths, G-ANLX should be deleted as it
constitutes little more than a wing. Work continues on G-ANDE and 7Q-YMY with the
addition of another from out of Africa. **John Bradshaw** gave up one of his Provost
spares-ships, with WV486/7694M moving to Thatcham to help out Alan House. The
other is thought to be still stored locally. Dave Pope moved his Chipmunk T.10 PAX
Trainer WP784 to Wellingborough on 25/8/88 and Tobago fuselage G-BGTB followed on
5/9/88. With no evidence to the contrary, it is thought the stored Jackaroo lives
on with Joe Iliffe.

G-AGNJ+ VP-YOJ Tiger Moth   ex Malawi, ZS-BGF, SAAF 2366. First noted 7/87. Restn.

G-ANDE	Tiger Moth	ex Stapleford, EM726, complex composite. Collision 22/7/84.
G-ANZT	Jackaroo	ex Thruxton, T7798, Wunstorf SF, 19 RFS, 5 RFS, 28 EFTS. CoA exp 15/3/68.
G-BRHW	7Q-YMY Tiger Moth	ex Malawi, VP-YMY, ZS-DLB, SAAF 4606, DE671.
WW447	Provost T.1	ex Exeter, CATCS, CNCS, RAFC. Stored.

SHAWDENE

(To the north of Newbury, on the old A34) Horizon 160 G-ASZS was flying by 1988, so had left the farm here. The Jodel is thought still to be stored.

| G-ATIC | CEA DR.1050 | ex F-BJCJ. CoA expired 1/6/81. |

THATCHAM

(North of the A4, west of Newbury) At a workshop here **Alan House** and friends completed their restoration of Provost T.51 178/G-BKOS during 1989 and it flew from a nearby strip, joining the already airworthy XF597/G-BKFW. Work is in hand on the force-landed XF836/G-AWRY and to this end, the fuselage of WV486/7694M has been acquired from John Bradshaw to help calibrate the jig. Alan acquired Whirlwind HAS.7 XN309/A2663 from Lasham by 7/89 and by 2/90 had used it in an exchange with the Irish Army Air Corps. XN309 moved to <u>Casement</u> for the dump 8/3/90 and coming the other way were the remains of Provost T.51 181 for use as spares.

WV486+	7694M Provost T.1	ex Reading, Halton, 6 FTS. Arrived by 7/89. See above.
XF836+	G-AWRY Provost T.1	ex Popham, Old Warden, 8043M, 27 MU, CATCS, CANCS, RAFC, Man UAS. Force-landed 28/7/87.
181+	Provost T.51	ex Casement, IAAC. Arrived 9/3/90.

WHITE WALTHAM

A story of migration here. Argus III G-AJPI was flying again in early 1989, in time to celebrate the 50th Anniversary of the establishment of the Air Transport Auxiliary. Chipmunk 22A G-ARMC was also made airworthy by 9/88. Colt 108 G-ARNG left by road on 17/5/88 for 'Somerset'. Chilton DW.1 G-AFGI has arrived for completion of its restoration. Gale damage here 1/90 may well provide some more candidates, but they will have to clock up a few more months before qualifying for entry. A withdrawn Apache now merits entry for similar reasons.

| G-AFGI+ | Chilton DW.1 | ex Woodlands Park, Booker. CoA expired 10/5/63. Arr 11/6/88. |
| G-ASMN+ | Apache 160G | ex 5N-AAT, 5N-ADA, N4464P. CoA expired 21/8/89. N772MM allocated. |

WINDSOR

Gordon King is still working on his Harvard project.

| B-163 | Harvard IIB | ex North Weald, Amsterdam, Dutch AF, RCAF FE930, 42-12417. |

WOODLANDS PARK

By 11/88 Chilton G-AFGI had moved to <u>White Waltham</u> ready for flight-testing.

WOODLEY

Plans are well in hand by the **Berkshire Aviation Group** to develop a small part of the former airfield site into a museum, which will have particular emphasis on Miles. Principal store for BAG remains Henley - which see. Magister 'L6906' was kept here only briefly and moved on to <u>Brooklands</u>. General enquiries about BAG can be made to : Secretary, BAG, 45 Malvern Way, Twyford, Reading, Berkshire RG10 9PY.

Others Bob Ogden continues to work on his Moth Major and to store Barry Welford's Minor Coupe.

| G-ABZB | Moth Major | ex Sweden, SE-AIA, G-ABZB. Under restoration. |
| G-AFNI | Moth Minor Coupe | ex W7972, 100 GCF, Foulsham SF, 241, G-AFNI. CoA expired 26/5/67. |

Buckinghamshire

AYLESBURY

At the TAVR Centre, **1365 Squadron ATC** keep their Hunter nose.

XF522	Hunter F.6	ex Bucks Ambulance Service, Aylesbury, Aylesbury Fire Service, Halton, 92, 66, 92. Nose section.

DENHAM

Both of the 'ITD' Cessna 310s have moved on. Having acted as a source of spares for G-XITD, C.310F G-OITD was scrapped here 21/11/89. G-XITD got up and flew away, only to undertake a wheels-up at Leavesden. This aircraft is thought to be the otherwise anonymous 310 now in use for instructional training at Cambridge Airport – which see.

FINMERE

J/1N Alpha G-AIGD had taken to the air by 5/88. The Xyla is still under restoration.

G-AWPN	Shield Xyla	Crashed 16/8/80. Under restoration.

HALTON

As Maggie continues to privatise everything under the sun and sell off everything else, there were worries that this historic site would be sold and the whole of **1 School of Technical Training** merged with the SoTT at Cosford. This mega-scheme appears to have disappeared up its own financial orifice and the School and the other units here all seem secure. With the advent of the Tucano-thing more JPs have come here and the trickle of Jaguars from Shawbury has continued. The Spitfire XVI restoration for San Diego was due to depart here as **W&R** went to press. The P-51D arrived here during 4/89 and is due to move to Hendon during 1990. Turnover in airframes has been less frantic than in previous editions : Jet Provost T.3 XM410/8054AM was broken up during 11/88 and was removed 1/89; XM468/8081M moved to St Athan by 3/90; Gnat T.1 XM706/8572M moved to Swinderby 8/11/89; XR569/8560M joined the dump at Linton-on-Ouse; XM709/8617M fetched £31,000 at the Sotheby's auction 9/3/90; XR984/8571M made £34,000 and XS110/8562M £29,000, buyers at present unknown, but thought to talk with Californian accents; Whirlwind HAR.10 XP405/8656M moved to Shorncliffe by 11/89. Going back to **W&R11** Gnats XR535/8569M and XR951/8603M are now thought very likely to have transitted through Bitteswell and Warbirds of Great Britain and both are now in the land of the dollar, with the former becoming N8130N and the latter N81298. Jet Provost T.3 XN594/8077M slipped the **W&R11** net, going to Cosford. Current line-up is :-

G-ASWJ	8449M Beagle 206 Srs 1	ex Rolls-Royce. wfu 8/75.
SL574	8391M Spitfire XVI	ex Bentley Priory, 'Battle of Britain', 11 GCF, North Weald SF, Biggin Hill SF, 3 CAACU, 103 FRS, CGS, EAAS. See above.
WT746	7770M Hunter F.4	ex St Athan, AFDS.
WV276	7847M Hunter F.4	ex Horsham St Faith, A&AEE, Rolls-Royce.
WZ559	7736M Vampire T.11	ex Oakington, 5 FTS, 94, 145. Gutted pod, moved to scrap compound by 11/89.
XD165	8673M Whirlwind HAR.10	ex SARTS, 202, 228, 22, 225, 155, Navy loan.
XE597	8874M Hunter FGA.9	ex Bentley Priory, Brawdy, 1 TWU, 2 TWU, TWU, 229 OCU, West Raynham SF, 1, 54, MoA, 208, 56, 63, 66. To the dump 6/89 - nose still with the School.
XE656	8678M Hunter F.6	ex 1 TWU, 229 OCU, DFLS, 92, 65.
XF319	7849M Hunter F.4	ex 229 OCU, 112, 66.
XF527	8680M Hunter F.6	ex 1 SoTT, Laarbruch SF, 4 FTS, CFE, 19, Church Fenton SF, Linton SF. Gate guardian.
XF974	7949M Hunter F.4	ex St Athan, 26, 3.
XG164	8681M Hunter F.6	ex Kemble, West Raynham SF, 74, 111.
XG274	8710M Hunter F.6	ex 4 FTS, 229 OCU, 66, 14.
XJ435	8671M Whirlwind HAR.10	ex 2 FTS, CFS, 1563 Flt, 22.
XJ727	8661M Whirlwind HAR.10	ex 2 FTS, CFS, 1310 Flt, 228, 22.

XM355	8229M Jet Provost T.3	ex Shawbury, 1 FTS, 7 FTS, CFS.
XM358+	8987M Jet Provost T.3A	ex 1 FTS, 3 FTS, 1 FTS, CFS, RAFC, CFS, 7 FTS, 2 FTS. First noted 6/89.
XM362	8230M Jet Provost T.3	ex Kemble, Shawbury, 3 FTS, 2 FTS. Sectioned and camouflaged.
XM369	8084M Jet Provost T.3	ex Shawbury, 2 FTS.
XM371+	8962M Jet Provost T.3A	ex CFS, RAFC, CFS, 3 FTS, 2 FTS. First noted 6/88.
XM375	8231M Jet Provost T.3	ex Shawbury, RAFC, 3 FTS, 2 FTS.
XM381	8232M Jet Provost T.3	ex Kemble, Shawbury, RAFC, 2 FTS.
XM386	8076M Jet Provost T.3	ex Shawbury, 2 FTS, CFS, Huntings, Luton.
XM402	8055AM Jet Provost T.3	ex Newton, Shawbury, 6 FTS, 2 FTS.
XM404	8055BM Jet Provost T.3	ex Newton, Shawbury, 3 FTS, 2 FTS.
XM408	8333M Jet Provost T.3	ex Kemble, Shawbury, MoA, 2 FTS. Marked as '8233M'.
XM409	8082M Jet Provost T.3	ex Shawbury, 2 FTS.
XM411	8434M Jet Provost T.3	ex St Athan, Shawbury, Kemble, CFS.
XM412+	9011M Jet Provost T.3A	ex 1 FTS, 3 FTS, 2 FTS. Allocation.
XM414+	8996M Jet Provost T.3A	ex 7 FTS, RAFC, 1 FTS, 6 FTS, RAFC, 2 FTS. Allocation, due here.
XM417	8054BM Jet Provost T.3	ex Shawbury, 6 FTS, 7 FTS, 2 FTS.
XM425+	8995M Jet Provost T.3A	ex 7 FTS, 1 FTS, RAFC, 3 FTS, CFS. Allocation, due here.
XM467	8085M Jet Provost T.3	ex Shawbury, 6 FTS, 1 FTS, RAFC.
XM473+	8974M Jet Provost T.3A	ex 7 FTS, 1 FTS, 7 FTS, 1 FTS, CFS, 3 FTS, 1 FTS. Composite. First noted 6/89.
XM478+	8983M Jet Provost T.3A	ex 1 FTS, 7 FTS, 1 FTS. Allocation, due here.
XM480	8080M Jet Provost T.3	ex 6 FTS, 1 FTS.
XN126	8655M Whirlwind HAR.10	ex 2 FTS, Queens Flt.
XN467	8559M Jet Provost T.3	ex Kemble, Shawbury, CFS, A&AEE, Huntings, Luton.
XN512	8435M Jet Provost T.3	ex St Athan, Shawbury, CFS.
XN548+	8971M Jet Provost T.3A	ex 7 FTS, 1 FTS. Arrived 13/1/89.
XN549	8335M Jet Provost T.3	ex Shawbury, 1 FTS, CFS. Marked as '8235M'.
XN554	8436M Jet Provost T.3	ex St Athan, Shawbury, CFS.
XP354	8721M Whirlwind HAR.10	ex 22, 202.
XP442	8454M Argosy T.2	ex Kemble, Benson SF, 114, Benson Wing, 114, MoA, 114.
XP503	8568M Gnat T.1	ex 4 FTS.
XP504	8618M Gnat T.1	ex 4 FTS, CFS, 4 FTS.
XP511	8619M Gnat T.1	ex 4 FTS, CFS, 4 FTS.
XP530	8606M Gnat T.1	ex 4 FTS, CFS.
XP534	8620M Gnat T.1	ex 4 FTS, CFS, 4 FTS, CFS, 4 FTS.
XP540	8608M Gnat T.1	ex 4 FTS.
XP557	8494M Jet Provost T.4	ex 6 FTS, RAFC.
XP567	8510M Jet Provost T.4	ex CATCS, 6 FTS, RAFC.
XP573	8336M Jet Provost T.4	ex Kemble, Shawbury, Rolls-Royce, 1 FTS, CFS. Marked '8236M'.
XP585	8407M Jet Provost T.4	ex St Athan, RAFC, 6 FTS, RAFC.
XP640	8501M Jet Provost T.4	ex CATCS, 6 FTS, CAW, CFS, 3 FTS.
XP672	8458M Jet Provost T.4	ex SoRF, CAW, CATCS, CAW, 2 FTS.
XP686	8502M Jet Provost T.4	ex 8401M, CATCS, 6 FTS, CAW, CATCS, CAW, 3 FTS.
XR140	8579M Argosy E.1	ex 115, 114, 242 OCU, 114. Broekn up 6/88 and removed to dump.
XR458	8662M Whirlwind HAR.10	ex 2 FTS, CFS, 28, 110, 103.
XR538	8621M Gnat T.1	ex 4 FTS.
XR574	8631M Gnat T.1	ex Cosford, Kemble, 4 FTS.
XR643	8516M Jet Provost T.4	ex Kemble hack, 3 CAACU, RAFC, 6 FTS.
XR650	8459M Jet Provost T.4	ex SoRF, CAW, CATCS, 3 FTS, CAW, 7 FTS.
XR651	8431M Jet Provost T.4	ex SoRF, CAW, CATCS, 3 FTS, 7 FTS.
XR662	8410M Jet Provost T.4	ex SoRF, CAW, CATCS, RAFC, CAW, 6 FTS, 7 FTS.
XR669	8062M Jet Provost T.4	ex Shawbury, BAC Warton, Huntings, Luton.
XR670	8498M Jet Provost T.4	ex SoRF, CATCS, 3 FTS, 1 FTS, 2 FTS, 7 FTS, CFS.
XR672	8495M Jet Provost T.4	ex SoRF, 6 FTS, CAW, CATCS, 3 FTS, 1 FTS.
XR704	8506M Jet Provost T.4	ex St Athan hack, CAW, CFS.
XR953	8609M Gnat T.1	ex 4 FTS.
XR954	8570M Gnat T.1	ex 4 FTS, CFS, 4 FTS.
XR980	8622M Gnat T.1	ex 4 FTS, CFS, 4 FTS, CFS, 4 FTS.
XR998	8623M Gnat T.1	ex 4 FTS.

XS100	8561M Gnat T.1	ex 4 FTS.
XS109	8626M Gnat T.1	ex Cosford, Kemble, 4 FTS, Red Arrows, CFS, 4 FTS.
XS176	8514M Jet Provost T.4	ex CATCS, 3 FTS, 2 FTS.
XS179	8337M Jet Provost T.4	ex Kemble, Shawbury, CAW, RAFC. Marked as '8237M'.
XS180	8338M Jet Provost T.4	ex Kemble, CAW, 6 FTS. Marked as '8238M'.
XS186	8408M Jet Provost T.4	ex St Athan, Kemble, Shawbury, CAW.
XS209	8409M Jet Provost T.4	ex St Athan, Kemble, Shawbury, CAW.
XS210	8339M Jet Provost T.4	ex Kemble, CAW. Marked '8239M'.
XS215	8507M Jet Provost T.4	ex CAW.
XS218	8508M Jet Provost T.4	ex Shawbury hack, 3 FTS.
XT257	8719M Wessex HAS.3	ex A&AEE.
XX110"	BAPC169 Jaguar GR.1 rig	engine systems rig, made of GRP.
XX118	8815M Jaguar GR.1	ex Shawbury, 6, Indian AF JI018, G-27-318, XX118, 226 OCU, JOCU. Centre section. Marked '8821M'.
XX726	8947M Jaguar GR.1	ex Shawbury, 6, 54, 14, 54, 6, JOCU.
XX739	8902M Jaguar GR.1	ex Shawbury, Gibraltar Det, 6.
XX743	8949M Jaguar GR.1	ex Shawbury, 6.
XX746	8895M Jaguar GR.1A	ex 226 OCU, 14, 17, 6, 31, 226 OCU.
XX747	8903M Jaguar GR.1	ex Gibraltar Det, 6, 20, 31, 226 OCU.
XX757	8948M Jaguar GR.1	ex Shawbury, 20, 226 OCU, 14.
XX818	8945M Jaguar GR.1	ex Shawbury, 31, 20, 17.
XX837+	8978M Jaguar T.2	ex Shawbury, 226 OCU. First noted 6/89.
XX956	8950M Jaguar GR.1	ex Shawbury, 17, 31, 14, 17.
XX966	8904M Jaguar GR.1A	ex Shawbury, 6, 54, 20, A&AEE, 20, 17.
XX975	8905M Jaguar GR.1	ex 226 OCU, 31, 17, 226 OCU.
XX976	8906M Jaguar GR.1	ex Shawbury, 17, 31.
XZ382	8908M Jaguar GR.1	ex Shawbury, 14, 17.
XZ389	8946M Jaguar GR.1	ex Shawbury, 17, 31, 20.
473415+	N6526D P-51D-25-NA	ex California, RCAF 9289, 44-73415. Damaged 19/3/77 - restored for RAFM - see above. Arrived via RAF C-130 at Lyneham 2/89 and here on 20/4/89. Stored.

MARLOW

Yet another **Staravia** depot has been discovered. By 1/89 two Hunters were to be found in store here. See also Bawdsey.

| PH-NLH+ | Hunter T.7 | ex Exeter Airport, NLR Amsterdam, Neth AF N-320, XM126 ntu. |
| E-420+ | G-9-442 Hunter F.51 | ex Ascot, Dunsfold, Aalborg, Danish AF ESK.724. Fuselage. |

MILTON KEYNES

The Sea Fury sections mentioned under this heading in **W&R11** have moved to Colchester to help in a restoration project.

NEWPORT PAGNELL

Spitfire historian and restorer **Peter R Arnold** has added a Spitfire Mk XII to his long term Seafire restoration project.

| EN224+ | G-FXII Spitfire XII | ex Cranfield, 595, 41. |
| LA564 | Seafire F.46 | ex Redbourn, Newark, Southend, Charnock Richard, Carlisle, Anthorn, 738, 767, A&AEE and cancelled Spitfire F.22 PV585. |

PINEWOOD

It is thought that the Jet Provost and Hunter nose are still to be found at the film studios.

| XP683 | Jet Provost T.4 | ex Finchampstead Ridges, Lasham, Bicester, 1 FTS, 6 FTS. Fuselage. |
| | Hunter F.6 | nose section. |

TWYFORD

(Previously listed under 'Berkshire', now amended.) **Peter Woods'** Seafire restoration project continues in the area.

| SX336 | G-BRMG Seafire XVII | ex Newark, Warrington, Stretton A2055, Bramcote. Rear fuselage of LA546. |

WORMINGHALL

(North of the A40 east of Oxford) Even though the Beverley is now an endangered species, a 'body count' at the **Fred Ford** yard here has revealled that the remains of C.1 XB288 are really too fragmentary to merit inclusion.

WYCOMBE AIR PARK

(Or Booker) From this issue we will bow to modernity and rename the airfield. At the excellent **Booker Aircraft Museum** three more nose sections have been taken on, two care of Barry Parkhouse. As well as the airframes, the internal contents of the BAM deserve dwelling over - very well presented material.   BAM is open Saturdays, Sundays and Bank Holidays 1030 to 1730.   Parties at other times by appointment.   Contact : David King, Chairman, Booker Aircraft Museum, 3 Spearing Road, High Wycombe, Buckinghamshire HP12 3JP.

KF435	Harvard IIB	ex Camberley, Sandhurst, 1 FTS, 2 FTS, 22 SFTS, 20 FTS, 11 PAFU. Composite.
WG789+	Canberra B.2/6	ex Kew, Burgess Hill, Bedford Airfield, RAE, 231 OCU. Nose section. Arrived 16/12/89.
WV495	7697M Provost T.1	ex St Merryn, Tattershall Thorpe, Strensall, Halton, 6 FTS.
WZ550	7902M Vampire T.11	ex Slough, Ewyas Harrold, CATCS, CFS, 8 FTS, 7 FTS, 202 AFS.
XA571	7722M Javelin FAW.1	ex Sibson, Aylesbury, Halton 7663M, 87, 46. Nose.
XM665	Whirlwind HAS.7	ex Chelsfield, Chertsey, Wroughton, Fleetlands, 829, 847, 848, 846, 737, 700H Flight. On loan.
6W-SAF+	C-47A-65-DL	ex Kew, Cranfield, Le Bourget, Senegalese AF, USAF MAAG Brussels VC-47A, USAAF 42-100611. Nose section. Arrived 16/12/89.
417657+ N99218	B-26K Invader	ex Canterbury, Southend, Chino, USAF 64-17657. Nose section. Arrived 16/4/88.

Under the care of Personal Plane Services, the late **Hon Patrick Lindsay Collection** is now being slimmed down. Fiat G.46 G-BBII was sold to Vic Norman and was flown out to Staverton 14/7/89; Spitfire IA AR213/G-AIST was bought by Victor Gauntlett in 1989, but will probably stay at Booker; the SE.5E/A and Fury replica have been entered into the Christie's Duxford auction of 28/4/90.   Stampe G-AZGC had an accident in Italy in 1988 during the making of a film. It returned and then moved to Hungerford. Current situation :

G-BIIZ	Great Lakes 2T-1A	ex N603K, NC603K.
B4863"	G-BLXT SE-5E	ex Orlando, N4488, USAAC 22-296. Airworthy. See above.
K1930+	G-BKBB Fury replica	ex Land's End. Arrived during 1988 - see notes above.
45	G-BHFG SNCAN SV-4C	ex F-BJDN, French military. Airworthy.
1076	G-AVEB MS.230	ex F-BGJT, French AF. CoA expired 21/8/87.

Naturally, most of the other notable aircraft on the airfield come under the realm of **Personal Plane Services** (PPS). Tony Bianchi has developed a close relationship with Florida-based collector Kermit Weeks and a two-way street is developing. EKW C-3605 C-499 was packed for Kermit and was exported during 1989. The other has been entered in the Christie's Duxford auction of 28/4/90. The former Northolt gate guardian Spitfire is here for preparation for Kermit's collection. Also with PPS is the long 'lost' Sheffield T-28C which is also entered into the Duxford auction.   Dornier Do 27A-4 3460/G-BMFG moved to Old Buckenham 22/5/89.   Other removals have been as follows : Stampe SV-4C G-AYCK to 'Cheshire'; Chipmunk 22 cockpit Section G-BDBL to Compton Abbas; Jungmann G-BJAL active at Gransden by 1989 and Cherokee Six G-KENS and Tomahawk C-GVXN had both perished on the dump by 7/88.

G-AZIO	SNCAN SV-4C Coupe	ex Redhill, Billingshurst, Croydon, F-BACB. Conversion to SV-4L.
G-USAF+	T-28C Trojan	ex 'Sheffield', USN 140589. First noted 7/89 - see above.
OK-JIK+	Yak C-11	first noted 7/89. Stored in PPS.
TE476+	G-XVIB Spitfire XVI	ex Northolt 8071M, Kemble, Henlow 7451M, 11 GCF, Martlesham SF, North Weald SF, Biggin Hill SF, St Athan, Kemble, 1 CAACU. Arrived 1989. For Kermit Weeks.
C-558	EKW C-3605	ex Lodrino, Swiss AF. See notes above.
	Yak C-11	ex La Ferte Alais (?), Egyptian AF. c/n 172623. Stripped frame.
BAPC 103	Pilcher Hawk rep	built by PPS. In store.

Cambridgeshire

ALCONBURY

The plastic Tiger on the gate is now well out of date with the Aggressors having gone to Woodbridge, converted to F-16s and then gone all peaceful and disbanded. Perhaps we shall see the vista of a plastic 'Warthog'. There has been no change in the BDR and instructional airframes at the base.

01534	F-5E Tiger II	mock up, pole mounted on gate, 527 TFTAS colours.
60312	F-101B-80-MC	ex AMARC Davis Monthan, Kentucky ANG. BDR.
63419	F-4C-15-MC	ex Texas ANG. BDR.
66692	U-2CT-LO	ex 5 SRTS/9 SRW, Beale. Instructional airframe.
153008	F-4N-MC	ex VF-154/USS 'Coral Sea'. BDR.

BASSINGBOURN

The former airfield, now **Allenbrooke Barracks,** has a Canberra displayed within the grounds. The **East Anglian Aviation Society** maintain the tower as a museum to the 91st BG and the 11 OTU and 231 OCU. Visits to this are by prior arrangement only, contact : M Reynolds, EAAS, 8 Pingle Lane, Northborough, Peterborough, PE6 9BW.

| WJ821 | 8668M Canberra PR.7 | ex RAE Bedford, 13, 58, 82. |

BOURN

On the airfield side, the stored Sea Prince has been joined by an engineless Cessna 337. On the heliport side, Bolkow 105s are the current trouble makers in terms of pinning them down. The original pod of G-BATC lies in the workshop here while the rejuvenated G-BATC is often to be seen flying from the pad outside! Another '105 has been converted to a roadable EMS (= ambulance) demonstrator and its identity is now thought to be proven. One of these two was the 'Soviet' machine mentioned in **W&R11.** A third machine is under restoration.

G-AXHA+	Cessna 337A	ex Luton, EI-ATH ntu, N5384S. Damaged 17/6/88. Derelict.
G-BATC+	MBB Bo 105D	ex D-HDAW. Original pod. See notes above.
G-BBJT	Robin HR.200-100	ex Rochester, F-WUQK. Damaged 14/1/87. Spares.
G-BGKJ+	MBB Bo 105D	ex D-HDDV. Ditched 25/4/89. Under rebuild.
G-BGKP+	MBB Bo 105D	ex D-HDGC. Crashed 16/2/81. EMS demonstrator - see above.
	Bell 47G	wreck. First noted mid-1988.
WP321	G-BRFC Sea Prince T.1	ex Kemble, 750, 744, Stretton. CoA expired 28/5/87. Stored.

CAMBRIDGE

Skycraft Services still store their Airedale in the area. Chipmunk T.10 WD356/7625M is more precisely located at St Ives - which see.

| G-ASRK | Airedale | ex Oakington area. CoA expired 29/7/84. Stored. |

CAMBRIDGE AIRPORT

(Or Teversham) The Canberra nose has been joined by an instructional Cessna 310. Note that the identity of the latter has not been 100% confirmed.

G-XITD+	Cessna 310G	ex Leavesden, Denham, G-ASYV, HB-LBV, N8948Z. Damaged.
		Instructional airframe. First noted 11/89.
WJ863	Canberra T.4 nose	ex 231 OCU, 360, Akrotiri SF, 231 OCU, Honington SF, Cottesmore SF.

CHATTERIS

(On the A141 south of March) At the strip the two derelict inmates live on.

| G-ARNH | Colt 108 | ex Elstree. Damaged 1/9/72. Dismantled. |
| G-AXNY | Fixter Pixie | ex Crowland area. Fuselage only, poor state. |

DUXFORD

Regular readers of **W&R** are probably tired of the plaudits the compiler rains down on the **Imperial War Museum** airfield complex. Suffice it to say that Duxford is the site to see a wide range of aircraft being restored and, where appropriate, flown. Regular special exhibits, events and air days add to the appeal of this very special airfield. As ever, there is much to talk of in terms of comings and goings, and these are listed below. Duxford is open daily 1000 to 1800 from mid-March to the end of October and 1000 to 1600 the remainder of the year. It is closed New Year's Day and December 24-26. During flying days different entrance charges are made. On days other than special events two of the civil airliner collection are open to inspection free of charge, one of which is normally Concorde. A large SAE will bring a leaflet on special events and opening times. Contact : IWM, Duxford Airfield, Duxford, Cambs, CB2 4QR. Telephone 0223 833963.

Major event for the IWM since **W&R11** has been the return early in 1989 to South Lambeth of several airframes that have 'lodged' here while major reconstruction of the 'parent' IWM went on. These aircraft are as follows : BE.2c 2699; Halifax A.VII nose PN323; He 162A-1 120235; Fw 190A-8 733682; the anonymous Zero cockpit section and joining them P-51D Mustang '472258'/9246 which previously had been a Duxford-only exhibit. Major acquisition under the direct IWM banner must be the immaculate Spitfire F.24 from Hong Kong. Other removals have been : loaned Bleriot XI G-AVXV to Hatch for overhaul and flight; Hunter F.2 WN904/7544M to the gate at Waterbeach in 1989; loaned Pembroke C.1 XK884/G-BNPG flew to Sweden as SE-BKH in 1988; loaned Venom J-1605/G-BLID by road to Charlwood 27/10/89 and loaned Venom J-1616/G-BLIF to the USA as N202DM during 1988.

Working on the Duxford site are a wide range of other organisations, all working in co-operation with the IWM. As with **W&R11**, all aircraft are listed as one list, but briefer details of happenings within all components on the site are given in narrative form below. Abbreviations are used to denote ownership of aircraft within the main list.

Central to all operations at Duxford is the **Duxford Aviation Society** (DAS). DAS members can be found volunteering their efforts towards every aspect of the site, from the fire crews, to the motor vehicle section, to aircraft restoration. DAS own the impressive airliner collection and undertake the awesome task of restoring and maintaining them. Main restoration efforts on the airliner side are still the Ambassador and the York. Loaned Bristol 170 G-BISU was flown out to Lympne 8/12/88 in preparation for its sale to Canada as C-FDFC. Membership enquiries can be made to : DAS, Duxford Airfield, Duxford, Cambridge, CB2 4QR. Telephone : 0223 835594.

During 1989 the British Aerial Museum renamed itself to reflect more properly its activities, becoming **The Aeroplane Restoration Company** (TARC). Main effort lies with the restoration to flying condition of Blenheim G-BPIV, with progress viewable in Building 66 and the hangars. TARC are undertaking a series of restoration tasks for the IWM itself, recent examples being the P-51 and Fw 190 in preparation for their display at South Lambeth and the Hunter F.2 going to the gate at Waterbeach. The Lysander is underway as a static exhibit for the IWM. Additionally, work for other operators on the airfield is undertaken, eg the crating of the Old Flying Machine Company's P-40. Several Harvards have been acquired and their restoration is underway. The TARC Beech 18 has also received a major restoration and is immaculate in a new USAAC scheme. Returning to the Blenheim project, in support of this is the **Blenheim Society** which also serves to unite former aircrew, groundcrew and Blenheim enthusiasts. Contact : TARC, Building 66, Duxford Airfield, Cambs, CB2 4QR. Telephone 0223 835313.

Duxford was host to no less than five airworthy B-17 Flying Fortresses during 1989 for the filming of the epic 'Memphis Belle'. Central to the 'cast' and to the maintenance of the others while they were in the UK was **B-17 Preservation Ltd** (B-17) operators of 'Sally B'. Backing the operation of this famous aircraft is a very active support group, the **Friends of Sally B** who publish an excellent magazine and offer other activities. Contact : B-17 Preservation Ltd, PO Box 132, Crawley, Sussex, RH10 3YD. Telephone : 0293 883213.

Viewable on Sundays is the excellent display of aviation archaeology and other artefacts of the **Essex Aviation Society**. Contact : Mick Skeels, 142 Leigham Court Drive, Leigh-on-Sea, Essex, SS9 1PU.

September 1, 1989 saw the first flight of Hurricane XII 'Z3781'/G-HURI in the
hands of Paul Day, a long-term and painstaking restoration by the team from **The
Fighter Collection** (TFC) well exhibiting their restoration capabilities. Prior to
this, Spitfire XVI G-CDAN/TB863 had been flown following restoration and was
shipped to New Zealand 13/10/88. A firm accolade was bestowed upon TFC when the
RAF Museum chose them to restore to static condition their former Indian Tempest
II.   A support organisation, **Friends of the Fighter Collection**, has been
established, producing a fine members' magazine and offering a range of activities.
TFC should take delivery of their Hellcat during 1990 with work continuing at Chino
on their P-38.   Other TFC happenings have been as follows : G-PSID P-51D Mustang
was sold in France 2/88; SM832/G-WWII Spitfire XIV moved to the Charles Church
workshop at Winchester; C-3605 C-551 arrived from Lodrino 13/3/88 by road and was
joined by fellow C-483 by 8/88. Both left by road for the USA 29/11/88. Enquiries
about TFC and the Friends should be made care of the IWM.
   Old Flying Machine Company (OFMC) continue to expand their operation which now
includes a Yak 11 and two more World War One replicas. Delivered in May 1988, the
OFMC Avenger will appear during 1990 in the markings of the TBM that a certain US
President used to fly.   Late in 1988 OFMC also took on the late Nick Grace's
Buchon. Well-known airshow performers, OFMC also undertake a lot of film work,
Mark Hanna being in charge of the aerial side of 'Memphis Belle'.   PT-13D NC88ZK
imported from the USA in 6/86 had moved on, destination unknown, by 1989.   OFMC
imported another Stearman, N53127, also from the USA in 4/88, but this too had
moved on by 1989. P-40 AK899/N94466 was crated and returned to the USA in 1989.
As foretold in **W&R11** T-6G MM54099 moved down to MAPS at Rochester 8/8/88. What was
not foretold was that OFMC were exchanging this for Meteor F.8 WK914, which they
plan to restore.
   With the arrival of Tigercat N6178C, **Plane Sailing/Lea Aviation** (PS) suddenly
found themselves as the operators of a 'stable'. The Tigercat quickly took on the
fin markings 'JW' in memory of a remarkable man, John Watts, who was killed in the
Tornado collision of 9/8/88.   His career in the RAF was exceptional, but his
determination to operate the Cat in the UK and the staging of the annual Fighter
Meet at North Weald will be his best monuments. The **Catalina Club** exists to bring
together all who are interested in PBYs and the Duxford-based one in particular.
Contact : 24, Batts Hill, Reigate, Surrey, RH2 OLT.
   Operations by the **Russavia Collection** (RUS) have continued to scale down,
following the Dragon Rapide accident on 21/6/87 and the subsequent halting of
tailwheel pleasure flying from Duxford. Drone G-AEDB moved during 1988 to Bishop's
Stortford. Airworthy Chipmunk T.10 WZ868/G-BCIW flew out 10/89 for a new base.
Further details can be found under Bishop's Stortford.
That said, the current situation is as follows :-

G-ACUU	Cierva C.30A	ex Staverton, HM580, 529, 1448 Flt, G-ACUU. CoA exp 30/4/60. IWM.
G-AFBS	Magister I	ex Staverton, G-AKKU ntu, BB661, G-AFBS. CoA exp 25/2/63. IWM.
G-AGJG	Dragon Rapide	ex X7344, 1 Cam Flt. CoA expired 15/5/74. Under rebuild. IWM.
G-AGTO	J/1 Autocrat	airworthy. DAS.
G-ALDG	Hermes 4	ex Gatwick, cabin trainer, Silver City/Britavia, Falcon, Airwork, BOAC. Fuselage only. CoA expired 9/1/63. DAS.
G-ALFU	Dove 6	ex CAFU Stansted. CoA expired 4/6/71. DAS.
G-ALWF	Viscount 701	ex Liverpool Airport, Cambrian, British Eagle, BEA. CoA expired 16/4/72. DAS.
G-ALZO	Ambassador	ex Lasham, Dan-Air, Handley Page, Jordan AF 108, BEA. CoA expired 14/5/72. Under restoration. DAS.
G-ANTK	York	ex Lasham, Dan-Air, MW232, Fairey Aviation, 511, 242. CoA expired 29/10/64. Under restoration. DAS.
G-AOVT	Britannia 312	ex Monarch, British Eagle, BOAC. CoA expired 11/3/75. DAS.
G-APDB	Comet 4	ex Dan-Air, MSA 9M-AOB, BOAC G-APDB. CoA expired 7/10/74. DAS.
G-APWJ	Herald 201	ex Norwich, Air UK, BIA, BUIA. CoA expired 21/12/85. DAS.
G-ASGC	Super VC-10 1151	ex BA, BOAC. CoA expired 20/4/80. DAS.
G-AVFB	Trident 2E	ex BA, Cyprus 5B-DAC, BEA. CoA expired 30/9/82. DAS.
G-AXDN	Concorde 01	ex BAC/Aerospatiale. CoA expired 30/9/77. DAS.

G-BFPL		Fokker D.VII rep	ex Lower Upham, Sandown, Land's End, Chertsey, D-EAWM. A/w. OFMC.
G-BOML+		Hispano HA-1112-MIL	ex Nick Grace, N170BG, Spanish AF C4K-107. Flew in 11/88. Airworthy. OFMC.
G-BPHZ+		MS.505 Criquet	ex F-BJQC, French military. Flew in 14/10/88. Luftwaffe colours and appropriately coded 'TA+RC'. Airworthy. TARC.
G-36-1		SB.4 SHERPA	ex Staverton, Bristol, Cranfield, G-14-1 and SB.1. Stored. IWM.
CF-EQS		PT-17-BW	ex Canada, USAAF 41-8169. Stored. IWM.
CF-KCG		TBM-3E Avenger	ex Canada, Conair, RCN 326, USN 69327. Under restoration. IWM.
F-BCDG		MS.502 Criquet	ex TARC, USA, EI-AUY, F-BCDG, ALAT. Stored. IWM.
F-BIEO+		Broussard	ex 63/Aeronavale. First noted 9/89. Spares. TARC.
NX11SN+		Yak 11	ex USA. Arrived 4/90. Airworthy. OFMC.
N47DD		P-47D-30-RA	ex Chino, USA, Peru AF FAP.119, USAAF 45-49192. Major restoration project, including parts from other airframes. IWM.
N152JS+		Fokker Dr I replica	ex USA. Arrived 13/5/89. Airworthy. OFMC.
NX700HL		F8F-2P Bearcat	ex N1YY, N4995V, US Navy 121714. Airworthy, TFC.
N753JS+		Nieuport 24 replica	ex USA. Arrived by 9/89. OFMC.
N6827C+		TBM-3E Avenger	ex USA, USN 91110. Arrived 12/5/88. A/w. See notes above. OFMC.
N6178C+		F7F-3 Tigercat	ex USA, Kermit Weeks, Sis-Q, Cal Nat, USN 08483. Flew in 13/11/88. Airworthy. PS.
N7614C		B-25J-30-NC	ex Shoreham, Dublin, Prestwick, Luton, USAF 44-31171. Restn. IWM
N8297		FG-1D Corsair	ex N9154Z, USN 88297. Airworthy. TFC.
N62822		P-63C-5-BE	ex 44-4393. F/f in UK 11/5/88. Airworthy, Soviet c/s. TFC.
N88972		B-25D-30-ND	ex CF-OGQ, KL161, USAAF 43-3318. Airworthy. 'Grumpy'. TFC.
5964"	G-BFVH	DH.2 replica	ex 'Gunbus', Lands End, Chertsey. Airworthy. RC.
E2581		Bristol F.2b	ex South Lambeth, 2 GCF, 30 TS, HQ Flt SE Area, 1 Com Sqn. IWM.
F3556		RAF RE.8	ex South Lambeth. 'A Paddy Bird from Ceylon'. IWM.
K2567"	G-MOTH	Tiger Moth	complex composite, airworthy. RC.
N4877	G-AMDA	Anson I	ex Staverton, Derby Airways, Watchfield SF, 3 FP, ATA, 3 FPP. IWM.
R3950		Battle I	ex Sandown, Strathallan, Canada, RCAF 1899. On loan, due to leave for Belgium during 1990. Crated as such 4/90.
S1287"+	G-BEYB	Flycatcher replica	ex Middle Wallop, Yeovilton. Airworthy. Loan TARC.
V3388	G-AHTW	Oxford I	ex Staverton, Boulton Paul, V3388. CoA exp 15/12/60. IWM.
V6028"	G-MKIV	Bolingbroke IVT	ex G-BLHM ntu, RCAF 10038. Crashed 21/6/87. Spares. TARC.
V9300	G-LIZY	Lysander III	ex 'Y1351', Canada, RCAF 1558, V9300. Restoration by TARC for IWM.
Z2033	G-ASTL	Firefly I	ex Staverton, G-ASTL, SE-BRD, Z2033. IWM.
Z3781"	G-HURI	Hurricane XII	ex Coningsby, Coventry, Canada. First flown 1/9/89. TFC.
Z7015	G-BKTH	Sea Hurricane I	ex Staverton, Old Warden, Loughborough, Yeovilton, 759, 880. Under restoration to flying condition. IWM/Shuttleworth Collection.
FR870"	NL1009N	P-40N Kittyhawk	ex N1233N, Wright Patterson, RCAF 840, 43-5802. Airworthy. TFC.
JV928"	G-BLSC	PBY-5A Catalina	ex Barkston Heath, South Africa, C-FMIR, N608FF, CF-MIR, N10023, USN 46633. Airworthy. Plane Sailing.
KB889	G-LANC	Lancaster X	ex Bitteswell, Blackbushe, Niagara Falls, RCAF 107 MRU, 428. Under restoration. IWM.
KF487+		Harvard IIB	ex Sandhurst, Avex, 1 FTS, 66 GCF. 1st noted 9/89. Spares. TARC.
LZ766	G-ALCK	Proctor III	ex Staverton, Tamworth, HQ Bomber Command, 21 EFTS. IWM.
MH434	G-ASJV	Spitfire IX	ex Booker, OOGEA OO-ARA, Belgian AF SM-41, Fokker B-13, Netherlands H-68, and H-105 322, MH434 349, 84 GSU, 222, 350, 222. A/w. OFMC.
ML417	G-BJSG	Spitfire IX	ex Booker, USA, Indian AF Tr.IX HS543, G-15-11, ML417, High Ercall, 411, 442, 443. Airworthy, TFC.
ML796		Sunderland MR.5	ex La Baule, Maisden-le-Riviere, Aeronavale 27F, 7FE, RAF 230, 4 OTU, 228. Under restoration. IWM.
MV293	G-SPIT	Spitfire XIV	ex Sleaford, Blackbushe, G-BGHB ntu, Bangalore, Indian inst T20, Indian AF, ACSEA, 215 MJ, 33 MJ. Under restoration. TFC.
NF370		Swordfish II	ex South Lambeth, Stretton, RAF charge. IWM.
NH799		Spitfire XIV	ex Bitteswell, Blackbushe, Indian AF instructional, 9, ACSEA, 215 MJ, 9 MJ. Under restoration. TFC.
TA719	G-ASKC	Mosquito TT.35	ex Staverton, G-ASKC, Shawbury, 3/4 CAACU, 4 CAACU, Shawbury. Crashed 27/7/64. Under restoration. IWM.
TG263		SARO SR.A.1	ex Staverton, Cranfield, G-12-1, TG263. IWM.
TG528		Hastings C.1A	ex Staverton, 24, 24/36, 242 OCU, 53/99, 47. IWM.

TX226	7865M Anson C.19	ex Little Staughton, East Dereham, Colerne, Shawbury, FTCCF, OCTU Jurby, 187, Hemswell SF, Coningsby CF, CBE. Stored. IWM.
VN485+	7326M Spitfire F.24	ex Kai Tak, Hong Kong, RHK Aux AF, 80. Arrived 18/7/89. IWM.
VT260	8813M Meteor F.4	ex Winterbourne Gunner, 49 MU, 12 FTS, 209 AFS, 203 AFS, 226 OCU, 203 AFS. Under restoration. IWM.
WD686	Meteor NF.11(mod)	ex RAE Bedford, Wroughton, TRE Defford. IWM.
WF425	Varsity T.1	ex RAE Met Flt, RAE, CFS, 1 ANS, 2 ANS. IWM.
WG752	Dragonfly HR.3	ex Dulwich, Fleetlands, Britannia Flt, 727, Culdrose SF, 705. IWM.
WH725	Canberra B.2	ex Wroughton, 50, 44. IWM
WJ288	G-SALY Sea Fury FB.11	ex Lympne, Southend, Biggin Hill, Dunsfold, FRU, Lossiemouth, Anthorn, Donibristle. On loan to IWM, due to move 1990.
WJ945	G-BEDV Varsity T.1	ex CFS, 5 FTS, AE&AEOS, CFS, 115, 116, 527. DAS.
WK714"+	WK914 Meteor F.8	ex Rochester, Manston, 85, CAW, 5 CAACU, 19. Arrived 8/8/88. OFMC – see notes above.
WK991	7825M Meteor F.8	ex Kemble, 56, 46, 13 GCF, NSF. IWM.
WM969	A2530 Sea Hawk FB.5	ex Culdrose 'SAH-5', FRU, 806, 811, 898. Under restoration. IWM.
WZ515	Vampire T.11	ex Staverton, Woodford, Chester, St Athan, 4 FTS, 8 FTS, 56, 253, 16. Stored. Due to go to Carlisle in 1990. IWM.
WZ590	Vampire T.11	ex Woodford, Chester, St Athan, 8 FTS, 5 FTS, 228 OCU. IWM.
XB261+	Beverley C.1	ex Southend, HAM, A&AEE. Nose section. Arrived 9/5/89. DAS.
XE627	Hunter F.6A	ex Brawdy, 1 TWU, TWU, 229 OCU, 1, 229 OCU, 54, 1, 54, Horsham St Faith SF, 54, 229 OCU, 65, 92. IWM.
XF708	Shackleton MR.3/3	ex Kemble, 203, 120, 201. Under restoration. IWM.
XG577+	A2571 Whirlwind HAS.7	ex Waterbeach, Duxford, East Midlands, Duxford, Lee-on-Solent, Arbroath, 705, 737, 815, 705, 701, 'Albion' Ship's Flt. Returned by 9/89. Stored.
XG613	Sea Venom FAW.21	ex Old Warden, 766, 809. IWM.
XG743	Sea Vampire T.22	ex Brawdy SF, 736, 764. IWM.
XG797	Gannet ECM.6	ex Arbroath, 831, 700, 810. IWM.
XH648	Victor B.1A(K2P)	ex 57, 55, 57, 15. IWM. Repainted and restored 1990.
XH897	Javelin FAW.9	ex A&AEE, 5, 33, 25. IWM.
XJ824	Vulcan B.2	ex 101, 9/35, 9, 230 OCU, 27. IWM.
XK695	Comet C.2(RCM)	ex Wyton, 51, 216, G-AMXH. IWM.
XK936	Whirlwind HAS.7	ex Wroughton, 705, 847, 848, 701, 820, 845. IWM.
XM135	Lightning F.1A	ex Leconfield, 60 MU, Leuchars TFF, 226 OCU, 74, A&AEE, AFDS. IWM
XN239	8889M Cadet TX.3	ex CGS. IWM.
XP281	Auster AOP.9	ex AFWF, Middle Wallop. IWM.
XR222	TSR-2 XO-4	ex Cranfield, Weybridge. Unflown. Restored 1989/90. IWM.
XR241	G-AXRR Auster AOP.9	ex Shuttleworth, St Athan, 1 Wing HQ, 654, Middle Wallop. Yellow c/s. Airworthy. TARC.
XS576	Sea Vixen FAW.2	ex Sydenham, 899, Brawdy. IWM
XS863	Wessex HAS.1	ex A&AEE. IWM.
	Typhoon	ex South Lambeth. Cockpit section. IWM.
A-549	FMA Pucara	ex ZD487 ntu, ex Boscombe Down, Yeovilton, Stanley, FAA. IWM.
A68-192	G-HAEC Mustang 22	ex '592', VR-HIU, RP-C651, PI-C651, VH-FCB, RAAF. Airworthy. OFMC
9893	Bolingbroke IVT	ex Canada. Stored. IWM.
10201	G-BPIV Bolingbroke IVT	ex Strathallan, Canada, RCAF. Under restoration. TARC.
18393	G-BCYK CF.100 Mk IV	ex Cranfield, RCAF. IWM.
18671"	G-BNZC Chipmunk 22	ex Hampton, G-ROYS, 7438M, WP905, CFS, 664, RAFC. A/w. TARC.
20285+	G-BGPB Harvard IV	ex North Weald, Portuguese AF 1747, WGAF BG+050, AA+050, USAF 53-4619. Spares. TARC.
533+	Yak C-11	ex La Ferte Alais, Egypt AF. Stored. TFC.
57	Mystere IVA	ex Sculthorpe, FAF 8 Esc, 321 GI, 5 Esc. IWM.
14286	T-33A-1-LO	ex Sculthorpe, FAF CIFAS 328. IWM.
42165	F-100D-11-NA	ex Sculthorpe, FAF Esc 2/11, Esc 1/3, USAF. IWM.
133722	NX1337A F4U-7 Corsair	ex Aeronavale 722, USN. Airworthy. Lindsey Walton.
100143	Fa 330A-1	ex Farnborough. IWM.
191660	AM.214 Me 163B-1	ex South Lambeth, Cranwell, 6 MU, RAE. IWM.
"	Amiot AAC.1 (Ju 52)	ex Portuguese AF 6316. Luftwaffe c/s, 'IZ+NK'. IWM.
HA457+	Tempest II	ex Cardington, Chichester, Indian AF, RAF. Arrived by 12/89. Static restoration for RAF Museum by TFC.

92	G-BJGW Broussard	ex F-BMMP, ALAT, AIA, GAM.50. Moroccan c/s. Restn. TARC.
NZ5628"	N240CA F4U-4B Corsair	ex N97359, N5213V, USN 97359. Airworthy. OFMC.
B-168+	Harvard IIB	ex North Weald, Amsterdam, Dutch AF, FE984, RCAF, 2 FIS, 42-12471. First noted 9/89. Spares. TARC.
Fv16105+	Harvard IIB	ex Vasteras, RSwAF, RCAF, 6 SFTS, RAF FE695, 42-892. First noted 10/89. TFC.
Fv35075	SAAB J35A Draken	ex RSwAF F16. IWM.
164"	G-BKGL Beech 18 3TM	ex Prestwick, CF-QPD, RCAF 1564. Airworthy. TARC.
17899	VT-29B-CO	ex 513 TAW, Mildenhall, USAF. IWM.
60689	B-52D-40-BW	ex 7 BW Carswell and others, USAF. IWM.
122095+	F8F Bearcat	ex Thailand, R Thai AF, US Navy. Arrived by 8/88. Stored. TFC.
114526+	T-6G Texan	ex France. Arrived by 8/89. Under restoration. TARC.
226671"	NX47DD P-47D/N	ex 45-49192 but complex composite. 'No Guts, No Glory' A/w. TFC.
231965"	F-BDRS B-17G-95-DL	ex IGN F-BDRS, N68629, USAAF 44-83735. 'Mary Alice'. IWM.
315509	G-BHUB C-47A-85-DL	ex Aces High G-BHUB, 'Airline' 'G-AGIV', 'FD988' and 'KG418', Spanish AF T3-29, N51V, N9985F, SAS SE-BBH, 43-15509. IWM.
461748	G-BHDK TB-29A-45-BN	ex China Lake, 307th BG, Okinawa. 'Hawg Wild' IWM.
463221"	N51JJ P-51D-25-NA	ex N6340T, RCAF 9568, USAAF 44-73149. 'Candyman/Moose'. A/w. TFC.
485784	G-BEDF B-17G-105-VE	ex N17TE, IGN F-BGSR, USAAF 44-85784. 'Sally B'. A/w. B-17.
BAPC 90	Colditz Cock rep	ex Higher Blagdon. Stored.
BAPC 93	Fi 103 (V-1)	ex Cosford. IWM.

In the locality, stored Nord NC.854 G-NORD had moved on during 1988. Destination not confirmed.

ELY

The **RAF Hospital** is still guarded by its Meteor.

WS774	7959M Meteor NF.14	ex Upwood, Kemble, 1 ANS, 2 ANS.

EVERSDEN

(On the A603 west of Cambridge) The store of aircraft has been added to, with the hulk of a Cessna 150 returning from Bredhurst by 5/89.

G-ADJJ	Tiger Moth	ex BB819, G-ADJJ. CoA expired 20/3/75. Stored.
G-ATEV	CEA DR.1050	ex F-BJHL. CoA expired 13/8/71. Stored.
G-AYBV	YC-12 Tourbillon	unfinished homebuild project. Stored.
G-AZDY	Tiger Moth	ex F-BGDJ, French AF, PG650. CoA expired 25/6/82. Stored.
G-BAXV+	Cessna F.150L	ex Bredhurst, Eversden, Sandtoft. Crashed 25/7/82. Wreck.
G-BKKS	Mercury Dart	unfinished homebuild project. Stored.
F-GAIP	G-BKOT WA.81 Piranha	unflown in UK markings. Stored.

FULBOURNE

(South east of Cambridge) Home of **Historic Flying Ltd**, the company set up by Tim Routsis to manage the much-publicised gate guardian exchange with the Ministry of Defence. Another workshop is to be found in the Braintree area - which see. Here is the former Church Fenton 'guardian' which will be Tim's personal machine.

BM597+	G-MKVB Spitfire Vb	ex Church Fenton, Linton-on-Ouse, Church Fenton, St Athan 5718M, 58 OTU, 317. Arrived 1989.

HUNTINGDON

Work continues in the area on **Peter Jackson**'s two Tiger projects. Peter's beautifully marked G-ANZU flies from a local strip.

G-AMNN	Tiger Moth	ex Redhill, NM137. Crashed 27/5/64. See also under Shoreham.
G-BPAJ	Tiger Moth	ex Jackaroo G-AOIX and Tiger T7087, Henlow CF, 6 FTS, 3 EFTS, ACC CF, 170, 20 EFTS, 12 EFTS. Under restoration.

KIMBOLTON

(On the A45 north west of St Neots) No change at the two **W&R** locations here. The Cessna hulk can be found on the former airfield, the Meteor within Kimbolton School but remember to take your cap off!

G-ARRG	Cessna 175B	ex Great Yarmouth, N8299T. Crashed 3/11/70. Hulk.
VZ477	7741M Meteor F.8	ex APS, 245. Nose only.

KINGSTON
(On the B1046 west of Cambridge) **Laurie Taylor** still perseveres with his restoration to flying condition (and RAF colours) of Magister G-AKPF.

| G-AKPF | Magister | ex Bassingbourn, Duxford, Burnaston. Fuselage G-ANLT, ex N3788, 169, 2 FIS, 2 FTS, 5 EFTS, 8 EFTS, 27 ERFTS. Wings from G-AKPF. |

LITTLE GRANSDEN
(On the B1046 west of Cambridge) The Tiger continues to be a 'hangar queen'. Aztec G-AWDI left, by one means or another, by mid 1989.

| G-AIRI | Tiger Moth | ex N5488, 29 EFTS, 14 EFTS, 20 ERFTS. CoA expired 9/11/81. Stored. |

LITTLE STAUGHTON
The Skeeter mentioned in **W&R11** as having been here from 4/87 did not stay long. It is now thought to have been G-BLIX/XL809, which currently flies from Sywell. Cessna F.150G G-AVGU arrived here from Cranfield by 9/88, but had gone — destination unknown — by 8/89.

Situation here is as follows, both being 'new'.

| G-ATID+ | Cessna 337 | ex N6239F. Stored by 5/89. |
| G-BBVG+ | Aztec 250C | ex ET-AEB, 5Y-AAT. CoA expired 10/9/88. Stored. |

MOLESWORTH
By 5/88 the large compound here dealing in USAFE scrap took delivery of 14060 T-33A from Lakenheath. However, by 10/88, the entire compound had been cleared. (For posterity, other than the T-33 above, the last known users of the compound were as follows, with 'last noted' dates :   FT-37 T-33A ex Alconbury (1/87); 10"/No 97 Mystere IVA ex Mildenhall (1/88); 63935 F-100F ex Alconbury (1/87); 660014 F-111A ex 366 TFW (4/87); 702375 F-111F ex 48   TFW (1/88); 702418 F-111F ex 48 TFW (4/87); 720142 RF-4C ex 10 TRW/1 TRS (1/88).

OAKINGTON
Alan House acquired the abortive Provost restoration XF597/G-BKFW from here and moved it down to Thatcham where his team quickly restored it to immaculate flying condition. The Varsity nose section with the local ATC has not been noted since 10/82, so it may well be heading for LOST!. Additionally, there are reports that it is/was 'synthetic', ie built for the job and not a 'flyer'.

ST IVES
Here with **John Chillingworth** since about 1985 has been a Chipmunk restoration, previously listed under 'Cambridge'.

| WD356+ | 7625M Chipmunk T.10 | ex Bushey, Nostell Priory, Aldergrove, Queens UAS. See notes. |

SIBSON
(Or Peterborough Sport Airfield) Cessna hulks are now the over-riding flavour of this airfield. Long-term landmark for A1 travellers, Varsity T.1 WF372 was rescued by the Brooklands Museum and was roaded there 13/11/88. Cessna 310B N620GS flew out to Sywell 2/89 and has become active as G-BPIL. Emeraude G-ARRS was flying by 1989. The hulk of Cessna FA.150K G-AXVC arrived here by 3/88 but had moved on to Shobdon during 1989. Going back to **W&R11**, the Nene Valley Aviation Society Auster G-AGXT moved more precisely to East Kirkby.

Current situation is :

G-AWSD+	Cessna F.150J	ex Denham. Damaged 16/10/87. First noted 11/87.
G-BABD+	Cessna FRA.150L	ex Cranfield. Crashed 16/10/87. Wreck. First noted 7/88.
G-BCRA+	Cessna F.150M	ex D-ELOS ntu. Crashed 30/7/87. Wreck. First noted 3/89.
G-BDFJ	Cessna F.150M	ex Coventry. Crashed 13/4/86. Wreck.
G-BFWF	Cessna 421B	ex Staverton, ZS-JCA, N1567G. CoA expired 15/5/80. Stored.
G-BGLI+	Cessna 152 II	ex N64997. Crashed 30/6/86. First noted 7/87.
G-BLSS+	Cessna F.150J	ex OO-CBS. Damaged 16/10/87. Wreck. First noted 11/88.
G-HUNY+	Cessna F.150G	ex Denham, G-AVGL. Damaged 16/10/87. Wreck. First noted 11/87.
WW444	Provost T.1	ex Coventry, Bitteswell, St Athan, 6 FTS. Stored.

WATERBEACH
A far more appropriate gate guardian for the former airfield, now home of **39 Engineer Regiment**, was provided by the IWM Duxford by 9/89. Whirlwind HAS.7 XG577/A2571 returned to Duxford for storage.

WN904+	7544M Hunter F.2	ex Duxford, Newton, 257. Gate guardian - see above.

WHITTLESEY
(On the A605 east of Peterborough) Stored on a farm in the area is an Auster.

G-AOGV	J/5R Alpine	CoA expired 17/7/72. Stored.

WILLINGHAM
(South of the A1123, east of Huntingdon) The Cessna continues to be stored here.

G-ARAU	Cessna 150	ex Sibson, N6494T. CoA expired 14/9/84. Stored.

WISBECH
For some time the **Fenland Aircraft Preservation Society** have exhibited a wide range of aviation archaeology items at the Bambers Garden Centre. These include incredible engine restorations where the cranks turn and the metalwork glows - and all from several feet under the Fens! Aviation archaeology at its best. During 1989, FAPS took on a Vampire and a Grasshopper and entered the pages of **W&R**! Located at Bambers Carden Centre, Old Lynn Road, West Walton Highway, near Wisbech, the Museum is open every Saturday, Sunday and Bank Holidays, March to September 0930 to 1700. More details from : R. W. Willatt, Secretary, FAPS, 62 Queens Road, Wisbech, Cambs.

XD434+	Vampire T.11	ex Barton, Woodford, Chester, St Athan, 5 FTS, 7 FTS. Arrived 3/89.
XP488+	Grasshopper TX.1	ex Long Sutton, Halton, West Malling. Arrived 1989.

WITTERING
The famous RAF base has won its case over its Spitfire F.21. The machine, not on the gate, but kept indoors and shown off during the summer, and a genuine 1 Squadron example, will not be replaced by the planned bit of plastic and will stay. (Wittering's gain is Swanton Morley's loss as they are now getting the plastic!) On the dump, long suffering Varsity T.1 WJ902 gave up the ghost and was cleared by 2/89. The other inmates are unchanged.

LA255	6490M Spitfire F.21	ex West Raynham, Cardington, Tangmere, 1. See above.
XF383	8706M Hunter F.6	ex Kemble, 12, 216, 237 OCU, 4 FTS, 229 OCU, 65, 111, 263. BDR.
XV279	8566M Harrier GR.1	ex Farnborough, Culdrose, A&AEE. WLT.
XV281	Harrier GR.1	ex Filton, Rolls-Royce, A&AEE, BSE Filton, Dunsfold. Spares.
XV779	8931M Harrier GR.3	ex 1. Gate guardian. Corrects **W&R11**.
XW923	8724M Harrier GR.3	ex 1417 Flt, 1, 233 OCU, 1. Nose section, rescue training.

WYTON
With three Canberras on the gate, Wyton was bound to stick out like a sore thumb when the one-gate-one-aircraft ruling came in. PR.7 WH773/8696M and B.6RC WT305/8511M were both put up for tender. WT305 was dismantled during 10/89 and had gone a month later - destination unknown. WH773 has had a reprieve as the tender fell through, but will be offered again before too long. On the dump T.17 WJ977 had gone to Snailwell by 3/88. Also on the dump, B.2 WK162/8887M perished later in 1988 and took the trip to Snailwell. The two Canberra noses mentioned in **W&R11** have been identified. One was T.4 WT482, marked '160 CSC'. This was acquired by the traders in Hull and moved to Charlwood 21/6/89, then quickly on to Long Marston. The other is the long-lost example from St Mawgan and still present. Going back to **W&R11** the axed Comet C.2R XK697 was removed to Snailwell.

WH773	8696M Canberra PR.7	ex 13, 58, 80, 31, 82, 540. See notes above.
WH848+	Canberra T.4	ex 231 OCU, 7, 13, 100, 85, 231 OCU, CAW, 231 OCU, 232 OCU, Gaydon SF, Binbrook SF, Marham SF. wfu 2/8/88. Fuselage with Canberra Servicing School.
WJ817	8695M Canberra PR.7	ex 13, 58, 80, 17, 58. Dump by 3/89.
WK119	Canberra B.2	ex St Mawgan, 7, MoA, NECS, 103. Nose on dump. See above.
WK127+	8985M Canberra TT.18	ex 100, 7, 10. Accident 13/12/88, wfu. BDR.
XH170	8739M Canberra PR.9	ex 39, RAE, 58. Gate guardian.

Cheshire

CHELFORD
(On the A537 west of Macclesfield) At a farm here the **Macclesfield Historical Aviation Society** have established themselves and have acquired a small array of aircraft.   Visitors are welcome, but by prior arrangement only for the time being. Contact : Kevin Whittaker, 17 Pitt Street, Macclesfield, SK11 7PT.

WH850+	Canberra T.4	ex Samlesbury, St Athan, Laarbruch SF, Wildenrath SF, 14, 88, Marham SF. Arrived by 6/88.
XE584+	Hunter FGA.9	ex Macclesfield, Bitteswell, G-9-450, 208, 8, 1. Nose section, first noted 10/88.
XR654+	Jet Provost T.4	ex Macclesfield, Bournemouth, Coventry, Puckeridge, Hatfield, 27 MU, CAW, 3 FTS, 6 FTS. Fuselage. First noted 10/88.
ET-272+	Hunter T.53	ex Macclesfield, Bournemouth, Leavesden, Elstree, Hatfield, Aalborg, Danish AF ESK.722.

Stored in the area is the wreck of a a Cessna Centurion.

EI-BRY+	Cessna 210M	ex Dublin, G-BMGU, ZS-KRZ, N6262B. Crashed 16/10/86. Wreck. First noted 11/88.

CHESTER
Restoration of the Vampire T.11 is thought to continue in the area.

XH312	Vampire T.11	ex Knutsford, Woodford, Hawarden, St Athan, 8 FTS.

CONGLETON
Mike Abbott is still working on his Leopard Moth restoration. He has a second Leopard registered to him, which has so far eluded **W&R**. Both restorations are very much 'from the ground up'.

G-ACOJ+	Leopard Moth	ex F-AMXP. See notes above.
G-ACOL	Leopard Moth	ex HB-OXO, CH-368. See notes above.

HANDFORTH
'Parented' by Shawbury, **395 Squadron ATC** still keep their Chippax here.

WZ869	8019M Chipmunk T.10 PAX	ex 1 FTS, RAFC, Dishforth SF, Benson SF, OXF UAS, DUR UAS, 64 GCF, Colerne SF. Crashed 20/5/68.

LYMM
(On the A56 west of Altrincham) Former TAC Messenger IVA G-ALAH is here for restoration to flying condition after being held for many moons at Henlow.

G-ALAH+	Messenger IVA	ex Henlow, RH377. CoA expired 18/4/65. See above.

MACCLESFIELD
A bypass development in the town and centralising operations on the expanding Bournemouth Airport base are bringing about the winding down of **Lovaux Ltd** here. By 3/90 only the hulk of the Buccaneer remained at the yard, doubtless defying being moved! The fuselage of Canberra B.2 WJ722 is unaccounted for. The nose of Hunter FGA.9 XE584 moved to Chelford by 10/88. Composite Hunter FGA.9 XJ690 moved to Bournemouth Airport - amending **W&R11**. The fuselage of Jet Provost T.4 XR654 also moved to Chelford and MHAS. The two-seat Hunter here was ET-272 (from Bournemouth) and this too has moved to Chelford. (Basis of the Biggin 'gate guardian' being ET-273 which did come through here, ex Cleethorpes - see **W&R9**. Not noted here previously is the nose of Hunter FGA.9 XE650. This was delivered to Seighford 3/90. That leaves :

XV155+	8716M Buccaneer S.2B	ex Brough, St Athan, 12, 237 OCU, 12. Arrived 2/89. See notes above.

In Park Street, **Macclesfield College of Further Education** should still have their Vampire, although it has not been reported for some time.

XD624	Vampire T.11	ex CATCS, CNCS, Church Fenton SF, 19.

MALPAS

(East of the A41 north west of Whitchurch)   **617 Squadron ATC** at Malpas School still
have their Whirlwind HAS.7.
XK944   A2607 Whirlwind HAS.7   ex Brunel Tech Bristol, Lee-on-Solent, Fleetlands, Arbroath,
                                 Fleetlands, Lossiemouth SF, Fleetlands, Yeovilton, 824, 'Ark Royal'
                                 Flight.

SAIGHTON

(South east of Chester) At **Saighton Camp**, the Army took delivery of a Wessex HU.5
in 3/87. But see also under Birmingham.
XS521+   Wessex HU.5   ex Wroughton. See notes above.

WARMINGHAM

(South of Middlewich in between the A530 and the A533) Located at the Warmingham
Craft Centre, **The Aeroplane Collection** continues to flourish. This is TAC's main
centre of restoration activity. A small store is still maintained in Wigan and of
course they have several aircraft in the Manchester Museum of Science and Industry.
Ken Fern at Stoke-on-Trent took over the Chrislea Airguard G-AFIN during 1989 and
he has plans to fly it, using the drawings that TAC hold. In return he delivered a
static replica BAPC.203 by 7/89. TAC acquired Auster G-AGXT from store at East
Kirkby by 1/89. but it moved on to BCAR at Hedge End on 4/7/88. Also going to
Hedge End on that date was Auster 6A G-ARDX, which was moved from Wigan to
Warmingham on 26/6/88. TAC have loaned their Chipmunk WB624 to SAC at Long Marston
and it was delivered there 2/4/89. The Chrislea Skyjeep frame is now thought to be
from a Super Ace instead. Find the Craft Centre at The Old Mill, Warmingham. Open
1000 to 1700 weekdays and 1000 to 1800 at weekends. Further details of TAC from :
7, Mayfield Avenue, Stretford, Manchester, M32 9ML. Current situation is :-
G-AFIN+" B'203 Chrislea Airguard ex Stoke-on-Trent. Replica -see notes above.
G-AJEB   J/1N Alpha   ex Brize Norton, Wigan, Cosford. CoA exp 27/3/69.
G-BBUW+   SA.102 Cavalier   ex East Kirkby, Boston, Crowland. Incomplete homebuild. Arrived
                                 5/1/89.
G-BLHL   CP.301A Emeraude   ex Wigan, East Kirkby, Tattershall, Chinnor, Booker, F-BLHL, F-OBLM.
                                 Crashed 4/8/81. Under restoration.
              Chrislea Skyjeep   ex Bristol area. Fuselage frame only. See notes above.
K2572"   Tiger Moth replica ex Hereford, Lutterworth, Holme-on-Spalding Moor. Arrived 14/2/88.
XK319+   Grasshopper TX.1   ex Stoke-on-Trent. Arrived 20/2/88. Loan from THC.
XL811   Skeeter AOP.12   ex Southend, 9/12 Lancers, 17F, 652, 651.
XN298+   Whirlwind HAR.9   ex Stoke-on-Trent, Bournemouth, Yeovilton, Wroughton, Lee-on-Solent
                                 SAR Flt, Fleetlands, Lee-on-Solent, 846, 848. On loan from THC.
BAPC 15   Addyman STG   ex Wigan, Harrogate.
BAPC 192   Weedhopper JC-24   unflown homebuild.
BAPC 193   Hovey Whing Ding   uncompleted homebuild.

WARRINGTON

Still doing the rounds of local shows is **1330 Squadron ATC**'s Jet Provost nose. It
is stowed in a container when not 'on the road'. Parent is Shawbury.
XM474   8121M Jet Provost T.3   ex Shrewsbury, Shawbury, MinTech, 6 FTS, MoA, 6 FTS, CFS. Nose.

WILMSLOW

Stored in this area is a Meta-Sokol, pending restoration.
G-APVU   L.40 Meta-Sokol   ex Manchester Airport, OK-NMI. Accident 12/9/78. Stored.

WINSFORD

(On the A54 south of Northwich) Stored at a farm here is the hulk of a Musketeer.
G-ASFB   Musketeer 23   crashed 23/5/81. Wreck.

Cleveland

MIDDLESBROUGH
Tidying up the reference in **W&R11**, unaccounted-for MiG-15bis/LIM-2 01016 became N15YY.

TEES-SIDE AIRPORT
(Or Middleton St George) Just which airframes survive at the **Civil Aviation Authority Fire School** here is open to doubt. At least five Tridents, two Viscounts and a 'helicopter' (likely XP330) were noted 8/89, but only the two Viscounts could be identified, and then only by default. It is not known if the Aztec still lives on. Accordingly, repeated here is the list as given in **W&R11** but with the warning that it needs severe updating and confirmation.

G-ARPD	Trident 1C	ex BA, BEA. CoA expired 30/ 4/81. Poor state.
G-ARPO	Trident 1C	ex BA, BEA. CoA expired 12/ 1/86. Whole.
G-ARPR	Trident 1C	ex BA, BEA. CoA expired 19/ 6/81. Poor state.
G-ARPW	Trident 1C	ex BA, BEA. CoA expired 3/11/82. Whole.
G-AVFJ	Trident 2E	ex BA, BEA. CoA expired 18/ 9/83. Whole.
G-AWZR	Trident 3B-101	ex BA, BEA. CoA expired 9/ 4/86. Whole.
G-AWZS	Trident 3B-101	ex BA, BEA. CoA expired 9/ 9/86. Whole.
G-AZLP	Viscount 813	ex BMA, SAA ZS-CDT. CoA expired 3/4/82. Whole.
G-AZLS	Viscount 813	ex BMA, SAA ZS-CDW. CoA expired 9/6/83. Whole.
D-IOMI	Aztec 250	wreck. First noted 8/87.
XP330	Whirlwind HAR.10	ex Stansted, 21, 32, 230, 110, 225. Gutted.

THORNABY-ON-TEES
It is thought that the Fewsdale Gyro can still be found in store in the area.

G-ATLH	Fewsdale Gyro	accident 7/78, stored.

Cornwall

CALLINGTON
(On the A390 south west of Tavistock) Cornwall seems to have a great affinity for the Lightning, with a couple of locations gaining former Binbrook examples when the great wind-down took hold. A private owner here took delivery of an F.6 in 6/88.

XR755+	Lightning F.6	ex Binbrook, 5, 5-11 pool. Arrived 6/89.

CHACEWATER
(East of the A30, north east of Redruth) It is thought the Mooney and VP-2 are still stored here.

G-ARWY	Mooney M.20A	ex Bodmin, N1079B. CoA expired 6/8/80. Wreck.
G-BTSC	Evans VP-2	CoA expired 18/7/84. 'Spirit of Truro'. Stored.

CULDROSE
As ever, there is much to record regarding comings and goings at HMS 'Sea Hawk's' **School of Aircraft Handling.** SAH teaches the disciplines needed to handle the various and hectic movements on the flight deck of a carrier as well as other skills. For this, a dummy deck (hence the 'DD' codes on the airframes) is etched out on the airfield. In terms of movements, a Buccaneer, a P.1127, a Wasp and three Wessex outbound to record for four Wessex arrivals, all from Lee-on-Solent.

Leaving have been : Wessex HAS.1 XM874/A2689 to Lee-on-Solent 12/7/88; Buccaneer S.1 XN953/A2655 to Predannack care of a Chinook on 23/8/88; Wessex HAS.1s XP158/A2688 and XP160/A2650 both to Lee-on-Solent 13/9/88; P.1127 XP980/A2700 to join the other vertical risers at Yeovilton 6/3/89 and Wasp HAS.1 XT441 to Predannack by 4/87 (amending **W&R11**). That makes the current situation :-

WF225	A2645 Sea Hawk F.1	ex FRU, 738, 802. Gate guard.
WT711	Hunter GA.11	ex Shawbury, FRADU, 14, 54. SAH.
WT804	Hunter GA.11	ex Shawbury, FRADU, Lossiemouth, 247. SAH.
WV267	Hunter GA.11	ex FRADU, 738, 98, 93, 14. SAH.
WW654	Hunter GA.11	ex FRADU, 738, 229 OCU, 98, 4, 98. SAH.
XE668	Hunter GA.11	ex Yeovilton, FRADU, 738, 26, 4. SAH.
XM328	Wessex HAS.3	ex Wroughton. SAH.
XM870+	Wessex HAS.3	ex Lee-on-Solent, Wroughton, 737. Arrived 13/9/88. SAH.
XP137+	Wessex HAS.3	ex Lee-on-Solent, Wroughton, 737. Arrived 13/9/88. SAH.
XS695	A2619 Kestrel FGA.1	ex Manadon, Tri-Partite Evaluation Squadron, A&AEE, RAE. SAH.
XS866+	A2705 Wessex HAS.1	ex Lee-on-Solent, Wroughton, 771. Arrived 22/6/88. SAH.
XS876+	A2695 Wessex HAS.1	ex Lee-on-Solent, Wroughton, 771. Arrived 12/7/88. SAH.
XS877	A2687 Wessex HAS.1	ex Wroughton, 771. SAH.
XS885	A2668 Wessex HAS.1	ex 772. SAH.
XT762	Wessex HU.5	ex Lee-on-Solent, Wroughton, RAE. SAH.
XV588	Phantom FG.1	nose section only. Escape training.
XV669	A2659 Sea King HAS.1	ex Lee-on-Solent, 820. Engineering Training School. 'Mr Walter' - Mechanical Radio Weapons and Electrical Training Engineering Rig! Crashed 31/3/76.
XX466	Hunter T.7	ex Shawbury, FRADU, 1 TWU, Jordan AF, RSaudi AF 70-616, HSA, XL620, 74, 66. SAH.

HAYLE

By 2/89 the Cherokee with 1907 Squadron ATC had gone.

HELSTON

At **Flambards Triple Theme Park** a refreshing realism came about during late 1988 with a review of the number of airframes held. Three aircraft, Gannet ECM.6 WN464/A2540 and Sea Vixens FAW.2 XJ575/A2611 and XJ584/A2621 were offered for sale in 10/88. There being no museum takers, all were scrapped, the Gannet 12/88 and the 'Vixens being rolled back into Culdrose and scrapped there 1/89. The nose of XJ575 was acquired by SAC and moved to Long Marston. The restoration programme has continued here with the Sea Hawk FB.3 the latest to come off the 'line'. The Museum has plenty to offer all tastes, including the Flambard Victorian Village, the Britain in the Blitz exhibition, the Cornwall Aero Park and various special exhibitions. Open every day April 11 to October 29 1000 to 1700. Contact : Flambards Triple Theme Park, Clodgey Lane, Helston, Cornwall, TR13 OGA. Tel 03265 3404.

G-APIW	Widgeon	ex Southend, Westlands. CoA expired 26/9/75.
G-BDDX	MW.2B Excalibur	only flight 1/7/76, built Bodmin.
F5459"	B'142 SE.5A replica	ex Trevanen Bal.
WF122	A2673 Sea Prince T.1	ex Culdrose, 750, Sydenham SF, Arbroath SF, Lossiemouth SF, 700Z Flt, Lossiemouth SF, FOFT, 750, Eglinton SF, 744.
WG511	Shackleton T.4	ex Colerne, St Mawgan, MOTU, Kinloss Wing, MOTU, 120, 42. Nose.
WG725	N9987Q Dragonfly HR.5	ex Southend, Middle Wallop, Odiham, Colerne, Weeton 7703M, RAE. Will be restored as WG754:912/CU.
WN105"	WF299 Sea Hawk FB.3	ex St Agnes, Topcliffe, Catterick 8164M, Lee-on-Solent, A2662, A2509, Culdrose SAH-8, 802, 738, 736. Restoration completed, complex composite.
WK122+	Canberra TT.18	ex Samlesbury, 7, 15, 61. Arrived 8/89.
WV106	Skyraider AEW.1	ex Culdrose, 849, Donibristle, Abbotsinch, USN 124086.
XA870	A2543 Whirlwind HAS.1	ex Predannack, Lee-on-Solent, 'Protector' Flt, 705, 'Protector' Flt, 155, 848. Sectioned.
XD332	A2574 Scimitar F.1	ex Culdrose SAH-19, Lee-on-Solent, 764B, 736, 807, 804.

XE368	A2534 Sea Hawk FGA.6	ex Culdrose SAH-3, Shotley.
XG691	Sea Venom FAW.22	ex Chilton Cantelo, Yeovilton, FRU, 891, 894.
XG831	A2539 Gannet ECM.6	ex Culdrose SAH-8, 831.
XJ917	Sycamore HR.14	ex Wroughton, CFS, 275.
XN258	Whirlwind HAR.9	ex Culdrose SF, 'Endurance' Flt, Culdrose SF, 'Hermes' Flt.
XN647	A2610 Sea Vixen FAW.2	ex Culdrose SAH-10, 766, 899.
XN967	A2627 Buccaneer S.1	ex Culdrose SAH-20, Lossiemouth.
XP350	Whirlwind HAR.10	ex Chivenor, 22, 225.
XS887	A2690 Wessex HAS.1	ex Culdrose, Wroughton, 771.
XT427	Wasp HAS.1	ex Yeovilton, Wroughton.
BAPC 116	Demoiselle replica	ex 'Flambards', Wysall.
BAPC 129	Blackburn 1911 rep	ex 'Flambards', stored.
BAPC 130	Blackburn 1912 rep	ex 'Flambards', stored.

LAND'S END AIRPORT
(Or St Just)   The final two replicas have left here.   Sopwith Camel replica
B7270/G-BFCZ was sold after the Bournemouth auction 10/87 and was acquired by the
Brooklands Museum.   Hawker Fury replica K1930/G-BKBB moved through to Booker and
was entered in the Duxford auction of 4/90.   The Auster engine test-bed has not
been seen in recent visits, but is thought to be still here.

G-AHAP	J/1 Autocrat	CoA expired 8/2/74. Engine test bed.
G-ARZD	Cessna 175C	ex N1689Y. Crashed 28/5/77. Wreck.
G-AYMF	Airtourer	crashed 9/6/72. Wreck.
G-AZTN	Airtourer	ex Exeter. Crashed 27/6/77. Wreck.

LELANT
(On the A3074 south of St Ives)   Peter Channon's Swift is still stored in the area.

G-ABTC	Comper Swift	CoA expired 18/7/84. 'Spirit of Butler'.

LISKEARD
At the **Castle Air** pad and centre, a Lightning F.6 has been restored and
dramatically posed - a likely candidate for pole tax!

XS936+	Lightning F.6	ex Binbrook, 5, LTF, 5, LTF, 5, 11, 23. First noted 6/88. Plinth-mounted by 8/89.

LOWER TREMAR
(Near Liskeard)   Another Lightning collector here has two airframes and also
acquired the former Torbay Aircraft Museum Sycamore.

XG544+	Sycamore HR.14	ex Higher Blagdon, 32, MCS, 228, 275. First noted 1989.
XR751+	Lightning F.3	ex Binbrook, 11, LTF, 29, 226 OCU, EE. Arrived 6/88.
XS919+	Lightning F.6	ex Binbrook, 11, 5, 11, 5, 56, 11. Arrived 6/88.

PERRANPORTH
A recent visit to the gliding site could not reveal the anonymous Olympia.

PREDANNACK
With no known losses to report at the Navy fire school here and two additions to
add to the list, the introduction section continues to contract.   Readers are
reminded that the nature of the terrain here often 'hides' inmates.

WF125	A2674 Sea Prince T.1	ex 750, Brawdy SF, 750, Lossiemouth SF, Brawdy SF, Yeovilton SF, Lossiemouth SF, 700Z Flt, 750.
XE712+	Hunter GA.11	ex Lee-on-Solent, Shawbury, FRADU, 738, 43, 222. Arrived 9/2/88.
XL836	A2642 Whirlwind HAS.7	ex Fleetlands, Wroughton, 705, 848, 847, 848.
XL846	A2625 Whirlwind HAS.7	ex Yeovilton, Lee-on-Solent, Lossie SF, Brawdy SF, 705, 820, 824.
XL899	Whirlwind HAR.9	ex Wroughton, Culdrose SF, W'ton, A&AEE, 'Protector' Flt, 847, 848.
XM329	A2609 Wessex HAS.1	ex Lee-on-Solent, Arbroath, 771.
XM331	Wessex HAS.3	ex Lee-on-Solent, Fleetlands. Poor state.
XM667	A2629 Whirlwind HAS.7	ex Lee-on-Solent, Wroughton, Lee-on-Solent, 705, 846, 825, 824.
XM838	Wessex HAS.1	ex Lee-on-Solent, Wroughton, 737.

XM841	Wessex HAS.1	ex Wroughton. Forward fuselage, poor state.
XN314	A2614 Whirlwind HAS.7	ex Lee-on-Solent, Wroughton, Fleetlands, 781, Yeovilton SF, Culdrose SF, Brawdy SF, Lossiemouth SF, 781, Alvis, 846, 719, A&AEE.
XN635	Jet Provost T.3	ex Culdrose, Predannack, Culdrose, Aldergrove, 3 FTS, RAFC. Nose.
XN934	A2600 Buccaneer S.1	ex Culdrose, Lee-on-Solent, 736.
XN953+	A2655 Buccaneer S.1	ex Culdrose SAH-23, St Athan 8182M, Lossiemouth, 736. Flew in under a Chinook 23/8/88.
XP107	A2527 Wessex HAS.1	ex Lee-on-Solent, Fleetlands, 845. Crashed 5/2/63.
XP149	A2669 Wessex HAS.1	ex Lee-on-Solent, Manadon.
XS119	Wessex HAS.3	ex Lee-on-Solent, Wroughton, 737.
XS125	A2648 Wessex HAS.1	ex Yeovilton, Lee-on-Solent, 771.
XS873	A2686 Wessex HAS.1	ex Lee-on-Solent, Wroughton, 771.
XT441	A2703 Wasp HAS.1	ex Culdrose, Wroughton, 829.
XT450	Wessex HU.5	ex 845.
XT757	A2722 Wessex HU.5	ex Lee-on-Solent, Wroughton, 845.

ST MAWGAN

During 1989 St Mawgan received a gate guardian in the shape of fully restored Shackleton AEW.2 WL795 suitably engineered to look like an MR.2. The continued existence of the travelling replicas normally credited to here is now doubted and unless proof positive is received on Scout replica A1742"/BAPC.38 and Camel replica D3419"/BAPC.59 they will be abandoned to the bowels of LOST! in the next edition. In **W&R10** Canberra B.2 WK119 was noted as having passed away on the dump, the nose survived and commuted to <u>Wyton</u> – which see.

WJ870	8683M Canberra T.4	ex Marham, 231 OCU, 100, 231 OCU, Bruggen SF, 213, Ahlhorn SF, Laarbruch SF, 31, 102. BDR.
WL795	8753M Shackleton AEW.2	ex 8, 205, 38, 204, 210, 269, 204. See above.
XH132	8915M Short SC-9	ex RAE Bedford. BDR.

ST MERRYN

At the former airfield the para-trainer is still in use. Stampe Special G-STMP is being restored here on behalf of Caroline Grace.

G-MLAS	Cessna 182E	ex Bodmin, OO-HPE, D-EGPE, N2826Y. CoA exp 20/10/82. Para-trainer.
G-STMP	SNCAN SV-4A	ex F-BCKB. Under rebuild.

Cumbria

APPLEBY

As predicted in **W&R11**, Vampire T.11 WZ576/8174M was indeed sold in Canada after being put up for tender in 7/87. Sadly it was written off during shipment. The wings were acquired by Derek Leek and moved to Bridgenorth.

CARK

Up on the wind-swept airfield, the para-trainer is still thought to exist.

G-AWMZ	Cessna F.172H	ex Blackpool Airport. Crashed 18/1/76. Para-trainer.

CARLISLE

(Kingstown, on the A7 north of the City)   At the RAF station, Meteor NF.14 WS792/7965M was entered into the Cardiff auction of 9/89 and fetched £4,000. It moved north o' the border to <u>Borgue</u>. Otherwise, no change.

WT660	7421M Hunter F.1	ex 229 OCU, DFLS. Gate guardian.
XT255	8751M Wessex HAS.3	ex ETPS. BDR within the camp.

CARLISLE AIRPORT

(Or Crosby-on-Eden)   The collection of the **Solway Aviation Society** continues to grow.   In 1/89 they received one of the former Saudi Lightnings from Warton and are due to take delivery of Vampire T.11 WZ515 from Duxford during 1990 (see under Duxford).   The Vulcan is owned by Tom Stoddart, but is displayed by SAS.   The aircraft are open to inspection on Sundays 1400 to 1600.   Contact : Tony Nuttall, Secretary, Solway Aviation Society, Moorside Farm, Laversdale End, Irthington, Carlisle, CA6 4PS.   The Cessna 310 still serves the local fire crews.

G-BAYY	Cessna 310C	ex Hinton-in-the-Hedges, N1782H. CoA expired 6/12/85. Fire crews.
WE188	Canberra T.4	ex Samlesbury, 231 OCU, 360, 231 OCU, 360, 100, 56, 231 OCU, Upwood SF, 231 OCU, Upwood SF, Waddington SF, Hemswell SF.
WS832	Meteor NF.14	ex RRE Pershore, Llanbedr, 12 MU, 8 MU.
XJ823	Vulcan B.2	ex 50, Wadd Wing, 35, 27, 9/35, Wadd Wing, 230 OCU, MoA.
ZF583+	Lightning F.51	ex Warton, RSAF 53-681, G-27-51. Arrived 8/1/89.

SPADEADAM

(North of the B6318, north east of Carlisle)   All is believed to remain the same with the targets and decoys at the Range area.   There are two sites, one being the Weapons Range where two T-33As are secreted and have things hurled at them.   The remainder of the aircraft are located on what is called the Electronic Warfare Site, centred around the abortive Bluestreak launch pad. This is a mock-up airfield that aircraft must attempt to hit, despite having their day truly messed around by all sorts of electronic wizardry.   The final three Mysteres still cannot be conclusively pinned down to being Nos 184, 207 and 262.

FT-01	T-33A-1-LO	ex Prestwick, Belgian AF, USAF 51-4041. Range target.
FT-02	T-33A-1-LO	ex Prestwick, Belgian AF, USAF 51-4043.
FT-06	T-33A-1-LO	ex Prestwick, Belgian AF, Neth AF M-44, USAF 51-4231.
FT-07	T-33A-1-LO	ex Prestwick, Belgian AF, Neth AF M-45, USAF 51-4233.
FT-10	T-33A-1-LO	ex Prestwick, Belgian AF, USAF 51-6664.
FT-11	T-33A-1-LO	ex Prestwick, Belgian AF, Neth AF M-47, USAF 51-6661.
FT-29	T-33A-1-LO	ex Prestwick, Belgian AF, USAF 53-5753. Range target.
61	Mystere IVA	ex Sculthorpe, FAF.
64	Mystere IVA	ex Sculthorpe, FAF.
81	Mystere IVA	ex Sculthorpe, FAF.
139	Mystere IVA	ex Sculthorpe, FAF.
180	Mystere IVA	ex Sculthorpe, FAF.
	Mystere IVA	see notes above.
	Mystere IVA	see notes above.
	Mystere IVA	see notes above.

WINDERMERE

Don't be put off by the name, for the **Windermere Steamboat Museum** contains a water-glider!   (And the steamboats are wonderful anyway!)   Located in Rayrigg Road, the Museum is open Easter to October, Monday to Saturday 1000 to 1800 and 1400 to 1800 on Sundays.   Contact : Windermere Steamboat Museum, Rayrigg Road, Windermere, Cumbria, LA23 1BN. Tel 096 62 5565.

BGA.266	T.1 Falcon	Modified by T C Pattison 1943 and flown from the lake.

Derbyshire

BURNASTON
By the time these words are read the property developers will have completed their rape of this airfield and turning it into a car plant that nobody seems to want just where it is. Sitting out in the long grass was Rallye Commodore G-AXHX (CoA expired 6/7/86) which certainly still present in early 4/90 as the 'dozers got into gear.

BUXTON
Stored in the area is a Fauvel flying wing glider.
BGA 1999+   DCB Fauvel AV.36CR   ex RNGSA, F-CBSH. Stored. First noted 3/88.

DERBY
Located at the Silk Mill, off Full Street, is the **Derby Industrial Museum** which may well annoy the more funadmentalist readers of **W&R** as it contains no aircraft! The compiler has been here three times and is entranced every time. Only exception to the rules normally adopted for this tome, the Museum has a staggering array of aero engines (mainly Rolls-Royce) going from the Eagle to the RB.211. Well worth it! Open 1000 to 1700 Tuesday to Saturday, 1400 to 1700 Sundays and Bank Holidays. Contact: Derby Ind. Museum, The Silk Mill, off Full Street, Derby, DE1 3AR. Tel:0332 255308.

HADFIELD
(On the A621 east of Greater Manchester) Within the Hadfield Industrial Estate, the **Military Aircraft Preservation Group** have their workshop, where work is carried out on their two Vampire pods and on small components and sub-assemblies for other groups. Visits are possible by prior application only. Contact : Phil Maloney, 51 Bleak Hey Road, Peel Hall, Wythenshawe, Manchester M22 5FS. Of the other two aircraft projects being carried out in the mill buildings, Tiger Moth G-ANFC has moved to 'Staffordshire' and we await a more precise location. The Anson C.19/2 nose section VP519/G-AVVR can now be found in Dukinfield.

| XD534 | Vampire T.11 | ex Wythenshawe, Cheadle Hulme, Woodford, Chester, Shawbury, 7 FTS, CFS, 9 FTS, 10 FTS. Pod. |
| 333 | Vampire T.55 | ex Dukinfield, New Brighton, Chester, Iraqi Air Force. Pod. |

SHARDLOW
(On the A6 south east of Derby) It is thought that the Griffiths Gyroplane is still stored here.
G-ATGZ   Griffiths GH.4   stored. Unflown.

Devon

CHIVENOR
W&R status at this pleasant base has changed little with all bar one of those airframes listed in   still serving in their various roles. The nose of Canberra B.2 WJ635 had expired by mid 1989, with a Jet   T.4 arriving to replace it.

WJ629	8747M	Canberra TT.18	ex FRADU, 7, 6, 32, 40. BDR.
WT806		Hunter GA.11	ex FRADU, CFS, 14. Static display, but held airworthy.
XD186	8730M	Whirlwind HAR.10	ex 22, 202, 228, CFS, 155. On display inside the camp.
XF509	8708M	Hunter F.6A	ex Thurleigh, 4 FTS, MoA, AFDS, 54. Gate guardian.
XL567	8723M	Hunter T.7	ex Kemble, 1, Laarbruch SF, 4 FTS, 19, 229 OCU. Dump.
XN632+	8352M	Jet Provost T.3	ex St Athan, Kemble, Shawbury, 3 FTS. Arrived 6/12/89. Dump.
XX257		Hawk T.1	ex Halton, Red Arrows. Crashed 31/8/84. Hulk for BDR.

CHUDLEIGH
(East of the A38, south west of Exeter) At a private motor museum here the one-off Bird Gyrocopter is displayed.
G-AXIY+   Bird Gyrocopter   see above.

DUNKESWELL

The airfield makes a re-entry into the realms of **W&R**. By mid 1989 the former
Torbay Aircraft Museum Provost had arrived for restoration. Some months later a
Vampire T.11 arrived, reportedly to be displayed at the gate.

WV679+	7615M Provost T.1	ex Higher Blagdon, Halton, 2 FTS. First noted 5/89.
XE982+	7564M Vampire T.11	ex Hereford, St Athan, RAFC. First noted 7/89 – see above.

EAGLESCOTT

First-time entry for this airfield with a bent Grob and a stored Cadet.

G-ROBB+	Grob G.109B	crashed 4/7/88. Stored.
WT867+	Cadet TX.3	ex Syerston, 626 VGS. Stored. First noted 8/86.

EAST BUDLEIGH

The hulk of Navajo 350 G-BASU moved through to Exeter Airport.

EXETER

Bertram Arden's famous cache of aircraft is still stored in the general area.

G-AALP	Surrey AL.1	CoA expired 17/5/40. Stored.
G-AFGC	BA Swallow II	ex BK893, G-AFGC. CoA expired 20/3/51. Stored.
G-AFHC	BA Swallow II	CoA expired 20/3/50. Stored.

EXETER AIRPORT

Much to talk of here, mostly in the nature of subtractions. By 7/88 large sections
of Lancaster X KB994 had arrived from Canada for assessment by West Country
Aeroservices for use in the Charles Church rebuild following the accident to
KB976/G-BCOH at Woodford. Parts of the latter also arrived here for a short time.
In the end, CIT at Cranfield got the work and the sections all moved there. Dakota
3 G-ANAF did not take up the marks N170GP and was instead acquired by Aces High and
very quickly transferred to the Dakota-'hungry' Air Atlantique for return to
service. Both of the Heron 2Ds (G-ANUO and G-AOTI) got up and flew out to Biggin
Hill where they commenced more open storage! Queen Air A80 G-ASRX moved on to
Manston by 1/89. Kittiwake G-BBRN moved to a workshop in South Wales and was
flying again by mid 1989. Catalina C-FHNH was acquired by Aces High and was
ferried to North Weald 2/11/88 only to arrive there in spectacular fashion when the
starboard main gear collapsed! Staravia dismantled and removed their two-seat
Hunter PH-NLH by late 1989, moving it to Marlow.

G-AHAT	J/1N Alpha	ex Taunton, Old Sarum, HB-EOK ntu. Crashed 31/8/74. Stored.
G-AMZY	Dove 8XC	CoA expired 11/9/74. With fire crews, poor state.
G-AYTC	Aztec 250C	ex E Midlands, 5Y-ABL, 5X-UUZ, 5Y-ABL. CoA exp 16/11/79. Spares.
G-BASU+	Navajo 350	ex East Budleigh, N7693L. Crashed 12/5/87. Hulk. 1st noted 8/88.
N500LN	Howard 500	ex N381RD, USN 34670. Open store.
VH-BLF	Debonair	ex Dunkeswell, VH-MIL. Wreck.

HIGHER BLAGDON

Land values and the need to be nearer to the direct tourist trade forced Keith
Fordyce and team to offer up the bulk of the airframes of the **Torbay Aircraft
Museum** for auction via Sotheby's on 19/10/88. This does not mean the demise of
this pioneering collection, the search is currently on for a more compact, and more
central location, at which to establish those airframes that have been retained,
plus all the excellent artefacts assembled over the years. Details of re-location
can be had from : Torbay Aircraft Museum, Higher Blagdon, near Paignton, Devon TQ3
3TG. Tel 0803 553540. Note that static Pitts S-2A BAPC.134/'G-CARS' had returned
for display by 5/88, but was returned to the public relations company who owned it
and is thought to be the one travelling around in Toyota markings. The auction was
held at Sotheby's 'Summer Place' at Billingshurst in Sussex, with buyers taking a
look over the airframes on offer in the week previously. Below are listed all of
the airframes held by TAM when the auction was staged. Note that the bids given
are high bids and in some cases do not necessarily reflect a sale. Airframes noted
as 'Retained' are not available for inspection until the Museum re-opens. The
three 'Battle of Britain' replicas were not sold, moving to Hawkinge well after the

sale. We stray from the normal format here, with the first three columns as ever, fourth giving 'high bid' (if appropriate) and the fifth notes.

G-ALFT		Dove 6	£ 1,450	to Caernarfon.
G-CARS"+	B'134	Pitts S-2A static	–	see notes above.
L1592"	B' 63	Hurricane replica	£ 4,000	not sold, later to Hawkinge.
NP184	G-ANYP	Proctor IV	£ 950	to private collector.
RG333"	G-AKEZ	Messenger 2A	£ 480	to private collector.
TX235		Anson C.19	£ 220	to Caernarfon.
WB758	7729M	Chipmunk T.10	£ 5,200	to private collector.
WF877		Meteor T.7(hybrid)	£ 1,550	to Aces High North Weald.
WM961	A2517	Sea Hawk FB.5	£ 1,300	to Caernarfon.
WN499		Dragonfly HR.3	£ 550	to Caernarfon.
WV679	7615M	Provost T.1	£ 2,000	to Dunkeswell.
WV843		Sea Hawk FGA.4	–	nose section, retained.
XE995		Vampire T.11	£ 600	sold, destination unknown.
XG544		Sycamore HR.14	£ 1,200	to Lower Tremar.
XG629		Sea Venom FAW.22	£ 700	to Fleetlands 3/90.
XJ393	A2538	Whirlwind HAR.3	£ 800	to Pulborough.
XN299		Whirlwind HAS.7	£ 3,200	to Portsmouth 2/11/89.
		Varsity T.1 nose	£ ?	to Caernarfon.
425/17"	B'133	Fokker Dr I rep	–	retained.
100545		Fa 330A-1	–	retained.
BAPC 69		Spitfire replica	£ 4,500	not sold, later to Hawkinge.
BAPC 74		'Bf 109' replica	–	not sold, later to Hawkinge.
BAPC 167		SE.5A replica	–	retained.

MANADON
(near Plymouth) Things are much the same regarding the instructional airframes held by the **Royal Navy Engineering College** within HMS 'Thunderer' other than for the arrival of an early Lynx by 10/88.

XF321		Hunter T.7	ex RAE, 56, 130.
XL879		Whirlwind HAS.7	ex Lee-on-Solent, ex 824. Crashed 10/3/61. Cockpit section only.
XP984	A2658	Hawker P.1127	ex RAE Bedford.
XS122	A2707	Wessex HAS.3	ex Wroughton, 737.
XS153		Wessex HAS.3	ex Lee-on-Solent, 737.
XV625		Wasp HAS.1	ex 815.
XW839+		Lynx 00-05	ex Rolls-Royce, Filton. Arrived by 31/10/88.
XZ249		Lynx HAS.2	ex 'Avenger' Flt. 'Purdy'. Crashed 4/5/83. Wreck.

MORETONHAMPSTEAD
Auster J/1 G-AIPW moved to Bristol Airport by 7/89 and was flying shortly afterwards.

PLYMOUTH
Preserved within the harbour is the frigate **HMS 'Plymouth'** and the Trust that owns the ship acquired a Wasp which is displayed on the flight deck.

XS570+	A2699	Wasp HAS.1	ex Lee-on-Solent. First noted late 1988.

PLYMOUTH CITY AIRPORT
(Or Roborough) Having wound-down the entry in **W&R11, Plymouth Executive Aviation** have brought it back with a bang with the delivery of Lightning T.5 XS422 in 9/89. PEA intend to restore the machine to flying condition and the **Lightning Flying Club** has been set up to support this venture. An option is reportedly held on XS422 currently stored at Southampton – which see.

XS451	G-LTNG	Lightning T.5	ex Cranfield, Newton 8503M, St Athan, Binbrook, LTF, 11, 226 OCU, 5, AFDS. Arrived 9/89. See notes above.

WEMBURY
Lightning F.3 XP748/8446M, once proud gate guardian at Binbrook, arrived for use on the ranges here 29/6/88. It had moved on to Pendine by 6/89.

Dorset

BLANDFORD FORUM
With no information to the contrary, we assume the Nord continues its rebuild.

G-BIUP   SNCAN NC.854S   ex Henstridge, G-AMPE ntu, G-BIUP, F-BFSC. CoA expired 24/4/84.

BOURNEMOUTH
With the wind-down of the Wessex Aviation Society airframes at the Wimborne site, **Bill Hamblen** took back the Harvard II and Auster. They join his own Harvard restoration project. **W&R11** claimed the 'spares ship' was just small pieces. This is not so, it constitutes a fuselage frame, also ex Sandhurst.

G-AJPZ+	J/1 Autocrat	ex Wimborne, New Milton, Thruxton, F-BFPE. Damaged 2/3/84. Arrived by 9/89. Stored.
FX442	Harvard II	ex Sandhurst, Avex, 501, 226 OCU, 203 AFS, 61 OTU. Restn.
KF488+	Harvard II	ex Wimborne, Sandhurst, Avex. Cockpit section. Arrived 8/88.
+	Harvard II	ex Sandhurst. Frame. See notes above.

BOURNEMOUTH AIRPORT
Out of the ashes and the auction of the late Mike Carlton's Hunter One Collection (HOC) has come a new historic jet operation under the leadership of Adrian Gjertson and Eric Haywood, **Jet Heritage Ltd** (JHL). Several airframes and all of the ambitions of the previous pioneering operation have been taken on but JHL has a wider scope, not only operating and restoring aircraft for itself, but maintaining and operating vintage jets for other concerns and the buying and selling of such types. (For example, JHL look after Phil Meeson's Venom FB.50 G-GONE and see below for Hunter buying and trading.) When Mike Carlton was killed, negotiations were well in hand for the acquisition of the Connah's Quay Supermarine Swift and this was achieved early in 1989 with its restoration to flying condition planned as a long term project. Jet Provost T.4 XR658 was acquired to exchange for the Swift and it is currently being prepared for its new role as an instructional airframe. It will travel north in due course. Of the Hunter One fleet that was auctioned and listed in **W&R11** the following stayed at Bournemouth to live under the JHL banner : Hunter T.7 G-BOOM, reflown 16/8/89; Jet Provost T.52As G-JETP and G-PROV again now airworthy; Sea Hawk FB.5 G-SEAH under restoration; Meteor TT.20 G-LOSM and again now airworthy. The Sea Hawk is nominally with the amazingly-named Sark International Airways. This operation decided they were chronically short of seating capacity and bought a Gnat at the Sotheby's auction of 9/3/90. This has come here for restoration, dramatically increasing their potential uplift!

Hunter F.51 G-HUNT was acquired by the awesome Combat Jets Flying Museum in the USA as N611JR and now flies as 'WB188'. JHL acquired two Hunter T.7s from Cosford in 11/88. Of these XL617 became G-HHNT and was sold in the USA in 11/89. Very much a 'working' operation, JHL are not set up to take visitors, but their airworthy machines should be seen at flying displays throughout the season. Current situation is as follows, all are technically 'new' :

G-BOOM+	Hunter T.7	ex HOC, Stansted, Leavesden, Hatfield G-9-432, Dunsfold, Aalborg, Danish AF ET-274, ESK-724. Airworthy, reflew 16/8/89.
G-JETP+	Jet Provost T.52A	ex HOC, Singapore ADC 355, Yemen AF 107, XP666. A/w.
G-PROV+	Jet Provost T.52A	ex HOC, Singapore ADC 352, Yemen AF 104, G-27-7, XS228. A/w.
G-SEAH+	WM994 Sea Hawk FB.5	ex HOC, Southend, Swansea, Cranfield, Arbroath A2503, Abbotsinch. Under restoration - see notes above.
WM167+	G-LOSM Meteor TT.20	ex HOC, Blackbushe, RAE Llanbedr, 228, Colerne CS, 228 OCU. A/w.
WV795+	A2661 Sea Hawk FGA.6	ex Bath, Cardiff-Wales, Culdrose, Halton 8151M, Sydenham, 738, 806, 700. Arrived 10/89. For static restoration.
XE677+	G-HHUN Hunter F.4	ex East Kirkby, Loughborough, Dunsfold, 229 OCU, 111, 93, 4. Arrived 9/89.
XF114+	Swift F.7	ex Connah's Quay, Aston Down, CS(A), Cranfield. Arrived 1/89 - see notes above.
XL572+	G-HNTR Hunter T.7	ex Cosford 8834M, 1 TWU, 2 TWU, TWU, 229 OCU. Arrived 11/88.
XM697+	G-NAAT Gnat T.1	ex Woking, HSA, A&AEE, HSA. Arrived 11/12/89.

XR537+	8642M Gnat T.1	ex Cosford, Red Arrows, 4 FTS. Arrived 4/4/90. See notes above.
XR658+	8192M Jet Provost T.4	ex Wroughton, Abingdon RAFEF, 6 FTS, CAW, 7 FTS. See notes above.
XS231+	Jet Provost T.5	ex Scampton, Shawbury, A&AEE, RAE, G-ATAJ ntu. Arrived late 1989.
ET-273+	Hunter T.7	composite, ex Biggin Hill, Macclesfield. Arrived 8/11/89. Plus original nose section.

Already mentioned in the above, Bournemouth is the main base for **Lovaux Ltd** who have greatly expanded their operations. While still specialising in the product support of a range of out-of-production types, they are also a major sub-contractor for the Ministry of Defence. The base at Macclesfield should have been closed down by the time these words are read. It is in the Hunter theme that the company comes into the realms of **W&R** with no less than five currently in their care. The two Qatari Hunters arrived inside Heavylift Belfast G-HLFT.

G-BNCX	XL621 Hunter T.7	ex RAE Bedford, 238 OCU, RAE.
XJ690"	XG195 Hunter FGA.9	ex Macclesfield, Bitteswell, G-9-453, 208, 19, 1. Composite, nose of XG195, other parts largely from XJ690.
E-402	Hunter F.51	ex Macclesfield, Dunsfold, G-9-433, Aalborg, Danish AF ESK.724.
QA-10+	Hunter FGA.78	ex Qatar AF, G-9-286, Dutch AF N-268. Arrived 26/2/88 - see above.
QA-12+	Hunter FGA.78	ex Qatar AF, G-9-284, Dutch AF N-222. Arrived 26/2/88 - see above.

Elsewhere, as ever at Bournemouth Airport, there is much to report. Of the Sykes Aviation Wessex 60 cache, all have moved on : G-AWXX/G-17-6 left by road 10/89, thought bound for the USA; G-AYNC/'150225' moved to Biggin Hill or Redhill in airworthy condition with plans to join the airshow circuit during 1990; G-ATBZ/G-17-4, G-AWOX/G-17-2, G-AZBY/G-17-5 and G-AZBZ/G-17-7 all went to Weston-super-Mare by 9/88. Of the 'Others' aircraft listed in **W&R11** Sea Vixen FAW.2TT G-VIXN was placed into the Christie's Duxford auction of 28/4/90 - see the Appendix. Chipmunk T.10 PAX WK570/8211M moved to Southampton by 4/89. Sea Vixen FAW.2s XP924 and XS577, listed as stored with Flight Refuelling, were both flown out to RAE Llanbedr (XP924 going on 6/1/86) and are still airworthy. Wasp spares-ship XT415 is assumed to have gone to New Zealand. BAC 1-11 G-AYUW fuselage is with AIM Aviation for smoke hood/fire suppression development.

G-ASFD+	L-200A Morava	ex Shoreham. CoA expired 12/7/84. Under restoration.
G-ASLH	Cessna 182F	ex Ipswich, N3505U. Crashed 14/6/81. Rebuild.
G-ASLL	Cessna 336	ex Doncaster, N1774Z. CoA expired 6/1/74. Stored.
G-ATAH	Cessna 336	ex N1707Z. CoA expired 5/12/76. Stored.
G-ATLC	Aztec 250C	ex Alderney Air Carter, N5903Y. CoA expired 30/9/78. Stored.
G-AVDR	Queen Air B80	ex Shobdon, Exeter, A40-CR, G-AVDR. CoA expired 30/6/86. Stored.
G-AVDS	Queen Air B80	ex Exeter, A40-CS, G-AVDS. CoA expired 26/8/77. Stored.
G-AYUW+	BAC 1-11 476FM	ex Luton, Faucett OB-R-953, BAC G-AYUW, G-16-17. Fuselage, arrived by 6/89. See notes above.
G-BEZB	Herald 209	ex Channel Express 'Blossom', 4X-AHS, G-8-2. Spares. CoA expired 2/2/88.
G-BNNG	Cessna T.337D	ex G-COLD, PH-NOS, N86147. CoA expired 15/7/85. Under rebuild.
G-VIXN	XS587 Sea Vixen FAW.2TT	ex FRL, RAE Farnborough 8828M, FRL, ADS, 899. See notes above.
EL-AJC	Boeing 707-430	ex 3C-ABI, N90498, 9G-ACK. With fire service.
N1721Z	Cessna 336	ex Isle of Mull. Crashed 10/7/74. Wreck, in store.
1190	Bf 109E	ex Buckfastleigh, Canada, II/JG.26. Force-landed Sussex 9/9/40. Under restoration in a hut on the airfield.

BOVINGTON
(Off the A352 near Wool, west of Wareham) The Skeeter is still on the gate of the **Junior Leaders Regiment** (and opposite the entrance to the Royal Tank Museum).

| XM564 | Skeeter AOP.12 | ex 652, CFS, 12 Flt, 652. Gate guardian. |

CHRISTCHURCH
The **Sea Vixen Society's** XJ580 is displayed outside 'Queensway' on the A35 Southampton road.

| XJ580 | Sea Vixen FAW.2 | ex Bournemouth Airport, FRL, RAE Farnborough, Llanbedr, 899. |

COMPTON ABBAS

Provost T.1 XF877/G-AWVF was airworthy again by 1989. A Super Cub and a Chipmunk have arrived to take its place.

G-AYPT+	Super Cub 95	ex D-EALX ntu, ALAT 51-15533. First noted 5/89. Restoration.
G-BDBL+	Chipmunk 22	ex Booker, WK621, Oxf UAS, Lon UAS, 6 AEF, Lon UAS, Biggin Hill SF, Lon UAS, Oxf UAS, Bri UAS, 22 RFS. Crashed 21/1/84. Composite, with rear end of G-AOSN. First noted 6/89.

DORCHESTER

Brian Woodford's fleet of airworthy classics, the **Wessex Aviation & Transport Collection** is based at a private strip here. The collection is not open to public inspection on a regular basis but occasionally open days are staged. The aircraft are also regular attenders at displays and fly-ins.

G-ABEV	DH.60G Moth	ex N4203E, G-ABEV, HB-OKI, CH-217.
G-ACZE	Dragon Rapide	ex G-AJGS, G-ACZE, Z7266, 3 FP, 6 AONS, G-ACZE.
G-ADHA	Fox Moth	ex N83DH, ZK-ASP, NZ566, ZK-ADI.
G-ADPS+	BA Swallow II	ex Hungerford, Dorchester, Strathallan, Sandown.
G-AEDT+	DH.90 Dragonfly	ex Southampton, USA, N2034, G-AEDT, VH-AAD, G-AEDT.
G-AFOB+	Moth Minor	ex Old Warden, X5117, 10 OAFU, St A UAS, 613, G-AFOB.
G-AGAT	J3F-50 Cub	ex NC26126.
G-AIYS	Leopard Moth	ex YI-ABI, SU-ABM.
G-AZMH	MS.500 Criquet	ex Booker, EI-AUU ntu, F-BJQG, French military. Luftwaffe c/s.
G-BMNV	SNCAN SV-4L	ex Booker, F-BBNI.
N4712V	PT-13D Kaydet	ex 42-16931.
T5672	G-ALRI Tiger Moth	ex ZK-BAB, G-ALRI, T5672, 7 FTS, 21 EFTS, 7 FTS, RAFC, 4 EFTS.
V9281"+	G-BCWL Lysander IIIA	ex Booker, Hamble, Blackbushe, Booker, Canada, RCAF.

At his workshop, **Tim Lane** continues to restore the Auster.

TW439	G-ANRP Auster 5	ex Warnham, Bournemouth, TW439, 9 MU, TCDU, 47 GCF, CFS, 20 MU, 1 FP. CoA expired 11/5/73. Serial corrected from **W&R11**.

PORTLAND

Little change to record at the Fleet Air Arm helicopter station. Wessex HAS.1 XM326 had demised on the dump by 7/88. By that time, a sequentially-minded Wasp had taken its place.

XS537	A2672 Wasp HAS.1	ex WLT, 703. Dump.
XT786	A2726 Wasp HAS.1	ex Wroughton, 829. Dump.
XV623	A2724 Wasp HAS.1	ex Wroughton, 829. Dump.
XV624+	Wasp HAS.1	ex Wroughton. Dump by 11/86.

SHERBORNE

(On the A30 east of Yeovil) Instructional airframes at the **Westland Customer Training School** are unchanged. The 'Gyrocopter' has been present since at least 1985, is unflown and decidedly a 'one-off'.

G-BIWY	WG.30-100	ex Yeovil, BAH. CoA expired 30/3/86.
	'Gyrocopter'	see notes above.
XR526	8147M Wessex HC.2	ex RAE Farnborough, Odiham, 72. Damaged 27/5/70.
PA-12	ZE449 SA.330L Puma	ex Weston-super-Mare, Fleetlands, Portsmouth, Port Stanley, Argentine PNA.

THORNICOMBE

Hiller UH-12C G-ASTP moved out to <u>Biggin Hill</u> by 10/88.

WEST MOORS

(On the B3072 north of Bournemouth) Confirmed as present with the fire section of the **RAOC Fuel Depot** here is the Wasp.

XS535	Wasp HAS.1	ex Wroughton, 703. Fire training.

WIMBORNE

With John May selling up the Botanic Gardens and moving for a well-deserved rest in Scotland, the **Wessex Aviation Society** decided to merge its efforts and act as a 'support group' for the Hall of Aviation in Southampton. Moving over to Southampton by 10/88 were : Tiger Moth G-ADWO/BB807; Meteor F.8 WA984; Sea Venom FAW.22 WM571; Pembroke C.1 nose WV705 and Wight Quadruplane replica BAPC 164. Sioux AH.1 XT242 was acquired by Ken Fern/The Helicopter Collection and despatched to Long Marston. J/1 Autocrat G-AJPZ and Harvard II KF388 went to Bournemouth. The Rotabuggy replica remains on loan with the Museum of Army Flying at Middle Wallop. Details of WAS are to be found under the 'Southampton' banner.

Essex

ANDREWSFIELD

(Or Great Saling) By 9/89 the hulks of Cherokee 140B G-AXTK and Cessna F.172H G-AXWF had gone - the former to Southend. Contrary to **W&R11**, Rebel Air Museum were refused permission by the USAF to move Mystere IVA 319 to their new home at Earls Colne. So it remains here without an 'owner'. Current situation is as follows :

G-ALNA	Tiger Moth	ex 'N9191', T6774, 6 FTS, 3 EFTS, 25 RFS, 28 EFTS, 2 EFTS. Crashed 26/1/86. Stored.
G-AYRP+	Cessna FA.150L	crashed 2/8/87. Wreck.
319	Mystere IVA	ex Sculthorpe, French Air Force. See notes above.

AUDLEY END

Rebuild of the Russavia Dragon Rapide continues apace. Since late 1987, a Luscombe Silvaire has also been making progress here.

G-AGTM	Dragon Rapide	ex Duxford, Biggin Hill, Duxford, JY-ACL, OD-ADP, G-AGTM, NF875. Damaged 21/6/87. Under restoration.
G-BNIO+	Silvaire 8A	ex NC45593. Under restoration since 9/87.

BASILDON

Unique in the realms of ATC units, **2243 Squadron** have an Airtourer airframe.

G-AWVH	Airtourer T.2	ex Southchurch, Goodwood. Crashed 15/3/81.

BOXTED

(North of Colchester, between the A134 and A12) Near the former airfield and near the 'Wig and Figget' public house is to be found the **Colchester Military and Aviation Museum**. Details are only sketchy, they are reported to be "open most weekends". Their major aviation exhibit is a long lost Essex inmate.

9J-RGH+	Cessna F.150F	ex Lexden, Martlesham Heath. Cockpit, camouflaged. 1st noted 5/88.

BRAINTREE

Located in the area is the workshop of **Vintage Fabrics** who are working on at least two of the Spitfires in the Historic Flying Ltd gate guardian exchange (based at Fulbourn). As we close for press, there is a report that Spitfire Mk XVI TD248 had come here from Earls Colne - which see. RW382 is for David Tallichet/Military Aircraft Restoration Corporation of Chino, California who will be supplying the Beaufort for the RAF Museum.

RW382+	8075M Spitfire XVI	ex Uxbridge, Leconfield, Church Fenton 7245M, C&RS, 3 CAACU, 604. Arrived 26/8/88. See notes above.
TB252+	8073M Spitfire XVI	ex Bentley Priory, Leuchars, Boulmer, Acklington, Odiham, 7281M, 7257M, 61 OTU, 350, 341, 329, 84 GSU. Arrived 9/11/88.

CHELMSFORD

In Meteor Lane **276 Squadron ATC** maintain their twin-jet of the same name. The **Fire**

Station took delivery of a Queen Air fuselage by 11/89 from Manston. By 9/89 Tiger
Moth G-ANPK was flying.

G-ASRX+	Queen Air A80	ex Manston, Exeter. CoA expired 30/4/84. Arrived by 11/89.
WH132	7906M Meteor T.7	ex Kemble, CAW, CFS, CAW, 8 FTS, 207 AFS.

COGGESHALL
(On the A120 east of Braintree) At the yard of **Chelmer Transport Hauliers** the nose
sections of two former Arkia Viscounts are stored.

4X-AVB+	Viscount 833	ex Tel Aviv, Arkia, BUA G-APTB. Cockpit. First noted 9/89.
4X-AVF+	Viscount 831	ex Tel Aviv, Arkia, G-16-20, BMA G-APND, Alia JY-ADB, BUA G-APND. First noted 9/89.

COLCHESTER
In this general area a workshop is restoring a Spitfire XVIII for David
Tallichet/Military Aircraft Restoration Corporation. Also here are the chunks of
Sea Furies G-AGHB and G-FURY previously at Milton Keynes. A Sea Fury centre
section is being used as the basis of at least one Sea Fury restoration, using a
new set of wings and the parts from 'HB and 'RY. The centre section is reported to
have come from the Navy and this might well make it the long-lost D-CIBO, last
heard of in storage at Wroughton 10/77.

TP298+	Spitfire XVIII	ex USA, Wroughton, Kalaikunda, Indian AF, RAF. See notes.
+	Sea Fury FB.11	composite restoration. See notes above.

DOWNHAM
By 5/88 the much-travelled Blackburn B2 G-ACBH had moved to Wickham Bishops.

EARLS COLNE
From the Spring of 1990 the **Rebel Air Museum** was up and running again in a new 100'
x 70' exhibition building. It will take some time for Dave Brett and friends to
take up all of the space offered within, but the quality of displays from the
Andrewsfield days are assured. As W&R closed for press exact opening times etc
were not available, although the aim was to be open every weekend. More details
from : RAM, 14 Amyruth Road, Brockley, London, SE4 1HQ. Telephone 081 690 0917.
Contrary to **W&R11**, the Mystere did not come here - see under Andrewsfield. The
Meteor nose here is not identified.

N9606H	PT-26 Cornell II	ex Andrewsfield, Southend, FH768, 42-14361.
EE425	Meteor F.3	ex Andrewsfield, Foulness, MoS, 206 AFS, 210 AFS, 206 AFS, 63, 266, 1, 222. Nose.
BAPC 115	HM.14 Pou du Ciel	ex Andrewsfield, Balham, South Wales.

Over at Eddie Coventry's **BAC Aviation**, restoration of the Yak (a C-11, not an 18)
moves on apace. Former Sealand gate guardian Spitfire TD248 arrived here by 8/88
for restoration to flying condition. It may have moved to Braintree (which see) by
late 1989.

G-OYAK	Yak C-11	ex La Ferte Alais, Egyptian Air Force 705 - corrects identity given in **W&R11**.
TD248+	G-OXVI Spitfire XVI	ex Sealand, Hooton Park 7246M, 610, 2 CAACU, 695. Arrived 8/88. See notes above.

EAST TILBURY
The number of airframes with the **Thameside Aviation Museum** at Coalhouse Fort has
increased to the tune of a Proctor and a Pup. It is thought to be open on the last
Sunday of each month, more details are available from : Thameside Aviation Museum,
80 Elm Road, Grays, Essex, RM17 6LD.

G-ADXS	HM.14 Pou du Ciel	ex Andrewsfield, Southend, Staverton, Southend.
G-AVZO+	Pup 100	ex Southend Airport, Benendon. CoA expired 12/7/75. Fuselage.
NP303+	G-ANZJ Proctor IV	ex Byfleet, Caterham, Kenley, Nottingham, Royston, London Bridge, Southend. CoA expired 10/3/67. Fuselage, first noted 9/89.

FOULNESS ISLAND

First thing needed here is to amend the title to **Projectile Experimental Establishment**, which covers a multitude of sins! A series of reports from here allows for a comprehensive run-down of the inmates. PEE also has an out-station at Pendine, which see. **W&R10** reported Buccaneer S.1 XK536 leaving by road on 22/10/85 - it is now known to have gone to <u>Pendine</u>. The Welsh projectile men seem to have a penchant for 'Bricks' as S.1 XN933 left by road on 14/10/85 and S.1 XN926 left 17/10/85, both also bound for <u>Pendine</u>. **W&R11** noted the rear fuselages of Canberra B.2/8 WE121 and B.2E WK164 going to Abingdon on 28/8/86. During 12/89 only the rear and mid fuselage of WE121 was to be noted here! Not noted before, Scimitar F.1 XD228 was to be found in the scrap area 12/89, as wings only. Also in that pile was XD241, again as wings only. Listed in **W&R11**, but not present by 12/89 were Canberra T.4 WJ872/8429M, Scimitar F.1 XD333 and Wasp HAS.1 XS565 - the latter being very short-lived, first noted 5/88. The current situation is as follows, all noted late 1989 unless noted :

WH673		Canberra B.2	ex Farnborough, 7, CAW, RAFC. Fuselage only.
WJ642"	WH723	Canberra B.2	ex Upwood, Weeton 7628M, BAC, 231 OCU. Fuselage.
WJ643		Canberra B.2/8	ex Farnborough, RAE. Noseless fuselage.
WJ679		Canberra B.2	ex RAE.
WJ880	8491M	Canberra T.4	ex Halton, 7, 85, 100, 56 Laarbruch SF, RAE, 16, Laarbruch SF, Gutersloh, 104. Noseless fuselage. See Firbeck.
WJ990		Canberra B.2	ex RAE, RRE, RAE, 40. Fuselage.
WK121+		Canberra B.2	ex RAE. Fuselage.
WK164		Canberra B.2E	ex 100. Fuselage. See notes above.
WT507	8548M	Canberra PR.7	ex Halton 8131M, 31, 17, 58, A&AEE, 58, 527, 58. Noseless fuse.
WT534	8549M	Canberra PR.7	ex Halton, 17. Noseless fuselage.
WT859	A2499	Supermarine 544	ex Culdrose, Fleetlands, Culdrose, Lee-on-Solent, RAE Bedford. Fuselage only, poor shape.
XA937		Victor K.1	ex St Athan, 214, 57, A&AEE, 10. Fuselage.
XD215	A2573	Scimitar F.1	ex Culdrose, 764B, 800, 803, A&AEE. Fuselage.
XD219		Scimitar F.1	ex Farnborough, West Freugh, Brawdy, FRU, 736, A&AEE. Fuselage.
XD235		Scimitar F.1	ex FRU, 803. Fuselage.
XD244		Scimitar F.1	ex Brawdy, 803, 736, 803, 807. Fuselage.
XD267		Scimitar F.1	ex Farnborough, FRU, 764B, 803, 736, 800,736, 803, 804, 807. Fuselage.
XD322		Scimitar F.1	ex FRU, 803, A&AEE, 800, 807. Fuselage.
XD857		Valiant BK.1	ex 49. Nose section.
XK525		Buccaneer S.1	ex Holme-on-Spalding Moor, Brough, West Freugh, RAE.
XM271+	8204M	Canberra B(I).8	ex Halton, 16, 88, Wildenrath SF. Minus nose. Last noted in **W&R9**. Dismantled by 12/89.
XN259	A2604	Whirlwind HAS.7	ex Lee-on-Solent, Arbroath, 771, 829, 847, 848. Gutted.
XN726	8545M	Lightning F.2A	ex Farnborough, Gutersloh, 92, 19, CFE.
XN771		Lightning F.2A	ex Farnborough, Gutersloh, 19, CFE.
XN795+		Lightning F.2A	ex RAE Bedford, A&AEE, BAC. First noted 12/89.
XN955		Buccaneer S.1	ex RAE.
XN960		Buccaneer S.1	ex Farnborough, RAE.
XR756+		Lightning F.6	ex Binbrook, 5, 11, LTF, 5, LTF, 5-11 pool, 23, 11, 23, 11, 23, 5. Arrived 28/6/88.
XS421		Lightning T.5	ex RAE, 23, 111, 226 OCU.
XS580+		Sea Vixen FAW.2	ex Farnborough, 899. Pod only. First noted 6/89.
XS927+		Lightning F.6	ex Binbrook, 5-11 pool, 23, 11, 74. Arrived 28/6/88.
XV280		Harrier GR.1	ex Boscombe Down, A&AAEE, HSA. Fuselage.
XV357		Buccaneer S.2A	ex St Athan, 237 OCU, 208.
XV373+		Sea King HAS.1	ex Boscombe Down, A&AEE. Arrived 29/7/86.
XV417		Phantom FGR.2	ex 29, 17, 14, 17, 14, 2, 228 OCU. Crashed 23/3/76. Noseless.
XV798		Harrier GR.1	ex Dunsfold. Composite airframe - nose from XP832, wings from XW264. Ex PCB test rig.
XW541+	8858M	Buccaneer S.2B	ex Honington, St Athan, 12, 16, 15. Arrived 11/10/88 via Chinook.
XW837		Lynx 1/06	ex Boscombe Down, Yeovil.

XW922+	8885M Harrier GR.3	ex Enfield, 233 OCU, 1 233 OCU, 1. First noted 6/89.
XX153	Lynx AH.1	ex Westlands.
XX510	Lynx HAS.2	ex Boscombe Down. Last noted 6/89.
	Lynx rotor rig	ex Yeovil. Plate reads WA/E/32.

FYFIELD
(On the B184 west of Chelmsford) Now very long-term, is the derelict Cherokee.

N3850K	Cherokee 140	battered fuselage.

HALSTEAD
(North east of Braintree) The Tiger restoration continues.

G-APBI	Tiger Moth	ex Audley End, EM903. Crashed 7/7/80. Rebuild.

LAINDON
(North of the A127, near Basildon) At a farm here, **George French** has two Austers.

G-AIGT+	J/1N Alpha	ex Audley End. CoA expired 22/10/76. Restn. 1st noted 9/89.
G-AOBV+	J/5P Autocar	ex Stapleford Tawney, Benington. CoA expired 7/4/71. Stored.

LOUGHTON
(To the west of Junction 5 on the M11) More precisely located than the previous Enfield heading is the **Lippitts Hill Police Helicopter Base**. A crunched Bell 222 is held for questioning - sorry, spares!

G-META+	Bell 222	ex N5733H. Crashed 6/5/87. Spares use.

NAVESTOCK
(Between the A113 and A128 south of Chipping Ongar) Still stored at **Jenkins Farm** is the Moth Minor.

G-AFOJ	Moth Minor	ex E-1, E-0236, G-AFOJ. CoA expired 27/8/69. Stored.

NORTH WEALD
With the opening of The Squadron in March 1989, North Weald became an airfield offering an unparalleled number of historic aviation facilities. Largest operator on the airfield, and planning another hangar is **Aces High**. Their fleet is a 'working' one and constantly changing, but always offers an ever-increasing array of types. Visits to the hangar are possible by prior arrangement. Contact : 037 882 2949. Other enquiries to : Aces High, Building D2, Fairoaks Airport, Chobham, Surrey. Tel 09905 6384. By far and away the 'star' acquisition for a long time must be the MiG-21PF from Hungary which is fully capable of flight. A second machine (G-BRAN) arrived here in two ISO containers, but was not unpacked and went on to the USA as N316DM. A third 'Fishbed' (G-BRAO ex 1603) is thought to have gone direct to the USA. The PBY made a spectacular arrival on the ferry flight from Exeter when the starboard undercarriage collapsed on landing. Of the aircraft listed in **W&R11**, the following have moved on : Dakota G-AMPO was acquired by Air Atlantique and is now in service at Coventry; Lincoln 2 G-29-1 was sold to Charles Church for use in the Lancaster restoration project and left 6/12/88 for Cranfield; the hulk of Enstrom 280C D-HGBX had gone by 1988; Seneca 200 N503DM was flying by early 1989; Meteor T.7 VZ638/G-JETM moved to Charlwood by 7/88. Over at Duxford, Aces High's Venom J-1605 was moved during 1989, also to Charlwood. C-119G N3267U flew in from Stansted 24/10/88 to winter on the Aces High ramp. It received a contract to fly in Africa in mid 1989 and flew off. In the meantime, the owner acquired the Aces High C-119G for spares. There are hopes that the airframe will find its way to a museum once this process is finished. In addition to their own aircraft, Aces High are currently playing host to a US registered Paris and the wonderfully-named Butane Buzzard Aviation, who are restoring a Sea Vixen and a Gnat. Butane Buzzard have entered the 'Vixen into the Christie's auction at Duxford on 28/4/90. Aces High have entered the following for this auction : CASA 2-111 G-AWHB; Beech 18 G-BKRG; TB-25N N1042B; TB-25J N9089Z; Venom G-BLSD and MiG-21PF G-BRAM. Current status here is :-

G-AWHB	CASA 2-111	ex Royston, Southend, Spanish AF B2-157. Dismantled.

G-BKRG	Beech C-45G	ex Duxford, N75WB, 'Octopussy', N9072Z, 51-11665. See notes above.
	JetRanger	ex Fairoaks, static composite for 'Biggles'.
N212DM+ G-BPFY	PBY-6A Catalina	ex Exeter C-FHNH, F-ZBAV, N5555H, N2846D, USN 64107. Flew in 2/11/88 - see notes above. Airworthy.
N999PJ+	Paris 2	ex F-BJLY. Lodges with Aces High. Airworthy.
N1042B	TB-25N Mitchell	ex Tallmantz Aviation, 44-30823. 'Dolly'. Camera-ship. Airworthy. See notes above.
N2700	C-119G-FA Boxcar	ex Manston, G-BLSW, 3C-ABA, Belgian AF CP-9, 57-2700. See notes above.
EN398"	B'184 Spitfire IX rep	ex Duxford.
HD368"	N9089Z TB-25J Mitchell	ex Duxford, G-BKXW ntu, Southend, Biggin Hill, N9089Z, 44-30861. 'Bedsheet Bomber'. See notes above.
WF877+	G-BPOE Meteor T.7(mod)	ex Higher Blagdon, Tarrant Rushton, Chilbolton, 96, 11. Arrived by 1/89.
XN691+	8143M Sea Vixen FAW.2	ex Coventry, Cosford, Halton, Sydenham, 893, 899. Arrived 2/90. Butane Buzzard Aviation. See notes above.
XS104+	G-FRCE Gnat T.1	ex Cosford 8604M, Kemble, 4 FTS. Arrived 4/89. Butane Buzzard. Under restoration to flying condition.
VK+AZ"	G-BFHG CASA 352L	ex Duxford, Fairoaks, Blackbushe, Spanish Air Force T2B-262. A/w.
503+	N610DM MiG-21PF Fishbed	ex G-BRAM, Hungarian AF. Arrived 4/89. See notes above.
J-1758	G-BLSD Venom FB.54	ex N203DM, Cranfield, G-BLSD, Dubendorf, Swiss AF. A/w. See notes above.
100884	G-DAKS Dakota 3	ex Duxford, 'KG374', 'Airline' 'G-AGHY', TS423, RAE, Ferranti, Airwork, Gatow SF, 436, 1 HGSU, 42-100884. Airworthy.
483009"+G-BPSE	AT-6D-1-NT Texan	ex NWRF, Ashford, 42-44450. Acquired summer 1989.

As outlined above another major facility opened at North Weald on 25/3/89 - **The Squadron.** Acting as a centre for classic aircraft restoration and operation and headquarters for the Harvard Formation Team, this is combined with a unique, members only, clubhouse and bar. Membership is open to anyone and includes an excellent house magazine. Visits to inspect the aircraft at The Squadron by non members is by prior appointment. A wide series of fly-ins is arranged during the summer season. Details from : The Squadron, North Weald Airfield, Epping, Essex, CM16, 6AA. Telephone : 037 882 4510. With the opening of the hangars there has been an influx of based aircraft. For completeness, these are listed but an increasing number of transients is not. There has been only one removal from the list as given in **W&R11**, Harvard IIB B-168 was acquired by ARC at Duxford and had moved there by 9/89. All below are airworthy, unless noted.

G-AZSC	Harvard IIB	ex PH-SKK, Dutch AF B-19, FT323, 43-13064. Gary Numan.
G-BRKC+	J/1 Autocrat	ex F-BFYT. Arrived by 9/89 for rebuild.
G-BRLV+	Harvard IV	ex N90448, RCAF 20403. Arrived by 9/89. Lloyd Owens.
G-ONAF+	NAF N3N-3	ex N45192. Pete Treadaway.
F-BGRZ+ G-AHAR	J/1 Autocrat	ex France. Arrived by 9/89. For restoration.
N15799+	'Zeke'/Harvard IV	ex USA, 'Tora, Tora, Tora', RCAF 20326. Arrived early 1989.
EX280	G-TEAC Harvard IIA	ex Portuguese AF 1523, SAAF 7333, EX280, 41-33253. Euan English.
FE992	G-BDAM Harvard IIB	ex LN-MAA, Fv16047, FE992, 42-12479. Euan English & Norman Lees.
FT239"	G-BIWX Harvard IV	ex MM53846, USAF. Anthony Hutton.
HB275"	N5063N Beech D.18S	ex G-BKGM, CF-SUQ, RCAF 2324. Anthony Hutton.
53319+	N3966A TBM-3E Avenger	ex Ipswich, USN. Flew in 23/9/89. Anthony Haig Thomas.

Over at **Robs Lamplough's** hangar (not open to inspection), Yak C.18M G-BMJY made its first post restoration flight during 9/89. Robs has acquired Hawker Sea Fury N232J and he raced it at the 1988 Reno, but as yet it has not crossed the 'Pond'. The three former Thorpe Park replicas (Deperdussin BAPC.136, Macchi M.39 BAPC.141 and Supermarine S.6B BAPC.156) were all exported to the USA. Harvard G-BGPB/385 suffered an accident at Gransden 15/6/89 and was acquired by 9/89 by ARC at Duxford for use as spares. Current situation is as follows :-

G-BMFB	AD-4W Skyraider	ex Angelholm, SE-EBK, G-31-12, WV181, USN 126867. Stored.
G-BMFC	AD-4W Skyraider	ex Bromma, SE-EBH, G-31-2, WT951, USN 127949. Stored.

G-BMJY		Yak C-18M	ex La Ferte Alais, Egyptian AF 627. Airworthy.
G-KYAK		Yak C-11	ex Duxford, Booker, Israel, Egyptian AF 590, Czech AF. A/w.
MV370	G-FXIV	Spitfire XIV	ex Basingstoke, Whitehall, St Leonards-on-Sea, Henfield, Nagpur, Indian AF instructional T44, MV370.
152/17"	G-ATJM	Fokker Dr I rep	ex Duxford, Orlando, N78001, EI-APY, G-ATJM. Airworthy.
28		P-51D-20-NA	ex Fowlmere, Watton, Duxford, Israeli AF/DF. Restoration.
72216	G-BIXL	P-51D-20-NA	ex Duxford, Ein-Gedi, Israeli AF/DF 43, Fv 26116, 44-72216. A/w.
126912		AD-1N Skyraider	ex Chad, French AF. Stored.

With the sad death of Bill Miles in late 1988, the decision was taken to wind-up
the **North Weald Aircraft Restoration Flight.** Bill was a patient and persevering
individual determined to keep his 'beloved North Weald 'alive'. He was very proud
of the developments going on all around him. The Meteor TT.20 is being maintained
on the airfield by the **39 Squadron Association.** Other than the Meteor, disposals
have been as follows : BAPC 117 BE.2 replica to Brooklands; BAPC 179 Sopwith Pup
replica to Waltham Abbey; 'V7767'/BAPC.72 Hurricane replica to Brooklands;
WJ880/8491M Canberra T.4 nose to Firbeck 30/7/89; XK625 Vampire T.11 to Firbeck
10/6/89; 'C19/18'/BAPC.118 Albatros replica to Firbeck 30/7/89; the Hunter nose was
returned to the RAF - destination unknown; Texan '483009' to Aces High and moved
across the airfield - see above. That leaves :

WM311"	WM224 Meteor TT.20	ex East Dereham, CSDE Swanton Morley 8177M, 5 CAACU, 3 CAACU, 228 OCU. 39 Squadron Association.

PAGLESHAM

(North east of Rochford) By 9/89 there was no sign of either Pawnee wreck G-BFEX
or of stored Beaver N5595K. All that could be seen was :

G-BFOI	W-Bell 47G-3B1	ex XT811. Crashed here 31/7/86. Wreck.

RAYLEIGH

Clearing up the entry here, the nose of Lightning F.1 XG325 did not come here after
the closure of the Historic Aircraft Museum at Southend Airport in 1982, but stayed
on the airfield site, waiting until late 1989 to be 'rediscovered' by **W&R!**

ROMFORD

Nigel Towler has established the **Cockpit Collection** here, having gained two from
East Kirkby. There may be some confusion between this venture and the one at
Walpole - which see.

WD954+	Canberra B.2	ex East Kirkby, Tattershall, Bicester, 76, Upwood, Hemswell. Nose section. Arrived 1989.
XH670+	Victor B.2	ex East Kirkby, Tattershall, Woodford, Radlett, Wittering Wing, MoA. Nose section. Arrived 1989.

SOUTHEND

Here the **Southend Historic Aircraft Society** have a small workshop and continue to
work on the former HAM Scion.

G-AEZF	Scion II	ex Southend Airport. CoA expired 5/5/54. Under restoration.

SOUTHEND AIRPORT

(Or Rochford) Still unrivalled in terms of the number of long-term and very
dormant civilian hulks, Southend Airport continues to take up a large chunk of the
overly expanding 'Essex' entry. There have been many additions, but only a few
subtractions. Long expected, but sad nevertheless, was the scrapping of Beverley
C.1 XB261 in 4/89. The nose section was presented to the DAS and moved to Duxford
on 9/5/89. This loss was made all the worse by the unbelievable scrapping of the
Hendon example not much later. Other departures : Devon C.2/2 G-ALFM was flying by
6/88; Tri-Pacer 150 G-APXT has left for 'London' for conversion to a PA-20 Pacer;
the hulk of Cessna F.150G G-AVCT moved onto Shobdon; Pup 100 fuselage G-AVZO has
turned up as a museum piece at East Tilbury; Z37 Cmelak G-AVZB made its last flight
on 25/6/88 to Wroughton for the Science Museum; Agwagon G-AZZG moved to Inverness

some years back. Viscount 806 G-APEY, listed in **W&R11** was in open store for only a short while before going back into service. Viscount 806 G-APIM was hit by an impassioned Shorts 'Shoebox' 11/1/88. It was put into open store until donated to the Brooklands Museum, moving there 11/2/90. Current situation :-

G-ALJZ	J/1 Autocrat	ex Shobdon. Crashed 25/10/70. Under rebuild.
G-AOHL	Viscount 802	Withdrawn from use 6/2/81. BAF cabin trainer.
G-AOHT	Viscount 802	ex ZS-SKY, G-AOHT, BAF, BEA. CoA expired 16/5/86. Fuselage.
G-AOYL+	Viscount 806	ex BAF, BA, BEA. Donated tail to G-BBDK by 1/90. CoA exp 2/8/88.
G-APBW	Auster Alpha 5	ex Audley End. Crashed 25/7/82. Under rebuild.
G-APEX	Viscount 806	ex BAF, BA, BEA. CoA expired 12/5/84. Fuselage.
G-APWA	Herald 100	ex PP-SDM, PP-ASV, G-APWA. CoA expired 4/82. Stored.
G-ARAB	Cessna 150	ex Elstree, N6485T. Damaged 25/1/86. Wreck.
G-ASYN	Terrier 2	ex Sibson, VF519, 661. Damaged 2/1/76. Spares.
G-ATGG+	MS.885 Super Rallye	ex F-BKLR. CoA expired 14/10/83. Stored.
G-ATMN	Cessna F.150F	crashed 11/5/84. Wreck for spares.
G-AVWZ	Fournier RF-4D	crashed 11/1/81. Fuselage, stored.
G-AWCK	Cessna F.150H	crashed 30/9/75. Wreck.
G-AWJI+	MS.880B Rallye Club	CoA expired 26/11/84. Stored.
G-AWLJ	Cessna F.150H	crashed 20/11/84. Wreck.
G-AWOC	MS.892A Rallye	crashed 13/6/74. Wreck.
G-AXTK+	Cherokee 140B	ex Andrewsfield. Crashed 6/9/81. First noted 10/89.
G-AYJD+	Fournier RF-3	ex F-BLXA. CoA expired 19/8/77. Under rebuild.
G-AYOX	Viscount 814	ex Tees-Side, BMA, 4X-AVA, G-AYOX, D-ANAC. CoA expired 14/11/84. Fuselage. Spares use.
G-AYRK	Cessna 150J	ex 5N-AII, N61170. CoA expired 25/4/76. Stored.
G-AYYE	Cessna F.150L	crashed 26/4/78. Wreck, spares use.
G-AZDZ	Cessna 172K	ex 5N-AIH, N1647C, N84508. Crashed 19/9/81. Wreck.
G-AZRW	Cessna T.337C	ex 9XR-DB, N2614S. CoA expired 7/6/82. Stored.
G-BCAB	MS.894A Rallye	crashed 25/2/77. Wreck.
G-BCIH	Cherokee 140	ex PH-VRN, N6661J. Crashed 14/11/76. Wreck.
G-BDOZ	Fournier RF-5	ex Chinnor, 5Y-AOZ. CoA expired 5/9/83. Stored.
G-BEPE	Belfast	ex G-52-14, XR362, 53 Squadron, G-ASKE. Spares use.
G-BEYE+	Herald 401	ex BAF, RMAF FM1021. CoA expired 15/6/83. Open store.
G-BFAC+	F.177RG Cardinal	ex N177AB, G-BFAC, D-EDIS. Damaged 4/1/89. Stored.
G-BKME	Skyvan 3-100	ex Stansted, A40-SN, G-AYJN, G-14-57. Stored.
G-BNAA+	Viscount 806	ex BAF, C-GWPY, G-AOYH. BAF, BA, BEA. CoA exp 22/3/88. Stored.
G-LOND+	Viscount 806	ex BAF, G-AOYI, G-LOND, G-AOYI, BA, BEA. CoA exp 20/6/88. Stored.
G-MAST	Cherokee 180	crashed 14/7/81. Wreck.
N4806E	B-26C Invader	ex Rockford, Illinois, 44-34172, Davis Monthan, 3 BW, 17 BW, 7 ADW. Under restoration.
VS610+	G-AOKL Prentice 1	CoA expired 10/9/83. Stored.
WB670+	8361M Chipmunk T.10 PAX	ex MoS, 5 FTS, LAS, 12 RFS, 5 RFS. 1312 Squadron ATC, here since 1975 at least!
XG325+	Lightning F.1	ex Wattisham, Foulness, A&AEE. Nose section with 1312 Squadron ATC. See notes under Rayleigh.
XL426	G-VJET Vulcan B.2A	ex Waddington, 50, 617, 27, Scampton Wing, 83. Stored.
XR363	G-OHCA Belfast C.1	ex Kemble, 53 Squadron. Open store.

STANSTED AIRPORT

As the amazing concrete things go up, then down goes the number of **W&R** things. Well established part of the scenery, Boeing 707-436 G-APFG was reduced to a fuselage and left by road for Cardington 9/5/89. By 10/88 DC-8-55 5N-AVR had been scrapped. This leaves :-

G-ANPP	Proctor III	ex Duxford, HM354. CoA expired 5/5/69. Under restoration.
G-ANUW	Dove 6	ex CAA CAFU. CoA expired 22/7/81. Open store.
G-AWZU	Trident 3B-101	ex Heathrow, BA, BEA. Fire crews. CoA expired 3/7/85.

STAPLEFORD TAWNEY

Down to one **W&R** candidate here. By 5/88 Wassmer D.120 G-BFOP was flying and by early 1989 so was Cessna FA.152 EI-BIE, which had become G-STAP. This leaves :-

G-AXGD	MS.880B Rallye	CoA expired 22/1/86. Stored.

STONDON
(Off the A128 south east of Chipping Ongar)   At **Thurston Engineering,** the Tawney
Owl is still kept in the rafters.

G-APWU   Tawney Owl   Crashed on its first and only flight at Stapleford 22/4/60.

WALTHAM ABBEY
As owners of the airframe, Epping Forest District Council took delivery of the
former NWRF Sopwith Pup replica during 12/89.

BAPC.179+   Sopwith Pup replica   ex North Weald, 'Wings'. Arrived 12/89. Stored.

WICKHAM BISHOPS
(Near Brentwood) **Ricky Cole** moved Blackburn B2 G-ACBH here by 5/88.

G-ACBH+   2895M Blackburn B2   ex Downham, Ramsden Heath, Brentwood. Fuselage. CoA expired
                                        27/11/41. Stored.

Gloucestershire

COLEFORD
(On the A4136 east of Monmouth)   It was threatened in **W&R11** and now it is carried
out, even if it's a lovely Flea.   There having been no reports on the continued
existence of HM.14 BAPC.46 since 4/80, it is banished to LOST!

FAIRFORD
With 'glasnost' breaking out and the base going back to daisies, this may be the
last entry for the BDR Phantom.

37699   F-4C-21-MC   ex Oregon ANG. BDR.

GLOUCESTER
In the town, **Midas Metals** handled the hulk of Sea Prince T.1 G-TACA/WM739 from
Staverton (sorry, Gloucester/Cheltenham Airport!) on 14/4/89. It is thought to have
been dealt with quickly.

GLOUCESTER/CHELTENHAM AIRPORT
(Or Staverton)   The **W&R**-type aeroplanes continue to diminish at this lovely
airfield, once a significant proportion of the book.   Sadly, Classic Aeroplane
ceased trading and the restoration of Tiger Moth G-AMBB is thought to have been
taken off site - see below.   CARG's Messenger is close to test flight and Safaya
and Nick Hemming's ambitious DH.88 'Black Magic' project is held in one of the
hangars.   Long time part of the skyline at Staverton, the Sea Prince and solitary
Pembroke store was finally dispersed during 1989, as follows : Sea Prince T.1 G-
DACA/WF118 to Charlwood with G-GACA/WP308 11-12/11/89; G-RACA/WM735 to Long Marston
12/5/89; G-TACA/WM739 to Gloucester 14/4/89; Pembroke C.1 N46EA/XK885 to Charlwood
by 11/89.

G-ACSP+   DH.88 Comet   ex Bodmin, Chirk, Portugal, CS-AAJ, E-1. Major restoration project.
                                        'Black Magic'.
G-AJOE   Messenger 2A   ex Innsworth, 'RH378'. CoA expired 4/3/77. See notes above.
WL349   Meteor T.7   ex Kemble, 1 ANS, 2 ANS, CFE, 229 OCU. On display.

Nearby three separate Tiger projects are underway.

G-AMBB+   Tiger Moth   ex airfield, see above. Composite, but reported to be mostly T6801.
G-ANOM   Tiger Moth   ex airfield, Maidens Green, N6837, Finningley SF, 1 GU, 2 GS, 11
                                        RFS, 11 EFTS, 217. Crashed 17/12/61.
G-BNDW   Tiger Moth   ex airfield, Cranfield. Composite, some parts from N6688.

INNSWORTH

(West of the B4063, near Parton, north east of Gloucester) With their Messenger restoration nearly ready to fly at Staverton and having won a Scania Transport Trust award in 1989, the **Cotswold Aircraft Restoration Group** can rightly feel well pleased. Work in their workshop on the RAF camp goes on apace, ranging from the restoration of the Meteor for the main gate, through to supplying small components to other people's restoration projects. Visits to the workshop are possible only by prior application. Contact :- Steve Thompson, CARG, Kia-Ora, Risbury, Leominster, Herefordshire, HR6 0NQ. Two airframes have been loaned to the new museum at Long Marston : Flea 'G-ADRG'/BAPC.77 and Auster AOP.9 XK421/8365M. A Typhoon cockpit section has joined the restoration projects here.

G-ASIP	Auster 6A	ex Gloucester/Cheltenham, Nympsfield, Heathrow, VF608, 12 Flt, 652, 1904 Flt, Hague Air Attache. Damaged 7/5/73. Spares.
R9371	Halifax II	ex local, 10. Crashed 9/3/42. Cockpit section. Identity almost certainly confirmed.
VW453	8703M Meteor T.7	ex Salisbury Plain, Hullavington, Takali, 604, 226 OCU, 203 AFS. Under restoration, for eventual display on the gate.
XG331	Lightning F.1	ex Gloucester, Dowty, Foulness, A&AEE, EE. Nose section.
XN412	Auster AOP.9	ex Swindon, Dorchester, Middle Wallop, 20 Flt, 656, Seletar, HS.
XR267	G-BJXR Auster AOP.9	ex Staverton, Congresbury, St Athan, 655, 652. On rebuild.
XW264	Harrier T.2	ex Dowty, Boscombe Down, HSA. Damaged 11/7/70. Forward fuselage.
	Tiger Moth	anonymous frame.
+	Typhoon IB	ex Leeds, Cheltenham, Kemble. Cockpit section. Arrived 25/11/89.

At the gate to **RAF Innsworth** itself, the Javelin still serves as a guardian.

XH903	7938M Javelin FAW.9	ex Shawbury, 5, 33, 29, 33, 23.

KEMBLE

It's been just like old times here of late, with the hangars being used again for storing large numbers of aircraft. This time, they have been wearing stars-n-bars, not roundels. With the replacing of the charismatic F-5E Tiger IIs in the USAF Aggressor Squadrons with the droid-like F-16, Kemble has become a focal point for storing and preparing F-5s for new customers. Naturally enough, the first candidates to arrive did not have far to travel, the 527th AS from Bentwaters. Ten aircraft flew in, with seven ear-marked for Tunisia and Morocco. The Tunisian ones were as follows : 01532 arrived 5/88, out as Y92517:IM 8/6/89; 01535 arrived 5/88, out as Y92519:IN 8/6/89; 01559 arrived 9/88, out as Y92521:IO 23/8/89; 01566 arrived 9/88, out as Y92523:IP 23/8/89. To Morocco : 01543 arrived 5/88, out 23/3/90; 01549 arrived 9/88, out 23/2/90; 01551 arrived 5/88, out 19/10/89; 01560 arrived 9/88 out 19/10/89. On 19/4/89 a C-5A touched down at Fairford having flown from Clark Air Force Base in the Philippines via Elmendorf AFB in Alaska with four F-5Es from the 26th AS, also destined for Morocco. Amid all this, the Meteor on the gate took it all rather well....

WH364	8169M Meteor F.8	ex 601, Safi SF, Takali SF, Idris SF, Takali SF, Safi SF, 85. Gate guardian.
01538+	F-5E Tiger II	ex 26th AS. Arrived 20/4/89.
01553+	F-5E Tiger II	ex 527th AS. Flown in /88.
01569+	F-5E Tiger II	ex 527th AS. Flown in 5/88.
50612+	F-5E Tiger II	ex 26th AS. Arrived 19/4/89.
50613+	F-5E Tiger II	ex 26th AS. Arrived 20/4/89.
50617+	F-5E Tiger II	ex 26th AS. Arrived 19/4/89.

MORETON-IN-THE-MARSH

(On the A44 north east of Cheltenham) The collection of vintage gliders assembled by **Eric Rolfe** and **Paul Williams** are still to be found locally. Also here, the **Wellington Galley** took on the former Firbeck Wellington by early 1990, displaying the sections.

BGA 964	BGT Kranich II	ex Warwick, SE-STF, Fv 8226.
	Hutter H.17a	ex Chivenor. Under restoration.
BAPC.25	Nyborg TGN.III	ex Stratford. Under restoration.
L7775+	Wellington I	ex Firbeck, Braemar, 20 OTU. Crashed 23/10/40. Sections. See notes above.

QUEDGELEY

(On the A430 south of Gloucester)   On **No 1 Site** the Meteor still guards the complex.   The centre section of Britannia 308F G-ANCF is stored here, the rest of it is to be found at Brooklands.

| WF784 | 7895M Meteor T.7 | ex Kemble, 5 CAACU, CAW, FTU, 130, 26. Gate guardian. |

STONEHOUSE

Vampire T.11 XE979 confounded all the critics by getting up and moving to Birlingham from the grounds of the hospital here. (Is it NHS or BUPA?)

STROUD

Near 'The British Oak', in Bowbridge Lane, **1329 Squadron ATC** keep their Chippax.

| WP845 | Chipmunk T.10 | ex Nor UAS, AOTS, PFS, AOTS, ITS, 7 AEF, 2 FTS, HCCS, Lon UAS, RAFC, 14 RFS. PAX Trainer. |

Hampshire

ALDERSHOT

1990 marks the 50th Anniversary of the Airborne Forces, making it a very special year for the **Airborne Forces Museum** at Browning Barracks, east of the A325 immediately south of Farnborough airfield.   Several special events and exhibitions are planned.   Open every day, except Mondays and December 24-26, 1000 to 1630 Contact : The Airborne Forces Museum, Browning Barracks, Aldershot, Hampshire, GU11 2DS. Tel : 0252 24431 ext 4619.

KP208	Dakota IV	ex Kemble, AFNE, Air Adviser New Delhi, AFNE, HCCF, 24, MEAF, USAAF 44-77087. Displayed outside.
	Hotspur II	full nose section and part of troop bay.
	Horsa II	full nose section.

ANDOVER

Durney Collection's is still held under wraps here.

| G-ALAX | Dragon Rapide | ex Old Warden, Luton, RL948, ERS, 27 GCF. See notes above. |

CHILBOLTON

On the airfield, **Alpha Aerotech** have been joined by Ian Grace's **Chilbolton Aviation**.   The former specialise in the Hiller UH-12 and the latter in the restoration of classic biplanes.   Hiller UH-12E-4 G-ASAZ was rebuilt using parts from one of the Pakistani registered examples and was flying again by 10/88. Otherwise there has been no change in the rotary winged inmates here.

G-ACDA+	Tiger Moth	ex Malmesbury, Shobdon, BB724, G-ACDA. Crashed 27/6/79. Under restoration.
G-AKUE+	Tiger Moth	ex ZS-FZL, CR-AGM; Portuguese AF. Crashed 2/1/89. For restn.
G-AVKY	Hiller UH-12E	ex CN-MAP. Crashed 26/6/84. Wreck.
G-AZSV	Hiller UH-12E	ex Thruxton, EP-HAH, 5N-AGJ, ZS-HAV. Crashed 28/7/80. Cabin.
G-BBLD	Hiller UH-12E	ex N31703, N31705 ntu, CAF 112279, RCAF 10279. Crashed 19/4/79.
G-BDFO	Hiller UH-12E	ex XS703 705. CoA exp 1/4/84. Cabin only.
G-BEDK	Hiller UH-12E	ex XS706 705. CoA exp 14/6/85. Cabin only.
G-BGFS	W-Bell 47G-3B1	ex XW192. CoA exp 21/3/85. Stored.
G-BGOZ	W-Bell 47G-3B1	ex Bridge Hewick, XT545. Crashed 18/6/81. Wreck.
AP-ATV	Hiller UH-12E-4	ex Bangladesh Army. Cabin only. See notes above.
AP-AWQ	Hiller UH-12E-4	ex AP-AOF, Bangladesh Army, N9776Q. Cabin only. See notes above.

FAREHAM

It is possible that the Gnat T.1 nose that was kept here is one and the same with the nose now held at the Southampton Hall of Aviation - which see.

FARNBOROUGH

Now, of course, it is the **Royal Aerospace Establishment** which doesn't seem to sit quite right at this historic site.   Additionally, there is a thriving general aviation terminal boiling up here and its presence and building work generally on the RAE site may well mean that some of the long termers here may have been scrapped or otherwise dealt with. As will be seen momentarily, a goodly chunk of airframes not reported for a while have been tracked down to Pendine. Continuing the trend here, losses well outnumber the arrivals : MS.880B G-AZGJ was consumed in the rebuild of G-BIOR by the Apprentices here and was flying again by 11/89; Meteor T.7 WA662 arrived here by road 26/10/87 from Llanbedr (eluding **W&R11**) but moved out to Chalgrove by 9/89; Canberra PR.7 WH774 expired on the dump by 9/88; Canberra B.2 WJ728 with the Apprentices was broken up and removed as far back as 13/3/84; the majority of Meteor T.7 WL405 (with other parts at Sunderland) also moved out to Chalgrove; the wreckage of Hunter T.12 XE531 was last noted 4/82 and is thought long since gone; likewise the remains of Meteor T.7 XF274 which was held at the AAIU; the fuselage of Hunter F.6A XG158/8686M moved to Pendine; Whirlwind HAR.10 HAR.10 XJ411 also moved to Pendine; Wessex HAS.1 XM330 had appeared at the Structures Laboratory by 4/84, but had gone by 6/89, fate unknown; Wessex HAS.1 XM926 moved to Pendine 18/2/86; Whirlwind HAR.10 XP356 had expired on the dump by 1985 no less; Whirlwind HAR.10 XR479 was also a Pendine pilgrim; Gnat T.1 XR544 is another that should have been cleared out of the listings long back, thought to have expired in 1983!; Wasp HAS.1 XS565 moved to Foulness by 3/88. All of the above makes the current situation as follows :

G-ANNG		Tiger Moth	ex DE524. CoA exp 29/11/67. Stored, dismantled.
BGA.562		APW Olympia 1	ex G-ALJZ. Crashed 20/7/58. Stored in 'Q' Shed.
		Broburn Wanderlust	Stored in 'Q' Shed.
WE146		Canberra PR.3	ex RAE. Nose section only.
WJ865		Canberra T.4	ex ETPS. RAE Apprentices.
WT308		Canberra B(I).6	ex A&AEE. Stored.
XD860		Valiant BK.1	ex 214, 138, 214. Nose section.
XE587+		Hunter F.6	ex RAE, Hawkers. Withdrawn 1989.
XF844		Provost T.1	ex RAE, 6 FTS.
XJ396		Whirlwind HAR.10	ex RAE Lasham, XD776 ntu. Derelict.
XN453		Comet 2E	ex RAE, G-AMXD. Sectioned.
XN688	8141M	Sea Vixen FAW.2	ex Halton, 893, 899, 890. Dump, poor state.
XP166		Scout AH.1	ex RAE, G-APVL. Stored.
XP393		Whirlwind HAR.10	ex Wroughton, RAE, 28, 103, 225. Derelict.
XP516	8580M	Gnat T.1	ex 4 FTS. Structures Laboratory.
XP532	8615M	Gnat T.1	ex 8577M, 4 FTS. Derelict.
XS482		Wessex HU.5	ex A&AEE. RAE Apprentices.
XT272		Buccaneer S.2	ex RAE Bedford. Dismantled.
XV147		Nimrod prototype	ex Woodford, A&AEE. Sectioned.
XV631		Wasp HAS.1	ex Wroughton, 'Endurance' Flt.
XW566+		Jaguar T.2	ex RAE, A&AEE. Withdrawn from use 17/6/85.
XX907		Lynx AH.1	ex RAE. Stored.
XX910		Lynx HAS.2	ex RAE. Stored.
		TSR-2	nose section.

Locally, the former Swiss Pup should still be under rebuild.
| HB-NBA | Pup 150 | ex Redhill. |

FLEETLANDS

Through the concerted efforts of Curator Graham Cooper and friends, a collection of archives here blossomed into the **RNAY Fleetlands Museum** during 1989. Visits are strictly by prior application for the present, but there are hopes that the museum

area can be made to 'detach' from the remainder of the RNAY, allowing regular
opening. The aim is to show the scope of the work undertaken at the RNAY over the
years. Contact : Graham Cooper, Curator, RNAY Fleetlands Museum, Gosport, Hants.
Telephone 0707 822351, ext 44391.

VX595+		Dragonfly HR.1	ex Henlow, Fleetlands. Arrived 9/2/90.
WV783+	7841M	Sycamore HR.12	ex Henlow, HDU Old Sarum, CFS, ASWDU. Arrived 9/2/90.
XG629+		Sea Venom FAW.22	ex Higher Blagdon, Culdrose, ADS, 831, 893. Arrived 3/90.
XJ481+		Sea Vixen FAW.1	ex Southampton, Ilkeston, Yeovilton, Portland, Yeovilton, Boscombe Down, LRWE Woomera. Arrived 1989.
XK988+	A2646	Whirlwind HAR.10	ex Middle Wallop, Ilkeston, Middle Wallop, Lee-on-Solent, 103, 110, 103, CFS, JEHU. Arrived by 2/90.
XL738+	7860M	Skeeter AOP.12	ex Middle Wallop, Southampton, Middle Wallop. Composite airframe, boom from XM565/7861M. Arrived by 6/89.
XL853+	A2630	Whirlwind HAS.7	ex Southampton, Middle Wallop, Lee-on-Solent, Wroughton, Yeovilton SF, 824. Arrived by 6/89.

Meanwhile, at the **RNAY** proper there has been little movement, at least in terms of
W&R fodder. Of the aircraft listed in the previous edition, two have moved on,
both requiring a firm 'destination'. Wessex HAS.1 XS872/A2666 had gone by 1/90 and
the travelling display airframe Wessex HAS.1 XS888 was also no longer held at the
Yard by this time. That leaves :

XL600		Hunter T.7	ex Scampton, 12, 4 FTS, Wattisham SF, 65. Apprentices.
XM836		Wessex HAS.3	ex Wroughton, 737. Apprentices.
XM923		Wessex HAS.3	ex Wroughton. Fire dump.
XP110		Wessex HAS.3	ex Wroughton, 737. Apprentices.
XS568		Wasp HAS.1	ex 829. Boom of XS539. Apprentices.
XS569		Wasp HAS.1	ex Wroughton. Apprentices.
XS868	A2706	Wessex HAS.1	ex A2691, Wroughton. Gate guardian.
XT780		Wasp HAS.1	ex Wroughton, 703. Apprentices.

HAMBLE
Ron Souch's **Antique Aeroplane Company** has a new workshop, best located under the
'Southampton' banner - which see. Mounted on a pole outside the **British Aerospace**
plant is :-
XM693	7891M	Gnat T.1	ex Abingdon, Bicester, A&AEE.

HAVANT
The **Military Vehicle Conservation Group** are restoring an Auster here. Contact :
MVCG, 86 Priorsdean Crescent, Leigh Park, Havant, Hants, TO9 3AU.
G-AGYL	J/1 Autocrat	ex Lasham, White Waltham. Crashed 6/7/64. Fitted with wings of VF505 and VX110. Under restoration.

HEDGE END
(On the A334 east of Southampton) Established at a workshop here are **British
Classic Aircraft Restorations** who have a decidedly Auster bent. BCAR's first
restoration was Auster 5 G-AJGJ/RT486 acquired from Southampton in 1988. It was
finished off at Chilbolton and was flying by early 1990. No less than four other
airframes have been acquired and restoration on at least one is in process. Visits
are possible by prior appointment. Contact : Steve Challis, BCAR, 15 Steele Close,
Eastleigh, Hants, SO5 3AA.

G-AGXT+		J/1N Alpha	ex Warmingham, East Kirkby, Sibson, Wigan, Handforth. Crashed 7/6/79. Arrived 4/7/88.
G-ANLU+	TW448	Auster 5	ex Elvington. CoA expired 8/8/68. Arrived 6/2/88. Restoration.
G-ARDX+		Auster 6A	ex Warmingham, Wigan, Handforth, Cardiff, TW524, Austers, 1900 Flt, Austers. Crashed 1/1/64. Arrived 4/7/88.
G-ARLO+		Terrier 1	ex Slinfold, TW642, 663, deH. Crashed 10/7/79. Arrived late 1989.

HOOK
(North of the M3, near Junction 5) Rebuild of the Auster continues at the strip.
G-AJXC	Auster 5	ex TJ343. CoA expired 2/8/82. Under rebuild.

LASHAM

On their own site overlooking the gliding activity, and the occasional blast-off of a Dan-Air nature returning to Gatwick, the **Second World War Aircraft Preservation Society** now have a large building serving as a shop and clubhouse on site. Improvements to the displays and the site have been the main theme since the last edition. There have been a couple of departures, but a most welcome arrival. Vampire T.11 XE856 and Wessex HAS.3 XM833 (which did not go to Monkton Farleigh, as speculated in **W&R11**) are due to go to Long Marston some time during 1990. Whirlwind HAR.9 XN309/A2663 moved to Thatcham during 1989. SWWAPS are open Sundays, Bank Holidays and other times by prior arrangement. Contact : SWWAPS, Lasham Airfield, Alton, Hants.

G-APIT	Prentice 1	ex Biggin Hill, Southend, VR192, 1 ASS, 6 FTS, CFS, 2 FTS, Blackburns. CoA expired 7/9/67.
VH-FDT"	Drover II	ex Blackbushe, Southend, G-APXX, VH-EAS.
4X-FNA	Meteor NF.13	ex Israel, WM366, A&AEE, RRE. Centre section, wings and tail, nose from TT.20 WM234 ex Arborfield, 5 MU, 3 CAACU, 151, Odiham.
WF137	Sea Prince C.1	ex Yeovilton, Culdrose SF, Shorts Ferry Unit, Arbroath SF, 781.
WH291	Meteor F.8	ex Kemble, 229 OCU, 85, CAW, 257.
WV798	A2557 Sea Hawk FGA.6	ex Chertsey, Culdrose, FRU, 801, 803, 787.
XE856	Vampire T.11	ex Welwyn GC, Woodford, Chester, St Athan, 219, North Weald SF, 226 OCU. See notes above.
XK418	7976M Auster AOP.9	ex Basingstoke, Thruxton, Middle Wallop, 654.
XM833+	Wessex HAS.3	ex Wroughton. see notes above.
XP360	Whirlwind HAR.10	ex Fawkham Green, CFS, 225.
E-423	Hunter F.51	ex Elstree, Dunsfold G-9-444, Danish AF, Aalborg store, ESK-724.
22+35+	F-104G Starfighter	ex Manching, JbG34, KE+413, DD+105. Flew in 19/8/88 inside RAF C-130K XV191.

Over at **Dan-Air** the Dakota still proudly guards the busy maintenance base. HS.748 G-ARAY arrived during 1989 and is being used for spares - there are hopes that it may find a museum home. Over at the **Royal Aerospace Establishment** site, the Comet fuselage section lives on.

G-ALYX	Comet 1	ex Farnborough. CoA expired 21/7/54. Noseless fuselage.
G-AMSU"	Dakota IV	G-AMPP mostly, ex Dan-Air, trooping serial XF756, Scottish Airlines, KK136, 12 MU, Military Mission Belgium, 1 TAMU, 147, 43-49456.
G-ARAY+	HS.748-1A/200	ex OY-DFV, G-11, G-ARAY, PI-C784, G-ARAY, VP-LIO, G-ARAY, PP-VJQ, G-ARAY, YV-V-AMC, G-ARAY. Arrived 31/10/89. Open store.

LEE-ON-SOLENT

Despite several departures to record and almost as many arrivals, in comparison with previous editions life at **HMS 'Daedalus'** has been relatively quiet. More Wessex HU.5s and Wasp HAS.1s have arrived for the extensive Air Engineering School (the Navy's Halton) and the associated Metalcraft and Battle Damage Repair school. The Historic Aircraft and Gannets continue in undisturbed storage. Departures have been as follows : Sea Fury FB.11 VR930/8382M to Boscombe Down for spares use; Hunter GA.11 XE712 moved to Predannack 9/2/88; Wessex HAS.3 XM870 to Culdrose 13/9/88; Whirlwind HAS.7 XN302/A2654 to Corsham by 6/88; Whirlwind HAR.9 XN311/A2643 to Corsham by 6/88; Wessex HAS.3 XP137 to Culdrose 13/9/88; Wasp HAS.1 XS570/A2699 to Plymouth; Wessex HAS.1 XS866/A2705 to Culdrose 22/6/88; Wessex HAS.1 XS876/A2695 to Culdrose 12/7/88; Wessex HU.5 XT459 from the dump to Faygate by 2/88; and Wessex HU.5 XT762 to Culdrose 28/7/87. During 4/89 Hunter GA.11 WV382 was offered for tender, having last flown in 10/76 with 3,434 hours total time. Its fate beyond this is not known. Joining the AES almost by 'stealth' at an unknown date was SH-3D Sea King XV370 (ex ETPS). The first the compiler knew of its being here was a report of it leaving for Yeovil on 31/1/90! Current situation is therefore as follows :

EZ407	Harvard III	ex Yeovilton, Portuguese AF 1656, SAAF, EZ407, 42-84931. Stored.
NF389	Swordfish III	Stored.
VR930	8382M Sea Fury FB.11	ex Wroughton, Yeovilton, Colerne, Dunsfold, FRU, Lossiemouth, Anthorn, 801, Anthorn, 802. Stored.

WV903	A2632	Sea Hawk FGA.4	ex Culdrose, Halton 8153M, Sydenham. Stored.
WV911	A2526	Sea Hawk FGA.6	ex Fleetlands, Lee-on-Solent. Stored.
XE339	A2635	Sea Hawk FGA.6	ex Culdrose, Halton 8156M. Stored.
XG888		Gannet T.5	ex Culdrose, Lossiemouth, 849. Stored.
XL500	A2701	Gannet AEW.3	ex Culdrose, Dowty-Rotol, Culdrose, Lossiemouth, 849. Stored.
XL880	A2714	Whirlwind HAR.9	ex Wroughton, 'Endurance' Flt, 'Protector' Flt, 847, 848, 815. BDR.
XM843	A2693	Wessex HAS.1	ex Wroughton, 771. Gate guardian by 7/89.
XM868	A2711	Wessex HAS.1	ex Wroughton, 737. AES.
XM874+	A2689	Wessex HAS.1	ex Culdrose, Wroughton, 771. Arrived 12/7/88. AES.
XM917	A2692	Wessex HAS.1	ex AES, Wroughton, 771. Dump.
XN359	A2712	Whirlwind HAR.9	ex Wroughton, 'Endurance' Flt, Fleetlands, Arbroath, 'Protector' Flt, 847, 719. BDR.
XP116	A2618	Wessex HAS.3	ex AES, 737 '520'. Crashed 15/11/71. Minus tail. Metalwork school.
XP150		Wessex HAS.3	ex Wroughton, 829, 'Antrim' Flt. AES.
XP151	A2684	Wessex HAS.1	ex AES, Wroughton, 'Ark Royal' Flt. Dump.
XP157	A2680	Wessex HAS.1	ex Wroughton. AES.
XS483		Wessex HU.5	ex Wroughton, 845. AES.
XS496+		Wessex HU.5	ex 772. AES. First noted 7/88.
XS507+		Wessex HU.5	ex 772. AES. First noted 7/88.
XS508+		Wessex HU.5	ex Wroughton. AES. First noted 9/88.
XS510+		Wessex HU.5	ex 772. AES. First noted 7/88.
XS511		Wessex HU.5	ex 845. AES.
XS513		Wessex HU.5	ex 772. AES.
XS514		Wessex HU.5	ex 845. AES.
XS515		Wessex HU.5	ex 845. AES.
XS516		Wessex HU.5	ex 845. AES.
XS520		Wessex HU.5	ex 845. AES.
XS522		Wessex HU.5	ex Wroughton, 848. AES.
XS529		Wasp HAS.1	ex 829 'Galatea' Flt. AES.
XS538	A2725	Wasp HAS.1	ex 829 'Lowestoft' Flt. BDR.
XS539		Wasp HAS.1	ex 829 'Endurance' Flt. AES.
XS545	A2702	Wasp HAS.1	ex Wroughton. 'Willy-never-Fly' AES.
XS567		Wasp HAS.1	ex 829 'Endurance' Flt. AES.
XS862		Wessex HAS.3	ex gate, AES, Wroughton, 737. AES.
XS865	A2694	Wessex HAS.1	ex AES, Wroughton, 771. Dump.
XS867	A2671	Wessex HAS.1	ex Culdrose. Dump, poor state.
XS870	A2697	Wessex HAS.1	ex Wroughton. AES.
XS878	A2683	Wessex HAS.1	ex Culdrose. AES.
XT429+		Wasp HAS.1	ex 829 'Plymouth' Flt. AES. First noted 9/88.
XT434+		Wasp HAS.1	ex 829. AES. First noted 9/88.
XT437+		Wasp HAS.1	ex 829 'Diomede' Flt. AES. first noted 7/89.
XT449		Wessex HU.5	ex Wroughton, 845. AES.
XT453		Wessex HU.5	ex 845. AES.
XT455		Wessex HU.5	ex 845. AES.
XT458+		Wessex HU.5	ex 772. AES. First noted 7/89.
XT482		Wessex HU.5	ex Wroughton, 848. AES.
XT484		Wessex HU.5	ex 845. AES.
XT485+		Wessex HU.5	ex 772. AES. First noted 9/8.
XT487	A2723	Wessex HU.5	ex MIW, Wroughton. Dump.
XT752		Gannet T.5	ex Culdrose, Lossiemouth, 849, Indonesian Navy AS-14, G-APYO, WN365. Stored.
XT761+		Wessex HU.5	ex Wroughton. AES. Arrived 12/4/88.
XT765		Wessex HU.5	ex 845. AES.
XT771+		Wessex HU.5	ex 772. AES. First noted 9/88.
XT795		Wasp HAS.1	ex 829 'Leander' Flt. AES.
XV644	A2664	Sea King HAS.1	ex AES, Farnborough. Crashed 19/11/74. Metalwork school.
		Lynx TA	built by RNAW Almondbank. AES.
		Lynx TA	built by RNAW Almondbank. AES.

More correctly listed as an appendix to Lee is the **Naval Air Medical School** at Seafield Park. Used for instruction, are a Wessex and a Buccaneer nose.

XS869	A2649 Wessex HAS.1	ex Lee-on-Solent, Manadon, 771.
	Buccaneer S.2	ex 809. Nose section.

LOWER UPHAM
(On the A333 near Bishop's Waltham)   Fokker D.VII G-BFPL fled the store here and now flies from <u>Duxford</u> with the Old Flying Machine Company. Otherwise, no change.

G-AHUF	Tiger Moth	ex Yeovilton, A2123, Arbroath A750, NL750. Stored.
G-BILA	DM-165L Viking	ex F-PPZE. CoA expired 14/9/83. Stored.

MIDDLE WALLOP
Going from strength to strength, the **Museum of Army Flying** continues to make great strides towards its goal of showing the whole spread of army aviation, from World War One kites to the Westland Lynx and from World War Two assault gliders to the Falklands campaign. Recent acquisitions have continued to build on the World War One theme and through the Kirby Kite, Tiger Moth and Hawk Major into the training phase of pilots from the Glider Regiment. Along with this has come a rationalisation of 'back-up' airframes with the following leaving the store : Whirlwind HAS.7 XK988/A2646 to <u>Fleetlands</u>; Skeeter AOP.12 XL738/7860M also to <u>Fleetlands</u>; Sioux AH.1 XT150 to <u>Netheravon</u> for the gate; Sioux AH.1 XT190 to <u>Soest</u>, West Germany for the gate; Sioux AH.1 XT236 transferred to the SAE here for BDR training, see below: Sioux AH.1 XT548 to <u>Hildesheim</u>, West Germany, for the gate; Sioux AH.1 XT550 to the gate at <u>Detmold</u>, West Germany; Beaver AL.1 XV272 cockpit area to BDR training with SAE here, see below. Additionally, Auster AOP.6 TW536 became G-BNGE and following a superb restoration was flying again by 1988 and is based here. Following the clear-out from the RAF Museum stores, MoAF received the sections of Airspeed Horsa 8596M. These along with the previously listed LH208 are really too small to qualify for an entry and can be 'lumped' with the TL659 hybrid. The EP.9 Prospectors are all currently off site in a workshop near Andover, while a display example is created. The Museum is open 1000 to 1630 including weekends and holidays. Contact : Museum of Army Flying, Middle Wallop, Stockbridge, Hampshire, SO20 8DY. Telephone 0264 62121 extension 428.

G-APWZ	Prospector EP.9	ex Goodwood. Damaged 7-8/2/84. See notes above.
G-APXW	Prospector EP.9	ex Shoreham, Lympne. Remains. Crashed 30/9/73. See notes above.
G-ARDG	Prospector EP.9	ex Shoreham, Lympne. Under restoration. See notes above.
G-AXKS	W-Bell 47G-4A	ex Bristows, ARWF, G-17-8. CoA expired 21/9/82.
BGA 285+	ACH T.6 Kite I	ex G-ALNH, BGA.285. Arrived during 1989. On loan.
B-415"	B'163 AFEE 10/42 replica	ex Wimborne. Flying Jeep. On loan.
P-5	8381M Rotachute III	ex Henlow. On loan.
5984"	B'112 DH.2 replica	ex Chertsey.
B6291"+	G-ASOP Camel replica	arrived 10/89. Built by Desmond St Cyrien. On loan.
N5195"	G-ABOX Sopwith Pup replica	ex Redhill. Damaged 2/7/86. CoA expired 18/9/86. On loan.
N6985+	G-AHMN Tiger Moth	ex 2 EFTS, 22 EFTS, Andover SF. CoA expired 25/6/87. On loan.
DG590+	G-ADMW Hawk Major	ex Henlow 8379M, Ternhill, Swanton Morley SF, Wyton SF. CoA expired 30/7/65. On loan from RAF Museum.
TJ569	G-AKOW Auster 5	ex PH-NAD, PH-NEG, TJ569. CoA expired 26/6/82.
TK777	Hamilcar I	ex South Yorkshire, substantial sections, also parts from TK718 and centre section from NX836, ex Henlow.
TL659	B' 80 Horsa II	fuselage, composite. See notes above.
WJ358	G-ARYD Auster AOP.6	ex Perth, WJ358, 651, 657, 1913 Flt. Stored.
WZ721	Auster AOP.9	ex 4 RTR, 656, 6 Flt. 'Dragon'.
XG502	Sycamore HR.14	ex gate, Wroughton, Bristols, JEHU.
XK776	ML Utility Mk 1	ex Cardington. Fitted with 'Clouy' wing. On loan.
XL813	Skeeter AOP.12	ex ARWF, 4 Regt, 9 Flt.
XP821	Beaver AL.1	ex Shawbury, Kemble. White colour scheme.
XP822	Beaver AL.1	ex Shawbury.
XP847	Scout AH.1	ex AETW.
XT108	Sioux AH.1	ex Duxford, Yeovilton, Middle Wallop, D&T Flight, Middle Wallop.
	Scout CIM	ex AETW.

A-528	8769M FMA Pucara	ex Cosford, Abingdon, Stanley Airport, Argentine AF.
A-533	ZD486 FMA Pucara	ex Boscombe Down, Abingdon, Finningley, Portsmouth, Stanley Airport, Argentine AF.
AE-406	UH-1H Iroquois	ex Fleetlands, Stanley Racecourse, Argentine Army, 72-21491.
AE-409	UH-1H Iroquois	ex Duxford, Middle Wallop, 656, Stanley Racecourse, Argentine Army, 72-21506
11989	N33600 L-19A Bird Dog	ex Fort Rucker, Alabama.
243809"	B'185 WACO CG-4A	ex Burtonwood, Shrewsbury. Fuselage.
BAPC.10	Hafner R-II	ex Locking, Weston-super-Mare, Old Warden, Yeovil. On loan.

The fleet of the **Army Air Corps Historic Aircraft Flight** is unchanged. They are
not open to view at Middle Wallop, but do make the 'rounds' of the displays.

XL814	Skeeter AOP.12	ex 1 Wing, 2 Wing, 651.
XP242	Auster AOP.9	reserve aircraft.
XR244	Auster AOP.9	ex AFWF.
XT131	Sioux AH.1	ex D&T Flight.

Elsewhere on the base, the Headquarters of the **Army Air Corps** the major change is
one of nomenclature. AETW (Air Engineering Training Wing) is now SAE (School of
Aeronautical Engineering, still centred upon the impressive Stockwell Hall within
the camp.   In general the fleet of instructional airframes, including the large
number of purpose-built instruction modules, has changed little, but it should
again be pointed out that some have not been physically reported (as opposed to the
dreaded 'supposed') for some time.   For safety's sake, these are marked #.
Departures have been as follows : Scout AH.1 XT616 to Wroughton 9/85; Lynx 1-02
XW835/G-BEAD left by road on 30/9/88 - destination?; Gazelle AH.1 XW865 moved to
Fleetlands and then joined 670 Squadron as far back as 12/2/85.

WZ724	7432M Auster AOP.9	ex 'WZ670', 656, FEAF. Gate guardian.
XL847	A2626 Whirlwind HAS.7	ex BDR, AETW, MoAF, Lee-on-Solent, Lossiemouth SF, 771, 829, 820. Dump.
XP191	Scout AH.1	ex Shrivenham, Wroughton. Stored.
XP848	Scout AH.1	ex Wroughton
XP853	Scout AH.1	ex 655.
XP854	7898M Scout AH.1	TAD.043. Crashed 15/5/65. Hydraulic systems rig by 7/88.
XP856	Scout AH.1	#
XP857	Scout AH.1	ex Yeovil. Near dump.
XP884	Scout AH.1	ex ARWS.
XP888	Scout AH.1	ex Wroughton, 651.
XP905	Scout AH.1	ex Wroughton, 656.
XP907	Scout AH.1	on dump by 7/88. Fitted with boom of XR630.
XR436	SARO P.531/2	ex MoAF, A&AEE. BDR.
XR597	Scout AH.1	ex travelling display airframe, Wroughton, 654.
XR635+	Scout AH.1	ex 653. Omitted from W&R11.
XT236+	Sioux AH.1	ex MoAF, Sek Kong. For BDR 1989.
XT640	Scout AH.1	ex Wroughton, 640.
XV272+	Beaver AL.1	ex MoAF, 'Operation Drake'. Cockpit only. For BDR 1989.
XV629	Wasp HAS.1	ex Wroughton. BDR.
XW836	Westland 606	ex Yeovil, Sherborne, Yeovil. Civil Lynx mock-up. #
XW838	TAD.009 Lynx 1-03	
XW888	Gazelle AH.1	ex ARWF.
XW889	Gazelle AH.1	ex ARWF.
XW900	TAD.900 Gazelle AH.1	Crashed 25/5/76. #
XW908+	Gazelle AH.1	ex Wroughton. Arrived 30/6/88.
XW912	Gazelle AH.1	ex Wroughton, 3 CBAS.
XX411	Gazelle AH.1	ex Falklands, 3 CBAS. Shot down 21/5/82. BDR.
XX452	Gazelle AH.1	Crashed 24/8/82. Pod only. Dump.
XZ213+	TAD.213 Lynx AH.1	ex Wroughton, 659. Crashed 20/3/86. First noted 3/88.
TAD. 01	Gazelle CIM	or possibly TAU.01. #
TAD. 02	Gazelle CIM	#

TAD. 04	Gazelle CIM	#
TAD. 08	Gazelle CIM	#
TAD.007	Lynx CIM	fuselage number TO.42. #
TAD.010	Lynx CIM	#
TAD.011	Lynx CIM	#
TAD.012	Lynx CIM	#
TAD.018	Lynx CIM	#
TAU. 3	Gazelle CIM	ex Arborfield, Middle Wallop. #

ODIHAM

Restored into camouflage colours, Whirlwind HAR.10 XR453/8873M now adorns the gate here (although be warned it is well within the camp boundaries). There have been two departures, both annoying in that their destinations are as yet unknown (doubtless someone is putting pen to paper even now....). These were HAR.10s XK970/8789M on 17/7/87 and XK986/8790M in 6/87. Wessex HAS.1 XP159 is favourite for the machine listed under Brands Hatch – which see.

WK968	8053M Meteor F.8	ex gate, Kemble, CAW, 46, 56, 64. Dump.
XN387	8564M Whirlwind HAR.9	ex Wroughton, Lee-on-Solent SAR Flt, Lossiemouth SF, 846, 719. BDR.
XP159	8877M Wessex HAS.1	ex Fleet, Leatherhead, 'Ark Royal' Flt. BDR.
XR453	8883M Whirlwind HAR.10	ex Foulness Island, 2 AFTS, CFS, 230, 1563 Flt, CFS. Gate.
XR681	8588M Jet Provost T.4	ex Abingdon, RAFEF, CATCS, 6 FTS, RAFC. Nose section, 1349 Sqn ATC.
XS871	8457M Wessex HAS.1	ex Wroughton. 72 Sqn colours, instructional airframe.
	Scout AH.1	gutted fuselage, for BDR.
61-2414	Boeing CH-47A	ex Boeing. Instructional airframe.

In the locality, **Steve Markham** stores his SIPA pair.

| G-AMSG | SIPA 903 | ex OO-VBL, F-BGHB. |
| G-AWLG | SIPA 903 | ex F-BGHG. CoA expired 22/8/79. |

POPHAM

The airfield has seen radical changes since acquisition by the late Charles Church (see under Winchester) with a view to making it an historic aircraft centre – which it may well still become. Perhaps in the light of this, Cessna FA.150L hulk G-AYXV sportingly got up and left by road 8/10/88.

PORTSMOUTH

There are three separate centres to consider in the area. We shall kick off with the latest, the **Royal Marines Museum.** Located at Eastney Barracks, during 1989 they took on a former Torbay Whirlwind. This can be seen from outside, viewing of the museum itself is by prior application only – 0705 819385.

| XJ393 | A2538 Whirlwind HAR.3 | ex Higher Blagdon, Lee-on-Solent, Arbroath, Pershore, CS(A). |
| | | XD363/XD763 ntu. Arrived 2/11/89. |

At **HMS 'Phoenix'** is a ship-board fire school which became just that during 1988. Wessex HAS.1 XS882/A2696 which had been used for instruction/research work here was put on HMS 'Naiad' and set ablaze in a trial. It is unlikely to have returned.

In an amazing about-turn, Anson T.21 VS562 was saved from **John Pound**'s scrapyard and was returned to Llanbedr – not to the RAE but to restoration and display at the Maes Artro Craft Centre. By 1988 it has been replaced by something of less historical significance.

| G-OARV+ | ARV-1 Super 2 | stripped, hulk. Crashed 24/5/86. First noted mid 1988. |

SOUTHAMPTON

The city and its environs hold much of interest to **W&R** followers, by far and away the largest element being the excellent **Southampton Hall of Aviation.** In previous editions **424 Squadron ATC** (ATC) has been listed separately, but it is felt their airframes are best listed as part of the Museum itself. At nearby Ocean Village, the Museum maintains a store and between the main site and here can be found the

ATC's aircraft. From late 1988 the airframes of the **Wessex Aviation Society** (WAS) had moved in, either for display or storage and in consequence several items have moved on. WAS had to leave the Wimborne site following a reorganisation, and made the decision to become effectively a supporters' organisation for the Hall of Aviation. The following have moved on : Vampire T.11 XD614/8124M nose with the ATC, was acquired by a local collector, see below: Sea Vixen FAW.1 XJ481 and Whirlwind HAS.7 XL853/A2630 joined the new museum at Fleetlands; the amazing Walrus caravan/amphibian (now known to be W2718) had left by early 1989, going on to form the basis of a restoration, hopefully to flying condition, within the County. To clean up the reference to Jet Provost T.3 nose XM415 with 424 ATC, this was presented to another unit in the locality and eventually scrapped. The Museum is open daily except Mondays and over the Christmas period, 1000 to 1700 (Tuesday to Saturday) and 1400 to 1700 (Sundays). Contact : Southampton Hall of Aviation, Albert Road South, Southampton, SO1 1FR. Telephone 0703 635830. Enquiries relating to the Wessex Aviation Society can be made to : M Phipp, Secretary, 68 Glenwood Road, West Moors, Wimborne, Dorset, BH22 OEW.

G-ADWO+	Tiger Moth	ex Wimborne. Composite with G-AOAC and G-AOJJ. Under restoration as BB807. Arrived by 9/88. Stored. WAS.
G-ALZE	BN-1F	ex Cosford, Kemble, Bembridge Harbour. On loan.
VH-BRC	Sandringham 4	ex Lee-on-Solent, VP-LVE 'Southern Cross', N158C Antilles Air Boats, VH-BRC Ansett 'Beachcomber', TEAL ZK-AMH 'Auckland', Sunderland III JM715 - no operational service.
	Airwave Hang-glider	prototype.
N248	Supermarine S.6A	ex Cowes, Southampton, Henlow, Southampton Pier, 'S1596' in 'First of the Few', Calshot, RAFHSF.
PK683	7150M Spitfire F.24	ex Kingsbridge Lane, Kemble, Colerne, Changi, Singapore Aux AF.
WA984+	Meteor F.8	ex Wimborne, Tarrant Rushton, 211 AFS, 19. Composite, parts from VZ530. Arrived by 12/88. Stored. WAS.
WK570+	8211M Chipmunk T.10	ex Bournemouth Airport, Hamble, 663, Hul UAS, 663, RAFC. PAX trainer. Arrived by 4/89. ATC.
WM571+	Sea Venom FAW.22	ex Wimborne, Staverton, ADS, 831B, HS. Arr by 12/88. WAS.
WZ753+	Grasshopper TX.1	ex Halton, 'London'. Arrived early 1989.
XD596	7939M Vampire T.11	ex Calmore, St Athan, CATCS, CNCS, 5 FTS, 4 FTS. ATC.
XJ476	Sea Vixen FAW.1	ex Boscombe Down, A&AEE. Nose section. ATC.
XK740	8396M Gnat F.1	ex Hamble, Cosford, Bicester, Church Fenton, MoS, Filton.
XL770	8046M Skeeter AOP.12	ex Middle Wallop, Shrivenham, Wroughton, 15/19 Hussars, 652, 654.
XN246+	Cadet TX.3	ex Syerston. Arrived by 12/88.
+	Gnat T.1	nose section. Possibly ex Fareham. First noted 12/88. Stored.
BAPC. 7	SUMPAC	ex Old Warden, Southampton.
BAPC.164+	Wight Quadruplane	ex Wimborne. Arrived late 1988. Under completion. WAS.

More precisely located under the 'Southampton' banner is Ron Souch's **Antique Aeroplane Company** workshop, previously to be found under 'Hamble'. As ever, only long term items are listed here, otherwise it would be a chronicle of everything that went through the shop. Two of Ron's charges have taken to the air since the last edition saw the light of day : Dragonfly G-AEDT first flew from Lee-on-Solent on 15/7/88 and is now based at Dorchester with Wessex Aviation & Transport; Hawk Speed Six G-ADGP was flying by mid 1989 and moved on to be based at Old Warden. That leaves the situation as follows :-

G-AANL+	DH.60M Moth	ex OY-DEH, Danish AF S-107, S-357. Stored.
G-AANO+	DH.60GMW Moth	ex N590N, NC590N. Stored.
G-ABDX	DH.60G Moth	ex HB-UAS, CH-405 ntu, G-ABDX. Stored.
G-AFSW	Chilton DW.2	ex Chilton Manor. Stored.
G-AISX	J-3C-65 Cub	ex 43-30372. Parts from OO-ALY/43-30409. CoA expired 6/7/49.
G-AOJK+	Tiger Moth	ex Shoreham area, R4896, 19 RFS, 18 RFS, 18 EFTS, 8 EFTS. Crashed 27/10/62. Fuselage. First noted 11/89.
C-7	G-ACFM Avro Cadet	ex Abbeyshrule, Terenure, EI-AGO, EI-AFO, C-7. Stored.

Stored in the docks area is the long-lost T-33A/N G-WGHB which was last noted leaving Coventry Airport by road 3/8/84 heading in this direction, but thought bound for a containerliner. By 1989 it had been joined by the P.1B from Hendon, the Lightning gate guardian from Coltishall and the T.5 from Boscombe Down. The latter is on option for the Lightning Flying Club at Plymouth - which see. These aircraft are all held by **Wensley Haydon-Baillie** who has also acquired the balance of the Saudi Lightnings at Warton - which see.

G-WGHB+	T-33A/N S/Star	ex Coventry Airport, Duxford, Southend, CF-EHB, 21640. See notes.
XA847+	8371M EE P.1B	ex Hendon, Farnborough, A&AEE, makers. Arrived 1989. Stored.
XM172+	8427M Lightning F.1A	ex Coltishall, 226 OCU, 56. Arrived 1989. Stored.
XS422+	Lightning T.5	ex Boscombe Down, A&AEE, 56, 29, 111, 29, 111, 226 OCU. Arrived 1989. Stored.

With one exception, the store at **Crofton Aeroplane Services** is undisturbed. Auster 5 G-AJGJ moved on to BCAR at Hedge End.

G-AHHU	J/1N Alpha	ex Sandown. Crashed 10/6/63. Stored.
G-APAA	J/5R Alpine	Crashed 9/8/75. Stored.
9M-ANN	Chipmunk 22	ex N70727 ntu, R Malaysian AF FM1026, WP909, 19 RFS, 8 RFS. Stored.
18-1528	F-MBCH Super Cub	ex Kingsclere, ALAT. Stored.

To complete the scene, a local collector has the nose of the former Southampton ATC Vampire and the fuselage of a Gannet AS.1. A Terrier continues long term restoration at another location, and stored in another is a J-3C-65 Cub.

G-ARLH	Terrier 1	ex White Waltham, EI-AMB. Composite of TW528, VF635 and VX109.
G-BDMS	J-3C-65 Cub	ex F-BEGZ, 44-80753. Stored.
WN411+	Gannet AS.1	fuselage, first noted 1/89.
XD614+	8124M Vampire T.11	ex Southampton ATC, Chilean AF spares, 3 FTS, 7 FTS, 1 FTS, CFS, RAFC. Nose section. First noted 1/89.

SOUTHAMPTON AIRPORT

(Or Eastleigh) Work has halted on the two Sea Vixens here and both are now stored. On the fire dump, HS.125-3B/RA G-JSAX had expired by early 1989. It was replaced by another of the breed. This example, veteran G-ATPE, is without its nose, that having gone to BAe - but where?

G-ATPE+	HS.125-1B/522	ex Colt Executive, Shell. CoA expired 1/4/87. On the dump by 9/89. Noseless - see notes above.
XJ571	8140M Sea Vixen FAW.2	ex Cosford, Halton, Sydenham, 893, 892, 899. Stored.
XJ607	8171M Sea Vixen FAW.2	ex Cosford, Cranwell, 890, 892, 766, 892. Stored.

THRUXTON

A considerable expansion here in the helicopter side but more importantly in a new 'warbird' workshop, initially working on three Warbirds of Great Britain types and then the cache of Harvards from Mozambique. There have been no departures.

G-BCYY	W-Bell 47G-3B1	ex XV318. Crashed 6/7/83. Wreck.
G-BKZI+	B.206B JetRanger	ex 5B-CGC or 'CGD, G-BKZI, N6238N. Wreck. First noted 4/89.
G-ICRU	B.206A JetRanger	ex Carlisle, C-GXVE ntu, N7845S. Crashed 24/5/84. Wreck.
+	Hiller UH-12E-4	c/no 4463. Pod only. First noted 2/88.
D-HEAS+	AB.206B JetRanger	wreck. First noted 4/89.
BR601+	PV260" Spitfire IX	ex Biggin Hill, Bitteswell, Cape Town, SAAF 5631, BR601, 165, 316, 454, 64. Arrived 6/7/89. Restoration.
PP972+	Seafire III	ex Biggin Hill, Vannes-Meucon, Gavres, Aeronavale 12F, Bien Hoa, 1F, PP972, FAA, 767, 809. Arrived by 8/89. Restoration.
TE392+	8074M Spitfire XVI	ex Biggin Hill, Bitteswell, Blackbushe, Hereford, Kemble, Waterbeach 7000M, Wellesbourne Mountford, Church Lawford, 2 CAACU, 34, 695, 595, 164, 65, 126. Arrived 6/7/89. Restoration.
1681+	G-BSBD T-6G Texan	ex Mozambique, Portuguese AF (PAF) 1681, 51-15007. Arrived 21/12/89. Restoration.
1736+	G-BSBF Harvard IV	ex Mozambique, PAF 1736, WGAF BF+058, AA+058, 52-8590. Arrived 21/12/89. Restoration.
1753+	G-BSBG Harvard IV	ex Mozambique, PAF 1753, WGAF BF+053, AA+053, 52-8562. Arrived 21/12/89. Restoration.

1730+	G-BSBE Harvard IV	ex Mozambique, PAF 1730, WGAF AA+652, 52-8521. Arr 21/12/89. Restn.
1788+	G-BSBB Harvard IV	ex Mozambique, PAF 1788, WGAF AA+689, 53-4636. Arr 21/12/89. Restn.
1741+	G-BSBC Harvard IV	ex Mozambique, PAF 1741, WGAF, 53-4629. Compositr, with the rear end of 1780. Arr 21/12/89. Restoration.

WARSASH

(South of the A27 west of Fareham, or across the Hamble from Hamble!) Still in use at the **Naval College of Nautical Studies** is a Wessex.

| XM327 | Wessex HAS.3 | ex 829 'Kent' Flt. |

WHITCHURCH

At Ron Eastman's workshop, Auster AOP.6 TW536/G-BNGE was flying by 9/88 in immaculate condition and now lodges at Middle Wallop. Work on the Plus D continues.

| G-AHWJ | T'craft Plus D | ex Kingsclere, Wincanton, LB294. CoA expired 30/6/71. Restn. |

WINCHESTER

While on a local flight in Spitfire Mk Vc 'EE606'/G-MKVC from his strip here, Charles Church encountered engine trouble that shortly became catastrophic. Attempting to make Blackbushe, the aircraft force-landed and Church was killed in the impact. The aircraft, built essentially 'as new' by Dick Melton and team from Charles Church (Spitfires) Ltd had flown for the first time on 20/11/88. It had been presented to the CAA as a 'series prototype' and was widely acclaimed. With the passing of Charles Church, the warbird movement has lost a man of great dynamism who sought perfection. Shortly before his death, Church had transferred the workshop to Dick Melton and it continues to make lovely Spitfires under the banner of **Dick Melton Aviation**. Charles Church also acquired nearby Popham airstrip - which see - and this is still managed under his banner in the capable hands of Dick Richardson. The Hurricane project can still be found at Sandown but the Lancaster is no more at Woodford, see under Cranfield. Spitfire IX RR232 was disposed of to Sussex Spraying Services in 11/89 and has moved on, it may well appear at Shoreham in due course.

G-SUSY	P-51D-20-NA	ex NL12066, Nicaraguan AF GN120, USAAF 44-72773. Airworthy.
BL628+	Spitfire Vb	ex Australia, St Merryn, 719, 610, 401. Restoration.
MV262	Spitfire XIV	ex Bitteswell, Blackbushe, Calcutta, Indian AF, ACSEA, 9 MU.
PL344	Spitfire IX	ex Netherlands, Anthony Fokker School, 129, 130, 401, 442, 602. Under major rebuild.
PT462	G-CTIX Spitfire Tr IX	ex Nailsworth, Israel, Israel AF/DF 2067/0607, Italian AF MM4100, RAF PT462 73 (?), 253. Airworthy.
TE517	G-CCIX Spitfire IX	ex Nailsworth, G-BIXP ntu, Duxford, Israel, Israel DF/AF 2046, Czech AF, RAF TE517 313. Under restoration.
SM832	G-WWII Spitfire XIV	ex Duxford, Bitteswell, Blackbushe, Indian AF, Dehra Dun gate, RAF SM832, ACSEA, 222 MU, 29 MU. Arrived 1988. Stored.

Hereford & Worcester

BIRLINGHAM
(East of the B4080 to the west of Evesham) During 1989 **Graham Revill** took delivery of the former Stonehouse Hospital Vampire T.11.
XE979+   Vampire T.11   ex Stonehouse, Woodford, Chester, St Athan, 1 FTS, 8 FTS, RAFC.

DROITWICH
At the base of **Rotorspan** can be found two inert Bell 47s.
G-AWRZ+   Bell 47G-5   ex HB-XCK, N1344X. Crashed 26/4/86. Wreck. First noted 8/86.
G-BFVM+   W/Bell 47G-3B1   ex XT234. CoA expired 20/11/87. Stored. First noted 4/88.

EWYAS HAROLD
(On the A465 south west of Hereford) It is a problematical exercise to check if the Trident fuselage is still with **22 Regiment** Special Air Service here. To avoid annoying these nice people, we'll assume it is. Tread boldly...
G-AVYB   Trident 1E-140   ex BA, BEA, Channel. Fuselage. CoA expired 21/6/82.

FOWNHOPE
(On the B4224 south east of Hereford) **Mark Biggs** has two as yet anonymous Tiger Moth frames stored in the area.
                 Tiger Moth   frame.
                 Tiger Moth   frame.

HEREFORD
At **RAF Hereford** (or Credenhill) the Hunter continues to guard the parade ground. Vampire T.11 XE982/7564M was put up for tender 4/89 and moved to Dunkeswell 7/89.
XG252   8840M Hunter FGA.9   ex Cosford, 1 TWU, 2 TWU, 1 TWU, TWU, 45, 8, Wittering SF, MoA, 54, 66. Displayed.

Elsewhere, **Clive Hardiman** passed on his static Tiger Moth replica to TAC at Warmingham 14/2/88. His 'flyer' project from Shobdon arrived here by 10/88.
G-DHTM+   Tiger Moth replica ex Shobdon. See notes above.

SHOBDON
Much to talk of here, although it is a story of the removal of several classic airframes and the arrival of a lot of 'tin'. Outbound have been : J/1 Autocrat G-AHHK and Auster Kingsland G-AJIT had both left the airfield by 11/89, destination unknown; Tiger Moth G-ACDA (composite with G-ANOR) moved out initially to Malmesbury and then on to Chilbolton for restoration; Tiger Moth replica G-DHTM moved to Hereford by 10/88. Noted in **MiniWrecks** as being in store here, Twin Comanche N230ET/G-ATET is in fact airworthy, although its sojourns into the either are infrequent. Current situation here is :
G-APSO   Dove 5   ex N1046T ntu. CoA expired 8/7/78. Stored, dismantled.
G-AVCT+   Cessna F.150G   ex Southend. CoA expired 3/3/73. Arrived by 10/89 for restoration.
G-AWFF+   Cessna F.150H   ex Bredhurst, Leavesden. Damaged 12/2/85. Fuselage. First noted 2/89.
G-AXVC+   Cessna FA.150K   ex Sibson. Crashed 14/10/87. Wreck. Arrived by 10/89.
G-AYFA   Twin Pioneer 3   ex Flight One, Prestwick, G-31-5, XM285, SRCU, 225, Odiham SF, 230. CoA expired 24/5/82. Open store.
G-AYSZ+   Cessna FA.150L   ex Dubai. CoA expired 28/5/88. First noted 10/89, for restoration.
G-BEPN   Pawnee 235D   ex N54877. Crashed 11/2/78. Fuselage frame only.

UPPER HILL
(Between the A4110 and the A49 south of Leominster) Steadfastly guarding the premises of **Lion Motors** and **Sheppards Crane Hire** is the Swift.
WK275   Swift F.4   ex Hatfield, Filton, C(A).

WITHINGTON
(East of Hereford on the A4103 to Worcester) By 10/89 **Hereford Tiles** had gained a former Leuchars Lightning.
XN781+   8538M Lightning F.2A   ex Leuchars, 92, 19. Arrived by 10/89.

Hertfordshire

BENINGTON

(South of the B1037 east of Stevenage) John Evetts of **EMK Aeroplane** was killed in the crash of a Mooney M.20 on 23/7/88 and the business here was subsequently wound up. All but the C-47A are known to have moved on as follows : Sokol G-AIXN to Breighton by 4/88; Gemini 1A G-AKHW to somewhere in 'Essex'; SK.1 G-AOBG also to Breighton; Bleriot XI BAPC.132/'G-BLXI' moved to the Musee d'Automobile, France; SPAD VII N4727V/S4523 is also thought to have gone dans la France. Vampire T.11 XD459 (with the wings of WZ464) came here from Cranfield (not to Ware as given in **W&R11**). Its current status is unknown. Here by 4/88 was Cadet TX.3 WT899. It had moved to Rush Green by 1989.

N5595T	C-47A-85-DL	ex Thruxton, Blackbushe, G-BGCG, Spanish AF T3-27, N49V, N50322, 43-15536. Stored dismantled.

BERKHAMSTED

Under this heading we list **Stuart McKay's** airframe store.

G-AVPD	Jodel D.9 Bebe	ex Langley. CoA expired 6/6/75. Stored.
G-AWDW	Bensen CB-8M	CoA expired 7/10/71. Stored.
G-AZZZ	Tiger Moth	ex Langley, Maidenhead, F-BGJE, NL864. Wings from G-BABA. Stored.
G-BBGP	Berg Cricket	Damaged 21/9/73. Stored.

BISHOP'S STORTFORD

With the Dragon Rapide under restoration at Audley End (which see) and consequently no major form of income (from pleasure flying) to provide the capital to expand the pioneering **Russavia Collection** of gliders and light aircraft, the fleet has undergone some more rationalisation with further thought being given to the long term of the operation. It would indeed be a tragedy if this unique collection were to be dissolved. The DH.84 Dragon project is in its very formative stages, although much of the 'hardware' exists to bring it into being should the right backing be found for the venture. Martin Monoplane project G-AEYY moved to Hitchin and the Fauvel AV.36CR BGA.2500 has been sold off along with the Sirocco G-MNDV. Russavia aircraft can also be found listed under Duxford and Eaton Bray. Aircraft listed below are stored in and around the area and visits to see them are not possible at present. General enquiries can be made to : Russavia, Woodend Green, Henham, Bishop's Stortford, Herts, CM22 6AY.

G-EBQP	DH.53 Humming Bird	composite, with wings of G-AEYY. Stored.
G-ACET+	DH.84 Dragon	see notes above. Ex AW171, G-ACET.
G-AEDB+	BAC Drone 2	ex Duxford, BGA.2731. CoA expired 26/5/87. Stored.
G-AKKH	Gemini 1A	ex Duxford. CoA expired 1/10/84. Stored.
BGA 162	Willow Wren	'Yellow Wren'. Stored.
BGA 651	ATR Slingsby Petrel	ex Dublin, EI-101, IGA.101, G-ALPP. Stored.
BGA 1147	BQJ Kranich II	ex RAFGSA.215. Stored.
BGA 3166	FCZ Lippisch Falke rep	Stored. (Slingsby T.1 Falcon).

BUSHEY

Vintage Aircraft Team (see Cranfield) still have a small store here. Clarifying **W&R11**, Vampire T.11 XK632 pod turned up at Hemel Hempstead.

VZ304	7630M Vampire FB.5	ex Carlisle, 3 CAACU, 249. Stored.
	Venom FB.4	ex Tinwald Downs. Identity not confirmed. Pod only. Stored.
	Mystery Jet MJ-1	ex Southend. Fuselage mock-up. Stored.

Not too far away, at the breakers yard called **Breakers** the Sundowner still crowns the pile of cars.

G-BARI	Sundowner	Crashed 23/4/75. Battered fuselage only.

CLOTHALL COMMON

(On the A507 south east of Baldock) The Arrow and Tri-Traveler are still stored.

G-ALJS	J/4 Arrow	ex Compton. Stored, dismantled. CoA exp 14/12/71.
G-APYU	Tri-Traveler	ex Moreton-in-the-Marsh. Crashed 23/4/72. Stored.

ELSTREE
At the airfield, the junked Kachina was joined by a Sudanese Navajo in 1988.
G-CHIT	Varga Kachina	Crashed 27/4/86. Fuselage.
ST-AHZ+	Navajo 300	ex G-AXMR, N6558L. Stored. First noted 7/88.

FOWLMERE
(North of the A505, near Royston) Adding to **W&R11**, Robs Lamplough's P-51 fuselage
did indeed move to North Weald. His Hurricane restoration is still here.
	Hurricane	ex Israel. Bare frame and other components.

GOFF'S OAK
(On the B156 west of Cheshunt) Stored at a farm here is a Hiller UH-12.
G-ATKG	Hiller UH-12B	ex Brandis Corner, Thornicombe, Redhill, Thai AF 103. CoA exp 28/11/69. Stored.

HATFIELD
The Jetstream fuselage is still used for instruction at the **Polytechnic**. Locally,
Gerry Atwell and Frank Telling are still at work on their Auster.
G-AKXP	Auster 5	ex Claygate, NJ633. Crashed 9/4/70. Under restoration.
	Jetstream	fuselage. See above.

HATFIELD AIRFIELD
Plans for the proposed Heritage Centre here appear to have gone no further. The
British Aerospace/Shuttleworth Collection DH.88 Comet G-ACSS is now flying again
and continues to be based here. Tiger Moth G-APLU was flown following restoration
during 1989 and now flies from here. During 1989 the former Wroughton Trident
arrived and is used for fire suppression trials. Also arriving in 1989 was one of
the unfinished HS.748 fuselages from Woodford, for static testing. Hatfield is the
base for BAe's 'roadshow' airframes and they are listed below, although more often
than not are to be found at various trade shows the world over.
G-ACSS	DH.88 Comet	ex Farnborough, Old Warden, Leavesden, K5084, G-ACSS. a/w.
G-ARYB	HS.125 Srs 1	ex Astwick Manor, Hatfield. CoA expired 22/1/68.
G-AVYE+	Trident 1E-140	ex Wroughton, BA, Northeast, BEA, Channel. CoA expired 13/7/82. Arrived 22/6/89.
G-AWZO	Trident 3B-101	ex Heathrow, BA, BEA. CoA expired 13/2/86.
c/n 1808+	HS.748-2B	ex Woodford, Set 289. Arrived 5/89 for statis tests.
	ATP mock-up	ex Woodford, Kemble, St Athan, Kemble, 84, Handling Squadron. Based upon Andover C.1 XS647. Travelling demonstrator.
	HS.125-800	ex Chester Airport, IAAC 236, G-AYBH. Crashed 27/11/79. Based upon an HS.125-600A fuselage. Travelling demonstrator.
	Jetstream 31	ex East Midlands, N14234. Based upon Jetstream 1 fuselage. Travelling demonstrator.

HEMEL HEMPSTEAD
By 1988, the local **RAFA** here had received the pod of a former Bushey Vampire T.11.
XK632+	Vampire T.11	ex Bushey, Keevil, Exeter, 3/4 CAACU, CFS. Pod.

HERTFORD
Stored in the area is an L.200 Morava, used by **Martin Emery** as a source of spares
for G-ASFD (see under Bournemouth Airport) and the airworthy G-BNBZ.
OE-FBC+	L.200 Morava	stored. Spares use - see above.

HITCHIN
Restoration of Super Cub G-BKEZ continues in the general area. The former Russavia
Martin Monoplane project came here during 1989 for **D Braham** to work on.
G-AEYY+	Martin Monoplane	ex Bishop's Stortford, Meir. Restoration project - wings to G-EBQP at Bishop's Stortford.
G-BKEZ	PA-19-95	ex Kingsclere, OO-SPL, 51-15628. Under restoration.

HODDESDON

(On the A41 south of Ware) Opposite the John Warner School, **1239 Squadron ATC** have
a Vampire.

| XD616 | Vampire T.11 | ex Old Warden, Woodford, Chester, St Athan, 8 FTS, 1 FTS, 8 FTS, 65. |

KINGS LANGLEY

(On the A41 north of Watford) During 1988, the Sea Vixen kept on the Holme Park
Industrial Estate, near the canal, was joined by a Sea Hawk.

| XE327+ | A2556 Sea Hawk FGA.6 | ex Llangennech, Sydenham, 738. Arrived 1988. |
| XJ494 | Sea Vixen FAW.2 | ex Farnborough, FRL, A&AEE, HSA, Sydenham, 899, Sydenham, 892. |

LEAVESDEN

The Gnat influx listed in **W&R11** turned into an efflux during 1988. XR572 was
shipped to the USA, becoming N572XR; XP535 first flew as G-BOXP on 5/8/88 and
transferred to <u>Cranfield</u> with XR991/G-BOXO following it. The ATC still have their
Vampire pod and the Dove still serves as an engine test-rig.

G-AJPR	Dove 1B	ex Biggin Hill. wfu 30/10/69. Forward fuselage.
WZ415	Vampire T.11	ex Croxley Green, Bushey, Keevil, Exeter, 3/4 CAACU, 226 OCU, CS(A).
		2(F) Squadron ATC, kept on the airfield boundary.

LEVERSTOCK GREEN

(On the road between Abbotts Langley and Hemel Hempstead) During 1988 the Provost
on display in the grounds of the 'Swan at Pimlico' public house had been joined by
a Skeeter, last heard of at the Wilkins & Wilkins Luton auction of 3/10/87.

WW442	7618M Provost T.1	ex Cranfield, Booker, St Merryn, Houghton-on-the-Hill,
		Kidlington, Halton, CNCS, 3 FTS.
XL765+	Skeeter AOP.12	ex Leamington Spa, Leeds, Rotherham, Wroughton, 17 Flt, 654, 651,
		SARO. First noted mid 1988.

LETCHWORTH

"How did this one escape for so long?" asked contributor and arch-ATC airframe
sleuth Dave Pope, having 'discovered' another one, only to find he was too late.
248 Squadron ATC took delivery of 'Chippax' WP862 circa 1969 from 955 Squadron ATC
in Stevenage. Struck off charge on 19/4/63, it was issued to the Stevenage ATC
unit around that date. The airframe 'disappeared' from Letchworth in July 1989 –
having apparently been stolen by gypsies. It was found in a gutted and battered
state in a local scrapyard, too far gone to worry about. For the record, its
pedigree was : ex Stevenage, Leeds UAS, Birm UAS, 1 FTS, Lon UAS, Biggin Hill SF,
Hull UAS, Lon UAS, Birm UAS, CNCS, RAFC.

LONDON COLNEY

(Off the A6 between London Colney and South Mimms) For those brave enough to take
their eyes from the three lanes of 80mph+ car park in front of them, a glimpse of
sanity can be had from the north western sector of the anti-clockwise M25. It is,
of course, the **Mosquito Aircraft Museum.** Restoration work here continues to
produce high quality exhibition airframes with the Sea Venom being the latest to
complete the treatment. 1990 sees the 50th Anniversary of the first flight of the
Mosquito and here must act as the centre shrine for such celebrations. Only major
note to make in terms of the 'fleet' is that the fuselage of Horsa TL615 was one
and the same as the one listed under <u>Robertsbridge</u> in **W&R11** and should be deleted
from here. MAM is open from Easter to the end of October on Sundays and from July
to the end of September on Thursday afternoons and is also open Bank Holidays.
Groups are welcome at other times by prior arrangement. Opening times are Sunday
1030 to 1730 and Thursdays 1400 to 1730. Contact : Mosquito Aircraft Museum, PO
Box 107, Salisbury Hall, London Colney, near St Albans, Herts, AL2 1BU. Telephone
0727 22051 during Museum opening hours as outlined above.

G-ABLM	Cierva C.24	ex Hatfield. CoA exp 16/1/35. Science Museum loan.
G-ADOT	Hornet Moth	ex Hatfield, Southampton, X9326, 5 GCF, 23 OTU, 24GCF, Halton SF,
		2 CPF, G-ADOT. CoA expired 15/10/59.

G-ANFP	Tiger Moth	ex Denham, Rush Green, N9503, 2 RFS, 7 RFS, 2 RFS, 4 RFS, 4 EFTS. CoA expired 1/7/63. Fuselage frame.
G-ANRX	Tiger Moth	ex Belchamp Walter, N6550, SLAW, 25 EFTS, 18 EFTS, 241, 14 EFTS, 56 ERFTS. CoA expired 20/6/61. Under restoration.
G-AOJT	Comet 1XB	ex Farnborough, Air France F-BGNX. Fuselage only.
G-ARYC	HS.125 Srs 1	ex Hatfield, Filton, Rolls-Royce. CoA expired 1/8/73.
G-AVFH	Trident 2	ex Heathrow, BA, BEA. Forward fuselage.
D-IFSB	Dove 6	ex Hatfield, BFS, D-CFSB, Panshanger, G-AMXR, N4280V.
A1325	RAF BE.2e	ex Norway, Norwegian AF '37' and '133'. Under restoration.
K3584"	B'186 Queen Bee	ex Hadfield, Redhill. Under restoration.
W4050	Mosquito I	ex Hatfield, Chester, Radlett, E-0234. Prototype.
TA122	Mosquito FB.6	ex Soesterberg, 4, 2 GCS, 48, 4, 605, 417 ARF. Fuselage, being rebuilt with the wing of TR.33 TW233 ex Israel.
TA634	Mosquito TT.35	ex Liverpool, G-AWJV, Aldergrove, 3 CAACU, APS Schleswigland, APS Ahlorn, APS Sylt, 4 CAACU. Under restoration.
TJ118	Mosquito TT.35	ex Elstree, Exeter, 3/4 CAACU, 3 CAACU. Nose. See also Oxford.
WP790	Chipmunk T.10	ex Rush Green, G-BBNC, WP790, Bir UAS, Wales UAS, PFTS, AOTS, 1 ITS, RAFC, Man UAS, G&S UAS, Stn UAS, 24 GCF, 5 RFS, 17 RFS.
WX853	7443M Venom NF.3	ex Debden, Shawbury, 23.
XE985	Vampire T.11	ex Woodford, Chester, St Athan, 5 FTS. Composite, wings of WZ476.
XG730	Sea Venom FAW.22	ex Southwick, ADS, 893, 894, 891.
XJ565	Sea Vixen FAW.2	ex RAE Bedford, 899, 893, 766B.
J-1008	Vampire FB.6	ex Hatfield, Swiss AF.
BAPC 146	Toucan MPA	ex Hitchin, Old Warden, Radlett. Centre body plus props.

PANSHANGER

This book relies on inputs from readers. The compiler gets around as much as he can, but when it comes down to it, it is observations from the roaming scribes who are good enough to write in that help to assemble the reports on each location. Every edition is full of amendments and modifications to the last one – that's part of the fascination of trying to track down the fates and circumstances of **W&R**-type airframes. And so it was that in the last edition it was decreed that the famous former Danish S-55s had gone, just their booms remaining. Not so, dear reader. Covered in layers of dust that make them look more like relics from ancient Egypt than retired rotorcraft, they live on! Boomless they are and in a very dark hangar, but very much here! The airfield has been sold for housing meanwhile, and this may be the last time they are listed here anyway! Bell UH-1H G-BMLA/VP-FBD moved on to Australia as VH-UHE and Bell 212 LN-OQS/G-GLEN became P2-PAV. There is just the addition of a Rallye to record.

G-ASOL	Bell 47D-1	ex N146B. CoA expired 6/9/71. Stored.
G-AYYY+	MS 880B Rallye Club	CoA expired 28/4/86. Stored.
G-BARJ	Bell 212	ex BEAS, VR-BGI, G-BARJ, EI-AWM, G-BARJ, EI-AWN, G-BARJ. Crashed 24/12/83. Wreck, stored.
G-BJYO	Tomahawk 112	Crashed 31/5/84. Cockpit section with Flying Club.
N5052P	Comanche 180	ex G-ATFS, N5052P. Stored.
XT148	Sioux AH.1	ex Wroughton. Stored.
XT803	Sioux AH.1	ex High Melton, Wroughton. Stored.
S-881+	S-55C	ex Elstree, Danish Air Force ESK.722. See notes above.
S-882+	S-55C	ex Elstree, Danish Air Force ESK.722. See notes above.
S-884+	S-55C	ex Elstree, Danish Air Force ESK.722. See notes above.
S-885+	S-55C	ex Elstree, Danish Air Force ESK.722. See notes above.
S-886+	S-55C	ex Elstree, Danish Air Force ESK.722. See notes above.
S-887+	S-55C	ex Elstree, Danish Air Force ESK.722. See notes above.
U-708	B.206 JetRanger	ex Ugandan AF. Wreck. Stored. With parts of U-705.

POTTERS BAR

Gerry Twyman's Auster is nearing the end of its restoration. It is thought that the D.120A can still be found in the area.

G-AGYH	J/1N Alpha	CoA expired 10/10/72. Under restoration.
F-BNZM	Wassmer D.120A	c/n 319. Under rebuild.

PATMORE
(North west of Bishop's Stortford)   Should still host a stored Cricket.
G-AYDJ	Cricket	CoA expired 13/4/72. Stored.

RABLEY HEATH
(Off the A1M south of Stevenage)   In open store here is an Auster AOP.9.
XP241	Auster AOP.9	ex St Athan, 653, Aden.

ROYSTON
At **Skycraft Services**, it is thought the contents of the workshop are unchanged.
G-ASBY	Airedale	CoA expired 22/3/80. Under rebuild.
G-BKXP	Auster AOP.6	ex Oakington, Belgian AF A-14, VT987. Under restoration.
A-20	Auster AOP.6	ex Oakington, Belgian AF, VT994. Spares use.

RUSH GREEN
The airfield makes a re-entry into the pages of **W&R**. Much-travelled Dragon Rapide G-AEML is now here, under restoration for Victor Gauntlett. With the death of Jim Coates, his Swalesong is stored here.   The Pawnee frame is assumed to be a 'rediscovery' and not 'new' as such.   The reason for the Cadet being here is unknown - motorglider-to-be, perhaps?
G-AEML+	Dragon Rapide	ex Barrow-in-Furness Airport, Babbacombe, Land's End, Coventry, Liverpool, X9450, Armstrong Whitworth, AFEE, 6 AACU, G-AEML. CoA expired 2/4/71. Arrived by 2/89. See notes above.
G-AYDV+	SA.II Swalesong	CoA expired 11/4/89. See notes above.
+	Pawnee	fuselage frame. See notes above.
WT899+	Cadet TX.3	ex Benington. Stored.

ST ALBANS
Auster G-APJZ moved to an owner in 'Kent', leaving just the three Vampire T.11s at the **College of Further Education** here to list.
WZ584	Vampire T.11	ex Hatfield, CATCS, 1 FTS, 2 CAACU, 32.
XE956	Vampire T.11	ex Hatfield, CATCS, 1 FTS, 8 FTS, 3 CAACU, APS, 67.
XH313	Vampire T.11	ex Hatfield, CATCS, Wattisham SF, 111.

WARE
Contrary to **W&R11**, Vampire T.11 XD459 did not come here, instead settling upon Benington, which see. Contributor Alan Allen acquired Vampire T.11 XE849/7928M and it moved to Monkton Farleigh 3/9/88.

Humberside

BEVERLEY
Very suddenly the Blackburn Beverley C.1 held by the **Museum of Army Transport** is the only whole one on the planet. With both the Hendon and Southend ones no more, this exhibit is now all the more precious. The 'Bev' forms the centre-piece of the outside displays here. Located in Flemingate, Beverley, the Museum is open 1000 to 1700 every day except Mondays in November, December, January and is closed December 24-26. Telephone 0482 860445.
XB259	Beverley C.1	ex Paull, Luton, Court Line, RAE, Blackburns, G-AOAI.
XP772	Beaver AL.1	ex Middle Wallop, 6 Flt.

Bensen B.8M G-ASME, which was stored locally, was fitted with a Rotax 503 and flew again by 4/88.

BILTON
After many years of storage, **Neville Medforth** offered Tiger Moth G-ANEJ for sale in 1988. It was acquired by the Royal Malaysian Air Force Museum at Kuala Lumpur and is now one of its star exhibits.

BREIGHTON
The scenery at the airfield has been transformed, at least from the point of view of the classiness of the aircraft that now live here! Breighton acts in a similar way to Tattershall Thorpe, holding civil aviation hulks while insurance settlements/disposals are underway, hence the small accumulation of such airframes. Several transitory airframes fall into that category and deserve mention here : Rallye Club G-BAOT was first noted 6/88; AA-5A Cheetah G-JULY first noted early 1988; Tomahawks G-BGZE and G-BGZH. All moved on to Tattershall Thrope. Nord 3202B N2254X/G-BMBF moved through to Kings Cliffe by 1988. Aeronca 100 G-AEVS arrived from the Sherburn area during 1988. It made its first post restoration flight in 11/89. Current situation is as follows :

G-AIXN+	M.1C Sokol	ex Benington, Booker, OK-BHA. CoA expired 13/4/77. First noted 3/89. For restoration.
G-AOBG+	Somers-Kendal SK.1	ex Benington, 'Sussex', Eaton Bray, Cranfield. Arr by 10/89.
G-ATKY	Cessna 150F	ex Sherburn, N8513G. Damaged 15/12/79. Under rebuild.
G-BBWZ	AA-1B Trainer	CoA expired 3/8/81. Stored.
T9738+ G-AKAT	Magister	ex Sherburn area, Winthorpe, Leicester East, 24 EFTS, 15 EFTS. CoA expired 13/11/65. Arrived by 3/89. Under restoration.

BROUGH
With Hawk work very much to the fore at this busy **British Aerospace** plant, not surprisingly a Hawk fatigue rig is now in operation here, alongside the older generation of airframes that have a support 'home' here. Adding to **W&R11**, the nose section of Buccaneer S.2B XK527 moved initially to Lutterworth and then to an owner in 'Hampshire'. The Apprentices Buccaneer, S.2B XV155/8716M moved to Lovaux at Macclesfield for canopy trials 2/89. Current situation is as follows :

XN982	Buccaneer S.2C	ex Holme-on-Spalding Moor, RAE Farnborough. Fatigue rig.
XT858	Phantom FG.1	ex Holme-on-Spalding Moor, Leuchars, Aldergrove, Hucknall, A&AEE, RAE Bedford, Hucknall, 700P, RAE Bedford. Fatigue rig.
+	Hawk	fatigue rig. First noted 7/89.
E-427	Hunter F.51	ex Holme-on-Spalding Moor, Brough, Dunsfold, G-9-447, Danish AF, ESK.724. Customer training airframe.
XP345+ 8792M	Whirlwind HAR.10	ex Tattershall Thorpe, Lee-on-Solent, Cyprus, Alexander Barracks, 84 'B' Flt, 1563 Flt, 202, CFS. Arrived 28/8/87.

CLEETHORPES
As foretold in **W&R11** the majority of the airframes held here made the move with the **Bomber County Aviation Museum** to Hemswell, as follows : Bristol Babe replica 'G-EASQ'/BAPC.87, Flying Flea G-AEJZ/BAPC.120, Stewart Ornithopter BAPC.161, Canberra T.19 WJ975, Vampire T.11 XD445, Hunter FGA.9 composite XG195, Sycamore HR.14 XG506 and Mystere IVA 101. Flying Flea 'G-AFFI'/BAPC.76 moved to Elvington to join YAM; the fuselage of Canberre B.6(M) went to a local scrapyard. The fates of Canberra PR.7 WH796 nose and the anonymous Wessex forward fuselage.

GRIMSBY
After much hard work, Christian Brydges and friends of the **Grimsby Aircraft Preservation Group** have established the **Museum of Weapon Technology** here. Things are at an early stage yet and visitors cannot be accommodated without prior arrangement. Arriving on site were by 3/90 were the Lightning F.6 and T.5 nose from Laceby and the F-104G from Skegness airfield. Contact : 31, Montgomery Road, Cleethorpes, South Humberside, DN35 9JG.

XR770+	Lightning F.6	ex Laceby, Binbrook, 11, 5-11 pool, 56, 23, 74. Arrived by 3/90.
XS457+	Lightning T.5	ex Laceby, Binbrook, 5, 11, 5, LTF, 11, 226 OCU. Nose section. Arrived by 3/90. Under restoration.
22+57+	F-104G Starfighter	ex Skegness, Laceby, Binbrook, Manching, JbG34, DD+239, KE+438. Arrived by 3/90.

HULL

In Hedon Road, **Aviation Marine Specialist Spares** have begun to live up to the first
bit of their name. By 9/88 they had acquired Whirlwind HAS.7 XN311/A2643 from its
brief sojourn at Corsham, but on 27/1/89 it had moved to 'Birmingham' - can anyone
be more precise? During 1989 two larger pieces of hardware arrived by road, with
perhaps Sea Prince T.1 WP314/8634M (ex Syerston arriving 18/2/89) substantiating
the 'Marine' part of the company's title! This validation was short-lived, as it
moved by 2/90. Destination unconfirmed, but most likely to be Charlwood. They are
held in store, looking for customers.
WL627+   8488M Varsity T.1   ex Newton, 6 FTS, 2 ANS, 1 ANS, BCBS. Arrived 5/3/89.

HUMBERSIDE AIRPORT

(Or Kirmington) Cessna 404 Titan G-PATT (accident 29/10/86) was in store here from
at least 3/87. Its sojourn continued until 15/12/88 when it left for Glasgow with
the ultimate intention of going to Kenya.

LACEBY

Another location where the inmates have come and gone in between editions. At the
J H Food Equipment plant on the by-pass, F-104G 22+57, Lightning F.6 XR770 and
Lightning T.5 nose XS457 (all ex Binbrook) were stored during 1988/1989. The F-
104G moved during 1989 to Skegness Airport, while the Lightnings moved to Grimsby
by 3/90.

STORWOOD

(South east of York) **Melbourne Autos** now have two Dragonflies and the report of a
Whirlwind HAR.10, mentioned in **W&R11**, has turned out to be correct.
WH991+   Dragonfly HR.3   ex Tattershall Thorpe, Tattershall, Wisbech, Taunton, Fleetlands,
                            Culdrose SF, 705, 700, Eglinton SF, 'Centaur' Flt, 705,
                            'Illustrious' Flt. First noted 11/88.
WP503   Dragonfly HR.3   ex Cleethorpes, Elsham Hall, Stansted, RAE Bedford, North Coates,
                            Lee-on-Solent, Lossiemouth SF.

Isle of Man

ISLE OF MAN AIRPORT

(Or Ronaldsway) Main source of attention here is the **Aeroservice (IoM) Ltd** hangar
where the restoration of Percival Q6 G-AFFD continues apace. Also within is a
collection of withdrawn or damaged airframes, all in long term store. The Leopard
Moth also remains flightless, elsewhere on the airfield.
G-ACLL   Leopard Moth   ex AW165, AFEE, 7 AACU, 6 AACU, Ringway SF, G-ACLL. CoA expired
                            7/9/84. Stored.
G-AFFD   Percival Q.6   ex Sutton Coldfield, Duxford, Redhill, G-AIEY ntu, X9407, MCS, 510,
                            Old Sarum SF, Halton SF, Heston SF, Northolt SF, 6 AACU, G-AFFD.
                            CoA expired 31/8/56. Under restoration.
G-APSZ+   Cessna 172   ex Barton, N6372E. Damaged 2/3/84. Stored.
G-AYVV+   ST-10 Diplomate   ex Cippenham. Crashed 30/9/79. Stored.
G-BAEO   Cessna F.172M   ex Manchester, Barton. Crashed 7/5/78. Fuselage.
G-BCGA+   Seneca 200-2   ex Panshanger, N41975. Crashed 18/12/77. Wreck. Stored.
+   Stits Playboy   ex USA. Fuselage frame.

Isle of Wight

BEMBRIDGE
Stored at the owner's home is a Rallye. Reports indicate that there may be an Aztec fuselage here also. (In which case, it is most likely to be G-AVVT.)

G-AXHI+   MS.880B Rallye Club CoA expired 7/6/87. Stored.

BEMBRIDGE AIRFIELD
Of the stored BN-2 Islander airframes, c/nos 2042 and 2043 disappeared to join the Philippines assembly line by 2/88. The others are thought to remain, however.

G-BJOG	BN-2 Islander	stored.
c/no 917	BN-2 Islander	stored.
c/no 920	BN-2 Islander	stored.
c/no 2036	BN-2 Islander	stored.
c/no 2041	BN-2 Islander	stored.

COWES
Early in 1987 the **Westland Aerospace/British Hovercarft Corporation** plant here received former Bristows Wessex 60s 5N-AJN and 5N-ALO from Redhill for storage. They left by road in 7/88, bound for the USA as N251HL and N252HL respectively.

NEWPORT
Still stored in the immediate area in two separate places are two homebuilds.

G-AZJE	JB.01 Minicab	ex Sandown. CoA expired 7/7/82. Stored.
G-BCMF	Levi Go-Plane	One and only flight 16/11/74. Stored.

SANDOWN
A very varied airfield, offering an increasing **W&R** population. Backtracking to **W&R11**, Charles Church (Spitfires) Ltd did not operate a workshop here. Working on their (now Dick Melton Aviation) Hurricane is Ron Clark's **RGC Ltd.** 'Buchon' G-HUNN went on to be based at Winchester after it had finished test flying. Steve Vizzard's **Airframe Assemblies** specialises in Spitfire wings and sub-assemblies and all of Mk XVI TE184 did not come here, moving instead from Chichester to East Midlands Airport. ARV Aviation became **Island Aviation** and another Super 2 became a derelict feature of the airfield by 4/88 when G-BMWI was placed on the dump. It was cut up and removed 10/89. The two frustrated Norman Freelances arrived for storage in 1/90. Stored here for many years has been Cessna 172B G-TOBY, this moved during 1989 to Shoreham for use as an instructional airframe. Current situation is as follows :

G-AMXT+	Dove 6	ex G-BJXI ntu, XJ347, G-AMXT, N1561V. CoA expired 5/12/86. Stored since arrival.
G-AYTD	Aztec 250C	ex Southend, 5Y-ACA, N5727Y. CoA exp 24/2/83. Hulk with firemen.
G-NACA+	NAC-2 Freelance	ex Cardiff. Arrived 22/1/90.
G-NACI+	NAC-1 Freelance	ex Cardiff, BN-3 G-AXFB. Arrived 22/1/90.
	ARV-2 Super 2	stress test airframe.
5481+	G-ORGI Hurricane XII	ex Winchester, Canada, RCAF. Bare frame. Under restoration.

Kent

ASHFORD
Work continues on the restoration of **Brian Knock**'s Jackaroo.

G-ANFY	Jackaroo	ex NL906. CoA expired 25/5/68. Under restoration.

BRANDS HATCH
By 4/88 a Vampire T.11, a Whirlwind HAR.10 and a Wessex coded '47/R' were to be found in a compound on the race track perimeter. They were to be seen again 4/89 and clearly deserve more investigation. Favourite for the Wessex is XP159 ex Odiham and Fleet.

BREDHURST
(South of Junction 4 of the M2, south of Gillingham) **RE Aviation** moved to Lydd in 1988 and took the opportunity to sell off some of their hardware at the same time. Cessna F.150H G-AWFF went to Shobdon; F.150L G-BAXV back to Eversden; and F.150L G-BLAL destination unknown. RE took with them Wilgas G-BHUN and G-BJAU which were only fleetingly here. The Cherokee and Zlin are still stored. **Aerocrafts** are working on the restoration of a long-dormant Jodel.

G-AXVS+	SAN DR.1050	ex Headcorn, Rochester, F-BJNL. CoA expired 13/6/77. Restn.
G-BEYT	Cherokee 140	ex West Germany, D-EBWO, N6280W. Stored.
G-BEZA	Zlin Z.226T	ex D-EMJD, OK-MJA. Stored.

BRENZETT
(On the A2070 north west of New Romney) Continued expansion and refinement at the **Brenzett Aeronautical Museum** will help put them firmly on the 'rounds' for the 50th Anniversary of the Battle of Britain during 1990. In readiness for this, the Hurricane cockpit section from Robertsbridge has arrived. Arriving late in 1989 was a Vampire T.11 from North Weald via Firbeck. The museum is open Sundays and Bank Holidays from Easter to October 1100 to 1700 and additionally Tuesdays, Wednesdays and Thursdays July to August from 1400 to 1700. Contact : Brenzett Aeronautical Museum, Ivychurch Road, Brenzett, Romney Marsh, Kent TN29 OEE.

G-AGPG	Avro XIX Srs 2	ex Southend, Pye, Ekco, Avro. CoA expired 13/12/71. Stored.
G-AMSM	Dakota 4	ex Booker, Brenzett, Duxford, Brenzett, Lydd, Skyways, Eagle, Starways, KN274, TCDU, 77, St Eval SF, Azores SF, 43-49948. Damaged 17/8/78. Nose.
V7350+	Hurricane I	ex Robertsbridge, 85. Crashed 29/8/40. Forward fuselage. Arrived 1989.
WH657	Canberra B.2	ex Godalming, RAE, 231 OCU.
XK625+	Vampire T.11	ex Firbeck, North Weald, Southend, Woodford, St Athan, 8 FTS, 7 FTS. Arrived 11/89.

CANTERBURY
The nose section of B-26K Invader N99218 moved to Booker 16/4/88.

CHALLOCK LEES
(On the A251 north of Ashford) The amazing Alaparma Baldo was joined in 1988 by an Auster from West Malling and the following year by a Falke from Maidstone nearing the end of its restoration.

G-AGYK+	J/1 Autocrat	ex West Malling, Rochester. Damaged 14/1/87. Arrived by 8/88.
G-AYYL+	T.61A Falke	ex Maidstone, Sittingbourne, Manston. Damaged 9-10/12/82. Arrived by 9/89. Restoration.
G-BCRH	Baldo 75	ex Little Snoring, Hardwick, Challock Lees, I-DONP, Italian AF MM53647.

CHATHAM
While the Sioux is still held in store off-site, the **Royal Engineers Museum** is well worth a visit. Open Tuesday to Friday and Spring/Summer Bank Holidays 1000 to 1700 and Sundays 1130 to 1700. Contact : Caroline M Reed, Curator, Royal Engineers

Museum, Brompton Barracks, Chatham, Kent ME4 4UG. Telephone 0634 44555 ext 2312.
XT133   7923M Sioux AH.1   ex Arborfield, Middle Wallop. Stored.

In Boundary Road can be found **1404 Squadron ATC** who keep a complete Chipmunk
fuselage here. The Squadron have a detached flight at Manston.
WZ846   8439M Chipmunk T.10   ex G-BCSC, Bicester, Manston, Wales UAS, AOTS, 202, 228, CFE, West
                                 Raynham SF, G&S UAS, Bri UAS, 1 AEF, St Athan hack, Nott UAS, 63
                                 GCF, Edn UAS, S'tn UAS.

Locally, the store of light aircraft is undisturbed.
G-AXDB   J-3C-65 Cub   ex Whitwell, Bembridge, F-BMSG, history beyond this unconfirmed.
                                 Damaged 13/12/72. Stored.
G-AYVP   Woody Pusher   Unfinished homebuild project.
G-BCNC   GY-201 Minicab   ex F-BICF. Under rebuild.

CHATTENDEN
(On the A228 north of Rochester) Within the grounds of the **Defence Ordnance
Disposal School** at Lodge Hill Camp are three 'guardians'.
WT301   Canberra B.6(mod)   ex 51, 192. Gate guardian.
BAPC 158 Fieseler Fi 103   gate guardian.
BAPC 159 Yokosuka Ohka II   ex Cranwell. Gate guardian.

CHISLET
(North of the A28 south of Herne Bay) At the strip here, a Tiger Moth is being
rebuilt for **Aero Vintage.** Its identity is now resolved.
G-ANOR   Tiger Moth   ex Shobdon, Billingshurst, DE694, Finningley SF, 2 GU, 16 RFS, 16
                                 EFTS. CoA expired 19/12/68. Under restoration.

HAWKINGE
(On the A260 north of Folkestone) **Kent Battle of Britain Museum** is in the vanguard
of marking the 50th Anniversary of the Battle of Britain. The assembly of
artefacts here is staggering and must rival that of the 'nationals'. Of particular
note is the uniform and flying clothing display while the array of machine guns and
other air weapons is spell-binding. The influx of more 'Battle of Britain' film
replicas from Torbay and Coventry and a Grunau Baby (representative of the training
phase of German pilots) has allowed for greatly extended dioramas within the hangar
area. The Museum is open seven days a week Easter to September 30 1000 to 17000
and October all week 1100 to 1400. Contact : Kent Battle of Britain Museum,
Aerodrome Road, Hawkinge Airfield, Folkestone, CT18 7AG. Telephone 0303 89 3140.
+   Grunau Baby   arrived 1989.
L1592"+   B' 63 Hurricane replica ex Higher Blagdon, 'Battle of Britain'. Arrived 1989.
N3289"   B' 65 Spitfire replica ex Chilham Castle, 'Battle of Britain'.
P3059"   B' 64 Hurricane replica ex Chilham Castle, 'Battle of Britain'.
XP701   8924M Lightning F.3   ex Binbrook, LTF, 5, 11, 56, 29, 111, 29, A&AEE.
1480"   B' 66 'Bf 109' replica ex Chilham Castle, 'Battle of Britain'.
6357"   B' 74 'Bf 109' replica ex Higher Blagdon, 'Battle of Britain'. Arrived 1989.
BAPC 36   Fi 103 (V-1) rep   ex Old Warden, Duxford, Old Warden.
BAPC 67+ 'Bf 109' replica   ex Coventry Airport, North Weald, Newark, 'Battle of Britain'.
                                 Arrived late 1988.
BAPC 69+ Spitfire replica   ex Higher Blagdon, Stoneleigh, 'Battle of Britain'. Arr 1989.

HEADCORN
(Or Lashenden) Early in 1990 a very proud Trevor Matthews of the **Lashenden Air
Warfare Museum** announced that a long series of patient negotiations were at last
showing fruit and the Museum was going to undertake a large expansion programme in
association with others, all leading to a combination of flying centre and museum.
Watch this space! LAWM is another Museum that is gearing up for the Battle of
Britain celebrations, having a fabulous internal artefact display that is always
evolving. The Museum also gives a commanding view of activities on the rest of

this pleasant airfield. Open Sundays and Bank Holidays 1030 to 1800 from Easter
until the end of October. Parties are welcome at other times by prior arrangement.
Contact : LAWM, Headcorn Airfield, Ashford, Kent TN27 9HX. Telephone 0622 890226.

WZ589	Vampire T.11	ex Woodford, Chester, St Athan, 56.
XN380	Whirlwind HAS.7	ex Wroughton, 705, 771, 829, 824, 825.
84	Mystere IVA	ex Sculthorpe, French AF. On loan from Robertsbridge AS.
63938	F-100F-16-NA	ex Sculthorpe, French AF.
BAPC 91	Fi 103R-IV	ex Horsham, Farnborough, Rechlin. Genuine piloted version.

On the **Airfield** itself, another major plus for this airfield is that it is now the
host to the Tiger Club, so it could be that several of the Redhill **W&R** inmates will
percolate here.   Auster 5 G-ANHZ moved to Lydd in mid-1988 to continue its
restoration. The Grampian Helicopters Pucara A-517/G-BLRP was advertised for sale
and left here in the container it arrived in, having never been unpacked. Its
destination is not known. A Bede BD-4 has been stored here since around 1984.

G-AHAV	J/1 Autocrat	ex HB-EOM ntu. CoA expired 21/6/75. Stored.
G-AJRE	J/1 Autocrat	ex Biggin Hill area. CoA expired 15/10/70. Under restoration.
G-ARRL+	J/1N Alpha	ex Maidstone, VP-KFK, VP-KPF, VP-KFK, VP-UAK. CoA expired 7/6/68. Arrived 10/6/89 for rebuild.
ZS-UAB+ G-BKZV	Bede BD-4	ex South Africa. Stored since 8/83.

LYDD
At the airfield **RE Aviation** moved in from Bredhurst during 1988. Currently, they
are hard at work on the restoration of three Wilgas that were damaged in the same
gale on the same airfield and an Auster from Headcorn.

G-ANHZ+	Auster 5	ex Headcorn, TW384, 1960 Flt, A&AEE. CoA exp 29/5/73. Arr 1988.
G-BHUN+	PZL-104 Wilga 35	ex Bredhurst, Booker. Damaged 27/3/87. Under restoration.
G-BJAU+	PZL-104 Wilga 35	ex Bredhurst, Booker. Damaged 27/3/87. Under restoration.
G-BKWG+	PZL-104 Wilga 35A	ex Bredhurst, Booker. Damaged 27/3/87. Under restoration.

LYMPNE
At the airfield, the Fiat G.46 is confirmed as resident in poor condition.

BAPC 79	Fiat G.46-IV	ex Southend, Shoreham, Italian AF.

MAIDSTONE
Exodus. Colin Woods moved his Falke G-AYYL to Challock Lees for completion. **Chris
Webb** and **Graham Smith** moved their Auster G-ARRL to Headcorn 10/6/89.

MANSTON
Needless to say, at **RAF Manston** the two guardians flanking the superb **Memorial
Building** were bound to fall foul of the 'one gate-one aircraft' policy. Canberra
PR.3 WE168/8049M and Javelin FAW.9 XH764/7972M were both offered for tender during
11/89 and were broken up in 3/90. There were hopes that the cockpit sections might
find their way into the hands of preservation group(s), but as **W&R** closed for
press, there were no details to hand. The brilliantly restored Hurricane II
'BN230' was used as the male mould for the plastic Hurricane gate guardians and was
subjected to poor treatment necessitating a spell away at Abingdon being re-
restored. The Memorial Building is open daily. This is as suitable a place as any
to say that Queen Air G-ASRX arrived from Exeter 1/89 for use as spares by Kent
Executive Aviation before the hulk was donated to the firemen at Chelmsford.

BN230"	LF751 Hurricane II	ex Rochester, Bentley Priory, Waterbeach 5466M, 27 OTU, 1681 BDTF. Composite aircraft, parts from Z3687 and PG593. See notes above.
TB752	8086M Spitfire XVI	ex Rochester, Manston 7256M/7279M, Lyneham, 5 CAACU, 103 FRS, 102 FRS, 403, 66.

With the closure of the fire school at Catterick, the newly amalgamated **Central
Training Establishment of the Air Force Department Fire Service** is now the centre
of RAF fire and rescue training for both Ministry and Air Force personnel.   To
clear up the reference in **W&R11**, Devon VP956, Hunter and Jet Provost noted as being

with 1404 Squadron ATC are in fact with the CTE, being located around the training
buildings and the dreaded 'smoke room'. The ATC have a base here, but at present
no airframes - see Chatham. Other than the addition of a former Bangladesh Biman
707 and the fuselage sections of the former Catterick VC-10, the 'fleet' here has
remained remarkably stable. Two airframes have given up the ghost, Victor K.1A
XH616 and Victor K.2 XL511, both by the end of 1988.

G-BDRC	Viscount 724	ex Exeter, Alidair, Air Inter F-BMCG, TCA CF-TGO.
+	Boeing 707-320	ex Bangladesh Biman. Arrived by 7/89.
VP953	Devon C.2/2	ex Kemble, 26, SCS, MCS, 12 Sector. Wings of VP960. Poor state.
VP956	Devon C.2/2	ex Kemble, 207, 21, WCS, MCS, AAFCE, MCS, FCCS, Wyton SF, Booker SF, MECS, Iraq CF.
VP963	Devon C.2/2	ex Kemble, 207, 21, 26, TCCS, NCS, 13 Sector, FCCF, 13 Sector, MCS, AAAFCE, FCCS, HCCS, 31, FCCS, BCCS, Paris Attache, 240 OCU, HS. Rear of VP960.
VP965	8823M Devon C.2/2	ex Northolt, 207, WCS, MCS, Upavon CF, MCS, 31.
XG327	8188M Lightning F.1	ex St Athan, RAE Bedford, Warton, A&AEE.
XH590	Victor K.1A	ex 55, 57, 55, 15. Poor state.
XJ430	Whirlwind HAR.10	ex Wroughton, 1310 Flt, 228, 275, 22, Westlands, 22.
XJ695	8738M Hunter FGA.9	ex CTE 8677M, Kemble, 1 TWU, TWU, 229 OCU, 58, 45, 20, 14, 20. Fitted with tail of XF519. See notes above.
XK968	8445M Whirlwind HAR.10	ex Wroughton, 28, 103, 110, 22, JEHU.
XK969	8646M Whirlwind HAR.10	ex Odiham, Abingdon, Wroughton, SAR Wing, 202, 230, 202, 228, CFS, 225, JEHU. Poor state.
XL386	8760M Vulcan B.2	ex 101, Wadd Wing, 230 OCU, 27, 230 OCU, 27, 230 OCU, Scamp Wing, 9.
XM657	8734M Vulcan B.2	ex 44, Wadd Wing, Cott Wing. On its nose.
XN602	8088M Jet Provost T.3	ex CTE, Brize Norton, Halton, Brampton, Shawbury, 6 FTS. See above.
XN855	8556M Argosy E.1	ex 115, 242 OCU, AOCU, 114.
XP333	8650M Whirlwind HAR.10	ex Odiham, 2 AFTS, CFS. Minus boom.
XP357	8499M Whirlwind HAR.10	ex Wroughton, 22, 230, 110, 225. Damaged 13/6/76.
XP394	Whirlwind HAR.10	ex Wroughton, CFS.
XP400	8444M Whirlwind HAR.10	ex Halton, Wroughton, 103, 110, 230. Poor state.
XP741	8939M Lightning F.3	ex 5, LTF, 11, 5, 111, Wattisham TFF, 111, Wattisham TFF, 111.
ZD233+	G-ASGC Super VC-10 1151	ex Catterick, Brize Norton, Prestwick, BA, BOAC. Fuselage. Arrived in 5/88.

ROCHESTER

Down on the slipway, Sunderland V G-BJHS made its first flight post restoration on
7/7/89 and made an appearance at the Great Warbirds Air Display at West Malling the
following month (flyby only!). Currently operating out of the Solent, it is up for
sale but is planning several airshow appearances during 1990.

ROCHESTER AIRPORT

The workshops of the **Medway Aircraft Preservation Society** continue to work on the
Spitfire PR.XI on behalf of Chris Horsley/Tangmere Flight and have received, as
predicted, the former Italian Harvard from Duxford, which is underway for Historic
Flying Ltd. Hurricane II LF738/5405M started restoration 4/90, the work being
undertaken jointly here and at Brooklands. Meteor F.8 'WK714'/WK914 travelled to
Duxford for OFMC 8/8/88. F-84F 6771"/FU-6 left by road 28/3/90 for Cosford. The
workshop facilities are open to the public on Sunday mornings and Monday and
Wednesday evenings, but Airport rules must be observed. Contact : Lewis Deal, 15,
Amethyst Avenue, Chatham, Kent, ME5 9TX. Telephone 0634 865028. Workshop on 0634 816492.

LF738	5405M Hurricane II	ex Biggin Hill, Wellesbourne Mountford, 22 OTU, 1682 BDTF. See notes above. Under restoration.
PL965	G-MKXI Spitfire PR.XI	ex Overloon, Bruggen, Overloon, Deelen, Twenthe, 16, 1 PP. Under restoration to flying condition.
MM54099+	T-6G Texan	ex Duxford, Lyneham, Decimomannu, Italian AF 'RR-56'. Arrived 8/8/88. Under restoration to flying condition.

Close to MAPS's area, but not part of their domain, is the stored Beech.

N96240	Beech D.18S (3TM)	ex Spain, Wellesbourne Mountford, Blackbushe, G-AYAH, N6123, RCAF 1559. Stored, poor state.

SEVENOAKS

Stored in this area are the airframes of the **Biggin Hill Air Museum** and **Friends of Biggin Hill**. With the continued strivings of Biggin Hill to become another Gatwick, plans to establish a museum at the former Battle of Britain airfield are still a long way from fruition. The Chipmunk PAX trainer previously listed under this heading can now be found under Croydon. Contact : Peter Smith, Curator, 3, Chatto Road, Battersea, London SW11 6JL.

G-AAXK	Klemm L25aI	CoA expired 29/11/60. Damaged 3/62. Fuselage. On loan.
G-BAYV	Noralpha	ex Booker, Hawkinge, Maidstone, Ford, F-BLTN, French AF. Crashed 23/2/74. Painted as a 'Bf 109'.
K5054"	B'190 Spitfire replica	built by Peter Smith. Static replica.
WP250	Vampire NF.10	ex Booker, Sandhurst, A&AEE. Pod only.
XD535	Vampire T.11	ex Preston, Croston, Woodford, Chester, St Athan, 4 FTS, 5 FTS, 1 ANS, 93.
	Typhoon IA	cockpit section, under restoration.

Locally, the Airedale spares-ship has been joined by an Auster on restoration.

G-APJZ+	J/1N Alpha	ex 5N-ACY, VR-NDR ntu, G-APJZ. Crashed 10/11/75. Restoration.
G-AWGA	Airedale	ex Biggin Hill, Bicester, EI-ATA, G-AWGA, D-ENRU. CoA expired 3/7/86. Spares for Biggin Hill-based G-ATCC.

SHORNCLIFFE

(Near Lydd) The Wessex (HC.2?) at the Junior Infantry Regiment, **Sir John Moore Barracks** which was offered for tender has gone, we know not where. In an example of reverse technology, it has been replaced by a Whirlwind!

XP405+	8656M Whirlwind HAR.10	ex Halton, 2 FTS, CFS, 228. First noted 10/89.

SMEETH

(On the A20 east of Ashford) In a garden here, an Aztec is used as a plaything.

G-ASER	Aztec 250B	ex Biggin Hill. Crashed 14/9/72. Hulk.

TUNBRIDGE WELLS

Work continues on the Tigers at **David** and **Mollie Wood**'s workshop. G-ADGT was the latest to roll off the 'production line' making its first flight during late 1988.

G-ANOD	Tiger Moth	ex New Milton, T6121, 19 RFS, 10 RFS, ULAS, 24 EFTS, Northolt SF, 60 OTU. CoA expired 7/2/60.
G-APJO	Tiger Moth	ex Bournemouth, NM126. Largely G-APJR, ex T7391, 1 GU, 2 GS, 14 RFS, 6 RFS, 6 EFTS. Crashed 28/5/61.
G-ISIS	Tiger Moth	ex G-AODR, Biggin Hill, NL779. Crashed 18/9/61.

WELLING

Continuing the god-like moving of locations, Welling is now rightly restored to Kent from 'Greater London'. **385 Squadron ATC** are located here and have the former White Waltham Chippax. They were omitted from **W&R11**.

WK626+	8213M Chipmunk T.10 PAX	ex White Waltham, Bicester, Odiham SF, Ox UAS, South Cerney SF, 1 FTS, Bicester SF, Odiham SF, FTCCS, Lon UAS, Cam UAS, Colerne SF, Leeds UAS, Nott UAS, 16 FRS, 18 RFS. SOC 31/10/72.

Work on the Auster AOP.9 continues, locally.

XN437	G-AXWA Auster AOP.9	ex Biggin Hill, Luton area, Odiham, Maghull, Hoylake, St Athan, Kenya.

WEST MALLING

Auster J/1 Autocrat G-AGYK moved to Challock Lees to continue its restoration.

Lancashire

BACUP

At Moorlands Park, the **Pennine Aviation Museum** are continuing with their aim of opening a regional museum to the public. For the moment, viewing is still by prior arrangement only. Contact : David Stansfield, School House, Sharneyford, Bacup, Lancashire OL13 9UQ. Telephone 0706 875967. Several airframes listed below are in fact stored off-site. Major acquisition during 1988 was a Canberra TT.18 from Samlesbury. The Hunter nose is used as a travelling exhibit. The frame of Piper Caribbean 150 G-ARHT was scrapped as being beyond use.

VV901	Anson T.21	ex Burtonwood, Cosford, Irton Holme, Leconfield, CFCCU, DUR UAS, 1 RFS.
WF911	Canberra B.2	ex Preston, Samlesbury G-27-161, 231 OCU. Nose section.
WJ721+	Canberra TT.18	ex Samlesbury, 7, 50, 40. Arrived 4/88.
WN149	Balliol T.2	ex Salford, Failsworth, RAFC. Nose section.
WN534	Balliol T.2	ex Salford, Failsworth, 22 MU, RAFC. Nose section.
XG297	Hunter FGA.9	ex Macclesfield, Bitteswell, HSA, 20, 28, 20, 4. Nose section only.
XK627	Vampire T.11	ex Hazel Grove, Woodford, Chester, St Athan, 8 FTS, CFS.
	Albemarle	ex Carlisle, Westnewton. Major restoration, composite.
BAPC 157	CG-4A Hadrian	ex Ormskirk. Complete fuselage frame.

BLACKBURN

Located in Preston Old Road, Witton Park, are **1262 Squadron ATC** with their anonymous Chippax.

| | Chipmunk T.10 PAX | identity unknown. |

BLACKPOOL AIRPORT

(Or Squires Gate) On the **W&R** front the major news from here is the establishment of **Wilkie Helicopters** run by Jim Wilkie of the Helicopter Museum of Great Britain. As all of the contents of the Museum (which was at Heysham) are to be found within the hangar it is assumed that the 'operational' side of business has come to the fore, at least for the time being. General maintenance and film work form part of the work undertaken by the company, although it also offers support facilities for 'geriatric' helicopters and a major refurbishment is underway on the former Wellingborough Widgeon. Of the former Museum airframes, Whirlwind HAR.21 WV198/G-BJWY moved through to Chorley, thankfully for, so far, non-destructive fire training. Current situation is as follows :

G-ANLW+		Widgeon 2	ex 'MD497', Wellingborough, Little Staughton, Tattershall Thorpe, Southend. CoA expired 27/5/81. Restoration for Sloane Helicopters.
G-AWRP		Grasshopper III	ex Heysham, Shoreham, Redhill. CoA exp 12/5/72.
G-AXFM		Grasshopper III	ex Heysham, Shoreham, Redhill. Ground running rig.
G-AZAU		Grasshopper III	ex Heysham, Shoreham, Redhill. Power and lift grouping only.
5X-UUW		Scout	ex Panshanger, Uganda Police Wing. Wreckage, for spares.
XK482	G-BJWC	Skeeter AOP.10	ex Heysham, Horsham, Ottershaw, Middle Wallop 7840M, HTF, Handling Squadron, MoS.
XK940	G-AYXT	Whirlwind HAS.7	ex Heysham, Carnforth, Panshanger, Elstree, Luton, Fleetlands, 771, Culdrose SF, 705, 825, 824, 845.
XN386	A2713	Whirlwind HAR.9	ex Wroughton, Yeovilton, Fleetlands, 'Endurance' Flt, 846, 814.
XX469	G-BNCL	Lynx 1-07	ex Lancaster, Sherborne A2657, Westlands.

Of the other airframes at the Airport, Messenger 2A G-AJWB was noted 'road running' southbound during 1989, destination unknown. While it cannot be confirmed, it is thought that stablemate Gemini 3A G-AKEK also disappeared at the same time, or shortly afterwards. Fairly long term 'hangar queen', Cessna 210 G-ASXR astounded everyone by flying again by 4/90. The ATC's Jet Provost T.3 nose XN511 was offered for tender during 1989 and the Newark Air Museum at Winthorpe snapped it up. Sundowner hulk G-AXSX is confirmed as having gone, thought scrapped. Otherwise, it is a case of the same old faces here.

| G-ATRS | Cherokee 140 | CoA expired 18/10/70. Stored. |

G-AVPH		Cessna F.150G	ex Woodvale. CoA expired 9/4/86. Stored.
F-BHMU	G-BHVZ	Cessna 180	ex N4793B. Under restoration.
F-BMGR	G-BHTC	CEA DR.1051/M1	ex Popham, Lydd. Under restoration.
XL391		Vulcan B.2	ex 44, 101, 44, 9/35, BCDU, MoA. Manchester Vulcan Bomber Society.

CHORLEY

At the **International Fire Training Centre**, Washington Hall, among an array of interesting goodies to test the skills of fire suppression operatives from the world over can be found a wonderful mock-up (see the photo-spread) and, sadly, Whirlwind HAR.21 WV198/G-BJWY, lying on its side for positioning and rescue training. There is a good chance that the Stoke-on-Trent based The Helicopter Collection have organised an exchange for this machine.

| WV198 | G-BJWY | Whirlwind HAR.21 | ex Blackpool Airport, '130191', Heysham, Carnforth, Gosport, Lee-on-Solent A2576, Arbroath, 781, 848, USN 130191. See notes. |

COCKERHAM

(Or Banks End, on the A588 between Lancaster and Fleetwood) The para-trainer still serves the **Black Knight Parachute Centre**.

| G-ARZE | | Cessna 172C | ex Blackpool Airport. Damaged 11/9/76. Para-trainer. |

ECCLESTON

(On the B5250 south of Leyland) The **Bygone Times Antique Warehouse** seemed to succeed where much more deserving causes failed, in taking on three airframes from the RAF Museum store. One of these was the former 'Battle of Britain' CASA 2-111 fuselage. Colin Waterworth of Newton-le-Willows managed to secure this and has placed it on loan to the South Yorkshire APS at Firbeck. The warehouse is open daily.

| E373"+ | | B'178 Avro 504K replica | ex Henlow, 'Aces High' (the film!). First noted 9/88. |
| BAPC 28+ | | Wright Flyer rep | ex Cardington, Finningley. First noted 9/88. |

HEYSHAM

Jim Wilkie has established Wilkie Helicopters and all of the airframes listed under this heading in **W&R11** moved on to Blackpool Airport – which see.

LANCASTER

It is thought that **Lancashire Fire Brigade Headquarters** still has its Lynx ground rig, acquired via Jim Wilkie and used for instruction on oil rig procedures.

| RG-05 | | Lynx static rig | ex Coventry Airport, Yeovil. |

RAMSGREAVE

(Between the A59 and the A6119 north of Blackburn) While the Dragonfly is thought still nestled in the grounds of a house here, confirmation would be useful.

| WG751 | | Dragonfly HR.3 | ex Ancoats, Wisbech. |

SAMLESBURY

Another dramatic change in the landscape to relate. With the exception of the gate guardian, the **British Aerospace** plant is now visibly empty of Canberras, surely the first time in a very long time. Offering a batch of the open store examples to the UK preservation movement for token payment, the balance were distributed among other BAe plants for their firemen. Legalities on the two Argentinian machines mean that they are most likely still to be found within the plant in dismantled state and they are still listed below accordingly. Only T.4 WE192 is unaccounted for at present. One of the former Saudi Lightnings at Warton is reported to be coming here for the gate. The Canberra exodus was as follows : T.17 WH665 to Filton by 3/10/88; T.4 WH846 to Elvington 5/88; T.4 WH850 to Chelford; TT.18 WJ639 to Sunderland; TT.18 WJ721 to Bacup 4/88; TT.18 WK122 to Helston 24/5/88; T.4 WT483 to Filton 10/6/88; T.4 WT488 to Dunsfold 6/88 and T.4 Q497 to Warton. Following up the Strikemaster notes in **W&R11**, the former Kuwaiti machines did not stay long, going on to Botswana during 1988. That leaves :

WH914 G-27-373	Canberra B.2	ex frustrated Argentine AF B.62, 231 OCU, 35, 76, 50, 61, 100. Dismantled and stored. See notes above.
WT537	Canberra PR.7	ex 13, 31, 17. Gate guardian.
XH583 G-27-374	Canberra T.4	ex frustrated Argentine AF T.64, St Athan, 231 OCU. Dismantled and stored. See notes above.

WARTON

As with the Canberras at Samlesbury, **British Aerospace** here offered a batch of the former Royal Saudi Air Force Lightnings to preservation groups and during late 1988/early 1989 they moved to their new locations. The bulk however have been acquired by a collector and during 1989 were carefully dismantled and placed into containers and moved to a former airfield in Cheshire for storage pending disposal arrangements. Three aircraft are held, one reportedly for the gate at Samlesbury, one possibly for the gate here and one for display by Ferranti at their Edinburgh plant in celebration of the AIRPASS radar. Going to 'Cheshire' were the following : F.53s ZF577/53-668, ZF579/53-671, ZF581/53-675, ZF582/53-676, ZF585/53-683, ZF586/53-688, ZF587/53-691, ZF589/53-700, ZF590/53-679, ZF591/53-685, ZF592/53-686; T.55s ZF595/55-714, ZF596/55-715, ZF597/55-711. Other disposals : F.53s ZF578/53-670 to <u>Cardiff-Wales Airport</u> by 3/89, ZF583/53-681 to <u>Carlisle Airport</u> 8/1/89, ZF588/53-693 to <u>East Midlands Airport</u> 8/1/89, ZF594/53-696 to <u>Sunderland</u> early 1989; and T.55 ZF598/55-713 to <u>Coventry Airport</u> 19/1/89. Still on the theme of Lightnings, F.3 XP703 last mentioned in **W&R9** as having been broken up after use as a fatigue rig, survived as a nose section and was acquired in 1989 by the Lightning Preservation Group and moved to <u>Bruntingthorpe</u>. Warton is now the only place on the planet to see Lightnings in their element, with several examples flying from here in an attempt to get the Tornado's radar systems up and working. Let us hope they are needed for some time yet. It would be a great shame to have all Lightnings in the UK listed in **W&R**! Going on to other types, the Strikemasters listed in **W&R11** all went on to Ecuador, not as given. Jaguar GR.1 XX740/G-27-331 slipped the net in **W&R11**, having been delivered to Oman as 225 in 11/86. Tornado GR.1 ZA403's secondment to the Saudi Support Unit was only brief and should be deleted. Jaguar GR.1 XX736/G-27-327 moved to <u>Shawbury</u> during 1989. All this makes the current situation as follows :

WJ857	Canberra T.4	ex Samlesbury, 231 OCU, Wittering SF. Nose section, dump.
XN973	Buccaneer S.1	ex EASAMS, Lossiemouth. Nose, dump.
XX765+	Jaguar GR.1(mod)	ex BAe fly-by-wire trials, RAE, A&AEE, 226 OCU, 14. Withdrawn from use 11/84 and stored.
ZA597+	Tornado GR.1	ex Honington. Cat 4 8/11/83. Spares use. Arrived 1988.
ZF580	Lightning F.53	ex RSAF 53-672, G-27-42. Open store. Reported for Samlesbury gate.
ZF584	Lightning F.53	ex RSAF 53-682, G-27-52. Open store. Reported for Ferranti.
ZF593	Lightning F.53	ex RSAF 53-692, G-27-62. Open store.
	Tornado ADV	fatigue rig, prod no AV.023, built in between ZE154 and ZE155.
	Strikemaster	composite airframe with Saudi Support Unit. Nose spare from BAC.167 prod line, centre section mock-up, rear end from JP T.3 XN634, one wing from a JP T.5 one from a JP T.3!
Q497+	Canberra T.4	ex Samlesbury, frustrated Indian AF B.52, Bracebridge Heath, Samlesbury, Kemble, WE191, 231 OCU, 237 OCU, 231 OCU, 245. Arrived 6/88. Dump.

Leicestershire

BITTESWELL

The predictions as to which new base Warbirds of Great Britain would find for themselves made in W&R11 - Biggin Hill and Bournemouth - turned out to be both correct, with a little time-stagger. Biggin Hill was the immediate choice of the organisation, but another move is now in hand, this time to Bournemouth. The reader is directed towards the entry under Biggin Hill in this edition for the full story of movements, but several unaccounted-for airframes from the narrative in W&R11 need some qualification. Of those left 'open' in the last edition, the following all moved on to Biggin Hill : Spitfire XVIII SM969/G-BRAF; Spitfire XVI RW386/G-BXVI; Spitfire XVI TE392; Bf 109K T2-124 and the former Yugoslavian Bf 109G-10. P-47D 13021 (also ex Yugoslavia) was exported direct from Bitteswell to the USA. Spitfire IX BR601, fresh from 'capture' at the Christie's auction of 31/10/86 in London, moved here and then to Biggin Hill.

BRUNTINGTHORPE

On 24/6/88 Lightning F.6 XR728 touched down here from Binbrook and the **Lightning Preservation Group** was born. LPG is unique in that it intends to concentrate its efforts on one aircraft and to develop an extensive array of artefacts around it. More importantly, '728 is being kept 'hot', LPG staging regular open days on which it is run up, or even taxied down the runway. A Lightning nose section has been acquired from Warton to back up the F.6. Details of the LPG from : Graham Jackson, 12, Badgers Close, Seaford, East Sussex, BN25 4DF.

XP703+	Lightning F.3	ex Warton, fatigue rig, MoD(PE), 29, 56, 74. Nose section. Arrived 8/89
XR728+	Lightning F.6	ex Binbrook, 11, LTF, 5, 56, 23, 11, 23. Flew in 24/6/88. See notes above.

The USAF 'repossessed' F-100D-15-NA 42239 during 6/88 and it was freighted out to West Germany. It may go on the gate at Hahn. The Mystere IVA, however, remains on the gate here.

85	Mystere IVA	ex East Midlands Airport, Sculthorpe, French AF.

COTTESMORE

The situation here is unchanged, although the inmates of the dump are beginning to show considerable signs of the stresses of the job!

WH791	8187M Canberra PR.7	ex St Athan 8165M/8176M, 81, 58, 82, 542. Gate guardian.
XJ582	8139M Sea Vixen FAW.2	ex Halton, Sydenham, 766. Fire dump, poor state.
XL618	8892M Hunter T.7	ex Shawbury, Kemble, 1 TWU, 229 OCU, Jever SF, Gutersloh SF. BDR.
XM656	8757M Vulcan B.2	ex 9, 35, Wadd Wing, 35. Nose. Dump.
XR716	8940M Lightning F.3	ex Binbrook, 5, LTF, 5, 11, 5, LTF, 56, 29, 226 OCU, 111, Wattisham TFF, 111. Dump.

EARL SHILTON

Auster J/5F G-AMUI moved out to a new owner in the Oakham area during 1989. More precise location awaited.

EAST MIDLANDS AIRPORT

At the **East Midlands Aeropark Visitors Centre**, delivery was taken of a former Warton Lightning during 1/89. The centre is still open daily from 1000. Closing times vary with the time of year. Contact : East Midlands Airport Aeropark, Castle Donington, Derby DE7 2SA. Telephone 0332 810621. Existing to support the Aeropark is the **East Midlands Aeropark Volunteers Association**, further details from : Upper Grange Farm, Markfield, Leicester, LE6 0RJ.

G-BEOZ	Argosy 101	ex ABC/Elan, N895U, N6502R, G-1-7. CoA exp 28/5/86.
G-FRJB	SA.1 Sheriff	ex Sandown. Incomplete and unflown.
VR-BEP	Whirlwind Srs 3	ex Cuckfield, G-BAMH, Bristows, Redhill, XG588.
WL626	G-BHDD Varsity T.1	ex Coventry, 6 FTS, 1 ANS, 2 ANS, 201 AFS.

| XM575 | G-BLMC | Vulcan B.2 | ex 44, Wadd Wing, Scampton Wing, 617. |
| ZF588+ | | Lightning F.53 | ex Warton, RSAF 53-693, G-27-63. Arrived 8/1/89. |

Of the Spitfires in **Trent Aero**'s care, Mk XVI TE356/G-SXVI flew to Biggin Hill 1/6/88. Next off the 'line' was Mk IX MJ730/G-BLAS which first flew 12/11/88 for new owner David Pennell, subsequently being re-registered as G-HFIX and now based on the airfield. Coming up from Chichester during 1989 was the former Nick Grace Mk XVI TE184/G-MXVI, which was due to fly during 1990 for Myrick Aviation. On the fire dump, Viscount 735 G-BFMW gave up the ghost in 1988 and was replaced by Merchantman G-APEG. Current situation is therefore :

G-APEG	Merchantman	ex Airfast, ABC, BEA. CoA expired 18/5/83. Dump.
G-AZLR	Viscount 813	ex BMA, ZS-SBU ntu, SAA ZS-CDU. BMA cabin trainer.
G-BKTJ	Cessna 404 Titan	ex Farnborough, Birmingham, LN-VIN, SE-GYL, N88721. Crashed 27/11/85. Wreck, stored.
TE184+	G-MXVI	Spitfire XVI	ex Chichester, Holywood, Aldergrove, Finningley, Royton, Newcastle-upon-Tyne, CGS, 607, 203 AFS. See notes above.

HUSBANDS BOSWORTH
The Brooklands Mosquito is still stored at the gliding site.

| G-AWIF | Mosquito | ex Shipdham, Tattershall Thorpe, Clitheroe. CoA expired 7/1/82. |

LEICESTER
A new development by Leicester Museums at nearby Coalville should see some of the Auster material held by the **Leicester Museum of Technology** in due course. Until then, the AOP.9, J/1N and newly-acquired J/4 remain in store, with G-AGOH airworthy at Leicester Airport and Plus C2 G-AFTN under restoration there. All of these may be viewed by prior arrangement with : Peter Stoddart, Leicestershire Museums, 96 New Walk, Leicester LE1 6TD. Telephone 0533 765532. The Museum itself, at the Abbey Pumping Station, Corporation Road, is open Monday to Saturday 1000 to 1730 and Sundays 1400 to 1730.

G-AJJK+	Auster J/4	ex Stratford-on-Avon. CoA expired 24/8/68. Arr 1988.
G-AJRH	J/1N Alpha	ex Harrogate, Wigan. CoA expired 5/6/69.
XP280	Auster AOP.9	ex St Athan, 2 Wing, Queen's Dragoon Guards, 2 RTR, 651.

LEICESTER AIRPORT
(Or Leicester East) As ever, the **W&R** situation is dominated here by all things Auster, thanks to Ron Neal's **RN Aviation** and the **Leicester Museum of Technology**. The latter bases their airworthy Auster J/1 G-AGOH here and work continues on the restoration of the Taylorcraft Plus C2. Two of Ron's charges are now flying, J/5L G-ANWX by early 1989 and Mk IV NJ695/G-AJXV by 6/89, returning to Nottingham Airport. Globe Swift G-ARNN has joined its brother at Tatenhill.

G-AEKZ	J/2 Cub	CoA expired 2/11/78. Under restoration, off-site.
G-AFTN	T'craft Plus C2	ex Heavitree, HL535, G-AFTN. Under restoration.
G-AGOH	J/1 Autocrat	Leicestershire Museums. Airworthy.
G-AGVG	J/1 Autocrat	ex Paull. Wrecked 2/1/76. Stored, off-site.
G-APMH	J/1U Workmaster	ex F-OBOA, G-APMH. Crashed 22/12/70. Stored.
G-ARDJ+	Auster D.6/180	crashed 30/5/86. Stored, pending restoration.
G-ATFU	Leopard Moth	ex off-site, HB-OTA, CH-366. Damaged 7/84.
XK417	G-AVXY	Auster AOP.9	ex Tattershall Thorpe, Wisbech, Henstridge, St Athan, 652, 9 Flt, 18 Flt, Middle Wallop. Under restoration.

LOUGHBOROUGH
Within the Department of Transport Technology at **Loughborough University**, the Jet Provost 1 still serves as an instructional airframe. It is part of the Shuttleworth Collection.

| G-AOBU | Jet Provost 1 | ex Luton, XM129, G-42-1. CoA expired 24/5/56. |

LUTTERWORTH
At a farm here, the two former Bruntingthorpe airframes held in store have been dispersed. Avro XIX Srs 2 G-AGWE is reported to have gone to the Valiant Air

Command in Florida, USA, in mid-1989. Hunter F.51 E-407 moved to Cranfield during 1989. At another location, a collector has the long-lost Bruntingthorpe Bensen gyroplane and during 7/88 acquired a Jet Provost nose section.

| G-AXCI+ | Bensen B.8M | ex East Midlands Airport. First noted 7/88. Stored. |
| XM426" | Jet Provost T.3 | ex Liversedge. Nose. Arrived 23/7/88. |

MARKET HARBOROUGH
The Vampire T.11 pod WZ608, previously held by the Kibworth Aviation Group, left by road 21/12/89 - destination unknown.

NARBOROUGH
(On the B4114 south west of Leicester) Wrongly placed under 'King's Lynn' in **MiniWrecks**, a yard here took on two Lightning T.5s and an F.6 nose from Binbrook during 1988. By early 1989 a Grasshopper TX.1 had joined them.

XK824+	Grasshopper TX.1	ex Halton. First noted 2/89.
XS420+	Lightning T.5	ex Binbrook, LTF, 5, LTF, 226 OCU. Arrived 25/7/88.
XS459+	Lightning T.5	ex Binbrook, 5, LTF, 56, 29, 226 OCU. Arrived 25/7/88.
XS933+	Lightning F.6	ex Binbrook, 5, 11, BAC, 5, 56, 11. Nose. Arrived 7/88.

NORTH LUFFENHAM
With the base taking on more (flightless) units and its future assured, there is a good possibility more airframes may join the collection at the Ketton end of the airfield. These are used for a variety of instructional purposes, including weapons and ordnance disposal.

WS776	7716M Meteor NF.14	ex Lyneham, 228 OCU, 85, 25. Gate guardian.
XG194	8839M Hunter FGA.9	ex Cosford, 1 TWU, TWU, 229 OCU, 1, 92, 111, 43.
XJ608	8802M Sea Vixen FAW.2	ex Bournemouth, FRL, Hatfield, RAE Llanbedr, 899. BDR.
XN699	8224M Sea Vixen FAW.2	ex Halton, Sydenham, 890. NBC training.
XP344	8764M Whirlwind HAR.10	ex Cranwell, Finningley, Chivenor, 22, SAR Wing, CFS.
XP921	8226M Sea Vixen FAW.2	ex Hereford, Halton, 890.

SOUTH WIGSTON
The Phoenix Aviation Museum folded here and much-travelled Vampire T.11 WZ553 moved to Winthorpe 19/3/89.

STANFORD
(Off the B5414 north east of Rugby) Centre-piece of the **Percy Pilcher Museum** within Stanford Hall is a Hawk replica. Open Easter to the end of September on Thursdays and weekends 1430 to 1800; Bank Holidays and the Tuesdays following them plus special event days. More details on 0788 860250.

| BAPC 45 | Pilcher Hawk rep | ex Coventry. |

Lincolnshire

BARKSTON HEATH
By 4/88 this satellite to Cranwell had gained a Canberra on the dump and the following year had acquired a Jet Provost nose for rescue training.

| WT339+ | 8198M Canberra B(I).8 | ex Cranwell, 16, 3, 14, 88. Dump. First noted 4/88. |
| XN643+ | 8704M Jet Provost T.3 | ex Cranwell, Abingdon, RAFEF, 1 FTS, 3 FTS. Crashed 30/7/81. Nose. First noted 2/89. |

BINBROOK

It's all over, no longer the sounds of the Lightning over the Wolds. Strangely quiet, Binbrook came briefly back to life when it became an airfield of the 'Mighty Eighth' during the filming of the epic 'Memphis Belle'. (Sadly during the making of that film, B-17G F-BEEA crashed on take-off 25/7/89 and was gutted – parts appearing later at Tattershall Thorpe, but that is another story.....). Now the mantle is down to F.6s XP693, XR724, XR773, XS904 and XS928 who fly out of Warton on target facilities duties in an attempt to get the Tornado ADV's intercept radar up to scratch. As the end of the Lightning loomed into sight, large numbers were put up for tender, and some found their way into the hands of 'collectors' who have since turned out to be dealers hoping to make a killing. It follows that ultimately the population of Lightnings 'preserved' around and about will diminish as assets are realised with scrappings – indeed this has already happened. To tell the story of final disposals from Binbrook needs a table. Below there is as near complete a list as is ever possible in **W&R** which breaks from the usual format and is made all the more possible by **Graham Jackson** of the Lightning Preservation Group. But, before that, there are two non-Lightnings to deal with. Gate guardian Spitfire F.22 PK664/7759M moved to St Athan 30/11/88 and stored F-104G 22+57 moved to Laceby.

Ignoring the five mentioned above that are still flying, the list below deals with the Lightnings that were still flying from, or stored at, Binbrook after 1/1/88, (ie a little back into the 'beat' of **W&R11**, but it is hoped that the overlap will be forgiven). Flying hours total generally includes the time up to touch-down on final flight, ie delivery away from Binbrook. Given below are serial, type, first flight, last flight, total hours, date of leaving Binbrook, notes and next destination (if applicable). Unless otherwise noted, the next destination is a forwarding reference so that the story can be picked up elsewhere in the book. If there is no forwarding reference, this is denoted by a <. For simplicity in this section, 'M' numbers and units are ignored.

XM969	T.4	f/f 28/ 3/61	1/f 22/ 7/74	TT 1,857	left	4/88	scrapped on site	<
							(was on fire dump)	
XP694	F.3	1/ 5/63	8/84	2,552		15/ 4/88	by road to	Otterburn
XP695	F.3	20/ 6/63	10/80	2,600		1/88	scrapped by Swefling Eng.	<
XP702	F.3	19/ 9/63	28/ 8/82	2,680		15/ 4/88	by road to	Otterburn
XP748	F.3	4/ 5/64	20/12/74	2,252		29/ 6/88	by road to	Wembury
							(former gate guardian)	
XP749	F.3	11/12/64	7/87	3,153		18/ 1/88	by road to	Sutton-on-the-Forest
XP750	F.3	3/ 1/64	12/84	3,456		18/ 1/88	by road to	Sutton-on-the-Forest
XP751	F.3	16/ 3/64	10/86	3,101		19/ 1/88	by road to	Sutton-on-the-Forest
XP764	F.3	19/ 9/64	10/86	2,923		21/ 1/88	by road to	Sutton-on-the-Forest
XR720	F.3	24/12/64	2/85	2,881		18/ 1/88	by road to	Sutton-on-the-Forest
XR725	F.6	19/ 2/65	17/12/87	3,870		7/88	by road to	Rossington
XR726	F.6	26/ 2/65	24/ 8/87	3,976		7/88	by road to	Rossington
XR727	F.6	8/ 3/65	10/ 5/88	3,944		10/ 5/88	flown to	Wildenrath
XR728	F.6	17/ 3/65	24/ 6/88	3,709		24/ 6/88	by road to	Bruntingthorpe
XR747	F.6	2/ 4/65	9/87	3,650		7/88	by road to	Rossington
XR751	F.3	31/ 5/65	22/ 9/82	2,060		6/88	by road to	Lower Tremar
XR753	F.6	23/ 6/65	24/ 5/88	4,285		24/ 5/88	flown to	Leeming
XR754	F.6	8/ 7/65	22/ 6/88	3,894		22/ 6/88	flown to	Honington
XR755	F.6	15/ 7/65	17/12/87	4,094		24/ 6/88	by road to	Callington
XR756	F.6	11/ 8/65	28/ 7/87	3,889		28/ 6/88	by road to	Foulness
XR757	F.6	19/ 8/65	21/12/87	4,316		7/88	by road to	Rossington
XR758	F.6	30/ 8/65	10/ 5/88	3,812		10/ 5/88	flown to	Laarbruch
XR759	F.6	9/ 9/65	9/87	3,749		7/88	by road to	Rossington
XR770	F.6	16/12/65	5/88	4,022		15/ 6/88	by road to	Laceby
XR771	F.6	20/ 1/66	15/ 3/88	3,554		29/ 6/88	by road to	Coventry Airport
XS416	T.5	20/ 8/64	21/12/87	3,088		6/88	by road to	Rossington
XS417	T.5	17/ 7/64	18/ 5/87	2,603		5/ 9/88	by road to	Winthorpe
XS419	T.5	18/12/64	27/ 2/87	2,609		6/88	by road to	Rossington
XS420	T.5	23/ 1/65	5/83	2,296		25/ 7/88	by road to	Narborough

XS423	T.5	31/ 3/65	6/ 9/74	1,441	1/88	scrapped by Swefling Eng.	<
XS449	T.5	30/ 4/65	4/ 9/74	1,435	1/88	scrapped by Swefling Eng.	<
XS450	T.5	25/ 5/65	2/ 9/74	1,786	1/88	scrapped by Swefling Eng.	<
XS452	T.5	30/ 6/65	29/ 6/88	3,011	29/ 6/88	flown to	Cranfield
XS454	T.5	30/ 8/65	6/75	1,449	1/88	scrapped by Swefling Eng.	<
XS456	T.5	26/10/65	4/87	2,314	20/ 7/88	by road to	Wainfleet
XS457	T.5	8/11/65	7/12/83	2,169	7/88	by road to	Laceby (nose only)
XS458	T.5	3/12/65	29/ 6/88	3,168	29/ 6/88	flown to	Cranfield
XS459	T.5	8/12/65	18/ 3/87	2,307	25/ 7/88	by road to	Narborough
XS895	F.6	6/ 4/66	4/12/86	3,275	7/88	by road to	Pendine
XS897	F.6	10/ 5/66	14/12/87	3,392	7/88	by road to	Rossington
XS898	F.6	20/ 5/66	30/ 6/88	3,488	30/ 6/88	flown to	Cranfield
XS899	F.6	8/ 6/66	28/ 6/88	3,702	28/ 6/88	flown to	Cranfield
XS901	F.6	1/ 7/66	10/ 5/88	3,781	10/ 5/88	flown to	Bruggen
XS903	F.6	17/ 8/66	18/ 5/88	4,055	18/ 5/88	flown to	Elvington
XS919	F.6	28/ 9/66	15/ 3/88	3,987	6/88	by road to	Lower Tremar
XS922	F.6	6/12/66	14/ 6/88	3,485	14/ 6/88	flown to	Wattisham
XS923	F.6	13/12/66	30/ 6/88	3,998	30/ 6/88	flown to	Cranfield
XS925	F.6	26/ 1/67	7/87	4,016	26/ 4/88	by road to	Hendon
XS927	F.6	15/ 2/67	20/10/86	3,576	28/ 6/88	by road to	Foulness
XS929	F.6	1/ 3/67	20/ 5/88	3,601	20/ 5/88	flown to	Akrotiri
XS932	F.6	20/ 4/67	7/11/87	3,636	7/88	by road to	Rossington
XS933	F.6	27/ 4/67	28/10/87	3,664	6/88	by road to	Narborough (nose only)
XS935	F.6	29/ 5/67	4/ 9/87	3,603	7/88	by road to	Rossington
XS936	F.6	31/ 5/67	24/11/87	3,962	23/ 6/88	by road to	Liskeard
XV328	T.5	22/12/66	29/ 6/88	3,021	29/ 6/88	flown to	Cranfield

Note : Those dealt with by Swelfing Engineering are not given a forwarding reference to Swefling, as it is believed that several scrapmerchants shared out the pickings, and either way, proccessing in Suffolk is remarkably swift.

BOSTON

At his workshop, **Dick Yates** continues to be busy. A quick scan down the list will reveal a decided liking for the Jodel breed and for things French in general. By 1989 two bent-wing-wonders were flying again, D.11A G-BDBV and DR.1050M-1 G-BIOI. Current situation here is thought to be as follows :-

G-AWUB	Gardan GY-201	ex F-PERX. CoA exp 23/10/80. Fuselage, stored.
G-AXDY+	Falconar F-11	unfinished homebuild. First noted as far back as 3/80!
G-BFDM	Wassmer D.120	ex F-BHYB. CoA expired 26/7/84. Spares use.
G-BGEW	SNCAN NC.854S	ex F-BFSJ. Stored.
F-BBGH	Brochet MB.100	ex F-WBGH. Stored.
F-PFUG	Adam RA-14	spares use.
37+	MAB Nord 3400	ex Stixwould, Breighton, Coventry, La Ferte Alais. Arr 3/90.

BOSTON AIRFIELD

(Or Wyberton) As ever, an agricultural feel to the airfield. Correcting **W&R11** the frame referred to as Pawnee G-BGPO was not, 'PO had been scrapped circa 1984. By 1989 a highly appropriately registered Pawnee had arrived for rebuild!

G-ASFZ	Pawnee 235	ex N6672Z. CoA expired 8/2/80. Frame only, stored. Original frame, rest of the original G-ASFZ rebuilt using spare frame 25-6309 and re-registered as G-BSFZ.
G-BDDT+	Pawnee 235C	ex Little Staughton, CS-AIX, N8820L. CoA expired 28/11/85. Arr by 9/89 for rebuild.
NJ673+ G-AOCR	Auster 5D	ex EI-AJS, G-AOCR, NJ673. CoA expired 3/7/86. Stored.

BURGH-LE-MARSH

(On the A158 west of Skegness) By 6/88 a dismantled, but unidentified, Apache had arrived at a yard here, to act as a source of spares for G-ARCW and G-ARJT (both to be found at Skegness Airfield - the latter active). This is bound to be frustrated Geronimo PH-NLK from Ipswich....but confirmation would be nice.

CABOURNE
By 4/88 J/1 Autocrat G-AIPV had moved to Wickenby.

CASTLE BYTHAM
(East of the Al, north of Stamford) At the strip, a Cub is held as a spares-ship.

F-BBBN	J-3C-65 Cub	ex Boston, 43-1092.

CONINGSBY
Gaining more and more in popularity, and very rightly so, is the **Battle of Britain Memorial Flight Visitor Centre**. Now boasting a well-stocked shop and a very well presented Museum of its own, the Centre offers a way to see the Flight 'at home'. During the winter months it is possible to see the fleet stripped down and undergoing refit or modification ready for the new season. Note that although booking is not required it is advisable as it may be that the Flight in whole or in part are positioning to a show. Open Monday to Friday except Bank Holidays 1000 to 1700 with the last guided tour at 1530. Contact : BBMF Visits, RAF Coningsby, Lincoln LN4 4SY. Tel : 0526 44041. During 8/89 Spitfire PR.XIX PS853 made her first flight following restoration at Coningsby. Her presence will help considerably during 1990 - a heavy year for the Flight for obvious reasons.

P7350	Spitfire IIA	ex 'Battle of Britain' G-AWLJ, Colerne, John Dale Ltd, Colerne, 57 OTU, CGS, 64, 616, 603, 266.
AB910	Spitfire VB	ex 'Battle of Britain', Allen Wheeler G-AISU, 29 MU, RWE, 527, 53 OTU, 402, 242, 133, 130, 222.
LF363	Hurricane IIC	ex Biggin Hill SF, 41, 41 GCF, Waterbeach SF, Odiham SF, Thorney Island SF, FCCS, Middle Wallop SF, 61 OTU, 41 OTU, 62 OTU, 26, 63, 309, 63.
PA474	Lancaster I	ex 44, Wroughton, Cranfield College, RAE, Flight Refuelling, 82.
PM631	Spitfire PR.XIX	ex THUM Flt, Buckeburg SF, 206 OCU, 203 AFS.
PS853	Spitfire PR.XIX	ex West Raynham, CFE, North Weald SF, Biggin Hill SF, THUM Flt, 16, 268, 16. See notes above.
PS915	Spitfire PR.XIX	ex Samlesbury, Preston, Brawdy, St Athan, Coningsby, Brawdy, Leuchars 7548M/7711M, West Malling, Biggin Hill, THUM Flt, 2, PRDU, 541.
PZ865	Hurricane IIC	ex Hawker Siddeley G-AMAU.
VP981	Devon C.2/2	ex Northolt, 207, 21, WCS, Wildenrath CF, AAFCE, MinTech, AAFCE, Paris Air Attache, Hendon SF, AFWE. Flight 'mother ship'.
WK518	Chipmunk T.10	ex Man UAS, Lon UAS, Liv UAS, Lee UAS, Hul UAS, Cam UAS, 1 AEF, Coltishall SF, FWS, 63 GCF, RAFC. Flight 'hack'.

On the airfield itself, the ever-present blast huts tend to cut down the view, but it is thought the dump and the BDR machines remain the same. Vampire T.11 WZ549/8118M travelled as far afield as Newtownards during 1989.

WJ815	8729M Canberra PR.7	ex 13, 58, 82, 540. Fuselage on dump.
XM987	Lightning T.4	ex 226 OCU, LCS. BDR.
XN774	8551M Lightning F.2A	ex 92, 19. Surface decoy.
XW528	8861M Buccaneer S.2B	ex St Athan, 15. BDR.

CRANWELL
With three gate guardians on the airfield, something was bound to give when the new one gate-one guardian routine came in. It would seem that the Canberra in the grounds of Trenchard Hall is immune to the theory - try telling that to Locking..... Hunter F.51 'XF979'/E-408 moved to Sealand by 11/88. With the Engineering Wing, the nose of Jet Provost T.3 XN643/8704M moved to Barkston Heath. Otherwise, the situation is quite tranquil.

WH699"	WJ637 Canberra B.2	8755M, ex Wyton, 231 OCU, 35. Outside Trenchard Hall.
XD429"	XD542 Vampire T.11	ex Colerne, Melksham 7604M, FWS, CGS. On plinth.
XF375	8736M Hunter F.6	ex ETPS, Warton, Armstrong Whitworth, C(A).
XF516	8685M Hunter F.6A	ex 1 TWU, 229 OCU, 92, 56.

XG209	8709M Hunter F.6	ex Halton, Kemble, 12, DFLS, 111, 14.
XJ634	8684M Hunter F.6A	ex 1 TWU, TWU, 229 OCU, 92.
XJ639	8687M Hunter F.6A	ex 1 TWU, TWU, 229 OCU, 4.
XK149	8714M Hunter F.6A	ex 1 TWU, TWU, 229 OCU, 54, 1, AFDS.
XL577	8676M Hunter T.7	ex 2 TWU, 237 OCU, 1 TWU, TWU, 229 OCU.
XX821	8896M Jaguar GR.1	ex Coltishall, 41, 14, 17, 226 OCU, 17.

DIGBY
While there is every reason to believe that the Meteor T.7 is still on show
somewhere inside the base, it seems to be well hidden....

WH166	8052M Meteor T.7	ex CFS, 5 CAACU, CAW, 4 FTS, 205 AFS, 210 AFS, 208 AFS.

EAST KIRKBY
Considerable movement to talk of at the **Lincolnshire Aviation Heritage Centre**, all
of it outbound. Working in conjunction with the site owners is the **Lincolnshire
Aviation Society** who own the airframes marked (LAS). Not all of the airframes
listed as being on site are on public show. Opening times vary, details from :
LAHC, East Kirkby, near Spilsby, Lincs, PE23 4DE. Telephone 07903 207. Taking
part in the exodus have been the following : Cavalier G-BBUW to Warmingham 5/1/89;
Comet 4C nose G-BEEX to Sunderland; anonymous Knight Twister fuselage gone,
destination unknown; T.8 Tutor BGA.794 to Tumby Woodside; Canberra B.2 nose WD954
to Romford; Hunter F.4 XE677 to JHL at Bournemouth Airport; Victor B.2 nose XH670
to Romford; Hunter F.51 E-424 to Firbeck 9/88; Stewart Ornithopter BAPC.61 and HM.14
Pou du Ciel BAPC.101 both to Tumby Woodside. Auster G-AGXT came here from Sibson
on the fold of the Nene Valley collection, but moved to Warmingham 13/1/88. NX611
finally made it on to the site early in 1988 and is assembled in its own impressive
hangar. New in here for Brian Nichols to work on are substantial pieces of Hampden
I AE436. Current situation is as follows :

G-ADFV	2893M Blackburn B-2	ex Tattershall, Wigan, Caterham, 4 EFTS Hanworth. Forward fuselage. Stored. LAS.
G-AJOZ	Argus II	ex Tattershall, Wigan, Market Drayton, Wigan, Southend, Sywell, FK338, Kemble, ATA 2 FP, 42-32142. Crashed 16/8/62. Under restoration. LAS.
G-AXEI	Ward Gnome	ex Tattershall. Local homebuild.
AE436+	Hampden I	ex Henlow, Sweden, 144. Crashed 4/9/42. Remains. Arr 11/88.
NP294	Proctor IV	ex Tattershall, Friskney, Poynton, Andover Down, Cosford, 4 RS, 2 RS. Restoration. LAS.
NX611+ G-ASXX	Lancaster VII	ex Scampton, Blackpool Airport, Hullavington, Lavenham, Biggin Hill, Aeronavale WU-15, St Athan, Llandow. Arrived 1988.
VV119	7285M Supermarine 535	ex Tattershall. Cockpit section. Identity questionable. LAS.
WW421	7688M Provost T.1	ex Tattershall, Lytham St Annes, St Athan, 3 FTS. LAS.
XA909	Vulcan B.1	ex Tattershall, Waddington, Wadd Wing, 50, 101. Nose section.
XM561	7980M Skeeter AOP.12	ex Tattershall, Moston, Middle Wallop, Arborfield, Wroughton, HQ 1 Wing, HQ 2 Wing, 651. Store.
100502	Fa 330A-1	ex Tattershall, Wigan. On loan from TAC.
BAPC 43	HM.14 Pou du Ciel	ex Tattershall, Wellingore. Under restoration.
BAPC 154	D.31 Turbulent	ex Tattershall, Nottingham. Unfinished, PFA.1654. Stored. LAS.

FENLAND
(Or Holbeach St Johns) The two Cessna 150s continue their symbiotic association
and have been joined by a Caribbean. The cockpit section of F.172M G-LOOK had gone
by 5/88. Scrapped?

G-AREL+	Caribbean 150	ex N3344Z. CoA expired 16/5/85. Stored.
G-ASTV	Cessna 150D	ex Panshanger, Luton, N6005T. CoA expired 18/10/75. Under rebuild to 'taildragger', using G-AWAX below for spares.
G-AWAX	Cessna 150D	ex OY-TRJ, N4153U. Crashed 3/2/80. See above.

HEMSWELL
The newly-named Hemswell Aviation Society succeeded in relocating the **Bomber County
Aviation Museum** here from Cleethorpes during the early part of 1989. For the

moment visits are by appointment only, contact : 75 Sixhill Street, Grimsby, South Humberside, DN32 9HS. Refer to Cleethorpes for disposals/disappearances before the move here. During 4/90 composite Hunter FGA.9 XG195/WT741 moved to Seighford. Current situation is as follows :

G-AESQ'+ B'	87 Bristol Babe rep	ex Cleethorpes, Selby. Incomplete.
G-AEJZ+	B'120 HM.14 Pou du Ciel	ex Cleethorpes, Brough.
WJ975+	Canberra T.19	ex Cleethorpes, Cambridge, 100, 7, 100, 85, West Raynham TFF, 228 OCU, 44, 35, 231 OCU.
XD445+	Vampire T.11	ex Cleethorpes, Huddersfield, Woodford, Chester, St Athan, 4 FTS, 5 FTS, Buckeburg SF.
XG506+	7852M Sycamore HR.14	ex Cleethorpes, Misson, Halton, HDU, MCS, 72, 118, 225, 118, 275.
101+	Mystere IVA	ex Cleethorpes, Sculthorpe, French AF.
BAPC 161+	Stewart Ornithopter	ex Cleethorpes.

An antique dealer with premises next to BCAM on the former airfield site acquired Meteor NF.11 nose WM267, ex Misson. This was snapped up by SYAM and moved to Firbeck 7/1/90.

HOLBEACH

By 6/88, the workshops of **K&L Aero Services** were empty – at least of whole airframes. Chipmunk 22A G-ARMD fuselage had moved on – destination unknown, its wings have surfaced at Husbands Bosworth. During 9/89 they took delivery of Dave Pope's two airframes.

G-AOSN+	Chipmunk 22	ex Wellingborough, 'Surrey', Denham, WB574, 10 RFS, 22 RFS. Crashed 19/2/77. Cockpit only. Arrived 9/89.
WP784+	Chipmunk T.10	ex Wellingborough, Reading, Benson, Abingdon, 6 AEF, Leeds UAS, Abn UAS, 8 FTS, Man UAS, QUB UAS, Air Attache Paris, 5 RFS, 17 RFS. Arrived 9/89.

HORNCASTLE

Stored in the area is an L-4H Grasshopper.

G-BJAY+	L-4H-PI Grasshopper	ex F-BFBN, OO-EAC, 44-79790. Damaged 22/2/67. Stored.

MARKET RASEN

Circa 1988 the anonymous Vulcan nose held with an ATC unit here was scrapped due to its poor condition. What chance now of finding out which one it was?

ROPSLEY

(South of the A52 between Grantham and Boston) At the strip, the Pawnee frame was joined by Auster J/5G Autocar G-ARKG by 9/86. This was restored and flying again by mid-1989.

G-BFBN	Pawnee 235D	Crashed 22/3/79. Fuselage frame only. Stored.

SCAMPTON

Disaster struck the **Vintage Pair** again on 30/5/88 when Meteor T.7 WF791 crashed while displaying at Coventry Airport, killing its pilot. Since then work on the Vampire has been halted. The month before the accident the Meteor F.8 previously stored at Shawbury arrived. This has been held in store since. The gate is now bare, Lancaster NX611 having made the trek to East Kirkby during 1988. There are rumours that the Gnat displayed outside the Red Arrows' building will be moved to the gate, but as yet this has not transpired. Talking of the **Central Flying School** proper, the advent of the Shorts Tucano-thing has allowed for the retirement of several JPs, all of which 'came and went' in between editions. These were as follows : T.3A XM458 was in the scrapping area by 4/89 and was removed by 10/89; T.3A XN574 was offered for tender as a stripped out fuselage 3/89 and moved to Chassey, France, 10/89; T.3A XN605 was stripped down by 10/88 and offered for tender 3/89 - no fate recorded; T.5 prototype XS231 (ex Shawbury, arrived 18/3/88) was offered for tender 3/89 and was acquired by JHL at Bournemouth Airport; T.5 XW298 (ex 6 FTS) arrived 4/89 and was in the scrap area by 6/89 and had migrated to Abingdon by 11/89. It would seem that Scampton is to take on the job of disposing of dead JPs. Here for a long time, but only physically noted in 12/89, are two JP procedure trainers that look very substantive - see the listing. The Hunter fleet of the **Trade Management Training School** (TMTS) is unchanged.

VZ467+	Meteor F.8	ex Shawbury, 1 TWU, 229 OCU, 500, 54, A&AEE. Arrived 4/88 - see above.
XE653	8829M Hunter F.6A	ex Kemble, 1 TWU, 229 OCU, 111, 43. TMTS.
XE920	8196M Vampire T.11	ex Henlow, Shawbury, CATCS, 8 FTS, 5 FTS, 1 FTS. See notes.
XF515	8830M Hunter F.6A	ex Kemble, 1 TWU, 229 OCU, 43, 247. TMTS.
XG160	8831M Hunter F.6A	ex 1 TWU, 229 OCU, 111, 43. TMTS.
XG172	8832M Hunter F.6A	ex 1 TWU, 229 OCU, 263, 19. TMTS.
XL587	8807M Hunter T.7	ex 208, 237 OCU, 1 TWU, 229 OCU.
XL592	8836M Hunter T.7	ex 1 TWU, TWU, 229 OCU.
XR571	8493M Gnat T.1	ex Cosford, Kemble, Brampton, Kemble, 4 FTS. Displayed.
	Vulcan B.2	hulk on dump. Thought to be XL384.
+	Jet Provost T.3	procedure trainer. Marked 'LEE 301/1'. See notes above.
+	Jet Provost T.5	procedure trainer. Marked 'LEE 301/2'. See notes above.

SKEGNESS AIRFIELD
(Or Ingoldmells) By 1989 Auster J/1N G-AHAL was flying again, with G-AHSO swopping places with it. An Apache had arrived from Land's End for restoration to flying status by mid 1987 - see also Burgh-le-Marsh. Dominating the inmates during 1989 was F-104G Starfighter 22+57 transitting from Laceby. It moved to <u>Grimsby</u> early 1990.

G-AHSO+	J/1N Alpha	spares use by 8/87. Stored.
G-ARCW+	Apache 160	ex Land's End, N2187P. CoA expired 6/7/86. See notes above.

STIXWOULD
Appearing at a garden in the village here by early 1989 was one of the Coventry Airport Nord 3400s (No 37/MAB). Acquired via a very brief stop at Breighton, the Nord was stored here until moving to <u>Boston</u> for restoration early in 1990.

STRUBBY
The **Lincolnshire Lightning Society's** F.3 is held on the airfield.

XP706	8925M Lightning F.3	ex Binbrook, LTF, 11, 5, LTF, 23, 111, 74.

STURGATE
Two Cherokee variants are under restoration at the airfield, with another acting as a source of spares. The Cessna para-trainer serves on, but is still anonymous.

G-BCTF+	Warrior 151	CoA expired 24/3/88. Under restoration.
G-BEYS+	Archer II	ex Wickenby, N2658Q. Crashed 20/6/81. Under restoration.
G-BFXZ	Archer II	ex Staverton, N7548F. Crashed 11/7/84. Wreck. Spares use.
	Cessna single	para-trainer. See notes above.

SUTTON BRIDGE
(On the A17 west of King's Lynn) Lindsey Walton keeps his Nord spares-ships at his strip in the area.

G-ASTG	Nord 1002	ex F-BGKI, French AF. CoA expired 26/10/73. Stored.
G-ASUA	Nord 1002	ex Elstree, F-BFDY. Crashed 30/7/64. Stored.

SWINDERBY
During 7/89 Canberra PR.7 WT520/8184M and Lightning F.1 XG329/8050M were both put up for tender. Not having fates for them, and with continued sightings of both well up to the end of 1989, they are kept in the listing - for now! The dump was re-occupied during 11/89, with a former Halton gold-brick - sorry, Gnat!

WG362	8630M Chipmunk T.10 PAX	ex Filton, Bir UAS, Wales UAS, Oxf UAS, Swanton Morley, Carlisle, Mildenhall, 100, Edn UAS, 3 BFTS, 16 RFS, 3 BFTS, 7 RFS. Also allocated 8437M.
WT520	8184M Canberra PR.7	ex CAW, 31, 17, 31, 17, 31, 80. Also 8094M. See notes above.
XD506	7983M Vampire T.11	ex Finningley, CATCS, CNCS, 5 FTS, 206 AFS. Gate guardian.
XG329	8050M Lightning F.1	ex Cranwell, A&AEE, Warton. See notes above.
XM706+	8572M Gnat T.1	ex Halton, 4 FTS, CFS. Arrived 8/11/89. Dump.

TATTERSHALL THORPE

As can be seen from the listing below, the famous strip operated by **Roger Windley** has exploded in terms of contents. This gives the compiler more than a few headaches, bearing in mind that **W&R** is about long-term (ie at least more than a year) flightless wonders and many of the airframes here do not fall into that category, even though they are obviously well battered. As with the rest of the work, these will have to wait and prove themselves as really and truly inert, then they will merit listing in the **W&R13** safety net. Essentially, the role of the hangars and stores here is to act as a kind of 'bonded store' for insurance hulks that are open to dispute, claim, or held by brokers and companies while seeking settlement in terms of spares reclamation or potential rebuild. Add to this that Roger himself is a collector of airframes (particularly rotorcraft) and the variety here is astounding. **W&R** serves principally as a source-book on the whereabouts and fates of aircraft and not as a guide to what-can-we-put-in-our-grubby-little-logbook-today? and this location serves as a good illustration of this. The legal surroundings of these airframes is such that visits are not just not permitted, but impossible, so the listing below serves by way of record and not as an invite! Whole airframes are dealt with only in the listing below. Parts of aircraft outstanding in the insurance paperwork department also come here for example, bits from the unfortunate Charles Church Lancaster are known to have come here (refer to Cranfield/RAE Bedford for more details). Likewise the back-end of the very unfortunate B-17G F-BEEA that came to grief at Binbrook came here. Known departures are as follows : Flying Flea G-AEOH has gone, quoted as "sold off"; Luton Minor G-BDJG was sold off and was flying by late 1989; Stearman G-ROAN moved to Wickenby by 4/88; Dragonfly HR.3 WH991 moved to Storwood; Whirlwind HAR.10 XJ407/G-BKHB was sold off and became N7013H, flying from nearby to Lakenheath in 1988; Whirlwind HAR.10 XP345/8792M did indeed moved to Storwood on 28/8/87 - confirming **W&R11**; Whirlwind HAR.10 XP346/8793M moved to Long Marston 7/88. Three airframes here are now deemed too small to be listed, constituting rear fuselages only and have been dropped from the listing : F.150M G-BEYM (mentioned only in **MiniWrecks**); Rallye 180GT G-BFMS and F.172H D-ECIU. Cessna F.177RG G-OADE (damaged 27/4/86 ex G-AZKM) arrived by 1988, was registered G-TOTO 8/89 and may have moved on.

G-APMP	Hiller UH-12C	ex Chilbolton, Southend. CoA expired 23/7/76.
G-ASKJ	Terrier 1	ex Redhill, EI-AMC ntu, VX926, 664, AOPS, HS. Crashed 20/6/84.
G-ATHF	Cessna 150F	ex Cambridge, N6292R. Crashed 7/9/83.
G-ATJU	Cessna 150F	ex N8265S. Crashed 9/11/82.
G-AVVE	Cessna F.150H	crashed 14/5/83. First noted 3/85.
G-AWCL+	Cessna F.150H	crashed 16/10/87. Arrived 28/1/88.
G-AXGA	PA-18-95 Super Cub	ex PH-NLE, PH-CUB ntu, RNethAF R-51, 52-2447. Crashed 26/12/86.
G-AXRC	Cricket	crashed 22/10/77.
G-AYFY	EAA Biplane	ex Cardiff, unfinished.
G-AYJW	Cessna FR.172G	ex Leavesden. Damaged 13/12/83.
G-AYVT	Brochet MB.84	ex Sunderland, F-BGLI. Damaged 28/6/77.
G-AZSN+	Cherokee Arrow 200	ex N3083R. Crashed 2/10/88. First noted 6/89.
G-AZVV	Cherokee 180G	crashed 8/11/85.
G-AZYJ	Wilga 35	ex Studley, Bickmarsh, SP-WEA. CoA expired 5/3/76.
G-BAOT+	Rallye Club	ex Breighton. Crashed 4/7/87. First noted 10/89.
G-BAYX	Bell 47G-5	ex CF-XPN, N6216N. Crashed 7/6/86.
G-BDNE	Harker Hawk	ex Middlesborough, unfinished.
G-BFON	Turbo Navajo	ex SE-FHB. Crashed 11/6/86.
G-BGHA+	Cessna F.152 II	damaged 16/10/87. (Storm at Shoreham) First noted 8/88.
G-BGNS+	Cessna F172N II	damaged 16/10/87. (Same storm!) First noted 8/88.
G-BGZE+	Tomahawk 112	ex Breighton. Damaged 16/10/87. (Same storm, Cardiff!) First noted 2/89.
G-BGZH+	Tomahawk 112	ex Breighton. Damaged 16/10/87. (Same storm, same place!) First noted 2/89. (It's an ill wind......)
G-BHOC	Commander 112A	ex N1378J. Crashed 1/10/85.
G-BHUP+	Cessna F.152 II	ex Barton. Crashed 17/5/89. Arrived 28/10/89. Wreck.
G-BKVM+	Super Cub 150	ex PH-KAZ, RNethAF R-214. Damaged 16/10/87 (that storm again, this time at Southampton). First noted 8/88.
G-BOCA+	Tomahawk 112	ex N24336. Damaged 22/9/88. First noted 10/89.

G-HASL		AA-5A Cheetah	ex G-BGSL. Crashed 25/6/86.
G-JULY+		AA-5A Cheetah	ex Breighton, G-BHIZ, N26795. Crashed 21/10/87. First noted 10/89.
G-LINT+		Pitts S-1S Special	crashed 15/3/86. First noted 8/86.
G-PULL		Super Cub 150	ex PH-MBB, ALAT 18-5356. Crashed 13/6/86.
C-GOEA	G-BMSP	Hughes 369HS	Under restoration.
EI-BKL		Cessna FR.172F	ex D-EBTQ, F-WLIT. Damaged 11/84.
5X-UUX	G-BKLJ	Scout Srs 1	ex Heysham, Panshanger, Uganda Police Air Wing. Spares for XT788.
WV703	8108M	Pembroke C.1	'G-IIIM', ex Coningsby, St Athan, 32, MCS, El Adem SF, Levant CF, MECS. Poor state.
XL735		Skeeter AOP.12	ex Manston, Wroughton, Detmold, Middle Wallop.
XP329	8791M	Whirlwind HAR.10	ex Shawbury, Lee-on-Solent, Akrotiri, 84, 230, 110, 225.
XP395	8674M	Whirlwind HAR.10	ex Halton, SARTS, 22, 230.
XR486+	8727M	Whirlwind HCC.12	ex St Athan, 32, Queen's Flight. Arrived by 10/89.
XT788	G-BMIR	Wasp HAS.1	ex Wroughton. Under restoration.

Stop Press. As we close for press, there are reports that the whole insurance store is to be disbanded/moved on from here.

TUMBY WOODSIDE
(To the east of Coningsby) Several airframes previously at the LAHC, East Kirkby, moved into the area for storage during 1989.

BGA 794+	T.8 Tutor	ex East Kirkby, Tattershall.
BAPC 61+	Stewart Ornithopter	ex East Kirkby, Tattershall, Wigan.
BAPC 101+	HM.14 Pou du Ciel	ex East Kirkby, Tattershall, Sleaford. Fuselage.

WADDINGTON
Two major elements of the skyline have gone from the base. The Nimrod AEW.3s all got up and flew away as they would be far too embarrassing when the Boeing Spinning Coffee Table MFI.1s arrive for 8 Squadron here in 1991! Departures, all to meet their fate at Abingdon, were : XV259 10/1/89, XZ280 10/1/89, XZ281 19/12/88, XZ282 9/11/88, XZ283 9/12/88, XZ285 31/10/88 and XZ287 23/11/88. Displayed alongside the Vulcan on the gate was Victor K.2 XL189/8912M. It was put up for tender during 1989 - under the 'gate' rule - and was dismantled and removed by scrapmen on 28/9/89. Just who processed it is a matter of some debate, either the amorphous Glasgow mob or the yard at Thirsk. The **Vulcan Display Flight** continues to fly the majestic XH558 and long may she remain so. Acting as a support club for the Vulcan is the **Vulcan Association**, details of membership from : 207, Weoley Castle Road, Weoley Castle, Birmingham, B29 5QW.

XH558		Vulcan B.2	ex Marham, Waddington, 50, Wadd Wing, A&AEE, Wadd Wing, 27, 230 OCU, 27, Wadd Wing, 230 OCU. Airworthy.
XJ825	8810M	Vulcan K.2	ex 50, Wadd Wing, 35, 27, 35, Akrotiri Wing, Cott Wing, Wadd Wing, Cott Wing, 35, 27. BDR.
XM607	8779M	Vulcan B.2	ex 44, 101, 35. Display airframe.

WAINFLEET
(South west of Skegness) On the A52 road to Skegness can be found **T A Smith & Co (Farm Produce) Ltd** at Croft Bank. In July 1988 they were made all the more exciting by the addition of :

XS456+	Lightning T.5	ex Binbrook, LTF, 11, LTF, 11, 56, Wattisham TFF, 56. Arr 20/7/88.

WICKENBY
Another Auster has arrived for rebuild, along with a well-known Stearman. Archer II G-BEYS has moved to Sturgate. Otherwise, no change with the **W&R** inmates here.

G-AIGM		J/1N Alpha	damaged in hangar collapse 1/87. Stored, poor shape.
G-AIPV+		J/1 Autocrat	ex Cabourne. CoA expired 1/6/68. Arrived by 7/87.
G-ARLK		Comanche 250	ex EI-ALW, N7257P ntu. Crashed 29/3/81. Awaiting rebuild.
G-DCAT		Turbo AgCat	ex N8312K. Crashed 3/7/85. For spares.
G-ROAN+		Stearman B75N-1	ex Tattershall Thorpe, Shoreham, Yugoslavia, N4685N, BuAer 07790. Damaged 21/10/83. For restoration.
PH-TPR		AgCat 450	ex N6882Q. For spares.

Greater London

BENTLEY PRIORY
'One gate-one guardian' is the new ruling. It doesn't seem to apply here. For its
sins, the base has got itself two plastic replicas. The Lightning F.1A looks set
to stay on in the grounds, but Spitfire F.21 LA226 currently held at Shawbury is
due to come here as soon as covered accommodation can be arranged for it. Leaving
here to allow for all of this were Spitfire XVI TB252/8073M going to Braintree
9/11/88 and Hunter F.6 XG290/8711M joining CSDE at Swanton Morley.

N9926"+	Spitfire replica	installed 1989. Displayed in the grounds.
P3386"+	Hurricane replica	installed 1989. Displayed in the grounds.
XM173	8414M Lightning F.1A	ex Binbrook, Binbrook TFF, Leuchars TFF, 226 OCU, 56. Displayed in the grounds.

BIGGIN HILL
Tiger Moth G-BBRB, 'lost' under the heading of Biggin Hill Airport in W&R11 has
surfaced under restoration in the area. Also stored locally, but not at the same
place, is a Proctor.

G-BBRB+	Tiger Moth	ex Biggin Hill airport, Headcorn, OO-EVB, Belgian AF T-8, DF198, Belgian TS. Damaged 16/1/87. Under restoration.
NP181	G-AOAR Proctor IV	ex Headcorn, Biggin Hill. CoA expired 25/10/63.

BIGGIN HILL AIRPORT
At the RAF Memorial Chapel, shortly to be the only RAF presence at the airfield,
Spitfire XVI SL674/8392M moved to store at St Athan in mid-1989. It has been
replaced by two suitably shaped credit cards. In W&R11, the previously Bitteswell-
based Warbirds of Great Britain (WoGB) had just moved into a new hangar. Now it
would seem that the ever-moving collection must move on again and Bournemouth is
the hot-tip for the new venue. As W&R went to press Spitfire XVI G-SXVI/TE356,
which arrived from East Midlands Airport on 1/6/88, was sold to the blossoming
Evergreen Ventures collection of Oregon, USA, as N356EV. Reported also to be going
to Evergreen are the Bf 109G-10, the Bf 109K and the P-38. A Catalina is reported
to be coming the other way some time in 1990 along with the long-expected P-40.
All but the former Yugoslavian P-47 Thunderbolt (which went to the USA) that were
unaccounted for under 'Bitteswell' in W&R11 did in fact move in here. Three
aircraft from the collection, moved to Thruxton for restoration, as follows :
Spitfire IX BR601 on 6/7/89, Seafire III PP972 by 8/89 and Spitfire XVI TE392/8074M
on 6/7/89. Of the other aircraft to be found at the airfield, there have been
several departures since W&R11 : Commander 520 G-ASJU on the dump was destroyed in
a fire fighting exercise during 1988; Hiller UH-12C G-ASTP arrived from Thornicombe
by 10/88, but travelled to Weston-super-Mare on 12/10/89; Aztec 250F G-BLXX was
flying again by 1988; the hulk of Short SD.360 EI-BEM was quickly processed here
and taken away by a Nottingham-based scrappy; Vampire T.11 XE998 moved out to
Charlwood, possibly via Peckham Rye; finally, the Brencham gate guardian Hunter,
now known to be mostly ET-273, moved to JHL at Bournemouth Airport 8/11/89. The
continued existence of the 'spares ship' Civilian Coupe (No 7) is now very much
doubted and is best taken out of the main listing. Sharing this fate is the
anonymous Scout pod, not noted for a long time. Current situation is :

G-AAOK+	Travel Air CW-12Q	ex Yugoslavia, N370N, NC370N, NC352M. Damaged 21/10/83. Stored.
G-ABYA+	DH.60G Moth	CoA expired 21/5/73. Crashed 21/5/72. Confirmed resident.
G-AKVZ	Messenger IVB	ex RH427. CoA expired 18/8/72. Under rebuild.
G-ANUO+	Heron 2D	ex Exeter. CoA expired 12/9/86. Stored.
G-AOGE	Proctor III	ex BV651,Halton SF, 2 GCS, FAA. CoA expired 21/5/84. Stored.
G-AOKH	Prentice 1	ex VS251, 3 FTS, CFS, 2 FTS. CoA expired 2/8/73. Spares use.
G-AOTI+	Heron 2D	ex Exeter, G-5-19. CoA expired 24/6/87. Arrived by 4/88. Stored.
G-APZR	Cessna 150	ex N6461T. Crashed 14/1/81. Engine test-bed with Airtech.
G-AREE	Aztec 250	CoA expired 6/6/81. External store.
G-ARWC	Cessna 150B	ex Exeter, N1115Y. Crashed 28/4/84. Wreck.
G-ASDA	Queen Air 65-80	CoA expired 8/11/79. External storage.

G-AVKB+	MB.50 Pipistrelle	ex Kingsclere. CoA expired 13/12/83. Stored. First noted 5/88.
G-AVWE	Cherokee 140	CoA expired 22/4/82. External storage.
G-AWCO	Cessna F.150H	CoA expired 29/8/75. Fuselage, poor state.
G-AWEK	Fournier RF-4D	crashed 25/10/72. Fuselage, stored.
G-AYRM	Cherokee 140D	crashed 12/1/84. Wreck.
G-BEAC	Cherokee 140	ex 4X-AND. CoA expired 20/11/83. External storage.
G-BGAU	Rearwin 9000L	ex N18548. Stored.
G-BHCX+	Cessna F.152 II	damaged 16/10/87. Stored.
G-BHYS	Cherokee 181	ex N8218Y. Crashed 7/12/85. Wreck.
NX55JP+ 88391	FG-1D Corsair	ex USA, Canada, MoTAT Auckland NZ, RNZAF NZ5648, USN 88391. Arrived 1988. Airworthy. WoGB.
N179JP+ 122179	F4U-5N Corsair	ex USA, Honduran AF FAH 604, USN 122179. Flew in 14/8/88. Airworthy. WoGB.
NL314BG+	P-51D-25-NA Mustang	ex USA, C-GZQX, CF-BAU, N51N, N169MD, N6337T, RCAF 9567, USAAF 44-73140. Flew in 8/9/88. Airworthy. WoGB.
N505MH+	P-38L-5-LO L'ning	ex USA, N62350, USAAF 44-53186. Flew in 16/5/89. Airworthy. Reported sold in the USA early 1990 - see notes above. WoGB.
NX49092	F4U-4 Corsair	ex USA, Honduran AF FAH 615, USN 97280. Airworthy. WoGB.
N52113+	P-63A Kingcobra	ex USA, 42-69097. Crated in 5/88. WoGB.
L1710"+	Hurricane replica	placed on the gate 5/89.
N3194"+	Spitfire replica	placed on the gate 23/2/89.
KZ321"+ G-HURY	Hurricane IV	ex Bitteswell, Blackbushe, Israel, Yugoslavia AF, RAF. Frame. WoGB.
NH238 G-MKIX	Spitfire IX	ex Bitteswell, Blackbushe, N238V, Harlingen, Hemswell, Winthorpe, Southampton, Andover, COGEA OO-ARE, Coxyde, Belgian AF SM-36, Netherlands AF H-60, Sealand, 76 MU, 9 MU, 49 MU, 84 GSU. Airworthy. WoGB.
PL983 G-PRXI	Spitfire PR.XI	ex East Midlands, Stonebroom, Duxford, Old Warden, Vickers G-15-109, NC74138, PL983 2, 4, 1 PP. Airworthy. WoGB.
RW386+ G-BXVI	Spitfire XVI	ex Bitteswell, Blackbushe, St Athan, Halton 6944M, 58 MU, 604. Stored. WoGB.
SM969+ G-BRAF	Spitfire XVIII	ex Bitteswell, Blackbushe, New Delhi, Indian AF HS877, RAF SM969, 47 MU, India, ACSEA, 76 MU. Stored. WoGB.
9663+	Bf 109G-6	ex Yugoslavia. Stored. Reported sold in the USA early 1990. See notes above. WoGB.
T2-124+	Bf 109G-10/U-4	ex USA, USAAF FE-124/T2-124. Stored. Reported sold in the USA early 1990. See notes above. WoGB.

CHESSINGTON

(On the A243 south of Surbiton) Joining the Zlin and the two Pitts frames here recently have been a long 'lost' Auster and a Taylorcraft Plus D.

G-AHUG+	T'craft Plus D	ex Tongham, Aldershot, LB282. CoA expired 12/7/70. Here since at least 11/86. Under restoration.
G-ANHR+	Auster 5	ex Jersey, MT192. CoA expired 20/7/86. Frame. First noted 2/90.
G-AWJX	Zlin Z.526	CoA expired 29/5/85. Under rebuild.
	Pitts S-1	fuselage frame.
	Pitts S-1	fuselage frame.

COULSDON

(On the South Circular, north of Croydon) The Edwards Gyrocopter still lives here.

G-ASDF	Edwards Gyrocopter	stored.

CROYDON

Here can be found **1924 Squadron ATC** who have had a Chippax here since at least 1985. It was briefly on loan to the Friends of Biggin Hill, hence its entry under Sevenoaks, which should now be amended.

WP921+	Chipmunk T.10 PAX	ex Henley-on-Thames, Benson, CoAT G-ATJJ, Colerne SF, Ox UAS, HCMSU, 10 RFS. See notes above.

ENFIELD

Both of the aircraft listed here in W&R11 have moved on. Harrier GR.3 XW922/8885M moved on to <u>Foulness</u> and did indeed spend time at the Ordnance Factory. Chipmunk

T.10 PAX trainer WK587/8212M, last noted as being with a college here, "went" in
the mid 1980s. The MoD still have this on charge, 'parented' by 5 AEF, so someone,
somewhere is deep in the proverbial.....

HAMPTON
Tiger Moth 'G-ADNZ' is thought to remain here.

| G-ADNZ" | Tiger Moth | ex Hayter, Christchurch, Tunbridge Wells, 6948M, DE673, 9 RFS, 22 |
| | | RFS, 22 EFTS, 19. No relationship to the original G-ADNZ. |

HANWELL
(On the A4020 east of Uxbridge) The famous Aeronca store is intact.

G-AETG	Aeronca 100	ex Booker. Crashed 7/4/69. Stored.
G-AEWV	Aeronca 100	substantial components. Stored.
G-AEXD	Aeronca 100	CoA expired 20/4/70. Composite, including parts from G-AESP.

HANWORTH
In the area, the Arkle Kittiwake continues its restoration.

| G-AWGM | Kittiwake II | ex Halton. Accident 18/1/86. |

HAYES
(On the A4020 south east of Uxbridge) No change to the aeronautical contents of
the **Science Museum Storage Facility** here.

G-ATTN	Piccard HAB	canopy only, basket and burner on display at South Kensington.
BAPC 52	Lilienthal Glider	ex South Kensington. Original.
	Gossamer Albatross	ex South Kensington.

HENDON
From this edition, with the upheaval of restyling the Battle of Britain Museum into
a new display dedicated to the 50th Anniversary of the conflict, entitled 'The
Battle of Britain Experience', the aircraft contents at the **Royal Air Force Museum**
will be treated as one listing. Under the Directorship of Dr Michael Fopp the
Museum has certainly received a new dynamism and new exhibits are finding their way
in. Likewise the galleries and displays have been receiving major rethinks with a
view to making the Museum a much more 'living' entity. The 'Battle of Britain
Experience' is central to this idea, with an extensive refurbishment to the hall
involved and a lot more inter-active exhibits, including 'talking' dummies to which
some people may take considerable objection. Such items are all part of broadening
the appeal and therefore concreting the security of the Museum as a major
attraction - the key being to bring people (be they 'buffs' or Joe Public) back
again. Hunter F.5 WP185/7583M went to Abingdon by 12/89 making way for an FGA.9.
Placing the English Electric P.1B XA847/8371M up for tender was not a popular move.
The first British aircraft to go trans-sonic in level flight, its space was needed
for a recently-retired Lightning F.6. It should really have gone to Cosford -
where the unremarkable pre-production XG337 could have been turned into saucepans
to pay for the move - but the Ministry thought otherwise. It was acquired by a
concerned UK collector and moved to storage in Southampton. By 11/89 the former
Polish MiG 15bis 01120 was moved out to South Lambeth in readiness for display at
the Imperial War Museum. This move towards the rationalisation of the national
collections came as a great source of relief to many as it seemed that the RAF
Museum had lost its routing somewhere.
    The RAF Museum is intended to be the principal beneficiary of the much-
publicised plastic-for-real gate guardian swop. In return for the Spitfires going
to Historic Flying Ltd a Bristol Beaufort and a P-40 will be appearing from
California in due course, apparently ready for display. Along with this have come
the plastic Hurricane and Spitfire replicas that now adorn several RAF bases. The
Spitfires held at St Athan are reported to be all held as exchange material for
future RAF Museum deals.
    During 11/89, Beverley C.1 XH124/8025M was offered for tender and outrage roamed
up and down the preservation world. In truth, the Beverley was in a terrible

state, no restoration work of any ilk having been carried out on it since it was
flown into Hendon. The space occupied by the 'Bev' will soon be occupied by two
further plastic replicas, a Hurricane and a Spitfire, to draw attention to the
'Battle of Britain Experience'. XH124 was beyond the means of the smaller groups
to move, let alone save its airframe from the creeping cancer it was suffering
from. With more time and a concerted effort at planned disposal, who knows. How
many visitors looked up and marvelled at the Beverley, little realising that nobody
was doing anything about conserving it? Management apathy over many years forced
Michael Fopp into acting in the only way he could toward what had become a fait
accompli. A scrapmerchant from Chelmsford carried out the deed in February and
March 1990.
       The whole of the Hendon complex is open 1000 to 1800 all week, with the
exception of Christmas. More details on the many activities going on during 'The
Battle of Britain Experience' can be had on receipt of an SAE at : RAF Museum,
Hendon, London, NW9 5LL. Telephone 081 205 2266.

G-EBMB	Hawker Cygnet	ex Cardington, Henlow, Lympne Trials No 14. CoA expired 30/11/61.
+	Nulli Secundus	airship gondola, 1907.
164	BAPC 106 Bleriot XI	RAeS loan.
168	G-BFDE Tabloid replica	ex Cardington, Hucknall. CoA expired 4/6/83.
433	BAPC 107 Bleriot XXVII	ex Cardington, RAeS loan.
2345"	G-ATVP FB.5 Gunbus rep	ex Cardington, Hendon, Weybridge. CoA expired 6/5/69.
3066	Caudron G.III	ex Henlow, Upavon, Heathrow, G-AETA, OO-ELA, O-BELA. RAeS loan.
A301	Morane BB	fuselage frame only.
E449"	Avro 504K	ex Henlow. Composite aircraft, including parts from 504K G-EBJE and 548A G-EBKN/E449.
F938	RAF SE.5A	ex Henlow, Heathrow, Colerne, 'B4563', Weybridge, Savage Skywriting G-EBIC. CoA expired 3/9/30.
A8226"	G-BIDW 1½ Strutter rep	ex Cardington, Land's End, '9382'. CoA expired 29/12/80.
C4994"+	G-BLWM M.1C Monoplane	ex Cardington, 'C4912', Hucknall. CoA expired 12/8/87. Arrived by 12/89.
E2466"	B'165 Bristol F.2b	ex Cardington, Weston-on-the-Green. Partially skeletal.
F1010	DH.9A	ex Cardington, Krakow, Berlin War Museum, 110.
F6314	Camel F.1	ex Heathrow, Colerne, Hendon, Tring, Waddon.
F8614"	G-AWAU Vimy replica	ex 'H651', VAFA Weybridge. CoA expired 4/8/69.
J9941"	G-ABMR Hart	ex HSA, 'J9933'. CoA expired 11/6/57.
K4232	Cierva C.30A	ex Cardington, SE-AZB, K4232 SAC.
K8042	8372M Gladiator II	ex 61 OTU, 5 (P)AFU, A&AEE.
K9942	8383M Spitfire IA	ex 71 MU, 53 OTU, 57 OTU, 72.
L5343+	Battle I	ex St Athan, Cardington, Leeming, Iceland, 98, 266. Crashed 13/9/40. Composite, with parts from P2183. Arrived 3/90.
L8756"	10001 Bolingbroke IVT	ex Boscombe Down, RCAF 10001.
N1671	8370M Defiant I	ex Finningley, 285, 307.
N5182"	G-APUP Sopwith Pup replica	ex Blackbushe, Old Warden. CoA expired 28/6/78.
N5628	Gladiator II	ex 263. Lost in Norway 4/40. Forward fuselage only.
N5912	8385M Sopwith Triplane	ex Henlow, 49 MU, 5 MU, Cardington, SAF Redcar, SAF Marske.
P2617	8373M Hurricane I	ex 71 MU, 9 FTS, 9 SFTS, 1, 607, 615.
P3175	Hurricane I	ex 257. Shot down by Bf 110 near North Weald 31/8/40. Wreck.
R5868	7325M Lancaster I	ex Scampton, 467, 83.
R9125	8377M Lysander III	ex 161, 225.
T6296	8387M Tiger Moth II	ex Yeovilton SF, BRNC, RNEC, Stretton, 7 EFTS, 1 EFTS.
W1048	8465M Halifax II	ex Henlow, Lake Hoklingen, Norway, 35, 102. Force-landed 9/4/44, recovered from lake bottom 1973.
X4590	8384M Spitfire I	ex Cosford, Finningley, 53 OTU, 303, 57 OTU, 66, 609.
Z7197+	8380M Proctor III	ex St Athan, Swinderby, Finningley, G-AKZN, AST, 18 EFTS, 1 RS, 2 SS. CoA expired 29/11/63. Arrived by 10/89.
KK995	Hoverfly I	ex Cranfield, 43 OTU, R-4B 43-46558.
MF628	Wellington T.10	ex Abingdon, St Athan, Biggin Hill, Heathrow, Hendon, Wisley, Vickers, 1 ANS.
ML824	Sunderland V	ex Pembroke Dock, Aeronavale, 330, 201.
MN235	Typhoon IB	ex Shawbury, Smithsonian, USAAF evaluation FE-491, 47 MU, 51 MU.

NV778	8386M Tempest V	ex Foulness Island, Middleton St George. Composite.
PK724	7288M Spitfire F.24	ex Finningley, Gaydon, Norton, Lyneham.
PM651+	7758M Spitfire PR.XIX	ex Benson, Bicester, Andover, Hucknall, Leconfield, Church Fenton, C&RS, 3 CAACU, 604. Arrived by 12/89.
RD253	7931M Beaufighter TF.10	ex St Athan, Portuguese AF BF-13.
TW117	7805M Mosquito T.3	ex Henlow, 3 CAACU, 58, 264, HCF, Linton-on-Ouse SF, APS Acklington.
VT812	7200M Vampire F.3	ex Cosford, Shawbury, Colerne, Cardington, 602, 601, 614, 32.
VX653	Sea Fury FB.11	ex Yeovilton, Lee-on-Solent, Lossiemouth, FRU, 811, 738, 736.
WE139	8369M Canberra PR.3	ex Henlow, 231 OCU, 39, 69, 540.
WH301	7930M Meteor F.8	ex Henlow, Kemble, 85, CAW, 609, DFLS/CFE.
WK281+	7712M Swift FR.5	ex St Athan, Swinderby, Finningley, Colerne, Northolt, 79. Arrived by 10/89.
WS843+	7937M Meteor NF.14	ex St Athan, Henlow, St Athan, Kemble, 1 ANS, MoA, 228 OCU. Arrived by 4/90.
XD818	7894M Valiant BK.1	ex Marham, 49 'A' Flt.
XG154+	8863M Hunter FGA.9	ex St Athan, 1 TWU, 229 OCU, 54, 43, 54. Arr by 12/89.
XG474	8367M Belvedere HC.1	ex 66, 26, 66.
XL318	8733M Vulcan B.2	ex Scampton, 617, 230 OCU, Wadd Wing, 617, 230 OCU, Scamp Wing, 617.
XP831	8406M P.1127	ex RAE Bedford, Dunsfold.
XS925+	8961M Lightning F.6	ex Binbrook, 11, 5-11 pool. Arrived 26/4/88.
	Beaufighter	ex Cranfield. Cockpit section.
A2-4	Seagull V	ex Cardington, Wyton, VH-ALB, RAAF A2-4.
A16-199	G-BEOX Hudson IIIA	ex Strathallan, VH-AGJ, VH-SMM, A16-199, FH174, 41-36975.
HD-75	Hanriot HD.1	ex Cardington, N75 (US civil), G-AFDX, OO-APJ, Belgian AF.
920	Stranraer	ex CF-BXO Queen Charlotte Airlines, RCAF 920.
HD5-1	Dornier Do 24T-3	ex N99225 ntu, Majorca, Spanish AF, HRS.1, 65-6, EC-DAF.
4101	8477M Bf 109E-3	ex St Athan, Henlow, Biggin Hill, Fulbeck, Wroughton, Stanmore Park, DG200, 1426 (EA) Flt, A&AEE, de H, Hucknall, RAE. Force-landed 27/11/40.
120227+	8472M He 162A-2	ex St Athan, Colerne, Leconfield, VH513, AM.65, Farnborough, Leck, JG.1. Arrived by 12/89.
360043	8475M Ju 88R-1	ex St Athan, Henlow, St Athan, Biggin Hill, Fulbeck, Wroughton, Stanmore Park, 47 MU, CFE-EAF, 1426 (EA) Flt, RAE. Defected 9/5/43.
494083	8474M Ju 87D-3	ex St Athan, Henlow, St Athan, Fulbeck, Wroughton, Stanmore Park, Eggebek.
584219+	8470M Fw 190F-8/U1	ex St Athan, Gaydon, Henlow, Fulbeck, Wroughton, Stanmore Park, Wroughton, Brize Norton, AM.29, Farnborough, Grove/Karup. Arrived by 12/89.
701152	8471M He 111H-23	ex St Athan, Henlow, Biggin Hill, Fulbeck, Stanmore Park, RAE, 56th FG USAAF Boxted.
730301	8479M Bf 110G-4/R6	ex St Athan, Biggin Hill, Stanmore Park, 76 MU, RAE, AM.34, Karup, I/NJG.3.
+	Fi 103 (V-1)	ex Cardington. (Likely BAPC.92) Arrived by 1/90.
MM5701	8468M Fiat CR-42	ex St Athan, Biggin Hill, Fulbeck, Wroughton, Stanmore Park, AFDU, RAE, BT474, 95 SCT. Force-landed Orfordness 11/11/40.
429366	8838M TB-25N-20-NC	ex Blackbushe, N9115Z, 'Hanover Street', Yesterday's Air Force, 'Catch 22', USAAF 44-29366.
483868	B-17G-95-DL	ex Stansted, N5237V, Andrews AFB, TBM Inc, Butler Aircraft, Aero Union, USN PB-1W 77233.
BAPC 82	Afghan Hind	ex Kabul, Royal Afghan AF, RAF.
BAPC 100	Clarke TWK	ex Cardington, Hayes. Science Museum loan.

HOUNSLOW
Held in store here for the **Imperial War Museum** is a Mosquito.

TV959	Mosquito T.3	ex South Lambeth, Bicester, 3 CAACU, HCEU, 228 OCU, 13 OTU.

HOUNSLOW HEATH
It doesn't seem that **W&R** sleuths feel safe walking on the Heath, even though it is home to the **Metropolitan Police Training Centre**, as there have been no reports concerning the Trident they have.

G-AVFK	Trident 2E	ex Heathrow, BA, BEA. CoA expired 15/8/83.

KENLEY
There are interesting reports of a mega-museum going to be built here, perhaps in time to celebrate the 50th Anniversary of the Battle of Britain..... We shall see. No news on the Cadet which is based here and used as a travelling recruiting aid.
VM791"   XA312 Cadet TX.3   8876M. Travelling airframe.

KEW
Collector and restorer Barry Parkhouse has a yard here, which has seen a fair bit of 'action' of late. On 4/8/89 Barry took on the nose of Canberra B.2/6 WG789 from Burgess Hill, but moved it on to **Booker** 16/12/89. On 1/7/89 he received two former Senegalese Air Force Dakota noses from brief transit through Cranfield. 6W-SAF was despatched on the same lorry that took WG789 to **Booker.** Current here are :

WD935+	Canberra B.2	ex Burgess Hill, St Athan, 360, 97, 151, CSE, EE, BCDU, RAAF A84-1 ntu. Nose. Arrived 1/90.
6W-SAE+	C-47A-25-DK	ex Cranfield, F-GEFY, Le Bourget, Senegalese AF, French AF, CSA OK-WAR, USAAF 42-93510. Nose. Arrived 1/7/89.

KINGSTON-UPON-THAMES
Confirmed as being with **British Aerospace** here is the nose of a Harrier T.2.
XW272   8783M Harrier T.2   ex Cranfield, 4, 20. Crashed 29/6/82. Nose.

LONDON AIRPORT
(Heathrow) The situation here is unchanged from that given in **W&R11**, ie

G-APDT	Comet 4	ex XA-NAB, G-APDT. Stored.
G-AVFG	Trident 2E	ex BA, BEA. CoA expired 2/ 7/85. Ground school airframe.
G-AWZK	Trident 3B-101	ex BA, BEA. CoA expired 14/10/86. Training airframe.

NORTHOLT
Spitfire XVI TE476 had left the gate by 11/89 and moved to **Booker** in readiness for shipping to the USA. It was replaced by :
MH777"+   Spitfire replica   gate guardian.

ORPINGTON
(On the A224 in south east London) The Auster 3 is still stored in the area.
G-AHLI   Auster 3   ex Rush Green, NJ911. CoA expired 26/4/73. Stored.

PECKHAM RYE
The compiler takes it all back.... **W&R11** described the location here as a scrapyard. Not so, it was somebody's garden! Both aircraft mentioned have gone, but are believed to have been Vampire T.11 XE998 transitting from Biggin Hill and Whirlwind HAR.10 XP398 transitting from Shawbury, both bound for **Charlwood.**

RUISLIP
Vampire collector, restorer and historian **Alan Allen** works on his two nose sections here.

WM729	Vampire NF.10	ex Bingley, Bradford, Church Fenton, CNCS, 2 ANS, 25, 151. Nose.
WZ581	Vampire T.11	ex Bushey, Keevil, 3/4 CAACU, 229 OCU, 233 OCU, 25. Nose.

SOUTH KENSINGTON
Within **The Science Museum**, the National Aeronautical Collection remains much as it was, with plans for the refurbishing of the gallery still apparently some time away. The SE.5A has been restored, very pleasingly, to Savage Skywriting colours. Refer also to Wroughton, where the Transport Collection is kept.   The Museum is open daily 1000 to 1800 and Sundays 1430 to 1800. Contact, The Science Museum, South Kensington, London SW7 2DD. Telephone 071 938 8000.

G-EBIB	SE.5A	ex Hendon, Savage Skywriting, F939. CoA expired 6/6/35.
G-AAAH	DH.60G Moth	CoA expired 23/12/30. 'Jason'. Amy Johnson's aircraft.
G-ANAV	Comet 1A	ex CF-CUM. Nose section only.
G-ATDD	Beagle 206-1	ex Leeds-Bradford. Nose section only.
G-ATTN	Piccard HAB	basket and burner. 'Red Dragon'. See also Hayes.

G-BBGN		Cameron A-375 HAB	gondola only. 'Daffodil II'.
G-9-185		Hunter F.6	ex Kingston-upon-Thames, Dutch AF N-250. Nose section only.
OO-BFH		Piccard Gas	gondola only.
304	BAPC 62	Cody Biplane	with the Museum since 1913.
D7560		Avro 504K	ex Waddon.
J8067		Pterodactyl 1	ex Yeovil, Farnborough.
L1592		Hurricane I	ex 615, 56.
P9444		Spitfire IA	ex Sydenham, 53 OTU, 61 OTU, 58 OTU, 72.
S1595		Supermarine S.6B	ex RAFHSF. Schneider Trophy winner 1931.
W4041/G		Gloster E.28/39	ex Farnborough.
AP507		Cierva C.30A	ex Halton, Sydenham, 76 MU, 5 MU, 529, 1448 Flt, Duxford Calibration Flt, RAE, G-ACWP.
EE416		Meteor III	ex Martin Baker. Nose.
KN448		Dakota IV	ex Ottawa, RCAF, 436, 10, 44-76586. Nose.
VX185	7631M	Canberra B.8	ex makers. Nose.
XN344	8018M	Skeeter AOP.12	ex Middle Wallop, 654, 652.
XP505		Gnat T.1	ex RAE Bedford, MinTech, Dunsfold, CFS.
		Short Bros Gas	balloon basket.
		Airship No 17	'Beta II'. Gondola only.
210/16	B '56	Fokker E.III	captured 8/4/16. Stripped airframe.
100509		Fa 330A-1	ex Farnborough. In store at the Museum.
191316		Me 163B-1a Komet	ex Halton, 6 MU, Farnborough, Husum, II/JG.400.
442795	B'199	Fi 103 (V-1)	
BAPC 50		Roe No 1 Triplane	Roe's second, first flown 13/7/09.
BAPC 51		Vickers Vimy IV	Alcock and Brown's trans-Atlantic machine, 1919.
BAPC 53		Wright Flyer rep	Hatfield-built.
BAPC 54		JAP-Harding Mono	Bleriot-based.
BAPC 55		Antoinette	1909 model.
BAPC 57		Pilcher Hawk rep	
BAPC 124		Lilienthal	replica, built by the Museum.

SOUTH LAMBETH

The major rework of the Imperial War Museum was completed and the building officially re-opened on 4/11/89. The new aviation gallery offers excellent light and dramatically presented airframes, several new to Lambeth. The Camel, the Spitfire, the Lancaster and the V-1 did not emigrate during the restoration work, all the others arrived back on site by 6/89. It need not be said that the IWM also operates the huge Duxford complex! The Museum is open 1000 to 1800 daily. Contact : Imperial War Museum, Lambeth Road, London SE1 6HZ. Tel: 071 735 8922.

2699+	RAF BE.2c	ex Duxford, South Lambeth, 192, 51, 50.
N6812	Camel 2F1	ex 'F4043'. Culley's aircraft.
R6915	Spitfire I	ex Cardiff, RNDU, 57 OTU, 61 OTU, 609.
DV372	Lancaster I	ex 1651 CU, 467. SOC 4/1/45. Nose.
PN323+	Halifax A.VII	ex Duxford, South Lambeth, Duxford, Staverton, Radlett, Standard Telephones, HP. SOC 28/5/48. Nose.
120235+	He 162A-1	ex Duxford, South Lambeth, Cranwell, Brize Norton, Farnborough AM.68, JG.1, Leck.
733682+	Fw 190A-8	ex Duxford, South Lambeth, Biggin Hill, Cranwell, Brize Norton, Farnborough AM.75.
01120+	MiG 15bis	ex Hendon, Middlesborough, Polish AF.
472258"+	P-51D-25-NA Mustang	ex Duxford, RCAF 9246, USAAF 44-73979.
+	A6M Zero	ex Duxford, South Lambeth. Cockpit.
BAPC 198	Fi 103 (V-1)	omitted from W&R11.

SOUTHALL

(On the A4020 south east of Uxbridge) At the **Technical College** the instructional airframes remain as they were.

G-AREF	Aztec 250	ex Biggin Hill. CoA expired 17/1/86.
G-ARMN	Cessna 175B	ex N8294T. CoA expired 16/12/77.
G-MBTY	American Eagle	bought from new 1982.

WB763	G-BBMR Chipmunk T.10	ex 2 FTS, 4 FTS, AOTS, 1 ITS, 1 AEF, Bri UAS, 3 AEF, AAC, 652, Odiham SF, 24 RFS, 14 RFS.
XD536	7734M Vampire T.11	ex Reading, Oakington, 5 FTS, Geilenkirchen SF, 234.
XL763	Skeeter AOP.12	ex Wroughton, 15/19 Hussars, HQ 1 Wing, 654.

STAINES
The former Saudi Arabian Auster is thought still held in store here.

| VP-KKO | J/5G Autocar | ex Saudi Arabia, AP-AHK, VP-KKO. Stored. |

STANMORE PARK
(On the A4140 in north west London) Still on the parade ground is the Javelin.

| XA553 | 7470M Javelin FAW.1 | ex Yatesbury, Gloster. |

SUNBURY-ON-THAMES
In Fordbridge Road, Lower Sunbury, **Sunbury Salvage Company** still show off their anonymous Adams-Wilson Hobbycopter.

| | Hobbycopter | displayed. |

UXBRIDGE
(On the A4020 south of the town) At the RAF base, Spitfire RW382/8075M moved to Braintree 26/8/88. In return they got a plastic one.

| BR600"+ | Spitfire replica | gate guardian. |

WEST DRAYTON
(Off the A4/M4 north of London Airport) The **London Air Traffic Control Centre** proudly shows off its immaculately painted and displayed Lightning.

| XN769 | 8402M Lightning F.2 | ex Leconfield, 92, 19, 92. |

WOOLWICH
At the **Royal Artillery Institution,** the Museum located at The Rotunda displays an Auster AOP.9 and a Canberra B.6 in the grounds. Details from : The Old Royal Military Academy, Woolwich, London SE18 4JJ. Telephone 081 854 5533.

| WH952 | Canberra B.6 | ex RAE Bedford, BAe Warton, RAE. |
| XR271 | Auster AOP.9 | ex Larkhill, St Athan, Middle Wallop. |

Greater Manchester

ALTRINCHAM
Held in the area is **Alan Ellis's** Vampire T.11 pod.

| XD595 | Vampire T.11 | ex Woodford, Chester, St Athan, 1 FTS, Oakington SF, 7 FTS, 4 FTS. Pod only. |

ASHTON-UNDER-LYNE
247 Squadron ATC maintain their Chipmunk T.10 PAX in Darnton Road.

| WP927 | 8216M Chipmunk T.10 PAX | ex Woodvale, Crosby, Hamble G-ATJK, MCS, Oxf UAS, Lon UAS, Detling SF, Lon UAS. |

BARTON AERODROME
As the aircraft population of this delightful airfield continues to rise, so does the number of attendant **W&R** candidates. A dramatic sight on the airfield for some time was the unfortunate Keenair Warbirds Broussard G-BKPU which suffered a spectacular forced-landing on the M62 nearby on 7/6/88. The hulk was brought to the airfield and stayed until at least 9/89 before moving on - destination unknown.

Across at the University hangar, the decision was taken during late 1988 to dispose
of Vampire T.11 XD434. It moved to Wisbech during 3/89.

G-APVV	Mooney M.20A	ex N8164E. Crashed 11/1/81. Stored.
G-ASAV+	MS.880B Rallye Club	CoA expired 20/1/89. Stored by 4/89.
G-AXWE	Cessna F.150K	damaged 2/1/76. Hulk, poor state.
G-AYWD+	Cessna 182N	ex N8928G. CoA expired 6/6/88. Stored.
G-BJXB+	Slingsby T.67A	CoA expired 6/11/88. Held for spares.

DUKINFIELD
Restoration of the Anson nose previously held in the mill at Hadfield, moved here
during 1989.

VP519+	G-AVVR Anson C.19/2	ex Hadfield, Stockport, Peel Green, Cosford, Wigan, Irlam, Shawbury, FCCS, 11 GCF, MCS, 31, Malta CF, TCDU. Nose.

LEVENSHULME
(On the A6 south east of Manchester) Unique in the world of ATC units, **1940
Squadron** in St Oswald's Road keep a Tiger Moth fuselage.

N6720	7014M Tiger Moth	ex Kings Heath, West Bromwich, 9 AFTS, 2 GS, Lon UAS, Queens UAS, 11 RFS, 11 EFTS, 4 CPF, 206. Fuselage.

MANCHESTER
The Aviation Gallery of the **Museum of Science and Industry** continues to prosper
with the long-awaited addition of TAC's Dragon Rapide coming down from East
Fortune. To make way for this, Pioneer CC.1 XL703/8034M moved to Cosford 4/89.
Viewing from within the superb building is excellent and redesigned walkways allow
for closer inspection and different photographic angles. The support displays are
excellent, with a series of wind tunnel models being particularly fascinating.
Basil Carlin and team have finished their restoration of the TAC Avian and picked
up a Scania Transport Trust award as proof of its excellence. Their next project
is the long-hidden Avro 504K G-ABAA/H2311 which arrived from Henlow 2/89. The
workshop is not generally available to public inspection. A major exhibition on
space flight is due to be opened during the summer of 1990. The Museum is open
every day from 1030 to 1700 including Bank Holidays but excluding December 23-25.
Contact : Museum of Science and Industry, Liverpool Road, Castlefield, Manchester
M3 4JP. Telephone 061 832 2244.

G-EBZM	Avian IIIA	ex Higher Blagdon, Peel Green, Lymm, Liverpool, Huyton, Manchester Airport, Hesketh Park, Giro Aviation, Merseyside Aero Club. CoA expired 20/1/38. TAC loan. See notes above.
G-ABAA+	H2311 Avro 504K	ex Henlow, Nash Collection. CoA expired 11/4/39. Arrived 2/89. Under restoration - see notes above.
G-ADAH+	Dragon Rapide	ex East Fortune, Peel Green, Booker, Allied Airways. CoA expired 9/6/47. Arrived 7/4/89. TAC loan.
G-APUD	Bensen B.7M	ex Firbeck, Nostell Priory, Wigan, Biggin Hill. CoA exp 27/9/60. TAC loan.
G-AWZP	Trident 3B-101	ex Heathrow, BA, BEA. Nose section.
T9707"	8378M Magister I	ex Hendon, G-AKKR, T9708, 51 MU, 16 EFTS, 239. CoA exp 10/4/65.
BL614	4354M Spitfire Vb	ex St Athan, 'AB871', Colerne, Credenhill, 118, 64, 222, 242, 611.
WB440	Firefly AS.6	ex Heaton Chapel, Newton-le-Willows, Salford, Failsworth, Anthorn, 812. Forward fuselage. On loan from Colin Waterworth.
WG763	7816M EE P.1A	ex Henlow, RAE Farnborough, RAE Bedford, A&AEE, EE Warton.
WP270	8598M Eton TX.1	ex Henlow, Hendon, 27 MU, 61 GCF.
WR960	8772M Shackleton AEW.2	ex Cosford, 8, 205, A&AEE, 210, 42, 228.
WT619	7525M Hunter F.1	ex Henlow, St Athan, 233 OCU, 222, 43. Partially sectioned.
WZ736	7868M Avro 707A	ex Waddington, Cosford, Finningley, RAE Bedford, A&AEE, Avros.
XG454	8366M Belvedere HC.1	ex Henlow, Abingdon, A&AEE, makers, Old Sarum, B'dere Trials Unit.
XL824	8021M Sycamore HR.14	ex Henlow, Wroughton, CFS, 1564 Flt, 103, 284.
8485M	B'98 Ohka II	ex Henlow, Cottesmore.
100549	Fa 330A-1	ex Liverpool Airport, Liverpool, Blackpool, Lavenham, Hullavington, Biggin Hill, Farnborough. MASL loan.

J-1172	8487M Vampire FB.6	ex Cosford, Colerne, Dubendorf, Swiss Air Force.
BAPC 6	Roe Triplane rep	ex London, Southend, Irlam, Peel Green, Old Warden, Woodford. TAC.
BAPC 89	Cayley Glider rep	ex Hendon, Lasham.
BAPC 175	Volmer VJ-23	ex Old Warden.
BAPC 182	Wood Ornithopter	ex Hale. Stored.

MANCHESTER AIRPORT
(Or Ringway) The three aircraft mentioned in **W&R11** steadfastly hold on to an existence here. Since 1988 an engineless BAC 1-11 has been held in open store outside the Dan-Air area. Another sign of the times was the dismantling of former Dan-Air HS.748 1/105 G-BEKC after a period of external storage here, during the spring of 1989. It moved through to Woodford 4/89.

G-ARPK	Trident 1C	ex BA, BEA. CoA expired 17/5/82. Fire service.
G-BAWV	Aztec 250B	ex Woodvale, G-BAWU ntu, 9J-REL, N5255Y. CoA expired 11/10/85. With the fire crews by 7/88.
G-BCCJ	AA-5 Traveler	accident 2/1/76. External store.
5N-AOK+	BAC 1-11-320AZ	ex Okada Air, G-BKAW, BCAL, G-AVBY, Laker. Arrived 11/2/88. Open store.

MOSTON
(On the B6393 north of Manchester) The Cherokee is still in use as an instructional airframe with **North Manchester Community College**, Moston Centre, Ashley Lane. Elsewhere in the area, an Ekin Airbuggy is stored as a source of spares for the airworthy G-AXYZ (correcting **W&R11**).

| G-ATOO | Cherokee 140 | ex Cark. CoA expired 24/9/84. Instructional airframe. |
| G-AXYX | Ekin Airbuggy | damaged 30/7/83. Spares for G-AXYZ. |

ROYTON
(On the A627 north of Oldham) In Park Lane, **1855 Squadron ATC** maintain their two aircraft. The Vampire is mounted on a moving rig. Both are 'parented' at Sealand.

| WS726 | 7960M Meteor NF.14 | ex Kemble, 1 ANS, 2 ANS, 25. |
| XK637 | Vampire T.11 | ex Woodford, Chester, St Athan, 4 FTS, 7 FTS. |

STOCKPORT
Kept in the area for use by **162 Squadron ATC** as an instructional airframe is John Mott's Jodel DR.100.

| G-AXUY | SAN DR.100A | ex F-BIZI. Crashed 3/9/78. Stored. |

TIMPERLEY
(On the A560 east of Altrincham) **145 Squadron ATC** keep their Chippax here.

| WD318 | 8207M Chipmunk T.10 PAX | ex Chorlton, Sealand, Wrexham, Shawbury, Dur UAS, Queens UAS, Acklington, Ouston SF, 19 RFS. |

WIGAN
TAC continue to wind down their store here, centralising their operation on Warmingham and the Manchester Museum of Science and Industry. Auster 6A G-ARDX moved through to Warmingham 26/6/88. Cadet TX.1 RA854 was due to join The Helicopter Collection at Stoke-on-Trent early in 1990, but, as **W&R** went to press, had yet to move.

G-AFIU	LA.4 Minor	ex Peel Green.
RA854	Cadet TX.1	ex RAFGSA, Woodvale, 41 GS.
BAPC 17	Woodhams Sprite	ex Irlam. Incomplete.
BAPC 60	Murray Helicopter	ex Salford.

WOODFORD
Hard work and patience by the **British Aerospace Avro Aircraft Restoration Society** could well see their immaculate Avro XIX rolled out, if not flown, during 1990. Work on the Vulcan continues, although the decision has been made not to fly her. These aircraft are not on public view, but general enquiries about the Society can be made to : Harry Holmes, British Aerospace plc, Woodford, Cheshire SK7 1QR. The

unfortunate Charles Church Lancaster KB976 was removed, initially to <u>Exeter</u> during
10/88. The aircraft is now awaiting a rebuild decision and it's held at Cranfield
and Thurleigh. HS.748-2A/LFD TJ-CCD was sold to Canadian operator Air Inuit as C-
FDOX during late 1988. Uncompleted HS.748-2B c/no 1808 moved to <u>Hatfield</u> 5/89 for
static testing. A former Dan-Air HS.748 arrived by road from Manchester Airport
during 4/89. The nose was despatched to Reflectone of Tampa, Florida, for use as
an ATP simular. The remainder sserves as a stress rig.

G-AHKX	Avro XIX Srs 2	ex Strathallan, Kemps Aerial Surveys, Treffield Aviation, Meridian Air Maps, Smiths Instruments. CoA exp 10/4/73. See notes.
G-BEKC+	HS.748 1-105	ex Manchester Airport, Dan-Air, LV-HHC, LV-PRJ, 'LV-PJR'. CoA expired 3/8/88. Arrived by road 4/89. Minus nose - see notes above. Stress rig.
c/no 06402	Comet 4	ex Nimrod development work. Fuselage. Stored.
c/no 1809	HS.748-2B	Set 290, uncompleted airframe. Stored.
XM603	Vulcan B.2	ex 44, 101, Wadd Wing, Scampton Wing, 9. See notes above.
XV148	Nimrod prototype	ex A&AEE, makers. Fatigue testing.
XV257	Nimrod MR.2	ex St Mawgan Wing, Kinloss Wing, 203, Kinloss Wing. Cat 4 at St Mawgan 3/6/84. Open store.
	Andover	test shell, ATP ground tests.

Merseyside

BIRKDALE
(On the A565 south west of Southport) A visit to Upper Aughton Road 11/89
confirmed the existence of **281 Squadron ATC**'s Chippax.

WG477	8362M Chipmunk T.10 PAX	ex Hamble G-ATDP, G-ATDI ntu, Marham SF, MECS, 114, Bri UAS, Abn UAS, 11 RFS, 2 BFTS, 25 RFS, Liv UAS, 25 RFS.

LIVERPOOL AIRPORT
(Or Speke) Amid much speculation about the size, shape and role of the Airport in
years to come, the essential nature of the **W&R** material here has changed
considerably. Two landmarks have gone. The fire crew's Viscount 802 G-AOJB was
removed by a scrap merchant during 1/89. It had surrendered not so much to the
firemen, more to the local kids! 'Maggie Mae', the Keenair Warbirds C-47A N54607
was auctioned during 1989, became G-BPMP and flew away to <u>Coventry Airport</u> for
restorative work where there are hopes to put it on the show circuit. The cache of
Nord 3202s continues to dwindle. G-BIZK/No 78 flew following restoration 15/12/88
and is now to be found in darkest Wales.. G-BIZJ/No 70 became G-BPMU and left
24/7/88. The recent re-registration of the third example may well indicate that it
is also to leave. With the addition of the SIPA from Chirk, that leaves :

G-AVWF	Cherokee 140	ex Caernarfon, PH-VRK, G-AVWF. CoA expired 23/5/81. Stored.
G-BDAO+	SIPA 901	ex Chirk, Winsford, F-BEPT. Crashed 20/6/76. Arrived 5/89 for restoration.
G-BRVA	Nord 3202	ex G-BIZL, Fort Lauderdale, N2255Y, FAF No 85 'AJG'. Stored.
G-OCME	Trislander	ex G-AYWI, G-51-262. Crashed 9/2/87. Spares.

MEOLS
Not far from the 'Railway Inn' can be found a Vampire in poor state in a garden.

WZ514	Vampire T.11	ex Irby, Bidston, Woodford, Chester, Shawbury, 5, 98.

WOODVALE
The local PAX trainer and the gate guardian are unchanged.

WA591	7917M Meteor T.7	ex St Athan CCAS, Kemble, CAW, 8 FTS, 5 FTS, CAW, 12 FTS, 215 AFS, 208 AFS, 203 AFS, 226 OCU, CFE. Gate guardian.
WG418	8209M Chipmunk T.10 PAX	ex Hamble, Jever SF, Lon UAS, 61 GCF, Qub UAS, Lon UAS, 3 BFTS, 16 RFS. 10 AEF trainer.

West Midlands

ALLESLEY
(On the A4114 north west of Coventry) **Carl Butler**'s store is unchanged.

G-AFHA	Mosscraft MA.1	uncompleted airframe, started 1938.
G-AFJV	Mosscraft MA.2	uncompleted airframe, started 1939.
G-AKUW	Super Ace 2	CoA expired 5/6/70. Under restoration.

BERKSWELL
(Between the A452 and the A45 west of Coventry) Careful and painstaking restoration continues on the Wicko at **Ken Woolley**'s workshop. The Dingbat hangs from the roof, awaiting its turn.

G-AFJA	Watkinson Dingbat	ex Headcorn. Crashed 19/5/75. Stored.
DR613 G-AFJB GM.1 Wicko		CoA expired 12/7/63. Under restoration.

BIRMINGHAM
As might be expected, the City of Birmingham dominates the references in the West Midlands. First off is the **Museum of Science and Industry** which, after many years of status quo with its airframes, loaned its Beaufighter nose to the Midland Air Museum at <u>Coventry Airport</u> during 1989. The Hurricane and Spitfire are still on display here. Open Monday to Saturday 0930 to 1700 and Sunday 1400 to 1700. Contact : Birmingham Museum of Science and Industry, Newhall Street, Birmingham B3 1RZ. Telephone 021 236 1022.

KX829	Hurricane IV	ex Loughborough, 631, 1606 Flt, 137.
ML427	6457M Spitfire IX	ex Castle Bromwich, St Athan, South Marston, Millfield, Hucknall, FLS, 3501 SU.

In Haslucks Green Road, Shirley, at Haslucks Green Barracks can be found the Navy establishment, the **Training Ship 'Gamecock'**. The Sea Cadets have a Wessex to play with. Also on the site is **492 Squadron ATC** who have a Canberra nose. Their anonymous Jet Provost nose section had gone by 11/89.

WT534	8549M Canberra PR.7	ex Halton, St Athan, 17. Nose.
XS886	A2685 Wessex HAS.1	ex Lee-on-Solent, Wroughton, 771.

There are two other ATC units to relate in the area. At the Barrows Lane TAVR Centre, Sheldon, **2030 Squadron** keep their Meteor. Over at Tile Cross, in Gressel Lane, are **2371 Squadron** with a Vampire pod.

WD646	8189M Meteor TT.20	ex 5 CAACU, 3/4 CAACU, CSE.
WZ450	Vampire T.11	ex Sealand, Wrexham, Woodford, Chester, Shawbury, RAFC, 233 OCU, 202 AFS. Pod.

The report given in **W&R11** relating to 202 Field Hospital in Kings Heath would seem to have been a red herring. Wessex HU.5 XS521 can be found at Saighton Camp, Cheshire. If it ever was here it was only a fleeting visit. Bensen G-ASLF and the anonymous example previously stored at a house in Shirley have moved on, destination/fate unknown.

BIRMINGHAM AIRPORT
(Or Elmdon) With MAPS's Humber-Bleriot still on show in the Terminal, the Trident with the firemen was joined by a Gulfstream I no less in 4/89.

G-AWZZ	Trident 3B-101	ex BA, BEA. CoA expired 21/5/84. Fire crews.
G-BOBX+	Gulfstream I	ex 9Q-CFK, N748M, N748MN, N73M, N706G, N777G. Flew in 29/12/87 for spares use. Towed to fire dump 12/4/89.
BAPC 9	Humber Monoplane	ex Yeovilton, Wroughton, Yeovilton, Coventry. MAM loan.

COVENTRY
In and around Coventry are several airframes of note. Restoration of Spitfire Tr 9 G-BMSB continues apace in the hands of **M S Bayliss** who is also restoring an anonymous Hurricane. **Roy Nerou** has a Chilton DW.1 stored. The **Mike Abbey** Flea has

not been physically confirmed for some considerable time and will find itself in
LOST! in **W&R13** unless we hear more. With **163 Squadron ATC** in Smith Street, the
anonymous Valiant nose had gone by 1988, leaving just the equally anonymous JP.

G-AFSV	Chilton DW.1A	CoA expired 12/7/72. Under restoration.
G-BMSB	Spitfire Tr IX	ex Stockbridge, Andover, G-ASOZ, Elstree, IAAC 158, Gormanston, 1 Fighter Squadron, G-15-171, RAF MJ627 29 MU, 441, 83 GSU. Restn.
+	Hurricane	under restoration. See notes above.
	Jet Provost T.3	ex Kemble. Fuselage number PAC/W/10169. Nose.
BAPC 27	HM.14 Pou du Ciel	ex Stratford. With some original parts. See above.

SOLIHULL

Abrasive Development Ltd should still have the Aztec for trials.

G-ASRE	Aztec 250C	ex Ipswich, Southend. CoA expired 12/4/81.

STONNALL

(On the A452 south east of Brownhills) Stored here is a sorry-looking Horizon.

G-AYOL	Horizon 180	ex St John, N3788, F-BNQU. CoA expired 29/6/83. Poor state.

SUTTON COLDFIELD

Another location with several points of interest. While keeping his ever-expanding
collection of flying aircraft at Cosford, **Bob Mitchell** keeps his two Miles
restoration projects in the area. **495 Squadron ATC's** Vampire T.11 XD602/7737M,
offered for tender 7/87, moved briefly to Southall 6/88 and was then exported. The
Scout is believed to still be kept at **St George's Barracks.**

G-AEUJ	Whitney Straight	ex Marple, East Midlands, Bournemouth. CoA expired 4/6/70.
G-AFRZ	Monarch	ex Shipdham, G-AIDE, W6463, Kemble, 10 GCF, FTCCF, 13 EFTS, G-AFRZ. CoA expired 29/6/70.
XR777"	XT625 Scout AH.1	ex 'XR625', Middle Wallop, TAD625.

Norfolk

BINHAM

(North of the A148, south east of Wells-next-the-Sea) A Leopard Moth has been
stored here since circa 1985.

G-ACMN+	Leopard Moth	ex X9381, 9 GCF, Netheravon SF, 297, 7 AACU, 6 AACU, 24, G-ACMN. CoA expired 8/5/85. Stored.

COLTISHALL

Gate guardian Spitfire XVI SL542/8390M left by road 7/12/88 for St Athan and was
replaced by a plastic Hurricane. The other guardian, Lightning F.1A XM172/8427M,
was offered for tender 4/89 (total time 2,083 hours, last flown 9/74) and was
acquired by a collector and moved to storage in Southampton. Hunter FGA.9 XG254
was airlifted out by Chinook 24/4/90, going to Weybourne. Remembering that
Canberras are beasts of great tenacity, the 'destruction' of PR.3 WE173 in **W&R11**
was premature. It was still to be found on the dump during 2/89.

V7467"+	Hurricane replica	arrived 21/3/89, unveiled 9/6/89. Gate guardian.
WE173	8740M Canberra PR.3	ex Farnborough, 231 OCU, 39, RAE, 39, 69, 82. Dump. See notes.
WT745	8893M Hunter T.8C	ex St Athan, Shawbury, Kemble, FRADU, 764, Yeovilton SF, 14. Rear end of XL565. ASF.
XV747+	8979M Harrier GR.3	ex St Athan, Wittering, 233 OCU, 1, 4, 233 OCU. Arr 29/9/88. BDR.
XX109	8918M Jaguar GR.1	ex Warton, A&AEE. WLT.
XX734	8816M Jaguar GR.1	ex Abingdon, Indian AF JI014, XX734, 6, JOCU. Fuselage. BDR.

FAKENHAM
Restoration of the Terrier continues.
G-ASCH   Terrier 2   ex Hinton-in-the-Hedges, Enstone, VF565, 654, 12 ILF, 1912 Flt, 652.
                                CoA expired 20/7/81. Under restoration.

FELTHORPE
And here, the Nipper continues its restoration.
G-ARBG   Nipper II   crashed 16/5/84. Under rebuild.

GREAT YARMOUTH AIRFIELD
(Or North Denes) British International Helicopters used the main hangar here for
storage of three WG.30s (G-BKGD, G-KATE, G-OGAS) during 1988 until all of them
moved through for more of the same at Beccles.

KING'S LYNN
Listed in **MiniWrecks** under this heading were two Lightning T.5s and the nose
section of an F.6. These aircraft were in fact delivered ex Binbrook to
Narborough, Leicestershire – which see.

LUDHAM
During 1989 the former St Leonards Spitfire IX was joined by one of a similar mark
from Belgium. Exchanged for the Bristol F.2b rebuilt by Skysport (see under
Hatch), MK912 arrived on board a Belgian Air Force C-130H at Coltishall and moved
to here for restoration on behalf of the Historic Aircraft Collection, Jersey. The
composite Chipmunk restoration here has gone, destination unknown. The fate of Fi
156 Storch G-FIST is a little clearer. The engine and fuselage have certainly
left. The remainder of the aircraft is believed to be in the Swindon area.
MK912+ G-BRRA Spitfire IX   ex Saffraanberg, Belgium, Belgian AF SM-29, RNeth AF H-59, H-119,
                                RAF MK912, 84 GSU, 312. See notes above.

TE566   G-BLCK Spitfire IX   ex St Leonards-on-Sea, Israeli DF/AF 32, Czech AF, RAF TE566, 312.

MARHAM
Other than the addition of a retired Victor K.2 to the dump during 1/89, there has
been no change to the **W&R** airframes here.
WH863   8693M Canberra T.17   ex 360, RAE, IAM. BDR.
XA917   7827M Victor B.1   ex Wyton, 232 OCU, 15, 101, RAE, A&AEE. Cockpit. Dump.
XH560   Vulcan B.2   ex Waddington, 50, Wadd Wing, 27, Akrotiri Wing, Cott Wing, Wadd
                                Wing, Cott Wing, 230 OCU, 12, MoA, 230 OCU. Dump.
XH673   8911M Victor K.2   ex 57, Witt Wing, 139, MoA. Outside SHQ.
XL160   8910M Victor K.2   ex 57, 55, Witt Wing, 100, MoA. BDR.
XL192+   9024M Victor K.2   ex 57, Wittering Wing, 232 OCU, 100. Towed to dump 4/1/89.
XX947   8797M Tornado P.03   ex Warton. WLT.

NEATISHEAD
(In between the A149, A1062 and A151 north east of Norwich) Guarding the base is :
WK654   8092M Meteor F.8   ex Kemble, 85, CFE, AWFCS, 247.

NORWICH AIRPORT
(Or Horsham St Faith) The **City of Norwich Aviation Museum** plan extended opening
times during 1990 – enquiries to the address below will bring details. The
collection of aircraft is unchanged. Open on Sundays October to April 1000 to
dusk and May to September 1000 to 1700 and on Thursday evenings during June, July
and August from 1930 to dusk. Contact : City of Norwich Aviation Museum, Old
Norwich Road, Horsham St Faith, Norwich, Norfolk.
G-ASKK   Herald 211   ex Air UK, PP-ASU, G-ASKK, PI-C910, CF-MCK. CoA expired 19/5/85.
TX228   Anson C.19   ex Duxford, Crawley, WCS, TCCF, Old Sarum SF, SLAW, FCCS, SLAW,
                                Hucknall SF. Stored.
XD375   7887M Vampire T.11   ex Cleethorpes, Elsham Hall, Duxford, Winterbourne Gunner, St Athan,
                                4 FTS, 1 FTS, 3 CAACU, 73.
XL840   Whirlwind HAS.7   ex Sibson, Blackpool Airport, Fleetwood, Wroughton, 705, Brawdy SF,
                                Culdrose SF, 705, 820.

XM612		Vulcan B.2	ex 44, Wadd Wing, Scampton Wing, 9.
XP355	G-BEBC	Whirlwind HAR.10	ex Faygate, 8463M, 38 GCF, 21, MinTech, CFS.
XP458		Grasshopper TX.1	ex Fakenham area. On loan.
XP919	8163M	Sea Vixen FAW.2	ex Chertsey, Halton, 766, 899, A&AEE.
121		Mystere IVA	ex Sculthorpe, French AF.
16718		T-33A-5-LO	ex Sculthorpe, Turkish AF ntu, French AF, 51-6718.

On the **Airport** site itself, Herald 201 G-APWH and the remains of Varsity T.1 WJ907
gave up the ghost on the fire dump by late 1987, being replaced by G-AVEZ. From
around 7/88 Herald 213 G-AVPN was put into external store here, but joined BAF on
16/11/89.

G-AVEZ	Herald 210	ex Museum, Air UK, BIA, BUA, PP-ASW, G-AVEZ, HB-AAH. CoA expired 5/1/81. Fire dump.

OLD BUCKENHAM
(On the B1077 south of Attleborough) Going back to **W&R11**, the Pawnee frame that
left for 'Lincolnshire' in 8/87 was in fact G-BFEY, not G-AVXA. The fate of the
latter is unknown. **Jim Avis** had made Skeeter AOP.12 XL812/G-SARO airworthy again
by 8/89. J/1 Autocrat G-AIBM was under restoration from 1987. Jim completed work
on it by June 1989 when it flew again and is now based at White Waltham. By 8/87
Tiger Moth G-AODT was also receiving the restorative treatment. This was flying by
1988 and is based. Current situation here is as follows :

G-APOI		Skeeter 8	ex Llandegla, Inverness, Blackpool, Southampton. CoA expired 30/3/61. Spares for G-SARO.
G-BENL+		Pawnee 235D	ex Sutton Bank, N54893. Crashed 10/7/85. Arr by 10/87.
G-BMFG+		Dornier Do 27A-4	ex Wycombe Air Park, Martlesham Heath, Portuguese AF 3460, Luftwaffe AC+955. Arrived 22/5/89. For restoration.

RAVENINGHAM
Inspection here 9/89 found the place well and truly empty of airframes. Both of
the Stampes (G-AYDR and G-BEPF) are believed to have gone to the Warminster area.
The fate of composite J-3C-65 N30228 is unknown.

REYMERSTON HALL
Based here is the pioneering fleet of autogiros of **W/C Ken H Wallis**. The listing
of withdrawn machines has been extended in this issue, reflecting those that have
been genuinely out of use for some time. See also Swanton Morley.

G-ARRT+		Wallis WA-116/McC	CoA expired 26/5/83. Stored.
G-ATHL		Wallis WA-116/F	ex Bury St Edmunds. Damaged 5/3/85. Spares use.
G-AVJW+		Wallis WA-118/M	CoA expired 21/4/83. Stored.
G-AYVO+		Wallis WA-120 Srs 1	ex South Kensington, Reymerston Hall. CoA expired 31/12/78.
G-AZBU	XR246	Auster AOP.9	ex Shipdham, 7862M, Middle Wallop, Beagle, 651. Stored.
G-AZVA		Monsun 150FF	ex D-EAAQ ntu. CoA expired 3/3/83. Stored.
G-BAHH+		Wallis WA-121/McC	CoA expired 15/7/88. Stored.
G-BGKT	XN441	Auster AOP.9	ex Shipdham, Scarning, St Athan, Aden, Kenya. Stored.
G-BLIK+		Wallis WA-116/F/S	CoA expired 15/5/88. Stored.

SCULTHORPE
End of an era. F-100D-11-NA 42212 left by road for Upper Heyford 1/9/89.

SHIPDHAM
Here the Tiger Moth store and the dusty Twin Comanche are without change.

G-AYAF	Twin Comanche 160C	ex N8842Y. CoA expired 8/5/77. Stored.
G-BINH	Tiger Moth	ex VT-DOW, Indian AF HU488. Crashed 19/6/84. Rebuild.
VT-CZV	Tiger Moth	ex G-AISY, N6740, 7 EFTS, 11 EFTS, 18 ERFTS. Stored.
VT-DOU	Tiger Moth	ex Indian AF HU483. Stored.
VT-DOX	Tiger Moth	ex Madras, Indian AF HU492. Stored.
VT-DOY	Tiger Moth	ex Madras, Indian AF HU498. Stored.
VT-DOZ	Tiger Moth	ex Indian AF HU504. US Mail colours. Stored.
VT-DPA	Tiger Moth	ex Madras, Indian AF HU511. US Mail colours. Stored.
VT-DPB	Tiger Moth	ex Madras, Indian AF HU708. Stored.
VT-DPC	Tiger Moth	ex Indian AF 'HU187'. Stored.

VT-DPE		Tiger Moth	ex Indian AF HU858. Stored.
VT-DPH		Tiger Moth	ex Indian AF HU887. Stored.
N9191	G-ALND	Tiger Moth	ex Panshanger, 5 SoTT, 19 EFTS, Duxford SF, 6 CPF. Crashed 8/3/81, under rebuild.

SWANTON MORLEY
At the **Central Servicing Development Establishment** Buccaneer S.2A XV152/8776M was scrapped mid-1988 and was to be ultimately replaced by the former Bentley Priory Hunter. The plastic Spitfire initially intended for Wittering was 'planted' during 4/90. The cockpit section of Chipmunk T.10 WB626 has not been seen for some time, it probably followed airworthy G-BCXN to its new home at Tibenham.

G-BFIP		Wallbro Monoplane	CoA expired 22/4/82. Stored.
+		Spitfire replica	unveiled 4/90.
WJ775	8581M	Canberra B.6RC	ex 51, 192. CSDE.
XG290+	8711M	Hunter F.6	ex Bentley Priory, Halton, Laarbruch SF, A&AEE. Arr 2/90. CSDE.

THORPE ABBOTTS
(On the A143 east of Diss) The **100th Bomb Group Museum** in the tower of the former 8th Air Force base still exhibits the Carvair cockpit section.

| CF-EPV | | Carvair | ex Fritton Lake, Southend, EI-AMR, N88819, 42-72343. Cockpit. |

WATTON
Still guarding the gate the RAF station is the Meteor.

| WS807 | 7973M | Meteor NF.14 | ex Kemble, 1 ANS, 2 ANS. |

WEST RAYNHAM
And still on guard at the Bloodhound base is a 'Flat Iron'. On 1/5/90 it was joined by a 'JP' from Halton for crash rescue training.

| XH980 | 7867M | Javelin FAW.8 | ex Stafford, Shawbury, 41. |
| XM402+ | 8055AM | Jet Provost T.3 | ex Halton, Newton, Shawbury, 6 FTS, 2 FTS. Arrived 1/5/90. Crash rescue training. |

WEYBOURNE
(On the A149 west of Cromer) The **Muckleborough Collection** of armoured fighting vehicles added an exhibit that could broadly be described as an AFV on 24/4/90. A Chinook flew in a hitch-hiking Hunter from Coltishall. The collection is open Easter to October 1000 to 1700 daily and weekends only during the winter. Telephone : 026 370 608 or '210.

| XG254 | 8881M | Hunter FGA.9 | ex Coltishall, St Athan, 1 TWU, 2 TWU, TWU, 229 OCU, 54, HS, 54. Arrived (via Chinook) 24/4/90. |

Northamptonshire

EAST HADDON
(North of the A428 north west of Northampton) The .Brantly is still stored here.

| G-AVIP | | Brantly B.2B | CoA expired 19/11/81. Stored. |

HINTON-IN-THE-HEDGES
The hulk of Cessna F.150H G-AWCJ was nowhere to be seen at the strip 5/89.

KINGS CLIFFE
(South of the A47, west of Peterborough) The Stampe can still be found at the strip. **John Tempest** now has his teeth into a Condor rebuild. Spares-ship Nord 3202B G-BMBF came here 4/88 from Breighton, moved to France with airworthy G-BEFH.

| G-AVJH+ | | D.62 Condor | ex Mona. Crashed 31/7/83. Under restoration. |
| G-BEUS | | AIA SV-4C | ex Gransden, Long Marston, F-BKFK, F-DAFK, French military. |

NORTHAMPTON
Restoration of the Moth Minor continues as a long-term project here.

G-AFPR   Moth Minor   ex Woodley, X5122, Langham SF, 1 TTU, 5 OTU, 16, G-AFPR. CoA expired
                              15/4/56. Under rebuild.

NORTHAMPTON AIRPORT

(Or Sywell) With **Sloane Helicopters** resident, helicopters now dominate the listing
here, although the airfield also hangs on to its long-adopted Auster image. J/1N
Alpha G-AIGR moved out to <u>Newark</u> by 10/88. By this time, brother G-AIZZ was in
residence for the completion of its restoration. It was flying by 7/89. Cessna
175A G-ARFG was flying by 4/88

G-AWRA   Pup 100   ex ZK-CYP ntu, G-35-020. Damaged 12/68. Stripped fuselage, in shed.
G-AYIA+   Hughes 369HS   Damaged 17/6/88. First noted 8/88. For spares.
G-BKJR   Hughes 269C   ex VR-HHT, VR-HHM, N8969F. Crashed 13/7/84. Spares.
G-HEWS+   Hughes 369D   damaged 5/12/87. Wreck. First noted 5/88.

SPANHOE

Much to his delight, the compiler has noticed his local airfield come back to life
with **Windmill Aviation** establishing a maintenance facility at the former 9th Air
Force base. Major project is the restoration of a former Indian Air Force Tempest
II for a local consortium.

G-AJDY+   J/1 Autocrat   ex Cossall, Sherburn. CoA expired 9/7/71. Under rebuild.
G-BNJJ+   Cessna 152 II   ex Nayland, Cranfield. Damaged 18/5/88. Hulk.
HA564+   Tempest II   ex Chichester, Indian AF, RAF MW376. Restoration.

WELLINGBOROUGH

Widgeon G-ANLW moved to <u>Blackpool Airport</u> for restoration by Jim Wilkie. The
Hiller remains in store in the area. **Dave Pope** moved here from Reading early in
1988. Tobago fuselage G-BGTB arrived 5/9/88 and Chipmunk T.10 WK626/8213M (note
amended identity) arrived 25/8/88. On 1/5/89 the cockpit section of Chipmunk 22 G-
AOSN arrived from 'Surrey'. Then came the decision to emigrate to Malta and the
airframes had to be disposed of. The Tobago was scrapped 10/89. The two Chipmunks
moved to <u>Holbeach</u> 9/89.

G-APKY   Hiller UH-12B   ex Northampton Airport, PH-NFL. CoA expired 7/5/74. Stored.

Northumberland

BOULMER

At the RAF base the Lightning is still proudly displayed.
XP745   8453M Lightning F.3   ex Leconfield, 29, 56.

CURROCK HILL

Still acting as a source of spares, at the gliding site, the Chipmunk lives in the
rafters of the hangar.
WK549   Chipmunk T.10   ex Kemble, BFWF, 651, 657, 63 GCF, 9 RFS, 5 BFTS. Stored.

OTTERBURN RANGES

(On the A696 north of Newcastle-on-Tyne) The exact status of airframes on the
ranges here is always open to doubt. What is known is that two former Binbrook
Lightning F.3s arrived during 4/88. The previous inmates are listed here with the
usual warning that they may well have long since passed on. Another complication
can be found under Thirsk.

XF386   8707M Hunter F.6A   ex Coltishall, Kemble, Laarbruch SF, 229 OCU, 92, 65.
XG264   8715M Hunter FGA.9   ex Brawdy, 2 TWU, TWU, 229 OCU, 58, 45, 54. Rear fuselage of XF445.
XP515   8614M Gnat T.1   ex Wattisham, Kemble, 4 FTS, CFS, 4 FTS, CFS, 4 FTS.
XP694+   Lightning F.3   ex Binbrook, 5-11 pool, LTF, 5-11 pool, LTF, 5, 56, 29, 11, 29,
                                    Wattisham TFF, 29, A&AEE, BAC. Arrived 4/88.
XP702+   Lightning F.3   ex Binbrook, 5, 56, 29, 56, 74. Arrived 4/88.
XS594   Andover C.1   ex Kemble, 84, St Athan Apps, A&AEE.
XS601   Andover C.1   ex Kemble, A&AEE, 46, Andover CU.

Nottinghamshire

BALDERTON
(On the A1 south east of Newark-on-Trent) In the dead and decaying yard previously used by **A1 Commercial Vehicle Sales,** the Lightning rots.
XN728   8546M Lightning F.2A   ex Coningsby, 92.

COSSALL
By 5/88 J/1 Autocrat G-AJDY had left here. It turned up eventually at <u>Spanhoe.</u>

LANGAR
Giving good service with the parachute club here is an exit-trainer Cessna.
G-BATD   Cessna U.206F   ex Isle of Man, Sibson, Shobdon, N60204. Crashed 5/4/80.

MANSFIELD
384 Squadron ATC keep a Canberra nose at their headquarters.
WT507   8548M Canberra PR.7   ex Halton 8131M, St Athan, 31, 17, 58, A&AEE, 58, 527, 58. Nose.

MISSON
The famous **Lou Jackson** yard gave up its long held (and long omitted from this tome) Meteor nose, it moving on to <u>Hemswell.</u>

NEWARK-ON-TRENT
Cliff Baker's famous store of Austers is largely undisturbed. His own J/1N Alpha G-AJAS is airworthy again. New addition is the original frame of J/1N Alpha G-AIGR from Northampton Airport.

G-AIGR+	J/1N Alpha	ex Northampton Airport, original fuselage frame. Arr by 10/88.
G-ALJI	J/1N Alpha	ex East Midlands, Elsham Hall, Goxhill, Kirmington. Damaged 12/1/75.
G-AIKE	Auster 5	ex Portsmouth, NJ728. Crashed 1/9/65.
G-AKOT	Auster 5	ex North Denes, TJ433, 657. Crashed 9/9/62.
G-AKWT	Auster 5	ex East Midlands, Elsham Hall, Goxhill, Stroxton Lodge, Tollerton, MT360. Crashed 7/8/48.
G-ALNV	Auster 5	ex Nottingham, Leicester, RT578. CoA expired 4/7/50.
G-AMUJ	J/5F Aiglet Trn	ex East Midlands, Winthorpe. Crashed 8/6/60.
G-ANHW	Auster 5D	ex Shipdham, TJ320, 664. CoA expired 9/3/70.
G-ANHX	Auster 5D	ex Leicester, TW519, 661, A&AEE. Crashed 28/3/70.
G-AOCP	Auster 5	ex TW462, 666. Damaged 4/70. Under rebuild.
G-ARGB	Auster 6A	ex Waddington, VF635, 662, 1901 Flt. CoA expired 21/6/74.
G-ARGI	Auster 6A	ex Chirk, Heathfield, VF530, 661. CoA expired 4/7/76.
G-AROJ	Airedale	ex Leicester, Thorney, HB-EOC, G-AROJ. CoA expired 8/1/76.
G-ARTM	Terrier 1	ex Chirk, WE536, 651, 657, Schwechat SF. Damaged 6/70.
G-ASWF	Airedale	ex Leicester. CoA expired 27/4/83.
EC-AXR	Auster 4	ex Shoreham, Spain, G-ANHU, MT255.
F-BBSO	Auster 5	ex Taunton, G-AMJM, TW452, 62 GCF. Frame only.
c/no 3705	Auster D.6/180	ex White Waltham, Rearsby. Frame only.
c/no 608	Terrier 2	ex White Waltham, Rearsby. Frame only.

NEWTON
The dog training Varsity T.1 WL627/8488M was put up for tender 12/88 and moved to <u>Hull.</u> It was replaced by a Hunter T.7 from Cosford. (Do the dogs notice the difference?) On the dump, the remains of Hunter F.2 WN901/7543M had expired by mid-1988. Current situation :
WT694   7510M Hunter F.1   ex Debden, 229 OCU, DFLS, 54. Gate guardian.
XL623+ 8770M Hunter T.7   ex Cosford, 1 TWU, 74, 19, 1, 43, 92, 208, 65. Arrived 4/88.
XN641   8865M Jet Provost T.3 ex Shawbury, 1 FTS, RAFC, 3 FTS. Fire dump.

NOTTINGHAM AIRPORT
(Or Tollerton) Another airfield that may well become a housing estate.... The

Auster is still stored in the main hangar.
G-AGVJ   J/1N Alpha   CoA expired 30/8/64. Fuselage. Stored.

SOUTH SCARLE
(In between the A46 and the A1133 south west of Lincoln) Rallye G-AZEE's original
fuselage is still stored at the strip here.
G-AZEE   MS.880B Rallye   ex Shipdham, F-BKKA. Original fuselage. Stored.

STAPLEFORD
(On the A453 south west of Nottingham) Tastefully camouflaged, **1360 Squadron ATC's**
Vampire is to be found in Cliff Hill Avenue.
XD463   8023M Vampire T.11   ex St Athan, CATCS, 3/4 CAACU, 5 FTS, 7 FTS.

SYERSTON
Sea Prince T.1 WP314/8634M was put up for tender 12/88 and was removed by road to
Hull 18/2/89. **Central Gliding School** have three demonstration airframes allocated
to them here, for possible preservation.
WZ791   8944M Grasshopper TX.1   ex Halton, High Wycombe, Hove.
XE799   8943M Cadet TX.3   ex CGS.
XN185   8942M Sedburgh TX.1   ex CGS, 643 VGS, 4 MGSP, 633 VGS, 635 VGS.

WINTHORPE
(On the A46 north east of Newark-on-Trent) On 11/4/90 (the very day these words
were going into the W/P) the **Newark Air Museum** celebrated the completion of their
prestigious display hangar with the 'roll in' of Safir 56321/G-BKPY. Now with a
well appointed entrance hall and shop, well presented artefact display and an
engine hall, Newark has very much come of age and offers a major attraction to
aviation 'buffs' and the general public alike. There have been several new
exhibits, most important being the acquisition of the Venom NF.3 from the RAF
Museum store at Henlow. Vampire T.11 WZ553 arrived from South Wigston 19/3/89 but
was acquired by a collector and moved to Lichfield 1/90. The Museum is open April
to October Monday to Friday 1000 to 1700, Saturday 1300 to 1700 and Sundays 1000 to
1800. November to March, Sundays only 1000 to dusk. All buildings are available
to the disabled, as are the toilets. Contact : Mick Smith, Curator, Newark Air
Museum, 35 Queen Street, Balderton, Newark, Notts, NG24 3NS. Museum telephone :
0636 707170.

G-AHRI+	Dove 1	ex Long Marston, East Kirkby, Tattershall, Little Staughton, 4X-ARI, G-AHRI. Arrived by 7/89.
G-AHMP	Proctor II	ex Honiton Clyst, BV631, Filton, Bristol, 758. Centre section.
G-ANXB	Heron 1	ex Biggin Hill, Fairflight, BEA Scottish, G-5-14. CoA expired 25/3/79. Under restoration.
VH-UTH	Monospar ST-12	ex Australia. Stored.
KF532	Harvard IIB	ex 781, 799, 727, 799, 758. Cockpit section.
TG517	Hastings T.5	ex 230 OCU, SCBS, BCBS, 202, 53, 47.
VL348 G-AVVO	Anson C.19	ex Southend, Shawbury, 22 GCF, 24 GCF, Colerne SF, 62 GCF, HCMSU, Reserve Command CF.
VR249 G-APIY	Prentice T.1	ex 1 ASS, RAFC. CoA expired 18/3/67.
VT229	7151M Meteor F.4	ex Duxford, Colerne, 12 FTS, 209 AFS, 207 AFS, 616, Lubeck SF.
VZ608	Meteor FR.9(mod)	ex Hucknall, Shoreham, MoS, Rolls-Royce. RB.108 test-bed.
VZ634	8657M Meteor T.7	ex Wattisham, 5 MU, MoA, Leeming SF, Stradishall SF, 41, 141, 609, 247.
WF369	Varsity T.1	ex 6 FTS, AE&AEOS, AES, 2 ANS, 201 AFS.
WH904	Canberra T.19	ex Cambridge, 7, 85, West Raynham TFF, 228 OCU, 35, 207.
WK277	7719M Swift FR.5	ex Cosford, Leconfield, 2.
WM913	8162M Sea Hawk FB.3	ex Fleetwood, Sealand, Culdrose A2510, Abbotsinch, 736.
WR977	8186M Shackleton MR.3/3	ex Finningley, 203, 42, 206, 203, 42, 201, 206, 201, 220.
WS692	7605M Meteor NF.12	ex Cranwell, Henlow, 72, 46, 38 MU, 33 MU.
WS739	7961M Meteor NF.14	ex Misson, Church Fenton, Kemble, 1 ANS, 2 ANS, 25.
WT933	7709M Sycamore 3	ex Sutton-in-Ashfield, Strensall, Halton, G-ALSW ntu.
WV606	7622M Provost T.1	ex Halton, 1 FTS.

WV787	8799M	Canberra B.2/8	ex Abingdon, A&AEE. Sapphire test-bed and other trials.
WW217		Sea Venom FAW.21	ex Cardiff-Wales, Ottershaw, Culdrose, Yeovilton, ADS, 891, 890.
WX905+	7458M	Venom NF.3	ex Henlow, Hendon, Yatesbury, 27 MU, 23. Arrived late 1989.
XD515	7998M	Vampire T.11	ex Misson, Linton-on-Ouse, 3 FTS, 7 FTS, 1 FTS, 5 FTS, 206 AFS.
XD593		Vampire T.11	ex Woodford, Chester, St Athan, 8 FTS, CFS, FWS, 5 FTS, 4 FTS.
XE317		Sycamore HR.14	ex Portsmouth, CFS, G-AMWO ntu.
XH992	7829M	Javelin FAW.8	ex Cosford, Shawbury, 85.
XJ560	8142M	Sea Vixen FAW.2	ex RAE Bedford, Farnborough, Halton, 893, 899, 892, 890.
XL149	7988M	Beverley C.1	ex Finningley, 84, 30, 84, 242 OCU. Cockpit section.
XL764	7940M	Skeeter AOP.12	ex Nostell Priory, Rotherham, 'Wallop, Arborfield, MoA, 'Wallop.
XM594		Vulcan B.2	ex 44, Scampton Wing, 617, 27.
XM685		Whirlwind HAS.7	ex Panshanger area, Elstree, Luton, G-AYZJ ntu, Fleetlands, Lee-on-Solent, 771, 'Ark Royal' Ship's Flt, 847, 848.
XN511+		Jet Provost T.3	ex Blackpool Airport, Kemble, CFS, 1 FTS, CFS. Nose. Arr 4/89.
XN819	8205M	Argosy C.1	ex Finningley, Shawbury, Benson Wing, 105, MoA. Cockpit section.
XN964		Buccaneer S.1	ex Bruntingthorpe, East Midlands, Brough, Pershore, 807. Amends identity quoted in W&R11.
XP226	A2667	Gannet AEW.3	ex Lee-on-Solent, Southwick, Lee, Lossiemouth, Ilchester, 849.
XS417+		Lightning T.5	ex Binbrook, LTF, 5, 11, 5, 11, LTF, 56, 23, 11, 23, 226 OCU. Arrived 5/9/88.
XT200		Sioux AH.1	ex Middle Wallop.
83		Mystere IVA	ex Sculthorpe, French AF.
19036		T-33A-1-LO	ex Sculthorpe, French AF.
42223		F-100D-16-NA	ex Sculthorpe, French AF.
56321	G-BKPY	Safir	ex Norwegian AF. See notes above.
BAPC 20		Lee Richards rep	ex 'Those Magnificent Men'. Dismantled.
BAPC 183		Zurowski ZP.1	ex Burton-on-Trent. Homebuilt helicopter, unflown.

Oxfordshire

ABINGDON

Continuing the evolution started in **W&R11**, the listing for RAF Abingdon is now as one list, without sub-headings. Still working hard on Jaguars, the **Abingdon Maintenance Unit** also works on Harriers and Hawks. The unit's storage role for several years, looking after mothballed VC-10s will shortly be coming to an end. Six of the seven Super VC-10s currently held will be going to Filton for tanker conversion by BAe, with presumably the seventh being scrapped here or moving on as well. During late 1988 and early 1989, the remaining Nimrod AEW.3s arrived from Waddington and by late 1989 at least one was reduced to a shell. XZ282 flew in 9/11/88, departing again, probably the last flight ever by the unfortunate type, to Kinloss 14/9/89. AEW.3 XZ286 had gone by 3/90, likely bound for the PEE at Foulness. Abingdon is the centre of battle damage repair training for the RAF, and the **Battle Damage Repair Flight** has several airframes with which to teach this artform. Going back to **W&R11**, Gnat T.1 XP541/8616M did leave here during 1987 and most likely did go via Bitteswell to the USA, becoming N8130Q. Canberra T.4 WJ867/8643M left by road 3/88 for Catterick. Inbound for BDR training have been several airframes, including Harrier GR.3s. Also based is the **Aircraft Salvage and Repair Unit**, responsible for moving airframes around the country – hence the many sightings of aircraft on the back of low-loaders here. The Inspectorate of Recruiting owns the airframes moved around the country by the **RAF Exhibition Flight.** Several of the 'plastic' airframes have changed identities recently and these are noted in the list below. RAFEF sent two of its airframes, Canberra nose WH903/8584M and Jet Provost T.4 XR658/8192M into store at Wroughton by 1988, where disposal arrangements were made. Two unflown Harrier GR.1 noses have arrived at Abingdon (listed below) and may well be for RAFEF. Gate guardian Spitfire F.24 PK624/8072M left for St Athan during 1989. It will be replaced by the Hunter F.5

previously on show at Hendon. By 8/89 a Spitfire IX had arrived from St Athan for
engineering assessment. If successful, the machine will be rebuilt to flying
condition for the BBMF at Coningsby.

MK356+	5690M Spitfire IX	ex St Athan, Henlow, Bicester, Hawkinge, Halton, 84 GSU, 443. Arrived 8/89 - see notes above.
TB382	7244M Spitfire XVI	ex Henlow, Ely, Middleton St George, 602. RAFEF.
TE311	7241M Spitfire XVI	ex Henlow, Wattisham, 2/3 CAACU, 103 FRS, 102 FRS, 83 GSU, 421. RAFEF.
WH703+	8490M Canberra B.2	ex Marham, 100, 85, 231 OCU. BDRF. Omitted from WSR11.
WH869	8515M Canberra B.2	ex St Athan, 7, 98, 245, 527, RAFC. ASRU.
WJ678	8864M Canberra B.2	ex Wyton, 100, 85, C(A). Overstressed 19/10/83. BDRF.
WJ876	Canberra T.4	ex 7, 13, 39, 13, 56, 13, Akrotiri SF, 39, Akrotiri SF, HS, 231 OCU, Waddington SF, 1 GCF, Binbrook SF, Scampton SF. Nose. RAFEF.
WK146	Canberra B.2	ex 59, 102. Nose. RAFEF.
WP185+	7583M Hunter F.5	ex Hendon, Henlow, 34, 1. Arrived 10/89. See notes above.
XE643	8586M Hunter FGA.9	ex 208, 56, 63, 66, 92. Accident 9/12/61. Nose. RAFEF.
XE670	8585M Hunter F.4	ex 7762M, 93, 26. Nose. RAFEF.
XG226	8800M Hunter F.6A	ex 1 TWU, TWU, 229 OCU, 92, 66, 92. Noseless fuselage and centre section. Nose at Faygate. BDRF.
XH537	8749M Vulcan B.2MRR	ex 27, 230 OCU, MoA. 'Preserved' on the airfield.
XK943	8796M Whirlwind HAS.7	ex BDRF, Lee-on-Solent A2653, Wroughton, 705, 848, 824. Fire dump.
XL569+	8833M Hunter T.7	ex Cosford, 2 TWU, 1 TWU, 12, 216, 237 OCU, Laarbruch SF, 15, 237 OCU, 12, MinTech, 2 TWU, 1 TWU, TWU, 229 OCU. Arr 18/3/88. BDRF.
XM191	8590M Lightning F.1	ex 7854M, Wattisham, 111. Crashed 9/6/64. Nose. RAFEF.
XN137	Jet Provost T.3	ex 3 FTS, CFS, makers. Nose. RAFEF.
XN503	Jet Provost T.3	ex MinTech, 4 FTS, 2 FTS, MinTech, 6 FTS, A&AEE. Nose. RAFEF.
XN962	8183M Buccaneer S.1	Nose. RAFEF.
XT274	8856M Buccaneer S.2A	ex St Athan, 237 OCU, 12, 237 OCU, 208, 237 OCU, 12. BDRF.
XT284	8855M Buccaneer S.2A	ex St Athan, 237 OCU, 15, 208. BDRF.
XT595	8851M Phantom FG.1	ex St Athan, Coningsby, A&AEE. Nose section - remainder can be found at Wattisham. RAFEF.
XV259+	Nimrod AEW.3	ex Waddington, Woodford, Kinloss Wing, St Mawgan Wing. Flew in 10/1/89. Stored.
XV261	8986M Nimrod AEW.3	ex Waddington, Woodford, Kinloss Wing, St Mawgan Wing, 203. Shell by 8/89 and sectioned by 3/90. BDR.
XV262	Nimrod AEW.3	ex Waddington, Woodford, Kinloss Wing, St Mawgan Wing, 203, Kinloss Wing. Shell by 8/89.
XV337	8852M Buccaneer S.2C	ex A&AEE, 208, A&AEE. BDRF.
XV338	8774M Buccaneer S.2A	ex St Athan, 237 OCU, 12. Nose. RAFEF.
XV740+	8989M Harrier GR.3	ex St Athan, 1, 4, 1. Arrived 19/4/89. BDRF.
XV753+	Harrier GR.3	ex St Athan, 1, 3, 233 OCU. Arrived 17/3/88. BDRF.
XV784+	8909M Harrier GR.3	ex St Athan, 233 OCU, 4, 1, 4. Damaged 2/4/86. Less nose. Arrived by 5/88. BDRF.
XW298+	9013M Jet Provost T.5	ex Scampton, 6 FTS, 1 FTS. Arrived by 11/89. BDRF.
XX115+	8821M Jaguar GR.1	ex Indian AF JI005, 226 OCU, JOCU. Hulk on dump. Omitted from WSR11.
XX263"	B'152 Hawk T.1 replica	ex XX162". RAFEF.
XX297"	B'171 Hawk T.1 replica	ex XX262". RAFEF.
XX344	8847M Hawk T.1	ex Dunsfold, RAE. Crashed 7/1/82. BDRF.
XX396	8718M Gazelle HT.3	ex 2 FTS. Crashed 30/6/81. RAFEF. Nominally based at Henlow.
XX718"	B'150 Jaguar GR.1 replica	RAFEF.
XZ135	8848M Harrier GR.3	ex 4. Nose, truck mounted. RAFEF.
XZ280+	Nimrod AEW.3	ex Waddington, Woodford, Kinloss Wing. Flew in 10/1/89. Stored.
XZ281+	Nimrod AEW.3	ex Waddington, Woodford, Kinloss Wing. Flew in 19/12/88. Stored.
XZ283+	Nimrod AEW.3	ex Waddington, JTU, Woodford. Flew in 9/12/88. Stored.
XZ285+	Nimrod AEW.3	ex Waddington, A&AEE, Woodford, St Mawgan Wing. Flew in 31/10/88. Stored.
XZ287+	Nimrod AEW.3	ex Waddington, JTU, Woodford. Flew in 23/11/88. Stored.
XZ363"	B'151 Jaguar GR.1 replica	ex XX824". RAFEF.
ZA600"	B'155 Tornado GR.1 rep	ex ZA322". RAFEF.

ZD230	Super VC-10 1151	ex G-ASGA, Prestwick, BA, BOAC. Stored. See notes above.
ZD235	Super VC-10 1151	ex G-ASGG, Prestwick, BA, BOAC. Stored. See notes above.
ZD239	Super VC-10 1151	ex G-ASGK, Prestwick, BA, BOAC. Stored. See notes above.
ZD240	Super VC-10 1151	ex G-ASGL, Prestwick, BA, BOAC. Stored. See notes above.
ZD241	Super VC-10 1151	ex G-ASGM, Prestwick, BA, BOAC. Stored. See notes above.
ZD242	Super VC-10 1151	ex G-ASGP, Prestwick, BA, BOAC. Stored. See notes above.
ZD243	Super VC-10 1151	ex G-ASGR, Prestwick, BA, BOAC. Stored. See notes above.
ZD472"	B'191 Harrier GR.5 rep	RAFEF.
	'Nimrod MR.1'	G-ALYW, ex Farnborough, Heathrow, BOAC. Comet fuselage suitably converted and fitted out.
+	Harrier GR.1	ex Hamble. Unflown cockpit. Marked '4 Spare Ser 41H/769733'. See above.
+	Harrier GR.1	ex Hamble. Unflown cockpit. Marked 'FL-R-41H/725624'. See above.

ARNCOTT
(South of the A41 south east of Bicester) Restoration of the Auster is thought to continue in the area.

G-ASEF	Auster 6A	ex Somerton, Bicester, RAFGSA, VW985, 664. CoA expired 19/12/66.

BENSON
The Bf 109G-2 here is nearing the end of a long and painstaking restoration to flying condition. In an historic link up of the Ministry of Defence and the Imperial War Museum, when flown, it will be operated from Duxford, until such time as it is retired when it will go on show at Hendon. The gate guardian Spitfire, PR.XIX PM651/7758M left for St Athan in 1989 and ultimately gained stardom at Hendon. As ever, it was replaced by a plastic replica, serialled as a PR.XI and looking for all the world like a Mk VIII!

EN343"+	Spitfire replica	unveiled 17/11/89.
XR509	8752M Wessex HC.2	ex 72, 240 OCU, 72, 18. Crashed 16/10/81. BDR.
XS642	8785M Andover C.1	ex Kemble, 84, SAR Flt, 84. Rescue training.
10639	8478M Bf 109G-2	ex Northolt, Lyneham, Henlow, Wattisham, Stanmore Park, 47 MU, CFE-EAF, 1426 (EA) Flt RN228, Sicily, I/JG.77. See notes above.
8669M	G-ARRV HS.748MF	ex Woodford, G-APZV. Fire dump.

BICESTER
The airframe situation at the headquarters of the **Royal Air Force Gliding and Soaring Association** has remained the same.

G-ASRI	Aztec 250B	ex Shoreham, N5287Y. CoA expired 30/8/87. Acquired for engines.
WB556	Chipmunk T.10	ex Oxf UAS. SOC 12/9/73 and presumed here since. Spares.
WG300	Chipmunk T.10	ex Shawbury, Kemble, Liv UAS, 19 RFS, 2 BFTS. Former RAFGSA engine test-bed.
WG303	8208M Chipmunk T.10	ex Shawbury, Kemble, Gatow SF, Wittering SF, Marham SF, Bir UAS, 5 RFS, 2 BFTS. Fuselage, RAFGSA engine test-bed.

BRIZE NORTON
Another place where the airframe stock has not changed. However, the narrative section from **W&R11** needs correcting. The resident **Air Movements School** teaches air movements personnel - what else? - not as given. Additionally, those initials JATE stand for Joint Air Transport Establishment and not as given.

6V-AEE	Cessna A.150M	ex N9860J. Spares ship for G-AYUY.
WT684	7422M Hunter F.1	ex Abingdon, Reading, 71 MU, 229 OCU, DFLS. Dump.
XS479	8819M Wessex HU.5	ex Wroughton, 845. JATE.
XS598	Andover C.1	ex Andover CU, Andover SF, HS, A&AEE. Cr 5/7/67. Fuselage. AMS.
XT141	8509M Sioux AH.1	ex Middle Wallop. AMS.
XT486	8919M Wessex HU.5	ex Wroughton, 845. JATE.
XT677	8016M Wessex HC.2	ex Lyneham, Thorney Island, 18. Crashed 25/4/68. Fire dump.
XV638	8826M Wasp HAS.1	ex Portland. Ditched 27/5/83. AMS.
XX914	8777M VC-10 1103	ex RAE Bedford, 9G-ABQ, G-ATDJ. Fuselage. AMS.
ZD232	8699M Super VC-10 1151	ex Heathrow, G-ASGD, BA, BOAC. Fuselage. Dump. Omitted from **W&R11**.
ZD234	8700M Super VC-10 1151	ex Heathrow, G-ASGF, BA, BOAC. Nose with 241 OCU as tanker simulator. Rear fuselage etc on dump.
ZD493	8977M VC-10 1101	ex Heathrow, G-ARVJ, Gulf-Air, BA, BOAC. BDR.

CHALGROVE

Keeping the **Martin Baker** bang-seat test-bed WL419 flying are the well known WA638 plus two RAE T.7s that were otherwise unaccounted for.

WA638	Meteor T.7(mod)	ex ETPS, RAE. Spares.
WA662+	Meteor T.7	ex Llanbedr, Farnborough, FCCS, 3, Wildenrath SF, Gutersloh SF, 3. First noted 9/89. Dismantled. Spares recovery.
WL405+	Meteor T.7	ex Farnborough, BCCS, 1 GCF, 231 OCU, Wittering SF, JCU, Hemswell CF. Nose and centre section. Spares recovery. Remainder at Sunderland with NEAM.
WL419+	Meteor T.7(mod)	ex 85, 13 GCF, CFE, 233 OCU. Ejector seat test-bed. Airworthy.

CULHAM

(On the A415 south east of Abingdon) With the UKAEA, the **Culham Lightning Studies Unit** should still have its Hunter GA.11.

WV381	Hunter GA.11	ex Kemble, FRADU, FRU, FWS, 222. Fuselage only.

ENSTONE

At the 'agricultural' end of this airfield, Pawnee 235D G-BEIH had gone by 12/88. The anonymous frame noted in **W&R11** cannot be pinned down, but it is highly likely to be one of those listed below, both of which are seemingly abandoned.

G-AVPY+	Pawnee 235C	ex N4636Y. Crashed 25/6/76. Stored.
G-AXBD+	Pawnee 235C	crashed 2/7/76. Stored.

HENLEY-ON-THAMES

Located here is the store of the **Berkshire Aviation Group**, who are working hard to establish a Miles-biased museum at Woodley - which see. The store is unchanged.

G-AHUI	Messenger 2A	ex Cranfield, Bushey, Caistor, Elsham Hall, Goxhill, Handforth, Wolverhampton. CoA expired 4/9/60. Fuselage.
G-AJFF	Messenger 2A	ex Cranfield, Bushey, Caistor, Elsham Hall, Egham, Elstree, Swanton Morley. CoA expired 16/3/68.
G-AKER	Gemini 1A	ex Cranfield, Bushey, Elsham Hall, Tattershall. CoA exp 18/9/65.
G-AKGD	Gemini 1A	ex Cranfield, Bushey, 'Sussex', Southend. CoA expired 14/11/66. Sectioned.
G-AKHZ	Gemini 1A	ex Cranfield, Bushey, Elsham Hall, Handforth. Complex composite, including parts from G-ALMJ, G-ALUG, G-AMME. 'HZ GoA exp 6/1/64.

OXFORD

David Elvidge continues to work on the rear fuselage and other parts of Mosquito TT.35 TJ118. The nose section is to be found at London Colney. New in the area are no less than three Spitfire restoration projects. Bearing in mind that these days a firewall and a maker's plate can constitute a viable rebuild, there may not be much to any or some of these. The former Gilze Rijen machine is more substantial and well-known. Ownership rests with three separate people.

LZ842+	Spitfire IX	ex Lanseria, South Africa, SAAF, RAF 232. See above.
MH603+	Spitfire IX	ex South Africa, SAAF, RAF 274, 331. See above.
MK732+	8633M Spitfire IX	ex Gilze Rijen, Abingdon, St Athan, Coningsby, Coltishall, Bicester, St Athan, Gutersloh, Einhoven, RNeth AF H-25, RAF 485. See above.

OXFORD AIRPORT

(Or Kidlington) Contents of the **Oxford Air Training Schoool** Ground Training School have not changed.

G-ARJR	Apache 160G	ex N4447P. CoA expired 24/10/78.
G-ARMA	Apache 160G	ex N4448P. CoA expired 22/ 7/77.
G-ASEW	Brantly B.2B	CoA expired 17/12/73.
G-AVBU	Cherokee Six 260	crashed 28/2/81. Fuselage.
G-BBVI	Enstrom F-28A	crashed 19/6/78.
G-BDBZ	Whirlwind HAR.10	ex Luton, XJ398, XD768 ntu.
G-BFSK	Apache 160	ex OO-NVC, OO-HVL, OO-PIP.
G-SHOE	Cessna 421C II	ex G-BHGD, D-IASC, OE-FLR, N3862C. Fuselage.
XT175	Sioux AH.1	ex TAD175, Middle Wallop.

SHOTTESWELL

(Off the A41 north of Banbury) The lovely Cessna 170 is still in store at the strip, clocking up seven years of immobility now.

G-BCLS   Cessna 170B   ex N8094A. CoA expired 27/1/83. External store.

SHRIVENHAM

(On the A420 north east of Swindon) The resident **Royal Military College of Science** (a joint services establishment) disposed of Whirlwind HAS.7 XN263 to <u>Wroughton</u> on 2/6/88. The three other airframes serve on.

WZ706   7851M Auster AOP.9   ex St Athan, 656, Far East.
XT151   Sioux AH.1   ex Wroughton, 664, ARWF.
XT621   Scout AH.1   ex Wroughton, 655, 656, 666, 664, 666.

UPPER HEYFORD

Acting alternatively as battle damage repair airframes and surface decoys, the four Mystere IVAs, the Thunderchief and the Phantom serve on. Joining them in 9/89 was the F-100D previously displayed at the main entrance to Sculthorpe. This will be placed on the gate during 1990.

36   Mystere IVA   EABDR.8, ex Chateaudun, French AF.
46   Mystere IVA   assumed EABDR.9, ex Chateaudun, French AF.
127   Mystere IVA   EABDR.7, ex Sculthorpe, Chateaudun, French AF.
129   Mystere IVA   EABDR.6, ex Sculthorpe, Chateaudun, French AF.
24428   F-105G-RE   ex Davis-Monthan 'FK095', 128 TFS, Georgia ANG.
42212+   F-100D-11-NA   ex Sculthorpe, French AF. Arrived 1/9/89. For the gate.
37449   F-4C-17-MC   ex 182 TFS, Texas ANG.

Shropshire

BRIDGNORTH

Derek Leek continues to work on his Vampire T.11. A new set of wings has been acquired for it, coming from the ill-fated WZ576 that was at Appleby.

XH330   Vampire T.11   ex Bushey, London Colney, Chester, Woodford, Chester, Shawbury, RAFC. Pod. Wings from WZ576.

CHETWYND

Still in use by the **Staffordshire Sports Skydiving Club** as a para-trainer is a Cessna 150 fuselage. It is not kept on the airfield.

G-ATIE   Cessna 150F   ex Market Drayton, N6291R. Crashed 28/7/79. Para-trainer.

COSFORD

The wind-down of the St Athan collection and the Henlow store has brought a lot more airframes into the superb **Aerospace Museum**. To accommodate this influx, several aircraft have been put into store on site, two have been disposed of and two transferred to the Fleet Air Arm Museum. Cosford now represents a staggering collection of aircraft, centred on three broad headings; captured Axis machines, trials and experimentals and the stunning transport collection. An air day is held each year and there are other events on the site - details from the Museum. Contact : Aerospace Museum, RAF Cosford, Shifnal, Shropshire, TF11 8UP. Telephone 090 722 4872 or '4112. During 2/90 the Supermarine S.517 VV106/7175M and the Hawker P.1052 VX272/7174M were moved to <u>Yeovilton</u> where they will help to illustrate the development of the Attacker and Sea Hawk respectively. Hunter F.1 WT555/7499M was auctioned off via the Phillips Cardiff sale of 21/9/89 and fetched £10,500. It is not known where it went. 'Regal Beagle' Basset CC.1 XS770 was offered for sale by tender and left by road for Cranfield on 1/2/89, becoming G-

HRHI. Current situation is as follows :

G-AFAP"	CASA 352L	ex Spanish AF T2B-272. British Airways (the original lot!) colours.
G-AGRU	Viking 1	ex Soesterberg, Channel, Lasham, Kuwait Oil, BWIA, VP-TAX, G-AGRU, BEA 'Vagrant'. BEA colours. CoA expired 9/1/64.
G-AIZE+	Argus II	ex Henlow, Hanwell, N9996F, 43-14601. Arrived by 1/90. Stored.
G-AJOV"	WP495 Dragonfly HR.3	ex Biggin Hill, Banstead, Warnham, Wimbledon. BEA colours.
G-AMOG	Viscount 701	ex Cardiff-Wales, BOAC, Cambrian, BEA 'Robert Falcon Scott', G-AMNZ ntu. BEA colours. CoA expired 14/6/77.
G-AOVF	Britannia 312F	ex Southend, Merchant Air, 9Q-CAZ, G-AOVF, Stansted, Donaldson, British Eagle, BOAC. BOAC colours.
G-APAS	8351M Comet 1XB	ex Shawbury, XM823, G-APAS, Air France, F-BGNZ, G-5-23. BOAC c/s.
G-APFJ	Boeing 707-436	ex British Airtours, BOAC. CoA exp 16/2/82. British Airtours c/s.
G-ARPH	Trident 1C	ex Heathrow, BA, BEA. CoA expired 8/9/82. British Airways colours.
G-ARVM	VC-10 1101	ex BA, BOAC. CoA expired 5/8/80. British Airways colours.
K7271"	B'148 Fury I replica	stored.
DG202/G	5758M F.9/40 Meteor	ex Yatesbury, Locking, Moreton Valance. Prototype Meteor, f/f 4/43.
HS503+	B'108 Swordfish IV	ex Henlow, Canada. Arrived by 1/90. Stored.
KG374"	KN645 Dakota IV	8355M, ex Colerne, AFN CF, MinTech, AFN HQ, SHAPE CF, Malta CF, BAFO CS, 2nd TAF CS, 44-77003.
KN751	B-24L-20-FO	ex Colerne, Indian AF 6 Squadron HE809, RAF KN751, 99.
MT847	6960M Spitfire XIV	ex Weeton, Middleton St George, Freckleton, Warton, 226 OCU, A&AEE.
RF398	8376M Lincoln B.2	ex Henlow, Abingdon, CSE, BCBS.
TA639	7806M Mosquito TT.35	ex CFS, 3 CAACU, Aldergrove TT Flt.
TG511	8554M Hastings T.5	ex 230 OCU, SCBS, BCBS, 202, 47.
TS798	York C.1	ex 'MW100', Shawbury, Brize Norton, Staverton, 'LV633', G-AGNV, Skyways, BOAC, TS798 ntu.
TX214	7817M Anson C.19	ex Henlow, HCCS, MCS, RCCF, Staff College CF, 1 FU, 16 FU.
VP952	8820M Devon C.2/2	ex St Athan, 207, 21, WCS, SCS, Upavon SF, TCCF, MCS, BCCS, HCCS, A&AEE, MCCF, AAFCE, TCCF, Hendon SF, HS.
VX461+	7646M Vampire FB.5	ex Henlow, Hendon, 8 FTS, 16, 26, Arrived by 1/90. Stored.
VX573	8389M Valetta C.3	ex Henlow, Wildenrath CF, Buckeburg CF. 'Lorelei'.
WA634	Meteor T.7(mod)	ex St Athan, Martin Baker.
WB188	7154M Hawker P.1067	ex St Athan, Colerne, Melksham. Hunter prototype.
WE600+	7602M Auster C4	ex St Athan, Swinderby, Finningley, Trans-Antarctic Expedition, 663. Arrived by late 1989.
WF408	8395M Varsity T.1	ex 2 SoTT, 6 SS, 2 ANS, 1 RS, 11 FTS, 201 AFS.
WG760	7755M EE P.1A	ex Binbrook, Henlow, Bicester, St Athan, Warton, A&AEE.
WG768	8005M Short SB.5	ex Topcliffe, Finningley, ETPS, A&AEE.
WG777	7986M Fairey FD-2	ex Topcliffe, Finningley, RAE Bedford.
WK935	7869M Meteor F.8(mod)	ex St Athan, Colerne, RAE Farnborough. Prone-pilot aircraft.
WL732	Sea Balliol T.21	ex Henlow, A&AEE, Lossiemouth, Anthorn. Stored.
WP912	8467M Chipmunk T.10	ex Hendon, Kemble, Man UAS, RAFC, ITS, Cam UAS, CFS, 2 FTS, Lon UAS, FTCCS, HCCS, 8 FTS.
WT346	8197M Canberra B(I).8	ex Shawbury, Colerne, 16, 3, 14, 88.
WV562	7606M Provost T.1	ex Cranwell, Henlow, 22 FTS.
WV746	8938M Pembroke C.1	ex 60, 207, 21, WCS, TCCF, FTCCS, BCCS, HS, 2 TAF CF.
WZ744	7932M Avro 707	ex Topcliffe, Finningley, RAE, Avros.
XA564	7464M Javelin FAW.1	ex 2 SoTT, Locking, Filton.
XA893	8591M Vulcan B.1	ex Abingdon, Bicester, A&AEE, Avro. Nose.
XD145	SARO SR.53	ex Brize Norton, Henlow, Westcott, A&AEE.
XD674	7570M Jet Provost T.1	ex St Athan, Swinderby, Finningley, 71 MU, Percivals.
XF785+	7648M Bristol 173	ex Henlow, G-ALBN. Arrived by 1/90. Stored.
XF926	8368M Bristol T.188	ex Foulness Island, RAE, A&AEE.
XG337	8056M Lightning F.1	ex 2 SoTT, Warton, A&AEE, Warton.
XH592	8429M Victor K.1A	ex 2 SoTT, St Athan, 232 OCU, TTF, 232 OCU, Marham Wing, 15.
XJ389	Jet Gyrodyne	ex Southampton, G-AJJP, makers. One time XD759.
XJ918	8190M Sycamore HR.14	ex 2 SoTT, 32, MCS, Kemble, Wroughton, 110, Seletar, A&AEE, 275.
XK724	7715M Gnat F.1	ex Cranwell, Bicester, Henlow, Follands.
XL703+	8034M Pioneer CC.1	ex Manchester, Henlow, 209, 230. Arrived by 4/89.

XL993	8388M Twin Pioneer CC.1	ex Henlow, Shawbury, 21, 78.
XM555	8027M Skeeter AOP.12	ex Shawbury, Ternhill, CFS, HQ BAOR, 654.
XM598	8778M Vulcan B.2	ex 44, Wadd Wing, Cott Wing, 12.
XN714	Hunting 126	ex RAE Bedford, NASA Ames and Moffett, Holme-on-Spalding Moor, RAE.
XP299	8726M Whirlwind HAR.10	ex 22, 230. 1563 Flt, Queen's Flt, 230, CFS, MoA. QF colours.
XP411	8442M Argosy C.1	ex 2 SoTT, 6 FTS, Kemble, 70.
XR220	7933M TSR-2 XO-2	ex Henlow, A&AEE. Never flown.
XR371	Belfast C.1	ex Hucknall, Kemble, 53. 'Enceladus'.
XR977	8640M Gnat T.1	ex 2 SoTT, Red Arrows, 4 FTS. Red Arrows colours.
ZD485	FMA Pucara	ex A&AEE, Yeovilton, Stanley Airport, Argentine AF A-515.
8469M	Fa 330A-1	ex Henlow, Farnborough.
8476M+	B'83 Ki 100-1b	ex St Athan, Cosford, Henlow, Biggin Hill, Fulbeck, Wroughton, Stanmore. Arrived by mid-1989.
8486M	B'99 Ohka II	ex St Athan, Cosford.
8583M	B'94 Fi 103 (V-1)	
+	P.1121	ex Henlow, Cranfield. Sections. Arrived by 1/90. Stored.
L-866	8466M PBY-6A Catalina	ex Colerne, Danish AF ESK.721, 82-866, 63993.
17473	T-33A-1-LO	ex Sculthorpe, French AF.
112372+	8482M Me 262A-2a	ex St Athan, Cosford, Finningley, Gaydon, Cranwell, Farnborough, VK893/AM.51, I/KG.51. Arrived mid-1989.
191614	8481M Me 163B-1a	ex Biggin Hill, Westcott, Brize Norton, Farnborough, Hussum, II/JG.400.
420430+	8483M Me 410A-1/U2	ex St Athan, Cosford, Fulbeck, Wroughton, Stanmore, Brize Norton, Farnborough, AM.72, Vaerlose. Arrived mid-1989.
475081+	7362M Fi 156C-7 Storch	ex St Athan, Coltishall, Bircham Newton, Finningley, Fulbeck, VP546, AM.101, Farnborough, 'RR+KE', 'GM+AK'. Arrived mid-1989.
5439+	8484M Ki 46 Dinah	BAPC.84, ex St Athan, Stanmore Park, ATAIU-SEA. Arr by mid-1989.
204	SP-2H Neptune	ex Dutch Navy 320 Sqn, Valkenburg, 5 Sqn, 321 Sqn.
6130+	AJ469 Ventura II	ex SAAF Museum, SAAF. Arrived by 1/90. Stored.
J-1704	Venom FB.4	ex Greenham Common and Swiss Air Force.
6771"+	F-84F-51-RE	ex Rochester, Southend, Beglian AF FU-6, USAF 52-7133. Arr 28/3/90.

More Jaguars and Jet Provosts have joined the 'fleet' of **2 School of Technical Training** and the **Weapons School.** There have been many disposals of older airframes, with the Argosies, Hunters and Shackletons going.   Two Gnats were offered for tender and six were auctioned at the Sotheby's Ministry of Defence sale in London on 9/3/90.   Disposals have been as follows :
Argosies E.1 XN816/8489M and C.1 XP444/8455M were both offered for tender 9/88 and were acquired by IPEC of New Zealand for spares and scrapped on site.   T.2 XR107/8441M was offered for tender at the same time, fate unknown.
Gnat T.1s XP514/8635M, XR987/8641M and XS104/8604M were offered for tender 9/88 and were all acquired by Arnold Glass, all moving to <u>Cranfield</u>. The following were offered at the Sotheby's auction of 9/3/90, with high bids as noted : XP533/8632M £102,000;   XP538/8607M £102,000;   XR537/8642M £105,000; XS102/8624M £88,000; XS105/8625M £84,000; XS107/8639M £122,000. No destinations/fates available as yet.
Hunter T.7s XL569/8833M by road to <u>Abingdon</u> 18/3/88; XL623/8770M to <u>Newton</u> by 4/88; XL572/8834M, XL576/8835M and XL617/8837M all offered for tender 6/88.   XL572 and XL617 went to JHL at <u>Bournemouth</u>; XL576 went to Ed Stead in the USA as N576NL.
Shackleton MR.3/3s, all offered for tender 9/88 : WR971/8119M removed, destination unknown; WR974/8117M and WR982/8106M both to <u>Charlwood</u> by 11/89; WR985/8103M to SAC at <u>Long Marston</u> by 12/89.
Vampire T.11s XD613/8122M which was on display in the parade ground, was offered for tender 9/88 and removed. Thought exported to France. XD377/8203M, which had been held for some time has not been reported since 6/84 and is also assumed to have moved on. That makes the current situation as follows :

WH740	8762M Canberra T.17	ex 360, RNZAF, Upwood SF, 40, 18.
WH775	8868M Canberra PR.7	ex 8128M, 100, 13, 31, 17, 31, 13, 82, makers.
WH957	8869M Canberra PR.7	ex 100, 98, Akrotiri Wing, 32, Hemswell SF, Upwood SF, 21, 542, 617.
WH960	8344M Canberra B.15	ex Akrotiri Wing, 32, 9, 12.
WH964	8870M Canberra E.15	ex St Athan, 100, 98, Akrotiri Wing, 32, 12.

WH984	8101M Canberra B.15	ex RAE, HS, 9, Binbrook SF, 9.
WJ565	8871M Canberra T.17	ex St Athan, 360, CA.
WJ640	8722M Canberra B.2	ex 100, 85, 51, 192, 231 OCU.
WJ756+	Canberra E.15	ex 100, 98, Akrotiri Wing, 32, 9, 101.
WK102	8780M Canberra T.17	ex 360, 45, RNZAF, 207.
WT532	8890M Canberra PR.7	ex 8728M, RAE Bedford, 13, Wyton SF, 58, 31, 13, 80.
WT536	8063M Canberra PR.7	ex 80, 31, 13, 17.
XG225	8713M Hunter F.6A	ex Weapons School, 2 SoTT, Kemble, 229 OCU, 92, 74, 20. On parade ground by 4/88.
XH136	8782M Canberra PR.9	ex 1 PRU, A&AEE, 39, 13, 58, MoA.
XH171	8746M Canberra PR.9	ex 39, 13, 39, MoA, 58.
XH593	8428M Victor K.1A	ex St Athan, 232 OCU, TTF, Marham Wing, 57, 15.
XM351	8078M Jet Provost T.3	ex Halton, Shawbury, 3 FTS, 7 FTS, 2 FTS.
XM367	8083M Jet Provost T.3	ex Halton, Shawbury, 3 FTS, 2 FTS.
XM455+	8960M Jet Provost T.3A	ex CFS, 3 FTS, CFS, 1 FTS, 3 FTS, RAFC. First noted 7/88.
XM471+	8968M Jet Provost T.3A	ex 7 FTS, 1 FTS, CFS, 3 FTS, 2 FTS, RAFC, 6 FTS, CFS. First noted 7/88.
XN472+	8959M Jet Provost T.3A	ex 7 FTS, 1 FTS, 3 FTS, 7 FTS, CFS. First noted 7/88.
XN492	8079M Jet Provost T.3	ex Halton, 6 FTS, RAFC.
XN501	8958M Jet Provost T.3A	ex CFS, 1 FTS.
XN577+	8956M Jet Provost T.3A	ex 7 FTS, 1 FTS, 7 FTS, RAFC. First noted 6/89.
XN582+	8957M Jet Provost T.3A	ex 7 FTS, 1 FTS, 3 FTS, RAFC. First noted 7/88.
XN593+	8988M Jet Provost T.3A	ex 7 FTS, 1 FTS, 2 FTS. First noted 6/89.
XN594	8077M Jet Provost T.3	ex Halton, Shawbury, 6 FTS, 7 FTS, 2 FTS. Omitted from W&R11.
XN640+	9016M Jet Provost T.3A	ex Church Fenton, 7 FTS, RAFC, 3 FTS, CFS, 6 FTS. Arr 3/90.
XP338	8647M Whirlwind HAR.10	ex Shawbury, 2 FTS, CFS, HDU, CFS, 225.
XP547+	8992M Jet Provost T.4	ex 1 TWU, SoRF, CATCS, RAFC, A&AEE. Arrived 3/89.
XR679+	8991M Jet Provost T.4	ex 1 TWU, SoRF, CAW, 3 CAACU, CAW, RAFC. Arrived 3/89.
XS178+	8994M Jet Provost T.4	ex 1 TWU, CATCS, RAFC, 7 FTS, CFS. Arrived 3/89.
XS219+	8993M Jet Provost T.4	ex 1 TWU, CATCS, CAW. Arrived 3/89.
XT277	8853M Buccaneer S.2A	ex Shawbury, 237 OCU, 12.
XT466	8921M Wessex HU.5	ex Wroughton, 847.
XW544	8857M Buccaneer S.2C	ex Shawbury, 16, 15.
XX110	8955M Jaguar GR.1	ex Shawbury, 6, A&AEE, BAC.
XX140+	9008M Jaguar T.2	ex Shawbury, 226 OCU, 54, JOCU. Arrived 1989.
XX669+	8997M Bulldog T.1	ex Bir UAS. Withdrawn after accident 6/9/88. Birmingham UAS inst.
XX727	8951M Jaguar GR.1	ex Shawbury, 6, 54, 6, JOCU.
XX730	8952M Jaguar GR.1	ex Shawbury, 6, JOCU.
XX751	8937M Jaguar GR.1	ex 226 OCU, 14.
XX756	8899M Jaguar GR.1	ex 14, 41, 14, 20, 226 OCU, 14.
XX819	8923M Jaguar GR.1	ex Shawbury, 20, 17.
XX826+	9021M Jaguar GR.1	ex Shawbury, 2, 20, 14. Arrived by 3/90.
XX844+	9023M Jaguar T.2	ex CIT Cranfield, 226 OCU, 17, 31. Arrived by 3/90.
XX948	8879M Tornado P.06	ex Warton. Weapons School.
XX958+	9022M Jaguar GR.1	ex Shawbury, 17, 14. Arrived by 3/90.
XX959	8953M Jaguar GR.1	ex Shawbury, 20, 14.
XX967+	9006M Jaguar GR.1	ex Shawbury, 14, 31. Arrived 1989.
XX968+	9007M Jaguar GR.1	ex Shawbury, 14, 31. Arrived 1989.
XX969	8897M Jaguar GR.1	ex 226 OCU, 3, 17, 31, 14, 31.
XZ368	8900M Jaguar GR.1	ex Coltishall, 14, 41, 14, 6, 14.
XZ370+	9004M Jaguar GR.1	ex Shawbury, 17. Arrived 1989.
XZ371	8907M Jaguar GR.1	ex Shawbury, 14, 17. Weapons School.
XZ374+	9005M Jaguar GR.1	ex Shawbury, 14, 20. Arrived 1989.
XZ383	8901M Jaguar GR.1	ex Coltishall, 14, 41, 54, 14, 226 OCU, 14, 17.
XZ384	8954M Jaguar GR.1	ex Shawbury, 17, 31, 20.
XZ390+	9003M Jaguar GR.1	ex Shawbury, 2, 20, 31. Arrived 1989.
	Lightning F.2A	cockpit section. Weapons School.
	Lightning F.3	cockpit section. Weapons School.
	Buccaneer S.2	cockpit section. Weapons School.

LUDLOW

In the area, three aircraft are on rebuild, the Comper Swift and the Pipistrelle with **H F Moffatt** and the Tiger Moth with **Robin Bailey**.

G-ABUS	Comper Swift	ex Heathfield. CoA expired 19/6/79. Restoration.
G-AHLT	Tiger Moth	ex Heathfield, Manston, Rochester, N9128, 19 FTS, 11 EFTS, 5 CPF. CoA expired 24/6/58.
G-BADV	MB.50 Pipistrelle	ex Dunkeswell, F-PBRJ. CoA expired 9/5/79.

OSWESTRY

A swop-around has taken place here, with a long-lost item from Shawbury surfacing in the process. Mr **D Higgins** loaned his Cessna cockpit section to the local ATC during 1989. He took delivery at his home late in the year of the cockpit of Whirlwind HAR.10 XJ758. This was recorded in **W&R10** as having been done to death on the dump at Shawbury. But this clearly was not the case!

G-AYOV	Cessna FA.150L	ex Sleap. Crashed 11/2/79. Oswestry ATC. Cockpit section.
XJ758+	8464M Whirlwind HAR.10	ex Shrewsbury, Shawbury, CFS, 230, CFS, 217, 1360 Flt, 22. Cockpit section - see notes above.

SHAWBURY

Much to report from the **Storage Site**. Many airframes have moved on. Largest input for storage has been the CATCS Jet Provost fleet, which just rolled across the airfield to effect delivery. While it is still a ground school CATC's flying element disbanded during 7/89. The Spitfire Mk 21 in store here is awaiting covered accommodation at Bentley Priory - hence its not being with the 'trade' examples at St Athan. See under Shrewsbury and Oswestry for details of a 'missing' inmate from here. Adding to **W&R11**, Whirlwind HAR.10 XP398/8794M eventually turned up at Charlwood. Removals from the store are best dealt with type by type :
Beaver AL.1s The final batch was put up for tender 9/89. Included in the list below are machines that would normally be too transitory for **W&R**, but are here for completeness. They were as follows :

XP769 ex NIBF	last flown 15/ 5/89, total time	9,053 hours	sold to Wipaire, USA, as N21190
XP771 in store	11/88,	9,743 hours	sold to Wipaire, USA, as N21200
XP778 ex Middle Wallop	15/ 5/89,	8,889 hours	sold to Auto Diesel, Essex
XP810 in store	11/85,	6,144 hours	sold to Wipaire, USA, as N21208
XP814 in store	/85,	6,205 hours	sold to Wipaire, USA, as N2123X
XP825 ex NIBF	15/ 5/89,	10,011 hours	sold to Wipaire, USA, as N2126S
XV270 ex NIBF	15/ 5/89,	7,697 hours	sold to Wipaire, USA, as N2126T
XV271 ex Middle Wallop	11/88,	7,845 hours	sold to auto Diesel, Essex

Three others have been here. XP775 was still present during 1988, but had gone by 11/89. XP779 and XV268 were still held at Shawbury 11/89 at least.
Buccaneer S.2B XT276 left by road 12/10/89 - destination unknown.
Bulldog T.1s XX538 left for 1 FTS at Linton-on-Ouse 3/88; XX539 to the CFS at Scampton 11/87.
Chipmunk T.10s WG458 went to Exeter 13/7/88; WK586 flew off to Swinderby by 3/88, later joining BBMF. It returned here by 6/89 but flew to Lossiemouth by 2/90 to join 8 Squadron; WP786 joined 6 AEF at Abingdon by 7/86; WP803 to Lossiemouth by 8/88; and WP891 to 5 AEF at Cambridge 22/6/88.
Jaguars T.2 XX140 to Cosford during 1989; T.2 XX150 to the JMU at Abingdon by 5/88; GR.1 XX727 (omitted from **W&R11**) to Cosford 11/2/88; GR.1 XX763 to St Athan by 9/89; GR.1 XX764 to St Athan; GR.1 XX824 (omitted from **W&R11**) moved to Halton as 9019M by 3/90; GR.1 XX825 to Halton as 9020M by 3/90; GR.1 XX826 to Halton as 9021M by 3/90; GR.1 XX841 to the JMU at Abingdon by 9/89; GR.1 XX956 to Halton; GR.1 XX967 to Cosford along with XX968, XZ370, XZ374 and XZ390; GR.1 XZ362 arrived by 1/89 but moved on to the JMU at Abingdon by 3/90; GR.1 XZ381 left 6/89 joining 54 Squadron. Delete XZ392 from the listing in **W&R11**, it has yet to turn up here!
Jet Provost T.5 XS231 was removed by road to Scampton 18/3/88.
Meteor F.8 VZ467 was moved to Scampton by road by 4/88.
Sycamore HR.14 Former display airframe XG540/8345M was offered for tender 3/88 and moved to Drighlington.
Vampire T.11 Gate guardian XD382/8033M was entered into the Phillips Cardiff auction of 21/9/89 and fetched £6,500, moving to Ripley.

Current status of the store and other airframes is as follows :

LA226	7119M Spitfire F.21	ex Abingdon, Biggin Hill, South Marston, London, South Marston, Little Rissington, 3 CAACU, 122. See notes above.
WH724	Canberra T.19	ex 100, 85, West Raynham TFF, 228 OCU, 15. Nose. Dump.
WK511	Chipmunk T.10	ex Kemble, BRNC, Wittering SF, Lon UAS, 61 GCF, Bri UAS, 22 RFS, 5 BFTS.
WT799	Hunter T.8	ex Kemble, FRADU, FRU, 759, RAE Bedford, 4, 111.
WV372+	Hunter T.7	ex FRADU, 237 OCU, 208, Laarbruch SF, RAE, 2, 222. Arr 20/2/87.
XM927	8814M Wessex HAS.3	ex Wroughton. Dump.
XN977	Buccaneer S.2B	ex St Athan, 15, 237 OCU.
XN983+	Buccaneer S.2	ex 12, 208, 12, 15, 12. Arrived 31/10/89.
XP351	8672M Whirlwind HAR.10	ex BDR, 2 FTS, SAR Wing, 22. Gate guardian.
XP556+	Jet Provost T.4	ex CATCS, SoRF, 6 FTS, RAFC. Arrived 7/89.
XP563+	Jet Provost T.4	ex CATCS, SoRF, 6 FTS, CATCS, RAFC. Arrived 7/89.
XP629+	Jet Provost T.4	ex CATCS, SoRF, CAW, 2 FTS. Arrived 12/7/89.
XP638+	Jet Provost T.4	ex CATCS, CAW, 6 FTS. Arrived 7/89.
XP688+	Jet Provost T.4	ex CATCS, CAW, RAFC. Arrived 7/89.
XP779+	Beaver AL.1	ex Middle Wallop. In store since 1986. Omitted from WKR11.
XR653+	Jet Provost T.4	ex CATCS, CAW, CATCS. Arrived 7/89.
XR673+	Jet Provost T.4	ex CATCS, SoRF, 6 FTS, RAFC, 2 FTS. Arrived 7/89.
XR674+	Jet Provost T.4	ex CATCS, 6 FTS, 1 FTS. Arrived 7/89.
XS181+	Jet Provost T.4	ex CATCS, RAFC, 3 FTS. Arrived 7/89.
XS217+	Jet Provost T.4	ex CATCS, CFS, RAFC. Arrived 12/7/89.
XT270	Buccaneer S.2B	ex St Athan, 208, 237 OCU, 12.
XT275	Buccaneer S.2B	ex St Athan, 15, 208.
XV157	Buccaneer S.2B	ex St Athan, 12, 208, 237 OCU, 12.
XV168+	Buccaneer S.2B	ex 237 OCU, 208, 12. arrived 13/10/89.
XV268	Beaver AL.1	ex BTF. See notes above.
XV334	Buccaneer S.2B	ex St Athan, 15, 237 OCU, 12, 237 OCU, 208, 12.
XV336	Buccaneer S.2B	ex St Athan, 12, 208, 237 OCU.
XV349	Buccaneer S.2B	ex St Athan, 12, 237 OCU, 15, 12.
XV356	Buccaneer S.2B	ex St Athan, 15, 208, 237 OCU, 12.
XV866	Buccaneer S.2B	ex St Athan, 16, 809.
XX121	Jaguar GR.1	ex 6, 54, 226 OCU, JOCU.
XX722	Jaguar GR.1	ex 6, 54, JOCU.
XX724+	Jaguar GR.1	ex 54, 14, 54, JOCU.
XX733+	Jaguar GR.1	ex 6, 54, A&AEE, 6, JOCU. SArrived 24/1/89.
XX736+	Jaguar GR.1	ex Warton G-27-327, Indian AF JI013, 6, 226 OCU, JOCU. Arr by road by 11/89.
XX737+	Jaguar GR.1	ex 54, Indian AF JI015, 6, 54, 226 OCU, 54, 226 OCU. Arr 17/5/89.
XX738+	Jaguar GR.1	ex 54, Indian AF JI016, 54, 6, JOCU. Arrived by 5/89.
XX744	Jaguar GR.1	ex 31, 17, 31, 6, 17, 14, 17, A&AEE.
XX748+	Jaguar GR.1	ex 54, 14, 226 OCU. Arrived by 2/89.
XX752+	Jaguar GR.1	ex 54, 6, 54, 6, 226 OCU, 54. Arrived by 12/88.
XX753	Jaguar GR.1	ex 226 OCU, 6.
XX836+	Jaguar T.2	ex 6, 17, 14, 226 OCU, 14.
XX846+	Jaguar T.2	ex 41, 226 OCU. Arrived 27/2/89.
XX847+	Jaguar T.2	ex ETPS, 226 OCU, 31, 20, 14, 2, 14, 226 OCU, 2, 226 OCU.
XX887	Buccaneer S.2B	ex Laarbruch, 16, 15.
XX888	Buccaneer S.2B	ex St Athan, 16, 15.
XX896	Buccaneer S.2B	ex St Athan, 12.
XX958	Jaguar GR.1	ex 17, 14.
XX977	Jaguar GR.1	ex 31.
XZ103+	Jaguar GR.1	ex 2. Arrived 1/89.
XZ106+	Jaguar GR.1	ex 2. Arrived 11/1/89.
XZ112+	Jaguar Gr.1	ex 2. Arrived 1/89.
XZ361+	Jaguar GR.1	ex 2. Arrived 1/89.
XZ391+	Jaguar GR.1	ex 54, 31. Arrived 12/2/90.

SHREWSBURY
An ATC unit (1330?) collected the cockpit section of Whirlwind HAR.10 XJ758/8464M from Shawbury in the mid-1980s. By 10/89 it was been acquired by Mr D Higgins and moved to Oswestry.

TERNHILL
The dump was cleared here in 1989 when a Vampire in poor state (T.11 XH274) and a Whirlwind were scrapped. The Whirlwind is most likely to be HAR.10 XJ757, last noted on the dump in 6/75.

TILSTOCK
Located in a hut off the airfield is the resident para-trainer.
G-ASNN   Cessna 182F   ex N3612U. CoA expired 3/5/85. Para-trainer.

WHITCHURCH
It is believed that the Vampire continues to live on with a private owner, Mr **R G A Mansell**, here.
XD452   7990M Vampire T.11   ex London Colney, Shawbury, 3 FTS, 7 FTS, 1 FTS, 8 FTS, 5 FTS.

Somerset

CHILTON CANTELO
Sea Hawk FGA.6 composite 'WM983' was exported to Soesterberg, Holland, 8/8/89.

GLASTONBURY
Whirlwind HAR.10 XP399 had left the garage here by early 1989. Where to?

HENSTRIDGE
Stored airframes at **Tony Young**'s airfield remain unchanged.
G-AHSD	T'craft Plus D	ex Wincanton, LB323. CoA expired 10/9/62.
G-AISC	Tipsy B Srs 1	ex Yeovil area. CoA expired 23/5/79. Under restoration.
G-ALYG	Auster 5D	ex Charlton Mackrell, London Airport, Irby-on-Humber, MS968. CoA expired 19/1/70. Stored.
G-ANEW	Tiger Moth	ex NM138. CoA expired 18/6/62. Stored.
G-ARJD	Colt 108	crashed 17/11/71. Frame stored.

TEMPLECOMBE
In answer to the question raised in **W&R11**, Wessex HAS.3 XS149 moved to Weston-super-Mare.

WELLS
Still bearing a typographical error instead of its serial, the Chipmunk T.10 is still with **1955 Squadron ATC** in Webbs Close.
WD355"   WD335 Chipmunk T.10   ex Dur UAS, Oxf UAS, G&S UAS, Not UAS, Lon UAS, G&S UAS, Abn UAS, StA UAS, G&S UAS, 11 RFS, 23 RFS.

WINCANTON
Auster J/1N G-AJIS moved on to Warminster.

YEOVIL
For the first time in many editions, the **Westland** plant is without an entry. Having out-lived its usefulness as an installations test-bed, the SH-3D Sea King XV372 was disposed of to a scrappy in Trowbridge. Simon Darch succeeded in flying his Tiger Moth G-AOXN again in 1988.

YEOVILTON

Major news from the superb **Fleet Air Arm Museum** is the extension of the impressive Concorde Hall to allow room for an exhibition on VTOL. With the based Sea Harriers viewablefrom the panoramic windows inside the Museum there could not be a more appropriate place for such an exhibition. Accordingly, there have been several arrivals to complete this theme. The World War One display is particularly impressive and the Skua has been 'returned' to its fjord in Norway in a vivid set-piece. There has been some reshuffling of airframes, with several moving through to the storage facility at Wroughton : Firefly TT.4 VH127 on 15/3/88; Whirlwind HAR.1 XA864 by 7/88; Wessex HAS.1 XS881/A2675 by 7/88 and UH-1H Iroquois AE-422 by 7/88 (AE-422 was to return in 6/89). Whirlwind HAS.3 XJ402/A2572 was scrapped during 1988. The Gannet cockpit section on show for many a long year here is now confirmed as being a purpose-built simulator and not an airframe conversion and therefore should be disregarded. Sea Fury 'WJ231' was registered as N57JB in the USA 3/89 - this is not the example here! FAAM is open every day (other than Christmas) March to October 1000 to 1730 and November to February 1000 to 1630. Contact : Fleet Air Arm Museum, RNAS Yeovilton, Ilchester, Somerset, BA22 8HT. Telephone : 0935 840 565.

G-ABUL"	XL717 Tiger Moth	ex G-AOXG, T7291, 33 MU, 24 EFTS, 19 EFTS.
G-AZAZ	Bensen B.8M	ex Mandon. Stored. (Amending **W&R11**)
G-BSST	Concorde 002	UK prototype, first flew 9/4/69. CoA expired 30/10/74.
8359	Short 184	ex Duxford, South Lambeth. Forward fuselage. IWM loan.
B6401"	G-AWYY Camel replica	ex Leisure Sport, N1917H, G-AWYY. CoA expired 1/9/85.
L2301	Walrus I	ex Arbroath, Thame, G-AIZG, Aer Lingus EI-ACC, IAAC N18.
L2940	Skua I	ex Lake Grotli, Norway, 800. Remains only. See notes above.
N1854	Fulmar II	ex Lossiemouth, Fairey's 'hack' G-AIBE, A&AEE.
N2078"	Sopwith Baby	ex Nash Collection. Composite of 8214 and 8215.
N4389"	N4172 Albacore	ex Land's End, Yeovilton.
N5220"	N5903 Gladiator II	ex Old Warden, 61 OTU. Shuttleworth Collection loan.
N5492"	B'111 Sopwith Triplane	ex Chertsey. Static replica.
N6452"	G-BIAU Pup replica	ex Whitehall. CoA expired 1/9/85.
P4139"	HS618 Swordfish II	ex 'W5984', Manadon A2001, Donibristle.
AL246	Martlet I	ex Loughborough, 768, 802.
DP872	Barracuda II	ex Northern Ireland. Remains. Omitted from **W&R11.**
EX976	Harvard IIA	ex Portuguese AF 1657, EX976, 41-33959.
KD431	Corsair IV	ex Cranfield, 716, 731.
KE209	Hellcat II	ex Lossiemouth, Stretton, Anthorn.
LZ551/G	Sea Vampire I	ex CS(A), DH, A&AEE, RAE. Science Museum loan.
SX137	Seafire F.17	ex Culdrose, Stretton, 759, 1831, Culham.
VR137	Wyvern TF.1	ex Cranfield. Eagle-powered prototype, never flown.
VV106+	7175M Supermarine 517	ex Cosford, St Athan, Colerne, Yatesbury. Arrived 2/90.
VX272+	7174M Hawker P.1052	ex Cosford, St Athan, Colerne. Arrived 2/90.
WA473	Attacker F.1	ex Abbotsinch gate, 736, 702, 800.
WG774	BAC 221	ex East Fortune, RAE Bedford, Filton, Fairey FD-2.
WJ231	Sea Fury FB.11	ex 'WE726', Yeovilton SF, FRU. See notes above.
WN493	Dragonfly HR.5	ex Culdrose, 705, 701, A&AEE.
WT121	Skyraider AEW.1	ex Culdrose, 849, USN 124121.
WV856	Sea Hawk FGA.6	ex RAE, 781, 806.
WW138	Sea Venom FAW.22	ex AWS, 831, 809.
XA127	Sea Vampire T.22	ex CIFE, 736. Pod.
XB446	Avenger AS.4	ex Culdrose SF, 831, 751, 820, USN 69502.
XB480	A2577 Hiller HT.1	ex Manadon, 705.
XD317	Scimitar F.1	ex FRU, RAE, 800, 736, 807.
XG574+	A2575 Whirlwind HAR.3	ex Wroughton, Lee-on-Solent, 771. Arrived by 7/89.
XG900+	Short SC.1	ex Wroughton, Hayes, South Kensington, RAE Bedford. Arrived 5/10/89. Science Museum loan.
XJ314+	R-R Thrust Rig	ex East Fortune, Strathallan, Hayes, South Kensington, RAE. Arrived 21/2/89. Science Museum loan.
XK488	Buccaneer S.1	ex BSE Filton and Blackburns.

XL503		Gannet AEW.3	ex RRE, 849 'D', 'A' Flts, A&AEE, 849 HQ Flt, C(A), 849 'A' Flt.
XN957		Buccaneer S.1	ex 736, 809.
XP142		Wessex HAS.3	ex 737. 'Humphrey'. Falklands exhibition.
XP841		HP.115	ex Cosford, Colerne, RAE Bedford.
XP980+	A2700	P.1127	ex Culdrose, Tarrant Rushton, RAE Bedford, Cranwell, A&AEE. Arrived 6/3/89.
XS527		Wasp HAS.1	ex Wroughton, 'Endurance' Flt.
XS590		Sea Vixen FAW.2	ex 899, 892.
XT176		Sioux AH.1	ex Coypool, 3 CBAS.
XT596		Phantom FG.1	ex BAe Scampton, Holme-on-Spalding Moor, A&AEE. (YF-4K).
+		Fairey III	fuselage frame.
A-522	8768M	FMA Pucara	ex St Athan, Stanley, Argentine AF. Falklands exhibition.
AE-422		UH-1H Iroquois	ex Wroughton, Yeovilton, Stanley, Argentine Army, 74-22520. Arrived 6/6/89 - see notes above. Falklands exhibition.
0729		T-34C-1 T'Mentor	ex Stanley, Pebble Island, Argentine Navy. Falklands exhibition.
0767		MB.339AA	ex Stanley, Argentine Navy. Composite airframe. Stored.
S.3398"	G-BFYO	SPAD XIII replica	ex Land's End, Chertsey, D-EOWM. CoA expired 21/6/82.
D.5397"	G-BFXL	Albatros D.Va rep	ex Leisure Sport, Land's End, Chertsey, D-EGKO. CoA exp 24/9/82.
102/17"	B'88	Fokker Dr I rep	scale replica, based on a Lawrence Parasol.
01420	G-BMZF	MiG 15bis (LIM-2)	ex North Weald, Gamston, Retford, Polish AF.
155848		F-4S-MC Phantom II	ex Lee-on-Solent (transit), VMFA-232, USMC.
159233		AV-8A-MC Harrier	ex VMA-231, USMC.
BAPC 58		Ohka II	ex Hayes, South Kensington. Science Museum loan.
BAPC 149		Short S.27 replica	ex Lee-on-Solent.

June and September 1989 were memorable months for the **Fleet Air Arm Historic Aircraft Flight**. On 10/6/89, while performing for the crowds at Prestwick, Sea Fury FB.11 TF956 encountered undercarriage problems - the starboard leg refused to come down. Despite violent 'g' manoeuvres and 'pogo-ing' the fighter down the runway, all to no avail. The pilot baled out off-shore and TF956 plunged into the bay. A Prestwick Sea King was there to pluck the pilot from the water. The wreckage was later salvaged and appeared briefly at HMS 'Gannet', Prestwick. An appeal has been launched to bring FAAHAF a replacement. The other date was much more pleasant when Sea Hawk FGA.6 WV908 flew again post restoration on 20/9/89. Sadly, budget considerations mean that it will not be performing during the 1990 season. On 1/2/90 a Sea Fury FB.11 arrived from Boscombe Down for spares use, formally for WG655, but it may for the vanguard of an FB.11 returning to the Flight. FAAHAF aircraft are not available for inspection at Yeovilton, but can be seen regularly at flying displays all over the country.

T8191		Tiger Moth	ex Yeo'ton SF, Culdrose SF, Yeo'ton SF, BRNC, Lossie SF, Arbroath SF, Culdrose SF, Bramcote, Gosport, 3 FF, 22 EFTS, 4 FIS, 3 EFTS.
LS326		Swordfish II	ex Westlands, Fairey G-AJVH, Worthy Down, 836.
VR930+	8382M	Sea Fury FB.11	ex Boscombe Down, Lee-on-Solent, Wroughton, Yeovilton, Colerne, Dunsfold, FRU, Lossiemouth, Anthorn, 801, Anthorn, 802. Arrived 1/2/90. See notes above.
WB271		Firefly AS.5	ex RAN Nowra, 723, 725, 816/817, 814.
WG655		Sea Fury T.20S	ex DLB D-CACU/ES3616, HSA Dunsfold G-9-65, Anthorn, Eglinton SF.
WV908		Sea Hawk FGA.6	ex Culdrose SF, Halton 8154M, Sydenham A2660, 738, 806, 898, 807. See notes above.

Elsewhere on the airfield in **W&R** terms, little has changed. A Harrier GR.1 has arrived for instructional purposes. The Sea Vixen was refurbished and is now the gate guardian for FONAC.

WJ677		Canberra B.2	ex St Mawgan, 7, 231 OCU, 50, 40, 103. Nose.
WP309		Sea Prince T.1	ex 750, Arbroath SF. Dump, poor state.
XE369	A2633	Sea Hawk FGA.6	ex Culdrose, Lee-on-Solent A2580, Halton 8158M, Arbroath. Dump.
XM845	A2682	Wessex HAS.1	ex Lee-on-Solent, Wroughton. Dump, very poor state.
XN308	A2605	Whirlwind HAS.7	ex Corsham, Lee-on-Solent, Wroughton, Lee-on-Solent, Arbroath, 771, 847, 848, 846, 814. Dump.
XN692	A2624	Sea Vixen FAW.2	ex Culdrose, 893. Gate guard for FONAC by 7/89.
XS128	A2670	Wessex HAS.1	ex Lee-on-Solent, 737. BDR.
XV277+		Harrier GR.1	ex Filton, HSA. Arrived 30/11/88.

AIRLINERS

Hulks at Southend. L to R: Viscount G-AYOX, Viscount G-APEX and Herald G- APWA *(Steve Harris)*
The last of the HS.748s. Sets 289 and 290 in store at Woodford *(Alan Curry)*
Museum-piece to life-saver. Trident 1E G-AVYE for smoke trials at Hatfield *(Ian Oliver)*

BAPC REGISTER 1

Short S.27 replica BAPC.149 and intrepid pilot at the Fleet Air Arm Museum, Yeovilton *(FAAM)*

BAPC.194, Santos-Dumont Demoiselle replica at Brooklands. It was built for the film 'Those Magnificent Men...' *(Ken Ellis)*

BAPC REGISTER 2

Former mount of Tony Hancock in 'Those Magnificent Men...', Dixon Ornithopter BAPC.8 laid out briefly at Old Warden *(Ian Oliver)*

Volmer VJ-23 Swingwing powered hang glider BAPC.175 at Manchester *(Alan Curry)*

Former 'Piece of Cake' Spitfire replica BAPC.202 on guard at Llanbedr *(Ken Ellis)*

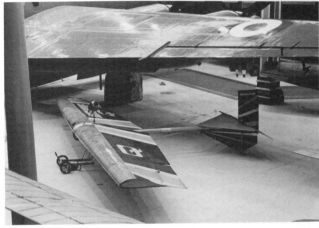

BUCCANEERS

Previously at Brough, S.2B XV155 moved to Lovaux at Macclesfield *(Alan Curry)*

Weapons loading trainer S.2B XT281 at Lossiemouth - 8705M is on the n.w.d *(John Chree)*

'Bricks' live up to their name - XV156 shows great tenacity on St Athan's dump *(Alan Curry)*

CANBERRAS

One-off Short SC-9 XH132 ready for battle damage repair training at St Mawgan *(Jim Simpson)*
St Mawgan's other Canberra is T.4 WJ870, which has seen better days *(Phil Stevens)*
Displayed within the base at Laarbruch, West Germany, B(I).8 XM264 *(Hywel Evans)*

CAERNARFON AIR MUSEUM

Imaginative plaything, Dragonfly HR.3 WN499 previously at the Torbay museum *(Ken Ellis)*

Fuselage of HM.14 Pou du Ciel BAPC.201, acquired from near Kidlington. Note non-standard undercarriage *(Ken Ellis)*

Dramatically-posed forward fuselage of Javelin FAW.7 XH837 *(Ken Ellis)*

CASEMENT IAC

Vampire T.11 198 outside the Officers' Mess *(Dave Allport)*

Provost T.51 181 hanging on to life on the dump *(Dave Allport)*

Pod of Vampire T.55 193 on the dump *(Dave Allport)*

CIVIL HULKS

Auster D.6/180 G-ARDJ awaiting its turn for attention at Leicester *(Alf Jenks)*

Forlorn Cessna 210 G-ASXR at Blackpool *(Darrel Bayley)*

Unflown since 1984, Beagle Pup G-AWKM at Swansea *(Ken Ellis)*

COMINGS AND GOINGS

Airedale G-ASAI ready to leave Dundee Airport for restoration nearby, 23 September 1989 *(Dave Allport)*

Readying Varsity WF372 for the move from Sibson to Brooklands on 13 November 1988 *(Ken Ellis)*

Dragon Rapide G-ADAH arrives at the Manchester Museum of Science and Technology from East Fortune 7 April 1989 *(Graham Sparkes)*

DOVES AND DEVONS

Sea Devon C.2 G-KOOL, ex VP967, at the East Surrey Technical College, Redhill *(John Dyer)*
Long part of the Stansted scenery, former CAFU Dove 6 G-ANUW *(Peter J Cooper)*
In open store at Sandown Sea Devon C.20 G-AMXT, ex XJ347 *(Chris Michell)*

DUXFORD

Awaiting its turn for restoration, The Fighter Collection's Yak C-11. *(Alan Curry)*
Battle R3950 from the late Charles Church's collection, briefly loaned to IWM *(Alan Curry)*
The first Hong Kong refugee? Spitfire F.24 VN485 arrived in July 1989. *(Alan Curry)*

FRENCH FLAVOUR

The unfortunate Broussard G-BKPU languishing at Barton *(Dave Allport)*
Nord 3400 No 37 at its new home of Stixwould, Lincs, ex Coventry Airport *(Ken Ellis)*
Rallye Commodore G-AXHX getting overgrown at Burnaston *(Alf Jenks)*

GATE GUARDIANS

Pole-mounted Gnat T.1 XM693 outside the British Aerospace plant at Hamble *(John Uncles)*
Britain's first Phantom guardian, FG.1 XT864 at Leuchars *(Dave Allport)*
Vampire T.11 'XD429' (really XD542) guards the South Airfield at Cranwell *(Bill Taylor)*

GONE

Beverley C.1 XH124 at Hendon. Axed January 1990 *(Ken Ellis)*
Sea Fury FB.11 TF956. Ditched off Prestwick June 1989 *(Alan Curry)*
Victor K.2 XL189 at Waddington. Axed September 1989 *(Alan Curry)*

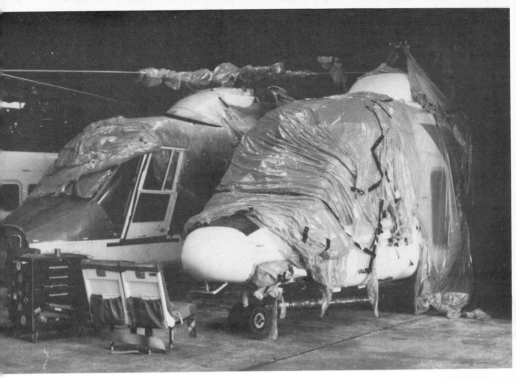

HELICOPTERS - CIVIL

Westland WG.30 cache at Beccles in December 1988. G-KATE and G-OGAS in the foreground with G-BKGD (since returned to service) at the rear *(Darrel Bayley)*

Cockpit pod of wrecked Enstrom F.28 G-BMIU at Coventry Airport *(Alf Jenks)*

'XWM 101' a rare Mockup Mk 1 at the International Fire Training College, Chorley, Lancs *(Dave Allport)*

HELICOPTERS - MILITARY

Early production Scout AH.1 XP191 on the dump at Middle Wallop *(Dave Allport)*
Whirlwind HAR.21 WV198 at the International Fire Training College, Chorley, *(Dave Allport)*
Unusual location. Wasp HAS.1 XS535 at the RAOC depot at West Moors, Dorset *(Greg Baddeley)*

HUNTERS
F.6 XG290 within the grounds of Bentley Priory *(Francois Prins)*
F.51 E-424 under restoration by SYAPS at Firbeck *(Ken Ellis)*
F.51 E-430 at Charlwood awaiting reassembly, wearing rogue Navy colours *(John Uncles)*

INTO THE VAT CAVE

Vintage Aircraft Team/Militair's ever-full hangar at Cranfield. On the restoration line, Provost T.1 G-BLFT and Alycon G-SHOW

Smashed hulk of the unique Miles Student G-MIOO

Ex Belgian Air Force CM-170R Magister MT-11/G-BRFU ready for restoration. *(All Alan Allen)*

INTERNATIONAL HELICOPTER MUSEUM

L to R: Wessex HAS.3 XS149, Wessex 60s G-AZBY, G-AVNE, WG.30 G- BGHF *(Ken Ellis)*
Hiller UH-12C G-ASTP *(Ken Ellis)*
Westland Widgeon 2 5N-ABW and Dragonfly HR.5 WG719 *(Ken Ellis)*

LEE'S TREASURE TROVE

General view of the 'historic' corner at Lee-on-Solent, Gannet T.5 XT752, Sea Hawk FGA.4 WV903, Gannet AEW.3 XL500 and Harvard III EZ407 in the foreground

Stored Sea Hawk FGA.6 WV911 is nearest the camera, with FGA.4 WV903 behind.

Gannet T.5 XT752 has been held at Lee since November 1978
(All Peter J Cooper)

LIGHTNINGS

Brilliantly re-assembled, the
Wainfleet T.5 XS456
(Tony McCarthy)

F.3 XR713 is displayed outside the
111 Squadron headquarters at
Leuchars *(Peter J Cooper)*

Rudderless F.3 XP741 has so far
escaped burning at Manston
(Tony McCarthy)

MANCHESTER AIRPORT

Okada Air BAC 1-11 5N-ADK held in open store, January 1990 *(Alan Curry)*
Scrapping of former Dan Air HS.748 G-BEKC, 1989 *(Alan Curry)*
Aztec 250B G-BAWV suffering C of G problems *(Graham Sparkes)*

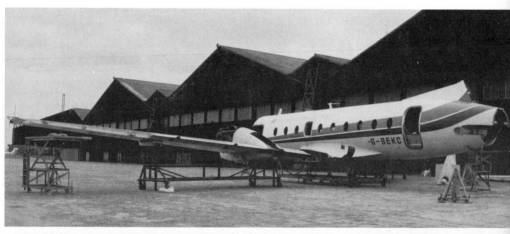

MARTIN BAKER'S METEORS

Spares ship for the airworthy WL419, T.7 WA638 hangared at Chalgrove *(Tim Hills)*

Centre section of former RAE Llanbedr T.7 WA662 with the majority of WL405 behind *(Tim Hills)*

T.7 WL405, ex RAE Farnborough. NEAM at Sunderland hold other parts to this aircraft *(Tim Hills)*

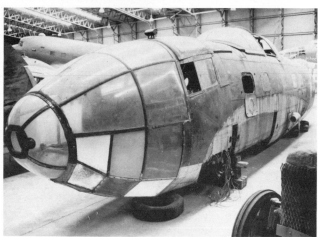

NORTH WEALD

Skyraider corner - Robs Lamplough's AD-4W G-BMFB ex SE-EBK

After use in the series 'Piece of Cake', CASA 2-111 G-AWHB in the Aces High hangar

Gnat T.1 XS104 under restoration for the Butane Buzzard Company *(All Alan Curry)*

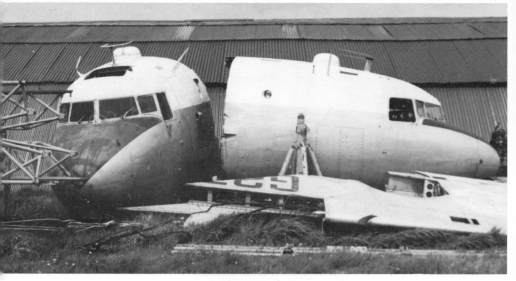

NOSES

Two former Senegalese Air Force C-47 noses (6W-SAE and 'F) were briefly at Cranfield, prior to moving to Kew *(Alan Allen)*

One of two ex Arkia Viscount noses (this one is 4X-AVB) held in a yard at Coggeshall, Essex *(Simon Murdoch)*

Showing all the signs of a lot of crash rescue training, the forlorn nose of Vulcan B.2 XM656 at Cottesmore *(Alan Curry)*

PIPER HULKS

Great registration for a 'bug bomber', Pawnee G-BDDT seen here at East Winch, is now at Boston on rebuild *(Bill Taylor)*

Battered Aztec fuselage G-AYTD out to graze at Sandown *(Chris Michell)*

Long-time part of the scene at Andrewsfield, Cherokee G-AXTK *(Darrel Bayley)*

RAF MUSEUM NEWCOMERS

Former Benson gate guardian Spitfire PR.XIX PM651 during installation, Dec 1989 *(Alan Curry)*
Swift FR.5 WK281 was previously with the St Athan collection *(Alan Curry)*
Complete with ADEN gun-pack, Hunter FGA.9 XG154 *(Alan Curry)*

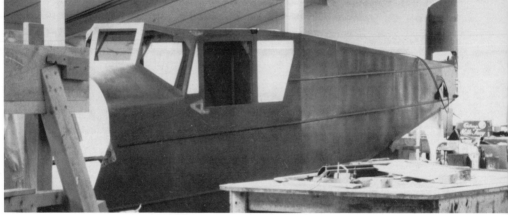

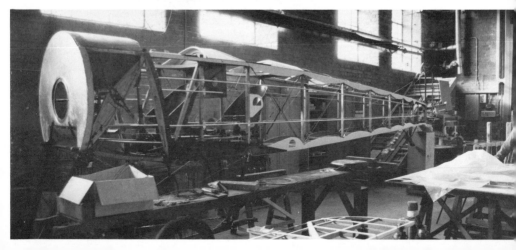

RESTORATIONS

Foster-Wikner GM.1 Wicko G-AFJB/DR613 undergoing near total restoration at Berkswell *(Alf Jenks)*

Visitors can monitor the progress of Desoutter I G-AAPZ in the workshop at Old Warden *(Alf Jenks)*

Restoration of the long-hidden Avro 504K G-ABAA well under way in the workshop of the Manchester Museum of Science and Industry *(Ken Ellis)*

SEA VIXENS

Smiling XJ604 which left Cranfield by road in April 1988. Bound for Otterburn? *(Ken Ellis)*

XJ582 in poor state on Cottesmore's dump *(Alan Curry)*

XJ580 on display at Christchurch *(Alan Curry)*

SHACKLETONS

8 Squadron's spares-ship MR.2C WL798 in its hangar at Lossiemouth *(John Chree)*

Once earmarked for the RAF Museum, the nose of MR.3/3 WR974 at Cosford during the long job dismantling it ready for the move to Charlwood *(Ken Ellis)*

'Zebedee', former RAE T.4 VP293 languishing at Strathallan *(Peter J Cooper)*

SOUTHALL TECH

Chipmunk T.10 WB763, allocated G-BBMR in 1973, but not fully converted for civil use, preferring life as an instructional airframe.

Trestled Vampire T.11 XD536, otherwise known as 7734M, has been here since 1986.

A 1960 model short-nose Piper Aztec 250 G-AREF, retired from active service in 1986
(All Alan Allen)

WESSEX

HU.5 XT486 masquerading as a HC.2 at Brize Norton
(Paul A Jackson)

Hulk of HAS.1 XM926 lying out on the ranges at PEE, Pendine
(Jim Henderson)

Out in the long grass at Fleetlands, HAS.3 XM923
(Peter J Cooper)

Staffordshire

ALDRIDGE
(On the A454 west of Walsall - **NB** omitted from the last two editions.) In Station Road, off Walsall Road, can be found **425 Squadron ATC**'s headquarters. they still have their Canberra nose, but readers are warned that a building extension makes it very hard to see!
WD931   Canberra B.2   ex Pershore, RRE, RAE. Nose.

BALDWINS GATE
Colt 108 G-ARKN was flying again by 5/88.

BURNTWOOD
The Vulcan nose is confirmed as still in residence in a garden in the town.
XM652   Vulcan B.2A   ex Sheffield, Waddington, 50, 35, 44, 9. Nose.

HALFPENNY GREEN
Airedale G-AVKP moved off to Sywell and by 6/88 was airworthy. That leaves just the T.31 with the local Air Scouts to record.
BGA.1346   T.31   ex Bickmarsh, RAFGSA.297. wfu 1/79. Air Scouts.

LICHFIELD
There are now three separate **W&R** items within the town. **1206 Squadron ATC** still have their PAX trainer in Cherry Orchard Road, near the City railway station. A private collector took delivery of the former Newark (and everywhere else!) Vampire T.11 during 1/90. The Gannet hulk was still to be seen in the scrapyard in mid-1988 at least.
WK576   8357M Chipmunk T.10 PAX   ex AOTS, 3/4 CAACU, Cam UAS, Oxf UAS, Lon UAS, Cam UAS, Lon UAS, Cam UAS, Hul UAS, Cam UAS, Bir UAS, Cam UAS, 22 RFS. See above.
WZ553+   Vampire T.11   ex Winthorpe, South Wigston, Bruntingthorpe, Loughborough, East Midlands Airport, Liverpool Airport, Woodford, Chester, St Athan, 4 FTS, 7 FTS, 202 AFS. Arrived 1/90 - see notes above.
XL471   Gannet AEW.3   ex Farnborough, 849 'B', HQ, 'D', HQ, 'A', 'D', A', 'B', HQ and 'C' Flts. Fuselage. wings at Tinwald Downs.

PENKRIDGE
The ATC Vampire moved to Stafford.

ROCESTER
(On the B5030 north of Uttoxeter) Still kept at the **JCB** plant is the Dove.
G-ARJB   Dove 8   ex East Midlands. CoA expired 10/12/73.

SEIGHFORD
At the former airfield, the **Staffordshire Aviation Museum** established themselves early in 1990. Due here is the Canberra at Locking - which see. On site so far are :
XE650+   Hunter FGA.9   ex Macclesfield, Bitteswell, 8, 208, 1, 263. Nose. Arr 3/90.
XG195+   Hunter FGA.   ex Hemswell, Cleethorpes, Macclesfield, Bitteswell G-9-453, 208, 1, 19. Composite, nose of GA.11 WT741 and other parts from XG297/G-9-452. Arrived 3/90.

STAFFORD
The former Penkridge Vampire T.11 (XD528/8159M) moved here during 1989 and was put up for tender during November. Its ultimate destination is unknown. Of the other aircraft here, the scrappy that did the Hendon Beverley to death was reported to have Stafford as his next port of call, "for a couple of Whirlwinds". Either these are machines we have no trace of, or he was using a generic term for a helicopter!
XA801   7739M Javelin FAW.2   ex St Athan, 46. Gate guardian.
XP359   8447M Whirlwind HAR.10   ex Abingdon, RAFEF, Wroughton, 103, 110, 103, 225. Dump - see notes above.

XS572   8845M Wasp HAS.1   ex Wroughton. Dump. See notes above.
XT469   8920M Wessex HU.5   ex Wroughton. Inst with Tactical Supply Wing. See notes above.

STOKE-ON-TRENT

In R J Mitchell's birthplace, the Spitfire continues to have pride of place in the
City Museum and Art Gallery. It is open daily 1030 to 1700 Monday to Saturday and
Sundays 1400 to 1700.   Contact : Stoke-on-Trent City Museum and Art Gallery,
Bethesda Street, Hanley, Stoke ST1 3DE. Tel 0782 273173.

RW388   6946M Spitfire XVI   ex Kemble, 71 MU, 19 MU, 5 MU, Andover, Benson, FC&RS, 612, 667.

Ken Fern has renamed his collection **The Helicopter Collection** although his love
light aircraft is still very much alive. Ken's aircraft can also be found at Long
Marston, Warmingham and Wigan – and see also Chorley. Visits to the Stoke workshop
are by prior permission only, contact : The Helicopter Collection, 311 Congleton
Road, Scholar Green, Stoke-on-Trent ST7 3JQ. Telephone : 0782 773140. Ken took
delivery of Chrislea Airguard G-AFIN from TAC at Warmingham in late 1987 and this
is being rebuilt to flying condition. In exchange, Ken built a non-flying replica
Airguard, BAPC.203/'G-AFIN' and this was delivered to Warmingham in 1989. Ken is
also building an Austin Whippet replica. Whirlwind HAR.9 XN298 was moved to
Warmingham in 1/89. Bensen BAPC.200 was loaned to SAC at Long Marston in 1989.
With the addition of a Jet Provost nose from Bournemouth the current situation here
is :
G-AFIN+   Chrislea Airguard   ex Warmingham, Wigan, Finningley. Arrived 12/87 – see above.
XN597+   7984M Jet Provost T.3 ex Bournemouth, Faygate, 2 FTS. Damaged 28/6/67. Nose. Arr 1/90.

SWYNNERTON

(East of the A519 south of Newcastle-under-Lyme) The Whirlwind should still be
inside the large Army camp here.
XK987   8393M Whirlwind HAR.10   ex Stafford, Brize Norton, 103, 110, 228, 22, 217, 1360 Flt, 22.

TATENHILL

With the arrival of long-term restoration G-ARNN from Leicester, this airfield is
now a centre for Globe Swift revivals!
G-ARNN+   GC-1B Swift   ex Leicester, VP-YMJ, VP-RDA, ZS-BMX, NC3279K. Crashed 1/9/73.
                             Arrived 1989. Restoration.
G-AVLM   Pup 160   ex Nottingham Airport, Cippenham. CoA expired 24/4/69.
G-BFNM   GC-1B Swift   ex Nottingham Airport, N78205. Restoration.

Suffolk

BARNHAM

(East of the A134, south of Thetford) During the summer of 1989 this out-station
of RAF Marham took on the former Bury St Edmunds Vampire FB.5.
VV217+   7323M Vampire FB.5   ex Bury St Edmunds, 'VV271', Oakington, DH. Arrived 6/89.

BAWDSEY

Shortly before the announcement of the closure of the base, a Staravia lorry
appeared in 1/90 and took away Hunter GA.11 XE673/8846M. Destination unknown, but
Marlow would seem a good bet....

BECCLES
The continued depression in the gas/oil industry has put some expensive hardware in store at the **British International Helicopters** heliport. Westland WG.30 Srs 100 G-BKGD was stored here from late 1988, be re-entered service (on the Scilly run) in mid-1989.

G-KATE+	Westland WG.30-100	ex Great Yarmouth, BIH. CoA expired 16/9/88. Stored.
G-OGAS+	Westland WG.30-100	ex Great Yarmouth, BIH, G-17-1, G-OGAS, G-BKNW. CoA expired 19/5/88. Stored.

BENTWATERS
With no definitive reports on the state of the BDR airframes within the base the situation is thought to be as before.

104	Mystere IVA	ex Woodbridge, Sculthorpe, French AF.
80260	F-101B-105-MC	ex Woodbridge, Davis-Monthan, Oregon ANG. BDR.

BURY ST EDMUNDS
During March/April 1989 **301 Squadron ATC** moved from Northgate Street to the TAVR Headquarters in the town. This occasioned a change around in airframes. Prior to this a Chippax arrived from Stowmarket 2/88, and it moved across to the new location. Vampire FB.5 VV217/7323M moved to <u>Barnham</u> by 6/89. The wreck of Chipmunk T.10 WK575 was scrapped 4/89.

WG471+	8210M Chipmunk T.10	ex Stowmarket, Leeming, Abn UAS, 1 FTS, 6 FTS, 220 OCU, Aston Down CF, MCCS, 4 SoTT, Nott UAS, Leeds UAS, 19 RFS, 24 RFS, 3 BFTS, 16 RFS, 4 BFTS. See notes above.

Continued proof that no stone should be left unturned, another 'Flea' has been 'discovered'! **N Hamlin-Wright** is working on the restoration of G-AEMY here.

G-AEMY+	HM.14 Pou du Ciel	ex Stowmarket.

FLIXTON
(On the B1062 west of Bungay) Another museum making great strides, the **Norfolk and Suffolk Aviation Museum** is hard at work on a major redevelopment of their site. Fund raising is underway for a hangar, which will be a large blister-type. To prepare the foundations, on land that was liable to flooding, several thousand tons of rubble have been laid. Work has continued on the airframes and displays during this busy period. Opening times : April, May, September and October open Sundays and Bank Holidays 1000 to 1700; July and August open Wednesdays and Thursdays 1900 to 2100; June, July and August on Sundays 1000 to 2100 and in July and August on Thursdays 1100 to 1700 - when the aircraft park will be open, if not the Museum building. Contact : John Reeve, Prospect Farm, Mettingham, Bungay, Suffolk.

N99153	T-28C Trojan	ex East Ham, France, Zaire/Congo AF FG-289, USN VT-3 146289. Crashed 14/12/77. Fuselage only, combined Zaire/USN colours.
P8140"	BAPC.71 Spitfire replica	ex 'P9390'.
VL349	N5054 Anson C.19	ex Norwich Airport, G-AWSA, SCS, NCS, North Coates SF, WSF, FCCS, HCCS, HCEU, 116, CSE, 1 FU.
VX580	Valetta C.2	ex Norwich Airport, MCS, MEAFCS, 114, HS. On loan.
WF128	8611M Sea Prince T.1	ex Honington, Kemble, Sydenham SF, A&AEE, 750.
WF643	Meteor F.8	ex Coltishall, Kemble, 29, Nicosia SF, 611, 56. Composite.
WV605	Provost T.1	ex Henlow, Higher Blagdon, 6 FTS, 3 FTS, 22 FTS.
XH892	7982M Javelin FAW.9R	ex Duxford, Colerne, Shawbury, 29, 64, 23. On loan.
XJ482	A2598 Sea Vixen FAW.1	ex Wimbourne Minster, 766, 700Y.
XK624	Vampire T.11	ex Lytham St Annes, Blackpool Airport, CFS, 3 FTS, 7 FTS, 1 FTS, 23 GCF, CFS, 7 FTS.
XN304	Whirlwind HAS.7	ex Bedford, Henlow, Wroughton, Shrivenham, Wroughton, 705, Old Sarum, 848.
XR485	Whirlwind HAR.10	ex Wroughton, 2 FTS, CFS.
79	Mystere IVA	ex Sculthorpe, French AF.
42196	F-100D-11-NA	ex Sculthorpe, French AF.

| 54433 | T-33A-5-LO | ex Sculthorpe, French AF. |
| BAPC 147 | Bensen B.7 | ex Loddon. |

HONINGTON

Much activity at this Tornado base to talk of. **W&R11** was about to confine the former MAPS Grunau Baby VT921 to LOST! It is now confirmed as having been burnt by the ATC unit that was looking after it, circa 1980. Buccaneer S.2B XW541/8858M flew off to Foulness on 11/10/88, courtesy of Chinook HC.1 ZA678. Tornado P.02 XX946/8883M left by road 21/3/90 bound for Harwich and Hamburg. The compound containing Tornado hulks was cleared out in March 1989, with both ZA408 and ZA555 being scrapped at this time. The hulk of ZA494 had moved to the main car park – further proof that the BAe take-over of Rover has given rise to identity problems! This was finally cleared 26/3/90. Not mentioned in **W&R11**, GR.1 ZA597 had been in use at the base for spares since 12/11/83, when it was declared Cat 4. It was removed in 1988 for similar purposes. Current situation :

XK526	8648M Buccaneer S.1	ex RAE Bedford. Gate guardian.
XN930	8180M Buccaneer S.1	ex BDR, St Athan, 736. Dump.
XR754+	8972M Lightning F.6	ex Binbrook, 11, 5-11 pool, 23, 5 A&AEE. Flew in 22/6/88.
XV338	8774M Buccaneer S.2A	ex 237 OCU, 12. Cockpit.
XX886	Buccaneer S.2B	ex 208, 16. WLT.

IPSWICH

188 Squadron ATC still keep their Chippax, at the TAVR Centre on the A12.

| WG463 | 8363M Chipmunk T.10 PAX | ex Hamble G-ATDX, Stn UAS, Not UAS, StA UAS, Cam UAS, Colerne SF, Oxf UAS, Abn UAS, Oxf UAS, 24 GCF, Cottesmore SF, 3 BFTS, 16 RFS. |

IPSWICH AIRPORT

Yet another airfield with problems about its future. Three Harvest Air Islanders noted in **MiniWrecks** as being in open store were all operational again by early 1989. (They were G-BJWL, G-BJWM and G-BJWN.) Dismantled Apache 160 PH-NLK had gone by mid-1988 and is thought to be the example to be found at Burgh-le-Marsh. DC-3-201A N4565L has continued to lie forgotten and has received more damage from gales. The Airport held an auction to sell the aircraft in 2/90, but this fell through.

G-ARKM		Colt 108	damaged 27/11/83. Under rebuild.
G-ATES		Cherokee Six 260	crashed 8/2/81. Para-trainer with Ipswich Parachute Centre.
N750M		Widgeon	ex Hal Far, N750, USN J4F-2 37711. Spares for N3103Q.
N3103Q	G-DUCK	Widgeon	ex Hal Far, N58337, OA-14 42-38217, NC28679. Restoration.
N4565L		DC-3-201A	ex Dublin, LV-GYP, LV-PCV, N129H, N512, N51D, N80C, NC21744. See notes above.

LAKENHEATH

Confirming the presence (or otherwise) of the myriad Mystere BDR airframes here is proving difficult. T-33A 14060 moved out to Molesworth by 5/88. Bearing in mind the Mystere situation, things should look like this :

16	Mystere IVA	ex Chateaudun, via Cambrai, French AF. Decoy.
75	Mystere IVA	ex Sculthorpe, Chateaudun, French AF.
99	Mystere IVA	ex Sculthorpe, Chateaudun, French AF.
113	Mystere IVA	ex Chateaudun, via Cambrai, French AF.
126	Mystere IVA	ex Sculthorpe, Chateaudun, French AF.
145	Mystere IVA	ex Chateaudun, French AF.
241	Mystere IVA	ex Chateaudun, French AF.
285	Mystere IVA	ex Chateaudun, via Cambrai, French AF.
300	Mystere IVA	ex Sculthorpe, Chateaudun, French AF.
309	Mystere IVA	ex Sculthorpe, Chateaudun, French AF.
24434	F-105G-RE	ex Davis-Monthan, 562 TFS.
37471	F-4C-18-M C	ex 163 TFS/122 TFW, Indiana ANG. BDR.
37610	F-4C-20-MC	ex 171 FIS, Michigan ANG. BDR.
63319"	42269 F-100D-16-NA	ex '54048', French AF. Gate guardian.

MILDENHALL
The little BDR 'fleet' here expanded somewhat with the arrival of a C-130A in 9/89.

16769	T-33A-1-LO	ex French AF, CIFAS-328. BDR.
24198	VC-140B-LM JetStar	ex 58 MAS, Ramstein. Inst.
40707	F-4C-22-MC	ex 171 FIS, Michigan ANG. BDR.
70524+	C-130A-LM	ex 143 TAS. Flew in 25/9/89. BDR.

MONEWDEN
(South of the A1120, north of Ipswich) At a farm strip, the Cessna hulk is still used for spares.

G-BENF	Cessna T.210L	ex Ipswich, N732AE, D-EIPY, N732AE. Crashed 29/5/81.

PARHAM
(Or Framlingham, on the B1116 north of Woodbridge) Cherokee 140 G-AVLI arrived here from Southend by 8/87, it was flying by 2/88. The former Lakenheath Aero Club Cessna is still stored.

N11824	Cessna 150L	stored, dismantled.

SNAILWELL
(North of Newmarket and listed under 'Newmarket' in **W&R11**) The famous yard of W E Knappett and Sons Ltd is now known as **Newmans**. Process rate is high here, but three confirmed 'inbounds' during 1988-1989 were all from Wyton : Canberra B.2 WK162/8887M; Canberra T.17 WJ977/8761M and Comet C.2R XK697.

STOWMARKET
Chipmunk T.10 PAX trainer WG471/8210M moved to Bury St Edmunds.

SUDBURY
Tony Ditheridge's **AJD Engineering** has acquired a former Canadian Hurricane IIB for long-term restoration to flying condition. Also held here is a Curtis Jenny for Aero Vintage Ltd.

+	Curtis JN4 Jenny	ex USA, 'The Great Waldo Pepper'. In store 1989.
BW853+	G-BRKE Hurricane IIB	ex Canada. For restoration.

SWEFLING
(On the B1119 east of Framlingham) Another well-known scrapyard is **Swefling Engineering** (and also known as Austin's). Processing of the former Binbrook Lightnings was swift and it is reported that not all of them came here – see under Binbrook for more details. Noted here 2/89 was the hulk of Mystere IVA '10' from Molesworth.

WALPOLE
(On the B1117 south east of Halesworth) The collection of noses at a private house here has grown more than a little and is known as the **Blyth Valley Aviation Collection**. (Readers should also refer to the 'Cockpit Collection' at Romford, these references may be linked/confused.)

WN907+	7416M Hunter F.5	ex Ascot, St Athan, Colerne, 257. Nose. First noted 9/88.
XL388	8750M Vulcan B.2	ex Honington, 50, Wadd Wing, Scampton Wing, 9. Nose.
XN696+	Sea Vixen FAW.2	ex Farnborough, Tarrant Rushton, ADS, 899. Nose. First noted 9/88.
+	Vampire T.11	Pod. '31'. First noted 9/88.

WATTISHAM
Gate guardian Spitfire V EP120/8070M was removed from the gate and moved to St Athan 1/2/89. It will not be replaced. Buccaneer S.2A XV154/8854M, while allocated for BDR here, preferred to stay in the land of the Malt and is listed under Lossiemouth. Former Leuchars-based Phantom FG.1s are arriving here as **W&R12** goes to press, but it is not clear if they will be long-termers or not. If they are – read all about them in **W&R13**! Adding to **W&R11** the fate of Lightnings XM139 and XM147, last recorded leaving here by road on 27/8/86, is now known as targets at Pendine.

WJ603	8664M Canberra B.2	ex 100, 85, 98, 85, 98, 6, 35, 115, 18. Dump, poor state.
XM192	8413M Lightning F.1A	ex Wattisham TFF, Binbrook TFF, 226 OCU, 111. Gate guardian.
XR718	8932M Lightning F.3	ex LTF, 11, LTF, 11, 5, LTF, 5, 11, LTF, 5, LTF, 5, 226 OCU, 29, 56. BDR.
XT595	8550M Phantom FG.1	ex St Athan, Abingdon, St Athan, Coningsby, A&AEE. Noseless hulk. (Nose – 8851M – is at Abingdon.)

WOODBRIDGE

Another USAF base where the job of compiling 'Who's Who in Mysteres' is proving problematical. With no contrary information, it is a case of status quo here.

9	Mystere IVA	ex Sculthorpe, Chateaudun, French AF. Decoy.
25	Mystere IVA	ex Sculthorpe, Chateaudun, French AF. Decoy.
50	Mystere IVA	ex Sculthorpe, Chateaudun, French AF. Decoy.
133	Mystere IVA	ex Sculthorpe, Chateaudun, French AF. Decoy.
276	Mystere IVA	ex Sculthorpe, Chateaudun, French AF. Decoy.
37414	F-4C-15-MC	ex New York ANG. Arrived 16/7/86. BDR.
70270	F-101B-80-MC	ex Davis-Monthan, Texas ANG.

Surrey

BANSTEAD

(On the A217 north of Reigate) An inspection here in 10/89 found the usual depressing pile of light aviation flotsam missing. They had been replaced by an even more depressing pile of junked road-building machines! As many a **W&R** reader knows, they may well survive elsewhere so for the purposes of completeness they were/are : G-APZE Apache 160; G-ATLN Cessna F.172G; G-ATRD Cessna F.150F; G-AXXA Cherokee 180E; G-AZDB Pup 100; G-AZWU Cessna F.150L; G-BAXW Cessna F.150L.

BROOKLANDS

(Or Weybridge) With a planned 'Preview' opening to the public for six months in 1991, aircraft and motor car enthusiasts alike are chomping at the bit for the **Brooklands Museum** to throw open its doors! For those that cannot wait that long, guided tours are available on a strictly prior arrangement basis, contact : Brooklands Museum, The Clubhouse, Brooklands Road, Weybridge, Surrey KT13 0QN. Telephone 0932 57381. As will be seen from the listing below, the aircraft acquisition programme has been in full swing, with the Varsity and Viscount dominating from a size point of view and the Harrier being the first with a non-service collection. Several airframes are on loan to the collection and are noted as such in the listing. The Britannia is held in store courtesy of the Museum while a permanent home is sought for it. The centre section is stored at RAF Quedgeley. Bleriot XI G-LOTI was purchased from Mike Beach by the Museum 12/89. Two loan aircraft have moved on : Comper Swift G-ACTF had moved out by 7/86, current whereabouts unknown; Mike Birch lent his Zlin Krajanek glider from 7/88, but it left during 1989. Current situation is as follows :-

G-AACA"	B'177 Avro 504K replica	ex 'G1381', Henlow. Under restoration.
G-ADRY"	B' 29 HM.14 Pou du Ciel	ex Aberdare, Swansea. On loan from Mike Beach (MB).
G-AEKV	DZQ Kronfeld Drone	BGA.2510 CoA expired 6/10/60. Loan Mike Beach.
G-ANCF	Britannia 308F	ex Manston, 5Y-AZP, G-ANCF, LV-GJB, LV-PPJ, G-ANCF ntu, G-14-1, G-18-4, N6597C ntu, G-ANCF. Roger Hargreaves/Proteus Aero Services. See notes above.
G-APIM+	Viscount 806	ex Southend, BAF, BA, BEA. Damaged 11/1/88. Arrived 11/2/90.
G-BJHV	Voisin replica	ex Old Warden. On loan.

G-LOTI	Bleriot XI replica	CoA expired 19/7/82. See notes above.
G-MJPB	Manuel Ladybird	On loan Bill Manuel.
G-VTOL+	ZA250 Harrier T.52	ex Dunsfold. Arrived 11/89. Loan from BAe.
BGA. 643	ATH Slingsby Gull 3	(Hawkridge Kittiwake) Loan Mike Beach.
BGA.3277+	FHQ Hols der Teufel rep	Loan Mike Beach. First noted 7/88.
	Curtiss Pusher rep	c/n PFA.119-10717. Loan Mike Beach.
+	VC-10	test shell, nose section. First noted 1987.
A40-AB	VC-10 1103	ex Sultan of Oman, G-ASIX.
D-12-354+	Rheinland	Loan Mike Beach. First noted 7/88.
B7270"+ G-BFCZ	Sopwith Camel rep	ex Lands End, Duxford, Thorpe Park. Arrived by 7/88. Made airworthy by PPS at Booker.
L6906"+ B' 44	Magister I	ex Woodley, Wroughton, Frenchay, G-AKKY, T9841, 11 EFTS, 16 EFTS. Arrived by 6/88. On loan from Berkshire Aviation Group.
N2980	Wellington 1A	ex Loch Ness, 20 OTU, 37, 149. Ditched 31/12/40. Under extensive restoration.
V7767"+ B' 72	Hurricane replica	ex North Weald, Coventry, 'Battle of Britain'. Arrived 20/7/89.
WF372+	Varsity T.1	ex Sibson, 6 FTS, 1 ANS, RAFC, 201 AFS. Arrived 13/11/88.
XA292+	FLR Cadet TX.3	BGA.3350. Loan Mike Beach. First noted 7/88.
XD816+	Valiant BK.1	ex Henlow, BAC, 214, 148. Nose section. Arrived 9/88.
R4	B'114 Vickers Viking rep	ex Chertsey, 'The Land Time Forgot'. Dismantled.
E-421+	Hunter F.51	ex Brooklands Tech, Kingston-on-Thames, Dunsfold, G-9-443, Aalborg, ESK.724, Danish Air Force. Arrived 18/3/89. On loan from BAe.
BAPC.117+	BE 2c replica	ex North Weald, BBC 'Wings'. Arrived 20/7/89.
BAPC.187	Roe I Biplane rep	Displayed in replica of Roe's shed.
BAPC.194	Demoiselle replica	ex Henlow, Gatow, 'Those Magnificent Men'. On loan.

Located nearby is **Autokraft Ltd** where work is well underway on two Hurricanes and two Tempests. One of the Hurricanes is LF738, underway in arrangement with the Medway Aircraft Preservation Society and also being work on at Rochester, where the airframe is listed for the purposes of **W&R!**. The other is a former Canadian MK XII. Both Tempests came from the Tangmere Flight cache.

5589+	Hurricane XII	ex Canada, RCAF. Under restoration.
HA586+ G-TEMT	Tempest II	ex Chichester, India, IAF, RAF MW763.
HA604+ G-PEST	Tempest II	ex Chichester, India, IAF, RAF MW401.

As can be seen from the above, the nearby **Brooklands Technical College** is down to just the Vampire now. Hunter F.51 E-421 moved to Brooklands 18/3/89.

XJ772	Vampire T.11	ex Wisley, Shawbury, CATCS, 1 FTS, 8 FTS, RAFC.

BYFLEET
Proctor IV NP303/G-ANZJ moved to East Tilbury by 1989.

CAMBERLEY
To be found near the town centre on the A30 is the headquarters of **1075 Squadron ATC**, who still have their 'JP' nose section.

XN493	Jet Provost T.3	ex Abingdon, 3 FTS, 7 FTS, RAFC. Nose section.

The locality is decidedly Auster-orientated, with three (quite separate) rebuilds going on is :-

G-AJUD	J/1 Autocrat	ex Tongham. CoA expired 18/5/74. Under restoration, by C Sawyer.
G-AYDW	Terrier 2	ex Cranfield, Bushey, G-ARLM, TW568, LAS, AOPS, 227 OCU, 43 OTU. CoA expired 1/7/73. Under restn by Barry Parkhouse - see also Kew.
G-JETS	Terrier 2	ex G-ASOM, Chirk, G-35-11, VF505, AAC, 652, 1909. CoA expired 19/9/79. Under restoration by Ted Tootel.

CHARLWOOD
(West of Gatwick Airport) More precisely located here is the ever-growing collection of aircraft at **Vallance Byways** in Lowfield Road, which **W&R11** had in West Sussex. Please note this collection is not open to the public. From Sea Hawk G-JETH in the last edition, the expansion rate here has been incredible. However, as

W&R closed for press, planning permission problems were threatening this collection. By 7/88 Vampire T.11 XE998 had arrived from the Biggin Hill area, but had moved on again by 1989 - destination unknown. A private house nearby received Canberra nose WT482/'160 CSE' from Wyton (via Aviation and Marine in Hull) on 21/6/89, but it had moved on to Long Marston by 9/89.G-DACA+ WF118 Sea Prince T.1   ex Gloucester-Cheltenham, Kemble, 750, A&AEE, 727, A&AEE, RAF Farnborough. Arrived 12/11/89.

G-GACA+	WP308 Sea Prince T.1	ex Gloucester-Cheltenham, Kemble, 750. Arrived 12/11/89.
G-JETH	Sea Hawk FB.5	ex Bournemouth, Southend, 'XE364', XE489, FRU, 899. Composite.
N46EA+	XK885 Pembroke C.1	ex Gloucester-Cheltenham, St Athan, 8452M, 60, 21, WCS, Seletar SF, B&TTF, Seletar SF, S&TFF, 209, 267. Arrived by 11/89.
VZ638+	G-JETM Meteor T.7	ex North Weald, Bournemouth, Southampton, Southend, Kemble, CAW, RAFC, 237 OCU, 501, Biggin Hill SF, FCCS, 85, 54, 25, 500. Arrived 7/88.
WH903+	8584M Canberra B.2	ex Hull, Wroughton, Abingdon, Bicester, 100, 85, MoA, 85, West Raynham TFF, 228 OCU, 102, 617. Nose section, first noted 12/88.
WR974+	8117M Shackleton MR.3/3	ex Cosford, Kinloss Wing, 203, 42, 203, ASWDU, MinTech, ASWDU, MinTech, CA. Arrived by 7/89.
WR982+	8106M Shackleton MR.3/3	ex Cosford, 201, 206, MoA, 205, 203, 206. Arrived by 11/89.
XN923+	Buccaneer S.1	ex Boscombe Down, West Freugh. Arrived 23/3/90.
XP398+	8794M Whirlwind HAR.10	ex Peckham Rye, Shawbury, 22, 1563F, 202, 103, 110, 225. First noted 7/88.
E-430+	Hunter F.51	ex Faygate, Chertsey, Dunsfold, G-9-448, Aalborg, ESK.724, Danish AF. Painted in FAA colours, GA.11-style.
J-1605+	G-BLID Venom FB.50	ex Duxford, Swiss AF. Arrived 27/10/89.

DUNSFOLD

A fair bit of expansion to talk of here, with a Canberra joining the dump and a Hunter 're-appearing' on the dump - albeit in poor state. This is almost certainly F.4 WV395, last noted on the dump in 6/83. The Trident is still used by RFD Ltd of Godalming for escape trials.

G-ARPZ	Trident 1C	ex Heathrow, BA, BEA. CoA expired 26/1/86.
WT488+	Canberra T.4	ex Samlesbury, CSF, 360, 98, 360, 231 OCU, 360, 98, 231 OCU, 360, 231 OCU, Wyton SF, 360, 98, 245, 527, CSE. Arrived by 8/88. Dump.
WV395+	G-9-428 Hunter F.4	ex Cosford, 8001M, MoS, 20. First noted 7/89, dump, poor state. See notes above.

EGHAM

With no information to the contrary, Peter Neilson's Auster AOP.9 continues to be rebuilt here.

XN435	G-BGBU Auster AOP.9	ex Amersham, Heston, St Athan, 6 Liaison Depot Flt, MoA.

FAIROAKS

Having written this location out of **W&R11**, it makes a re-entry this time with a predictable rotary bias. Alan Mann use an Agusta A109 as a travelling demonstrator and installations rig. It has been used for several ambulance (sorry, yah we're talking EMS here, yah) and military (who dares wins)' rig-outs.

G-GBCA+	Agusta A.109 Mk II	Crashed 7/6/85. See notes above.
G-JGFF+	AB.206B JetRanger	Crashed 17/7/86. Wreck. First noted 10/88.

GODALMING

Located in Hallam Road at the TAVR Centre is **1254 Sqn ATC**, who still have their Hunter nose.

WV332	7673M Hunter F.4	ex Dunsfold, G-9-406, Halton, 234, 112, 67. Nose.

REDHILL

Airframes used by the two elements of the **East Surrey Technical College** are unchanged. Note that they are at quite separate sites in the town. The Musketeer and Hiller are at **Redhill Technical College**, the Sea Devon at ESTC.

G-ANOA	Hiller UH-12A	ex Redhill Aerodrome, F-BEEG, N8170H. CoA expired 12/6/70. RTC.
G-AWTU	Musketeer A23-19A	ex Deanland, AP-AWT, G-AWTU, N2769B. wfu 5/85. RTC.
G-KOOL	VP967 Sea Devon C.2/2	ex Biggin Hill, Kemble, 781, 21, 207, SCCS, SCS, WCS, SCS, NCS, SCS, MCS, MoA, MCS, OCCF, 38 GCF, TTCCF, FCCS, 2 TAF CS, MCCS, RAFG CS, 2 TAF CS, Wahn SF, RCCF.

Locally, **Ian McLennan** has recognised the lure of the under-rated Turbulent and has two under restoration with a third incomplete.

G-ASSY+	D.31 Turbulent	ex Redhill. Damaged 8/5/83. Under restoration.
G-AWWT+	D.31 Turbulent	ex Redhill. Damaged 15/7/86. Under restoration.
G-BIVZ+	D.31A Turbulent	ex Redhill. Incomplete. Stored.

REDHILL AERODROME

All the charm and charisma of this airfield got up and left in December 1989 when the Tiger Club had to leave in favour of a more corporate image. (Thankfully those lovely people at Headcorn know a thing or two and have welcomed the Club with open arms.) Listed below are Tiger Moth G-AOAA and TSR.3 G-AWIV, although they may well have migrated to Headcorn by now. We must look now to Bristows to supply interest with the occasional 'vintage' helicopter.

Going back to **W&R11**, Wessex 60s 5N-AJN and 5N-ALO did indeed go to the Isle of Wight, a more precise location being Cowes. Tiger Moth G-AOBO was noted as departing to a destination unknown in mid 1987. This was West Chiltington. Departures since then have been several, counter-balanced by the additions. Much rebuilt Tiger Moth G-ASKP was flying again by late 1987 (not as given in **W&R11**) only to hit a vehicle on landing here 10/10/88! Undaunted, it was flying yet again by late 1989. Whirlwind Srs 3 G-AODA shocked everyone during late 1988 when it was restored to flying condition and was undertaking contract work during 1989. Apprentice Whirlwind Srs 3 G-ATLZ/5N-AJH had gone by mid 1989, destination unknown. Condor G-AXGS was sold off and was flying by 1989. Wessex 60 G-BGWT was exported to the USA by mid 1989. Finally, the hulk of Super Puma G-TIGD was removed during 1989, thought scrapped. Current situation :-

G-AOAA+	Tiger Moth	ex DF159, 24 GCF, 1 RS, 1 GTS, 20 PAFU, 5 GTS. Stored following accident. First noted 9/89. See notes above.
G-ASYW	Bell 47G-2	ex Bristows, VR-BBA, CP-704, VP-TCF, CP-671, VR-BBA. CoA expired 23/11/85. Stored.
G-AWIV+	Airmark TSR.3	CoA expired 26/7/85. Stored. See notes above.
G-AYNP	Whirlwind Srs 3	ex Bristow, ZS-HCY, G-AYNP, XG576. CoA expired 27/10/85. Stored.
5N-AHN+	AB.206B JetRanger	ex Bristow, G-AWFV. Damaged and stored. Present for quite some time.

REIGATE

Still in use for non-destructive fire fighting training at the **County Fire Brigade Headquarters** is the Trident 3 fuselage in black and gold colours.

| G-AWZI | Trident 3B-101 | ex Heathrow, BA, BEA. CoA expired 5/8/85. Fuselage. |

SMALLFIELD

Cessna 150A N41836 had gone from here by 1986 no less. It moved to Redhill, became G-ARFI again, moved to Shoreham, then to Haverfordwest and was made airworthy again.

TONGHAM

(On the A3014 south of Aldershot) Taylorcraft Plus D G-AHUG moved to Chessington 11/86. The two Austers remain in store at the farm.

| G-AJAB | J/1N Alpha | CoA expired 3/10/75. Stored. |
| G-ASEE | J/1N Alpha | ex I-AGRI. Crashed 9/2/74. Stored. |

VIRGINIA WATER

(On the A30 south west of Egham) It is believed the damaged Cessna 210 is still to be found at a private house here.

| G-OILS | Cessna T.210L | ex G-BCZP, N1736X. Crashed 29/1/82. |

WOKING
Gnat T.1 XM697 was acquired by Jet Heritage Ltd and left for Bournemouth 11/12/89.

East Sussex

BATTLE
A small workshop here is working on the restoration of a Spitfire IX and a former IAAC Seafire III. Spitfire Tr IX PV202/G-TRIX came here from St Leonards-on-Sea circa 1987 to continue its restoration. This was seen to fruition on 23/2/90 when it first flew at Dunsfold.

TA805+	Spitfire IX	ex South Africa, SAAF, 234, 183. Parts only.
157+	Seafire III	ex Dublin Tech, Casement, IAAC, RX158. Restoration.

HAILSHAM
Grenville Helicopters' pad at the Boship Manor Hotel still has its 'guardian' composite Bell 47.

G-AYOE	Bell 47G	ex F-OCBF. Crashed 16/7/77. Composite, including Sioux parts.

HASTINGS
John Wakeford (corrects **W&R11**) continues the restoration of his Klemm Swallow and on the Castleham Estate at the **Bo-Peep Garage** the Meteor can be found up the pole.

G-ACXE	L-25C-1 Swallow	CoA expired 7/4/40. Under restoration.
WL345	Meteor T.7	ex Hastings, Kemble, CAW, 8 FTS, 5 FTS, CFE, 229 OCU.

HOVE
Here since at least 1975 (but successfully escaping all manner of **W&R** sleuths) is a Chippax with **176 Squadron ATC.**

WD370+	Chipmunk T.10 PAX	ex 3 AEF, 2 SoTT, 1 AEF, Hull UAS, 2 BFFS. SOC 12/3/75.

LEWES
Paul Penn-Sayers' **Fun Airplane Company** is working on Linnet G-APNS here and has two other airframes in store.

G-APNS	Linnet	ex Chessington. CoA expired 6/10/78. Under rebuild.
G-BKCZ+	Wassmer D.120A	ex F-BKCZ. Stored.

ROBERTSBRIDGE
(On the A21 north west of Hastings) **Robertsbridge Aviation Society** have an exceptional collection of components, engines and items from digs etc on display at their small museum. Early in 1989 the cockpit section of Hurricane I V7350 moved to Brenzett. The museum is open to the public every Thursday evening from 1700 and on the last Sunday afternoon of each month except December. Contact : Dennis Woodgate, RAS, 'Cwmavon', Northbridge Street, Robertsbridge, East Sussex, TN32 5NY. See also Headcorn, where RAS's Mystere is kept.

G-AIVW	Tiger Moth	ex Redhill, T5370, 20 AFU, SAN, 10 EFTS, 25 PEFTS, 1 PFTS. Wrecked 27/8/82. Remains. Complex composite, largely based on G-ANLR/N6856.
TL615	Horsa II	ex London Colney, Brize Norton. Substantial fuselage section.
WZ822	Grasshopper TX.1	ex Syerston.

RYE
Restoration of Ian Addy's Norecrin continues here.

G-BAYL	Norecrin VI	ex Solihull, Bodmin, F-BEQV. Restoration.

ST LEONARDS-ON-SEA
Spitfire Tr IX PV202/G-TRIX moved to Battle. At **Aero Vintage** the restoration of
Bristol F.2b G-AANM is making great strides, with final assembly underway. The
frame of F.2b BAPC.19 was used as the basis of the superb static replica made by
Skysport Engineering at Hatch for Belgium.

D7889" G-AANM Bristol F.2b   BAPC.166, ex Old Warden. Under restoration.

SEAFORD
Riverside Metals still seduce customers with their Aztec fuselage mounted over the
offices. They can be found on the Cradle Hill Industrial Estate.

G-BHNG   Aztec 250E   ex Shoreham, N54125. Crashed 19/12/81. Fuselage only.

SEDLESCOMBE
(North of Hastings) Recent sightings have confirmed the existence of only the
HM.293 in store here. It is likely the Jodel and the Cessna survive, however.

G-AWFT   Jodel D.9   ex Hazeleigh Grange. CoA expired 22/7/69. See above.
G-AXPG   Mignet HM.293   ex Hazeleigh Grange, Southend. CoA expired 20/1/77.
F-BSIL   Cessna F.150K   dismantled, for spares. See above.

UCKFIELD
At Headley Court, **2530 Squadron ATC** should still have the Jet Provost nose.

XP677   8587M Jet Provost T.4   ex Abingdon, RAFEF, 2 FTS. Nose section only.

West Sussex

BURGESS HILL
Established here is a company called **Wing Spares.** During 1986 they acquired the
former RAE Bedford Canberra B.2/6 WG789. It was broken up for components, but
Barry Parkhouse managed to acquire the nose and it moved out to Kew on 3/8/89. The
company also acquired Canberra B.2 WD935 from St Athan and it arrived here on
24/11/89 for reduction to spares. Following the pattern, Barry got the nose of
this one as well and it has also ·gone to Kew. Being spares orientated, it is
doubted if airframes last long here.

CHARLWOOD
More God-like powers - this entry has upped and moved to Surrey!

CHICHESTER
A brilliant engineer and gifted flyer was taken from us in a motor accident on
14/10/88. This was Nick Grace, and we are all the poorer for his passing. In this
general area, **Tangmere Flight** keep a workshop and store. The hoard of former
Indian Tempest IIs are here, with hopefully at least one to fly in Nick's honour.
Nick's Spitfire XVI TE184, acquired from Holywood, Northern Ireland, did not go to
Sandown as reported in **W&R11**, but was kept here until going to East Midlands
Airport in early 1989. Of the Tempests, all were recovered in the late 1970s by
Warbirds of Great Britain and held 'somewhere in the UK' until acquired by Nick and
partner Chris Horsley. Several have moved on : HA564/MW376 to Spanhoe; HA586/MW763
and HA604/MW401 to Brooklands; HA591/MW810 went to the New England Air Museum at
Windsor Locks, Connecticut, in exchange for the Short Sealand that went to Holywood
in exchange for Spitfire TE184; HA457 went to the RAF Museum at Cardington
initially.

HA557+   Tempest II   ex India, IAF, RAF MW404. Stored.
HA580+   Tempest II   ex India, IAF, RAF MW758. Stored.

CRAWLEY

Crawley Technical College are still at work on the IHM SARO P.531.
XN334   A2525 SARO P.531   ex Weston-super-Mare, Yeovilton, Arbroath, Lee-
                                    on-Solent. Under restoration.

FAYGATE

(On the A264 between Horsham and Crawley) Little information to hand on the status
of the contents of the yard of **Park Aviation Supply.** There have been three
removals and one arrival. Going have been : Jet Provost T.3 nose section XN597
(not previously noted) moved to Bournemouth briefly and then to Stoke-on-Trent; Jet
Provost T.4 XP568 to Long Marston and Hunter F.51 E-430 to Charlwood.

G-BFTD	AA-5A Cheetah	crashed 30/3/79. Hulk.
WH911	Canberra E.15	ex St Athan, 98, 35. Forward fuselage.
XG226	8800M Hunter F.6A	ex Catterick, 1 TWU, TWU, 229 OCU, 92, 66, 92.
		Forward fuselage, rear section at Abingdon.
XP976	Hawker P.1127	ex Wittering, Foulness Island, Farnborough,
		Sevenhampton, Aston Down, 71 MU, BLEU, Dunsfold.
XT459+	Wessex HU.5	ex Lee-on-Solent dump, 845. Crashed 7/11/83. Arrived by 2/88.
XT866	Phantom FG.1	ex Leuchars, 43, Phantom TF. Crashed 9/7/81.
XX114	Jaguar GR.1	ex 226 OCU. Crashed 19/9/83. Hulk.
XX137	Jaguar T.2	ex 226 OCU. Crashed 5/2/76. Hulk.
XX293	Hawk T.1	ex 4 FTS. Crashed 17/4/85. Hulk.
XZ120	Jaguar GR.1	ex 2. Crashed 25/2/77. Hulk.
XZ438	Sea Harrier FRS.1	ex BAe. Crashed 17/5/82. Hulk.
	F-4D	ex 32 TFS. Forward fuselage.

GATWICK

While terminals seem to be blossoming everywhere at the **Airport,** the **W&R** situation
remains much the same. Perhaps predictably, the Aztec 250E hulk 'SX-BBD' (G-BBBD)
has not been noted for some time and is presumed scrapped or expired. The Trident
is used for non-destructive fire training and the Comet for handling training.
Over at the **Hilton Hotel** the DH.60 replica still 'flies' in the lobby.

G-AAAH"	B'168 DH.60G Moth rep	Gatwick Hilton lobby.
G-APMB	Comet 4B	CoA expired 18/5/79. Cabin trainer.
G-AWZX	Trident 3B-101	ex Heathrow, BA, BEA. CoA exp 30/4/84.

GOODWOOD

Amending **W&R11,** crated Tiger Moth ZS-BCU had gone by 1985.

PULBOROUGH

By 5/89 Whirlwind HAR.3 XJ393 had appeared at **Macari's Toat Cafeteria** on the A29
north of the town as an attraction/plaything.
XJ393+   A2538 Whirlwind HAR.3   ex Higher Blagdon, Lee-on-Solent, Arbroath,
                                   Pershore, CS(A), XD363 and XD763 ntu.

SHOREHAM-BY-SEA

Work continues on the Tiger Moth locally.
G-ALVP   Tiger Moth   ex Shoreham Lighthouse, R4770, 4 RFS, 4 EFTS, 10
                          FTS, 7 EFTS, 11 EFTS. CoA expired 15/2/61.

SHOREHAM AIRPORT

Air South (AS) have been busy. Robinson Redwing G-ABNX was flying again by 1988,
DH.60G Moth 'EM-01'/G-AAOR was repainted as '30-76' and first flew again on 30/4/89
and Tiger Moth G-ADXT was sold and moved to a Hampshire owner. Morava G-ASFD moved
by road to Bournemouth for restoration. Stored AB 47J Ranger G-APTH was flying
again by 9/88. Over at **Chelsea College** (CC), Seneca G-BBFF was a set of wings only
by 7/87 and should be disregarded. On the plus side, the College took on the
former Sandown Pembroke in 5/88 and later a Cessna from the same airfield. The two
Chipmunks from Nigeria are stored pending a decision on rebuild.

G-AMNN''	Tiger Moth	ex Redhill. Composite, real identity unknown. CC
G-AOIS	Tiger Moth	ex R5172, West Malling SF, 22 SFTS, 15 EFTS, 9 EFTS. CoA expired 7/6/81. Under restoration.
G-APNJ	Cessna 310	ex EI-AJY, N3635D. CoA expired 28/11/74. CC.
G-ARBO	Comanche 250	crashed 27/4/83. For rebuild.
G-ARRM	Beagle 206-1X	ex Duxford, Shoreham. Prototype. CoA expired 28/12/64. Stored.
G-AVDF	Pup 200	ex Duxford, Shoreham. Prototype. CoA expired 22/5/68. Stored.
G-AVUK	Enstrom F.28A/UK	ex Thruxton, N4460. Crashed 3/12/75. Wreck.
G-BDJP	J-3C-90 Cub	ex OO-SKZ, PH-NCV, NC3908K. CoA expired 18/5/84. Stored. AS.
G-BJAP	Tiger Moth	ex Slinfold. Composite, under construction. AS.
G-BNPU+	XL929 Pembroke C.1	ex Sandown, Shawbury, 60, Kemble, 207, SCCS, TCCS, FCCS, BCCS. Flew in 7/5/88. CC.
G-TOBY+	Cessna 172B	ex Sandown, G-ARCM, N6952X. Damaged 15/10/83. First noted 2/90. CC.
	Tiger Moth	fuselage frame with AS.
EC-AIU	Tiger Moth	ex Spain, Spanish AF, F-AQJX. First noted 2/88. Under restoration by AS.
VQ-SAC	BN-2A Islander	crashed 4/9/76. Forward fuselage. CC.
5N-AAE+	Chipmunk 22	ex Nigeria, VR-NBI, G-AOJS, D-EHOF, G-AOJS, WB745, Stn UAS, 14 RFS, Stn UAS, 14 RFS. Arrived 6/4/89. Stored.
5N-AGP+	Chipmunk 22	ex Nigeria, G-AOZV, EI-AHP, WD290, HCEU, 288, HCEU, HCCS, 1 RFS. Arrived 6/4/89. Stored.

SLINFOLD
Terrier 1 G-ARLO left the strip by late 1989, going to Hedge End. Otherwise, no change here.

G-AMKU	J/1B Aiglet	ex ST-ABD, SN-ABD, G-AMKU. CoA exp 21/9/84.
G-BBHJ	J-3C-65 Cub	ex OO-GEC. Under rebuild.

TANGMERE
1990 being the 50th Anniversary of the Battle of Britain, the **Tangmere Military Aviation Museum** should see a rightful upturn in visitors. Open daily 1100 to 1730 from March 1 to early November, parties can be accommodated at other times by arrangement. Contact : Tangmere Military Aviation Museum, PO Box 50, Tangmere Airfield, Chichester, West Sussex PO20 6ER. Telephone 0243 775223. Current plans are to try to exchange the T-33 for a more appropriate airframe.

XF314''	E-412 Hunter F.51	ex Dunsfold, G-9-439, Danish AF, Aalborg, ESK.724. 43 Squadron colours.
19252	T-33A-1-LO	ex Hailsham, Sculthorpe, French AF.
C4E-88	Bf 109E	ex Stubbington, Spain. Poor state.

WEST CHILTINGTON
(On the B2139 south of Horsham) The strip makes a re-entry with a former Redhill Tiger Moth arriving in 1987 for rebuild.

G-AOBO+	Tiger Moth	ex Redhill, Fareham, N6473, 10 RFS, 16 EFTS, 10 EFTS, 19 ERFTS. CoA expired 28/9/69. First noted 1987, under rebuild.

Tyne & Wear

GATESHEAD
The fuselage of Viscount 'G-WHIZ' continues to take all the kids can throw at it in **Saltwell Park**.

G-WHIZ" G-AMOE Viscount 701   ex Chester-le-Street, Newcastle, Northest, Cambrian, British Eagle, Channel, BEA. wfu 6/1/72. Rear fuselage of G-AOHJ.

NEWCASTLE AIRPORT
(Or Woolsington) By 1989 Super Baladou IV G-ATSY was flying again, leaving this entry all empty again.

SUNDERLAND
More exhibits, a couple of 'roll-outs' after major restoration and continued development of the site sums up the progress made by the **North East Aircraft Museum** at the former airfield. With the Meteor F.8 and Sea Venom newly restored, programmes underway at present include the Anson, the Gazelle and the F-86D. With the bulk of Meteor T.7 WL405 now known to be at Chalgrove, reference to it here has been dropped, although NEAM hope to have it all when Martin Baker have finished with it. Open every day for some time now, NEAM has made great strides in terms of both site and exhibit development. Further expansion on the former airfield site, now the Nissan plant, is being monitored. Still in use by the plant is the lamella hangar that was once the major structure on the airfield. This sort of construction is now somewhat rare and NEAM hope to be able to acquire it. This will mean moving it lock, stock and barrel onto their adjacent site - a major undertaking. John Stelling's two Austers have moved out to a local workshop (G-ANFU and the anonymous AOP.6 - see below). NEAM is open every day 1100-1800 (or dusk in winter). Group visits are welcome with prior notice. Contact : North East Aircraft Museum, Old Washington Road, Sunderland, Tyne & Wear SR5 3HZ. Telephone 091 519 0662 - note the new number.

G-AWRS	Avro XIX Srs 2	ex Strathallan, Kemps, Junex, Hewitts, TX213, WCS, 22 GCF, OCTU, 18 GCF, 2 TAF CS, 527, CSE, RCCF. CoA expired 10/8/73. Under rebuild.
G-BAGJ	Gazelle 1	ex Carlisle, G-SFTA, HB-XIL, G-BAGJ, XW858 ntu. Crashed 7/3/84. Under restoration.
G-BEEX+	Comet 4C	ex East Kirkby, Tattershall, Woodford, Lasham, Dan-Air, SU-ALM. Nose section. Arrived 1989.
+	Olympus hang glider	on site by 12/89.
+	AES Lone Ranger	microlight. On site by 12/89.
RH746	Brigand TF.1	ex Failsworth, CS(A), ATDU Gosport, Bristols, ATDU, A&AEE, makers. Fuselage, under restoration.
VX577	Valetta C.2	ex Northern Parachute Centre, MCS, 70, Malta CF, 70, MECS, Gibraltar CF, Malta C&TTS, 2 TAF CS, 30.
WA577	7718M Sycamore 3	ex Kings Heath, Shirley, St Athan, A&AEE, G-ALST ntu.
WB685	Chipmunk T.10	ex Leeds, Irlam, Edn UAS, Lyneham SF, 8 RFS, 1 RFS. Composite, rear fuselage of WP969/G-ATHC. On loan from Nigel Ponsford.
WD790	8743M Meteor NF.11	ex Darlington, Leeming, RAE Llanbedr, RS&RE, RRE, TRE. Nose.
WD889	Firefly AS.5	ex Failsworth. With rear fuselage of VT409.
WG724	Dragonfly HR.5	ex Chester-le-Street, Moor Monkton, Blackbushe, Lossie' SF, Ford SF.
WJ639+	Canberra TT.18	ex Samlesbury, 7, 57. Arrived 8/88.
WK198	7428M Swift F.4	ex Failsworth, 10 SoTT, Aldergrove, MoS. Fuselage.
WL181	Meteor F.8	ex Chester-le-Street, Acklington, Kemble, CAW, Tangmere SF, 34.
WN516	Balliol T.2	ex Failsworth, RAFC. Cockpit section.
WZ518	Vampire T.11	ex Chester-le-Street, Handforth, Pomona Dock, 5 FTS, Oldenburg SF, 2 TAF CF, 14. Composite, wings of WZ608.
WZ767	Grasshopper TX.1	ex Syerston.
XG518	8009M Sycamore HR.14	ex Balloch, Halton, Wroughton, CFS, Khormaksar SF, El Adem SF, Habbiniya SF, Amman SF.

XG523	7793M Sycamore HR.14	ex Hayes, Middle Wallop, Ternhill, CFS, JEHU. Damaged 25/9/62. Nose section. Identity now confirmed.
XG680	Sea Venom FAW.22	ex Sydenham, ADS, 891.
XL319	Vulcan B.2	ex 44, Wadd Wing, 35, 230 OCU, 617, 230 OCU, Scampton Wing, 617.
XM660	Whirlwind HAS.7	ex Almondbank, Fleetlands, Lee, Lossiemouth SAR Flt, 737, 700H, 824.
XP627	Jet Provost T.4	ex London Colney, Hatfield, Shawbury, 6 FTS, 3 FTS, 1 FTS.
XW276+	Gazelle 03	ex Wroughton, Southampton, Middle Wallop, Farnborough, Leatherhead, F-ZWRI. Arrived 12/88. On loan from MoAF.
ZF594+	Lightning F.53	ex Warton, RSAF 53-696, 2 Sqn Tabuk, 13 Sqn Dhahran, 2 Sqn Tabuk, 6 Sqn Khamis Mushayt, LCU Dhahran, 2 Sqn Dhahran, G-27-66. Arr 4/89.
	Canberra T.4	ex Marham. Nose section.
E-419	Hunter F.51	ex Dunsfold, G-9-441, Aalborg, Danish AF ESK.724.
146	Mystere IVA	ex Sculthorpe, French AF.
42157	F-100D-16-NA	ex Sculthorpe, French AF.
54439	T-33A-1-LO	ex Sculthorpe, French AF.
171	F-86D-35-NA	ex Hellenikon, Greek AF, USAF 51-6171. Under restoration. Note corrected serial.
541	F-84F-40-RE	ex Hellenikon, Greek AF, USAF 52-6541.
BAPC 96	Brown Helicopter	ex Stanley.
BAPC 97	Luton LA-4 Minor	ex Sibson, Sunderland, Stanley.
BAPC 119	Bensen B.7	ex Stanley.

Next door to NEAM is **2214 Squadron ATC**. They maintain a Vampire T.11 for instructional purposes.

XD622	8160M Vampire T.11	ex Leeming, Barkston Ash, Shawbury, 118, RAFC.

As related above, **John Stelling** moved his Auster AOP.6 restoration project from the NEAM workshop's to his own premises in the locality.

+	Auster AOP.6	ex NEAM, Bristol. See notes above.

Warwickshire

COVENTRY·AIRPORT

(Or Baginton) Museums either mature or they fade away. Those that reach maturity have the strength to re-assess and refine their aircraft stocks and are happy to make disposals for the sake of a more rounded collecting profile and to place airframes with more appropriate organisations. This is certainly so with the **Midland Air Museum** who have made exceptional strides in recent years. With a lesser emphasis on airframe acquisition, the theme of the past five years has been in developing their impressive site, restoring key airframes and firming up their 'made-in-Coventry' image plus the links with Whittle and the jet engine in general. A new gallery is currently underway which will centre on the 'Coventry' theme and will include upwards of twenty engines. Midland Air Museum has two phases of opening. During the Summer (April-October) Monday to Saturday 1000-1600 and Sundays and Bank Holidays 1100-1800. Winter (November-March) Saturday and Sunday 1100-1700. Further details from : Midland Air Museum, Baginton, Coventry CV8 3AZ. (0203 301033).

With all of this in train, it is not surprising that several airframes have been disposed of, and others will certainly follow. The fuselage of Fox Moth G-ACCB has gone to Ted Gautrey in Nuneaton for restoration to flying condition. As of this edition, we will drop Luton Minor G-BAPC from the listing. This really crossed through **W&R's** terms of reference, being only a set of pre-war LA.4 wings - but the registration was too close to our hearts to ignore! There is a good chance that by the time these words are read, the wings will have left MAM's care to join a fuselage and take to the air - dare it be too much to hope that the hallowed lettering G-**BAPC** will survive? Someday, someone in the UK will have to preserve types like the Aztec and the Cessna - for there can be no denying they are part of our aviation heritage - and MAM were first off in this league. Admitting such items are beyond their collecting policy (or were MAM just way ahead of their time?!) Aztec G-SHIP was sold off to an owner in the West Midlands during 1988 and Cessna F.172E G-ASOK"/D-EDCU went likewise to a gent in Scotland. Cadet TX.1 BGA.804 now flies as 'BAA' in Scotland. 'Bf 109' replica BAPC 67 travelled to Hawkinge in 1988 to join the ever-increasing KBBM. Finally, Sea Vixen FAW.2 XN691/8143M had arrived from Cosford by 4/88 for temporary loan/storage at MAM. It moved to North Weald in 2/90.

G-EBJG	Pixie III	ex Coventry, Stratford-on-Avon. CoA expired 2/10/36. Stored.
G-ABOI	Wheeler Slymph	ex Coventry, Old Warden. On loan. Stored.
G-AEGV	HM.14 Pou du Ciel	ex Coventry, Knowle, Northampton, Northampton Airport. Stored.
G-ALCU	Dove 2	ex airfield, VT-CEH. CoA expired 16/3/73. Stored.
G-APJJ+	Fairey Ultra-Light	ex Heaton Chapel, Coventry, Hayes. CoA expired 1/4/59. Arr 6/2/88.
G-APRL	Argosy 101	ex ABC/Elan, Sagitair, N890U, N602Z, N6507R, G-APRL. 'Edna'. CoA expired 23/3/87.
G-APWN	Whirlwind Srs 3	ex Cranfield, Redhill, Bristow, VR-BER, G-APWN, 5N-AGI, G-APWN. CoA expired 17/5/78.
VP-KJL	Messenger 4A	ex G-ALAR, RH371. Stored.
+	Chargus Vortex 120	powered hang glider. Acquired 1989.
H3426" BAPC 68	Hurricane replica	ex Wembley, Newark. On loan. Stored.
EE531	7090M Meteor F.4	ex Bentham, Coventry Airport, Birmingham, Weston Park, Birmingham, RAE Lasham, A&AEE, makers.
VF301	7060M Vampire F.1	ex Stoneleigh, Debden, 208 AFS, 595, 226 OCU.
VM325	Anson C.19	ex Halfpenny Green, WCS, NCS, WCS, TCCF, Upavon CF, 173, 4 FP.
VS623	G-AOKZ Prentice T.1	ex Shoreham, Redhill, Southend, VS623, CFS, 2 FTS, 22 FTS.
VT935	BP-111A	ex Cranfield, RAE Bedford.
WF922	Canberra PR.3	ex Cambridge, 39, 69, 58, 82.
WS838	Meteor NF.14	ex Cosford, Manchester, Cosford, Shawbury, Colerne, RAE Bedford, RRE, MoS, 64, 238 OCU.
WV797	A2637 Sea Hawk FGA.6	ex Perth, Culdrose, Halton 8155M, Sydenham, 738, 898, 899, Fleetlands, 787.
XA508	A2472 Gannet T.2	ex Yeovilton, Manadon, 737.

XA699	7809M Javelin FAW.5	ex Cosford, Locking, Shawbury, Kemble, Shawbury, 5, 151.
XA862	A2542 Whirlwind HAS.1	ex Wroughton, Lee-on-Solent, Seafield Park, Haslar, Lee-on-Solent, Fleetlands, 781, 771, 700, 'Protector' Flt, 700, 'Protector' Flt, 705, G-AMJT ntu.
XD626	Vampire T.11	ex Bitteswell, Shawbury, CATCS, CNCS, 5 FTS, RAFC, CFS.
XE855	Vampire T.11	ex Upton-by-Chester, Woodford, Chester, 27 MU, 22 MU, 10 MU, AWOCU. Pod only, spares use.
XE872	Vampire T.11	ex Long Itchington, Woodford, Chester, St Athan, 5 FTS, 3/4 CAACU, 8 FTS, 7 FTS, CFS. Stored, spares use.
XF382	Hunter F.6A	ex Brawdy, 1 TWU, TWU, 229 OCU, FCS, 65, 63, 92.
XK741	Gnat T.1	ex Leamington Spa, Fordhouses, Dunsfold, Hamble, Boscombe Down, Dunsfold. Minus wings.
XK907	Whirlwind HAS.7	ex Bubbenhall, Panshanger, Elstree, Luton, ETPS, RRE, Alvis. Stored - spares use.
XL360	Vulcan B.2	ex 44, 101, 35, 617, 230 OCU, Wadd Wing, 230 OCU, Scamp Wing, 617.
XR771+	Lightning F.6	ex Binbrook, 5, 11, 5, 56, 74. Arrived 15/7/88. On loan from Magnatec Ltd.
ZF598+	Lightning T.55	ex Warton, RSAF 55-713, G-27-72. Arrived 19/1/89.
+	Beaufighter	ex Birmingham, Coventry. Cockpit section. Arrived 10/89.
E-425	Hunter F.51	ex Dunsfold, G-9-446, Aalborg, Danish AF ESK.724.
R-756	F-104G	ex Aalborg, Danish AF.
70	Mystere IVA	ex Sculthorpe, French AF.
14419	T-33A-1-LO	ex Sculthorpe, French AF.
42174	F-100D-16-NA	ex Sculthorpe, French AF.
28368	Fl 282V-20 Kolibri	ex Coventry, Cranfield, Brize Norton. Frame only.
29640	SAAB J29F	ex Southend, R Swedish AF.
24535	HH-43B Huskie	ex Woodbridge, 40 ARRS, Det 2, Upper Heyford.
82062	U-6A Beaver	ex Mannheim, US Army.
BAPC 32	Crossley Tom Thumb	ex Coventry, Bewdley, Coventry, Banbury. Unfinished. Stored.
BAPC 126	Turbulent	ex Shoreham, Croydon. Static display airframe.

It is believed that John Coggins' **Aircraft Radio Museum** located just off the airfield is still available for inspection with prior permission. John's small collection of Percival types continues to be stored on the Airport site, but are not available for inspection. Contact : John F Coggins, Aircraft Radio Museum, Baginton, Coventry, Warwickshire.

G-AMLZ	Prince 6E	ex VR-TBN ntu, G-AMLZ. CoA expired 18/6/71.
G-AOKO	Prentice 1	ex Southend, VS621, CFS, 2 FTS, 22 FTS. CoA exp 23/10/72. Spares.
G-APIU	Prentice 1	ex VR200, 1 ASS, 2 ASS, CFS, 2 FTS. CoA expired 23/2/67. Spares.
G-APJB	Prentice 1	ex VR259, 1 ASS, 2 ASS, RAFC. CoA expired 4/9/77.

Let us not forget that Coventry is a thriving and expanding **Airport**. Dominating the scene is Air Atlantique, with their DC-6 freight operations, DC-3 charter and thier DC-3/Islander fleet for pollution control work. Air Atlantique have had three 'Daks' laid up for some time, but two are now undergoing preparation for return to service, with G-APML likely to join them. Tempete G-ASUS was flying again by mid 1988. Across at the former Armstrong Whitworth site; the Nord 3400 stock has found new owners, but the TB-25, Canuck, CASA 352 and T-6G remain in unresolved storage, decaying all the while. The '3400s went as follows : 37/MAB to

Breighton briefly before settling on Stixwould; 39/MOC to Sweden 7/89; 68/MHA unknown; 121/MJA to Sweden 7/89; 124/MOO/N9048P to a Sussex owner as G-BOSJ. Several of the non-flying World War replicas are still to be found rotting here (partially correcting **W&R11**), but just which is which is not clear.

G-AMPO+	C-47B-30-DK Dakota	ex North Weald, LN-RTO, G-AMPO, KN566, 44-76853. CoA expired 2/6/86, stored by Air Atlantique. For return to service 1990.
G-APML+	C-47B-1-DK Dakota 6	ex KJ836, 43-48359. CoA expired 27/7/84, stored.
G-ATUC+	Cherokee 140	crashed 2/4/88. Hulk, first noted 11/88.

G-AWSH" G-ASWH	Luton LA.5 Major	ex Sywell, Yeovilton. Crashed 3/7/77. Stored.
G-AYKZ	SAI KZ-8	ex HB-EPB, OY-ACB. CoA expired 17/7/81. Stored.
G-BMIU+	Enstrom F.28A	ex OO-BAM, F-BVRE ntu. Crashed 9/7/86. Cabin stored.
G-BPMP+	C-47A-50-DL	ex Liverpool, N54607, Blackbushe, N9842A ntu, 20669/CNA-LM Moroccan AF, CN-CCL, F-BEFA, 42-24211. Arrived by 7/89 for restoration.
CS-ACQ	Fleet 80 Canuck	ex Rochester, Blackbushe, Portugal, CF-DQP. Open store.
N9+AA" G-BECL	CASA 352L	ex Blackbushe, Spanish AF T2B-212. CoA exp 4/11/85. Open store.
114700	T-6G-NH Texan	ex 'Empire of the Sun', La Ferte Alais, FAF. Open store.
151632"NL9494Z	TB-25N-NC Mitchell	ex Blackbushe, USAAF 44-30925. 'Gorgeous George-Anne'. Open store.

LAWFORD HEATH

(Near Church Lawford)   The Hunter still guards **8 Group Royal Observer Corps.**

WT651	7532M Hunter F.1	ex Halton, Credenhill, 229 OCU, 233 OCU, 229 OCU, 222.

LEAMINGTON SPA

After its appearance at the Luton auction of 10/87, Skeeter AOP.12 XL765 did not
return here (correcting **W&R11**) but eventually settled on <u>Leverstock Green</u>.

LONG MARSTON

Amazing strides have been made with the establishment of the **Stratford Aircraft
Collection** here. Opening to the public is scheduled as this edition goes on sale.
Enquiries relating to opening times etc should be made to SAC, 32 Flaxley Close,
Winyates Green, Redditch, Worcs, B98 0QS. There has been a large influx of
airframes to the site and one departure, Dove G-AHRI moving on to <u>Winthorpe</u>.

G-ADRG"+	B'77 HM.14 Pou du Ciel	ex Innsworth, Ross-on-Wye, Staverton. Arrived 1989. CARG loan.
WB624+	Chipmunk T.10	ex Warmingham, East Midlands, Wigan, Dur UAS, Abn UAS, Henlow, St Athan, 22 GCF, Debden, Jurby SF, 8 FTS, 18 RFS. Arr 2/4/89, loan.
WM735+ G-RACA	Sea Prince T.1	ex Gloucester/Cheltenham, Kemble, 750, BTU, A&AEE. Arr 12/5/89.
WR985+	8103M Shackleton MR.3/3	ex Cosford, 201, 120, 206, 203, 206, A&AEE, 206. Arr late 1989.
WT482+	Canberra T.4	ex Charlwood, Hull, Wyton, '160 CSE', 231 OCU, 85, 231 OCU, Bruggen SF, 88, 17, Wahn SF, Wildenrath SF, Gutersloh SF, 103. SOC 6/1/76. Nose section only. Arrived by 9/89.
WT483+	Canberra T.4	ex Filton, Samlesbury, 231 OCU, 39, 231 OCU, 16, Laarbruch, 68, Laarbruch SF, 69. Arrived 1/10/88.
WZ779	Grasshopper TX.1	ex Syerston. Identity corrected from **W&R11.**
XA293	Cadet TX.3	ex Redditch.
XD447	Vampire T.11	ex East Kirkby, Tattershall, Woodford, Chester, St Athan, 8 FTS, RAFC, 5 FTS.
XJ575+	A2611 Sea Vixen FAW.2	ex Helston, Culdrose SAH-13, 766. Nose section. Arrived by 7/89.
XK421+	8365M Auster AOP.9	ex Innsworth, Bristol, Caldicote, St Athan, Detmold, Middle Wallop. Arrived 1989, on loan from CARG.
XP346+	8793M Whirlwind HAR.10	ex Tattershall Thorpe, Shawbury, Lee-on-Solent, Akrotiri, 84, 22, 225. Arrived by 8/88.
XP568+	Jet Provost T.4	ex Faygate, Hatfield, Hatfield Tech, Shawbury, RAFC. Fuselage. First noted 7/89. Stored.
XT242+	Sioux AH.1	ex Wimborne, Middle Wallop. Composite. Arrived by 8/88, on loan.
XW315+	Jet Provost T.5	ex 'Lincolnshire', CFS, 3 FTS, CFS. Cockpit section, first noted 7/89. Stored.
BAPC 200+	Bensen B.7	ex Stoke-on-Trent. Composite. Arrived 1988, on loan.

On the airfield itself, the **Midland Warplane Museum** continue to store their Sea
Venom. Enquiries relating to MWM can be made to : M J Evans, 7 Appleby Close,
Great Alne, Alcester, Warks B49 6HJ. The local parachute club still have their
para-trainer, the identity of which is now confirmed.

G-BAKK	Cessna F.172H	ex Coventry, 4X-CEB, 5B-CBK, N10658. CoA exp 20/4/85. Para-tnr.
XG692	Sea Venom FAW.21	ex Alcester, Wellesbourne Mountford, Sydenham, Castlereagh, Sydenham, 750. Stored.

NUNEATON
Two items of interest are to be found in the general area. **Ted Gautrey** has taken
on the former Midland Air Museum Fox Moth fuselage and is restoring it to flying
condition.   In Attleborough Road, **Smith's** scrapyard still holds onto the Turbo-
Porter wreck.

G-ACCB+	Fox Moth	ex Coventry Airport, Redhill, Blackpool, Southport. Ditched 25/9/56. Under restoration.
G-BHCR	PC.6-B2/H2	ex East Midlands, Sibson, HB-FFT, ST-AEW, HB-FFT. Crashed 15/2/81.

STRATFORD-ON-AVON
Auster J/4 G-AIJK was aquired by Leicester Museums and moved to Leicester.

STUDLEY
Vampire T.11 XE864 moved by road to Firbeck on 8/1/89.

WARWICK
Long term restoration of John Berkeley's Seafire continues in the area.

SX300	A2054 Seafire F.17	ex Leamington Spa, Warrington, Bramcote A646.

WELLESBOURNE MOUNTFORD
Major centre for **W&R** interest here is the **Wellesbourne Aviation Group.** Their
Vampire has now finished its restoration and is a shining example to one and all.
WAG have also restored the airfield underground control rooms and defence
strongpoint as the **Wellesbourne Wartime Museum.** . Enquiries to : Dell Paddock, 2
Longford Close, Bidford-on-Avon, Alcester, Warwickshire, B50 4EB. Telephone 0789
778816.   On the airfield itself, Super Cub G-BJTP was flying in US Marine Corps
colours by late 1988. The hulk of a Seneca has appeared on the airfield and the
Vulcan remains inert.

G-BJEO+	Seneca III	ex Birmingham Airport, PH-GEC, G-TOMF, G-BJEO, N8424Y. Crashed 16/5/86. On dump, first noted 5/86.
XK590	Vampire T.11	ex Witney, Brize Norton, CATCS, 4 FTS, 7 FTS. WAG.
XM655	G-VULC Vulcan B.2	ex N655AV ntu, 44, 101, 50, 44, 9. Open store.

Wiltshire

BOSCOMBE DOWN
Always a fascinating place, the **Aeroplane & Armament Experimental Establishment**
holds much of interest **W&R**-wise. First off, we must record the passing of an old
faithful : Hastings C.2 WD496 finally gave up the struggle on the dump and was
carted away by a scrapman on 11/7/89. More youthful, but clearly lacking the
staying power, Lightning F.3 XR717, which had lain beside the old girl, was reduced
to so much ash the year before. The Canberra B.6 nose noted in **W&R11** as being up
for tender in 10/87 has not been seen since and is therefore assumed to have moved
on.   ETPS's Lightning T.5 XS422 made its last flight in 8/87 and was offered for
tender in 10/88. It was carefully dismantled and moved by road to Southampton for
storage.   Another transitional Lightning was F.6 XR773 which was stored here from
mid-1988. It got up and flew to Warton to join the active ones in 9/89. Sea King
HAS.1 XV373, reported in **W&R11** as being due to move to a firing range, made a
truthful man of the compiler (so rare, these days!) and left on 29/7/86 for
Foulness. Buccaneer S.1 XN923 left by road on 23/3/90 for Charlwood. Sea Fury
FB.11 VR930 (ex Lee-on-Solent) was here for an undetermined period, doubtless
supplying parts for VZ345, before it moved to Yeovilton 1/2/90.

G-ALRX	Britannia 101	ex WB473 ntu, VX447 ntu. Crashed 4/2/54. Nose section, with Aeromedical & Safety School (note amended name).

FS890	7554M Harvard IIB	ex Little Rissington, Nott UAS, Man UAS, Nott UAS, Bir UAS, Nott UAS, 1 FTS, 2 FTS, 600, 21 FTS. Spares for flyers FT375 and KF183.
VP968	Devon C.2/2	ex Northolt, 207, 26, TCCS, NCS, SCS, FCCS.
VZ345	Sea Fury T.20S	ex DLB D-CATA, D-FATA, ES.8503, G-9-30, Hawkers, Dunsfold, 1832. Accident 19/4/85. Under restoration.
WH876	Canberra B.2(mod)	ex A&AEE, 73, 207, 115. Stored. Dismantled.
WT309	Canberra B(I).6	ex A&AEE, HS. Stored.
XL472	Gannet AEW.3	ex 849 'B', HQ and 'A' Flts. Rescue training.
XL629	Lightning T.4	ex ETPS, A&AEE. Gate guardian.
XL898	8654M Whirlwind HAR.9	ex Abingdon, Wroughton, 'Endurance' Flt, 847, 825, 824, 820.
XV784+	8909M Harrier GR.3	ex Wittering, 233 OCU, 4, 1, 4. Damaged 2/4/86. Nose section only, remainder at Abingdon.

CHILMARK
(South of the A303 between Wylye and Cricklade)   The Wessex remains in use for instructional purposes at the armaments establishment here.

| XP140 | 8806M Wessex HAS.3 | ex Wroughton. |

CHIPPENHAM
Chipmunk PAX trainer WP863/8360M had moved on to Marlborough during 1987. By 12/88 Flowers scrapyard had been cleared of all substantial aeronautica.

CORSHAM
(On the B3353 south west of Chippenham)   Briefly at **HMS 'Royal Arthur'** was Whirlwind HAS.7 XN311 from Lee-on-Solent, it moved to Hull by 9/88.   It was replaced by yet another Whirlwind for officer training by 6/88.

| XN302+ | A2654 Whirlwind HAS.7 | ex Lee-on-Solent, AES, Southampton, Culdrose, 771, Lossiemouth SF, 847, 848. Arrived by 6/88. |

CRUDWELL
(On the A429 south of Kemble) The Whirlwind is still extant in the first scrapyard on the southern edge of the village.   This explains the equal number of reports claiming there has never been one present and those not understanding why there should be reports that it has gone!

| XK912 | Whirlwind HAS.7 | ex Notton, Wroughton, 705, 'Centaur' Flt, 'Hermes' Flt, 737, 815, 824, 820, 845. |

KEEVIL
Ever dwindling, the Vampire store here has halved since **W&R11.** By 7/87 XE928 and XH329 had been scrapped, leaving only two still stored here.   Adding to the previous edition, XK632 travelled directly to Hemel Hempstead and not via Bushey and Croxley Green as noted.

| WZ620 | Vampire T.11 | ex Exeter, 3/4 CAACU. Stored. |
| XE921 | Vampire T.11 | ex Exeter, 3/4 CAACU, 1 FTS, CFS. Stored. |

LYNEHAM
Much to amend and restore here. Having successfully 'rediscovered' Meteor WF825 as being present here in **W&R11**, it got up and moved to Monkton Farleigh on 26/4/88. Despite an attempt to wipe them out of the last edition, the Hunter and Vulcan on the dump happily serve on.   The Wessex here for instructional use was XT470 (not '472) and it moved to Netheravon.

XJ676	8844M Hunter F.6A	ex 1 TWU, TWU, 229 OCU, 2, 93. Dump – see notes above.
XK699	7971M Comet C.2	ex Henlow, Lyneham, 216. Gate guardian.
XL445	8811M Vulcan K.2	ex 50, 44, 35, 230 OCU, Wadd Wing, Akrotiri Wing, Wadd Wing, 27. Dump, see notes above.

MARLBOROUGH
In London Road can be found **2293 Squadron ATC,** who since 1987 have had the former
Chippenham Chippax.
WP863+   8360M Chipmunk T.10 PAX   ex Chippenham, Shawbury, Hamble G-ATJI, RAFC, 664, RAFC.

MONKTON FARLEIGH
(East of the A363, east of Bath) By sheer magic this location has migrated from
Avon to Wiltshire! The **Avon Air Museum** is established here but must move in due
course. AAM have gained two more airframes. The Wessex from Lasham has still not
materialised. See also under Thatcham. Located at the Monkton Farleigh Mines,
further details from Paul Brown, 8 Hobbes Close, Malmesbury, Wilts, SN16 0DA.
WF825+   8359M Meteor T.7   ex Lyneham, Kemble, CAW, 33, 603. Arrived 26/4/88.
XE849+   7928M Vampire T.11   ex Conington, Ware, St Athan, CNCS, 5 FTS, 7 FTS, 1 FTS, 4 FTS.
                                  Arrived 4/9/88.
XH767   7955M Javelin FAW.9   ex Worcester, Shawbury, 228 OCU, 11, 25.

NETHERAVON
The home of **7 Regiment, AAC** and the Army Parachute Association. With the latter,
the Islander fuselage is still in use. With the former a gate guardian, in the
form of Sioux XT150, arrived on 24/4/89. On the dump Wessex HU.5 XT470 still
serves on, despite what **W&R11** may have said (the machine being referred to there
was XT472). Beaver AL.1 XP827 was too small to consider listing by 8/89 and should
be deleted.
G-BBRP   BN-2A-9 Islander   crashed 20/2/82. Para-trainer, fuselage only.
XT150+   Sioux AH.1   ex Middle Wallop, composite of 7883M & 7884M. Arrived 24/4/89 for
                                  the gate.
XT470   Wessex HU.5   ex Lyneham, Wroughton, 845. Dump. See notes above.

OLD SARUM
At the **Brooklands Aerospace** plant, two aircraft constitute long termers.
G-NRDC+   Fieldmaster   ex Cardiff-Wales. CoA expired 17/10/87. Stored.
G-TRAK+   Optica (mod)   ex G-BLFC. CoA expired 13/10/87. Stored.

SALISBURY
Cliff Lovell's **Hampshire Light Planes Services** continues to import and restore
aircraft from a workshop near here. The majority of Cliff's throughput is too
quick for the likes of **W&R,** so only the more tenacious tenants receive a mention
here. The Shuttleworth Gull Six G-ADPR is best listed under Old Warden, although
the wings have been worked on here. Globe Swift G-AHUN was flying by the summer of
1989. Super Cub frame 51-15431 is thought not to have made the move from
Kingsclere and should accordingly be deleted.
G-ADMT   Hornet Moth   ex Kingsclere, Perth, Strathallan, Southampton. CoA exp 27/3/60.
G-AEZJ   Vega Gull   ex Sweden, SE-ALA, PH-ATH, G-AEZJ.
G-AHUN   GC-1B Swift   ex Kingsclere, EC-AJK, OO-KAY, NC77764.
EC-ADE   Moth Major   fuselage, stored.

TROWBRIDGE
By 12/88 the yard of **E J Shanley & Sons** in Green Lane had taken on the former
Yeovil Sea King.
XV372+   SH-3D Sea King   ex Yeovil, Lee-on-Solent, RAE, Westlands. Arr by 12/88.

UPAVON
Stored not far from the airfield is an Auster.
G-AIGF   J/1N Alpha   CoA expired 19/5/85. Stored dismantled.

WARMINSTER
By 1987 an Auster and a Tiger Moth had moved to the area for restoration. The
Tiger Moth was the former Kingsclere G-AOJK. By early 1989 it had moved to White
Waltham and was airworthy. Auster J/1N G-AJIS arrived from Wincanton, but moved to
Chilbolton and was flying by 1/90.

WINTERBOURNE GUNNER
(On the A338 north of Salisbury) No change with the airframes held by the **Nuclear, Bacteriological and Chemical Defence Centre.**

XK531	8403M Buccaneer S.1	ex Boscombe Down, Honington, 736, 809, 700S.
XR478	Whirlwind HAR.10	ex Wroughton, 230. Crashed 9/8/67.
XR482	Whirlwind HAR.10	ex Wroughton, 28, 110, 103, 110, 103.
XT430	Wasp HAS.1	ex Wroughton, 829.

WROUGHTON
Regular open days and other events continue to be held at the **Science Museum Air Transport Collection and Storage Facility** Principal interest for the aviation-minded visitor· here must be the superb transport aircraft collection, but readers should force themselves to look at the vehicles and other machinery – you won't regret it! Trident 1E G-AVYE was removed during 1989 to Hatfield where it is being used for vital, life-saving smoke research work. Short SC.1 XG900 left for the VTOL exhibition at Yeovilton on 5/10/89 and Gazelle XW276 has gone on loan to NEAM at Sunderland. Both the Cmelak and the HS.125 promised in various parts of **W&R11** have arrived. Details of events planned at Wroughton can be had from : The Science Museum, South Kensington, London SW7 2DD, (071 938 8000) or from the local officer on 0793 814466. Entry to the Museum storage site is via the Red Barn Gate on the A361.

G-AACN	HP Gugnunc	ex Hayes and K1908.
G-ACIT	DH.84 Dragon	ex Southend, Beagle, ANT Blackpool, BEA, Scottish Airways, Highland Airways. CoA expired 25/5/74.
G-AEHM	HM.14 Pou du Ciel	ex Hayes, Whitchurch, Bristol.
G-ALXT	Dragon Rapide	ex Strathallan, Staverton, 4R-AAI, CY-AAI, G-ALXT, NF865, 5 MU, 18 MU, MCS.
G-APWY	Piaggio P.166	ex Southend, Marconi. CoA expired 14/3/81.
G-APYD	Comet 4B	ex Dan-Air, Olympic SX-DAL, G-APYD, BEA. CoA expired 3/8/79.
G-ASSM+	HS.125-1/522	ex Chester, Southampton, 5N-AMK, G-ASSM. Arr 16/3/89.
G-AVZB+	Z-37 Cmelak	ex Southend, OK-WKQ. Flew in 25/6/88.
G-AWZM	Trident 3B-101	ex Heathrow, BA, BEA. CoA expired 13/12/85.
G-MMCB	Huntair Pathfinder	microlight.
G-RBOS	Colt AS-105	hot air airship. Donated by Royal Bank of Scotland.
EI-AYO	DC-3A-197	ex Shannon, N655GP, N225J, N8695E, N333H, NC16071.
NC5171N G-LIOA	Lockheed 10A	ex Wings and Wheels Orlando, N5171N, NC243 Boston-Maine A/W, NC14959 Eastern.
N18E	Boeing 247	ex Wings and Wheels Orlando, Sky Tours, NC18E, NC18, NC13340 CAA, United/National Air Transport.
N7777G G-CONI	L-749A-79	ex Dublin, Lanzair, KLM PH-LDT, PH-TET.
VP975	Devon C.2/2	ex RAE Farnborough, A&AEE, CCCF, 19 GCF, CPE.
XD163	8645M Whirlwind HAR.10	ex CFS, Akrotiri SAR Flt, MoA, 228, 275, 155, MoA. Held for International Helicopter Museum, Weston-super-Mare.
BAPC 162	Newbury Manflier	MPA, major parts.
BAPC 172	Chargus Midas	hang glider.
BAPC 173	Birdman Grasshopper	powered hang glider.
BAPC 174	Bensen B.7	gyroglider.
BAPC 188	McBroom Cobra 88	hang glider.

From this issue, the **Royal Naval Aircraft Yard** and the **Fleet Air Arm Museum Storage Facility** have been fused into the same list as they use the same hangars! During 6/88, three airframes were offered for tender from here; Canberra T.4 nose WH903, Jet Provost T.4 XR658 both from Abingdon and an anonymous Canberra B(I).8. WH903 went to Charlwood, XR658 to Bournemouth, but the fate of the B(I).8 is unknown. During 2/89 former Shrivenham Whirlwind HAS.7 XN263 (which arrived here 2/6/88) was also offered up for tender. It was acquired· by a Mr Jelly of Sussex. Of the Museum stock Whirlwind HAS.3 XG574/A2575 and UH-1H AE-422 moved to Yeovilton, the latter on 6/6/89·. Of the large Scout store here, XR603 left for Nowra, Australia, on 6/6/88 for spares use. XP909 (ex AETW, Middle Wallop and noted in **MiniWrecks**) was first noted in store 9/85, but joined 658 Sqn 22/1/89. The Scout store is now quite long in the tooth and is believed to be a 'posturing' stock for arms talks.

Some of the Gazelles held are also well used to the place by now. Gazelle AH.1
departures have been as folows : XW893 (arrived 21/5/84 ex Garrison Air Sqn) left
21/3/89 for 665 Sqn; XX392 (arrived 3/1/88 ex 670 Sqn) left 7/3/89 for Yeovil;
XZ340 (accident 6/9/88, arrived 10/10/88 ex 670) to Yeovil for rebuild 9/2/89;
ZB691 arrived here off the production line in 1984 and left 18/5/89 for 670 Sqn;
ZB692 arrived fresh off the line in 1984 and left 23/6/89 to 670 Sqn. Lynx AH.1
XZ671 (ex Yeovil, accident 1/85, arrived 12/7/88) left 2/3/89 for Yeovil again to
became an AH.9.   See under Colchester for a likely destination for the centre
section of Sea Fury D-CIBO that was 'lost' from here some editions back. Most of
these items are new to our list, having taken quite some research to establish them
as long term inmates.

VH127+	Firefly TT.4	ex Yeovilton, Culdrose, FRU, 700, 737, 812. Arr 15/3/88. FAAM.
WP313	Sea Prince T.1	ex Kemble, 750, Sydenham SF, 750, Lossiemouth SF, 750. FAAM.
WS103	Meteor T.7	ex Lee-on-Solent, FRU, Kemble, Yeovilton Standards Squadron, Anthorn. FAAM.
XA129	Sea Vampire T.22	ex Yeovilton, CIFE, 736. FAAM.
XA466	Gannet COD.4	ex Yeovilton, Lee-on-Solent, Lossiemouth, 849. FAAM.
XA864+	Whirlwind HAR.1	ex Yeovilton, RAE Bedford, A&AEE, RAE, CA, G-17-1. Arrived by 7/88. FAAM.
XK911	A2603 Whirlwind HAS.7	ex Lee-on-Solent, Arbroath, 771, 829, 'Ark Royal' Flt, 824, 820, 845. Last HAS.7 held in non-Museum store.
XM916	Wessex HAS.3	ex RNAY. Fire dump, poor state.
XN332	A2579 SARO P.531	ex Yeovilton, Manadon, G-APNV. FAAM.
XN385	Whirlwind HAS.7	ex Culdrose, Wroughton, HS, A&AEE, 771, 824, 825, 824. FAAM.
XP190	Scout AH.1	ex Arborfield.
XP846	Scout AH.1	ex 660. Stored.
XP850	Scout AH.1	ex 660. Stored.
XP855+	Scout AH.1	ex 652. Stored.
XP890	Scout AH.1	ex ARWF. Stored.
XP893+	Scout AH.1	ex Garrison Air Sqn. Arrived 3/3/87.
XP902+	Scout AH.1	ex Garrison Air Sqn. Arrived 3/3/87.
XP903	Scout AH.1	ex 657. Stored.
XR595+	Scout AH.1	ex 666. Arrived 1/7/88.
XR602+	Scout AH.1	ex 659. First noted 9/85.
XR627+	Scout AH.1	ex Garrison Air Sqn. Arrived 4/3/87.
XR628+	Scout AH.1	ex 656. First noted 1984.
XR629	Scout AH.1	ex Garrison Air Sqn. Stored.
XR630+	Scout AH.1	ex 658. Stored.
XR632+	Scout AH.1	ex 666. Arrived 1/7/88.
XR637	Scout AH.1	ex 658. Stored.
XR639	Scout AH.1	ex 658. Stored.
XS120	8653M Wessex HAS.1	ex Abingdon, Wroughton. Dump.
XS881+	A2675 Wessex HAS.1	ex Yeovilton, Culdrose. Arrived 7/89. FAAM.
XT616	Scout AH.1	ex Middle Wallop, 658. Stored.
XT617+	Scout AH.1	ex 653. First noted 5/79.
XT623+	Scout AH.1	ex 655. Arrived 15/10/82.
XT626+	Scout AH.1	ex 656. First noted 9/85.
XT633+	Scout AH.1	ex 659. Arrived 7/1/81.
XT637	Scout AH.1	ex 657. Stored.
XT639	Scout AH.1	ex 658. Stored.
XT642	Scout AH.1	ex 656. Stored.
XT643+	Scout AH.1	ex 660. Arrived 6/4/88.
XT645	Scout AH.1	ex 656. Stored.
XT648+	Scout AH.1	ex 659. Arrived 7/1/81.
XV118+	Scout AH.1	ex 657. First noted 2/85.
XV119+	Scout AH.1	ex 659. First noted 5/79.
XV121+	Scout AH.1	ex Westlands. Arrived 17/2/88.
XV123+	Scout AH.1	ex 657. First noted 11/83.
XV124+	Scout AH.1	ex 656. Arrived 14/11/83.
XV131+	Scout AH.1	ex 660. Arrived 6/4/88.

XV138+	Scout AH.1	ex 658. First noted 9/85.
XW281+	Scout AH.1	ex 658. Arrived 9/11/88.
XW284	Scout AH.1	ex ARWF. Stored.
XW616+	Scout AH.1	ex Garrison Flt. Arrived 2/3/87.
XW795+	Scout AH.1	ex 659. Arrived 7/1/81.
XW796+	Scout AH.1	ex 660. Arrived 6/4/88.
XW846+	Gazelle AH.1	ex MoD(PE). Arrived 25/1/85.
XX378+	Gazelle AH.1	ex Westlands. Arrived 29/6/84.
XX399+	Gazelle AH.1	ex 3 CBAS. Arrived 14/11/84.
XZ290+	Gazelle AH.1	ex Garrison Flt. Arrived 7/8/84.
XZ320+	Gazelle AH.1	ex D&TS. Arrived 22/5/85.
XZ324+	Gazelle AH.1	ex Garrison Flt. Arrived 5/3/87.
XZ326+	Gazelle AH.1	ex 3 CBAS. Arrived 14/11/84.
ZB676+	Gazelle AH.1	ex Fleetlands. Arrived 12/7/84.
ZB693+	Gazelle AH.1	arrived off the line 1984.
AE-520	CH-47C Chinook	ex Fleetlands, Brize Norton, Fleetlands, Portsmouth, St Athan, Stanley, Argentine Army.

The Canberra continues to guard the patients at the **Princess Alexandra Royal Air Force Hospital.**

| WJ676 | 7796M Canberra B.2 | ex Colerne, Melksham, 245, 35, 50. |

North Yorkshire

CATTERICK

Long-expected, the days of the fire school here are over. The Fire & Rescue Training Squadron, as the unit here was last termed, moved to Manston on 18/11/88. Airframes continue to linger here, for what purpose, and for how much longer, is unknown. The yard at Thirsk has certainly handled some material from here and the reader should make reference there. Super VC-10 ZD233 fuselage moved to Manston by 4/88. Airframes are known to have expired : Hastings C.1 TG536/8405M; Canberra PR.7 WJ825/8697M and Whirlwind HAR.10 XD182/8612M; Sea Vixen FAW.2 XJ572/8803M; Sea Vixen D.3 XN652/8817M; . The following listing should be taken as a guide to what was left at the closure and not as a listing of what to find there the next time the car overheats on the A1.

VP971	8824M Devon C.2/2	ex Northolt, 207, 60, 207, SCCS, SCS, AAFCE, SCS, HS, MoA, SCS, MCS, MCCS, MCCF, BCCF.
WH794	8652M Canberra PR.7	ex Abingdon, 13, 58, 82, 540.
WH925	Canberra B.2	ex BCDU, 231 OCU, 35, 207. Nose section.
WJ867+	8643M Canberra T.4	ex Abingdon, Newton, A&AEE, ETPS. Arrived by 3/88.
WT362	Canberra B(I).8	ex 3, 14, 88. Nose section.
XA939	Victor B(K).1A	ex 214, 15, 10. Nose section.
XM997	Lightning T.4	ex Leconfield, 226 OCU, 92, 226 OCU, LCS. Poor shape.
XN925	8087M Buccaneer S.1	ex A2602. Nuclear Weapons training compound.

CHOP GATE

(On the B1257 north of Helmsley) During 1988 the **North Yorkshire Aircraft Recovery Centre** took delivery of a Jet Provost nose from Leeds. See also Thirsk.

WM145	Meteor NF.11	ex Rotherham, Finningley, 5, 29, 151, 219. Cockpit section.
WZ557	Vampire T.11	ex Huntingdon, Acaster Malbis, Woodford, Chester, St Athan, 5 FTS, 16. All black colour scheme.
XN600+	Jet Provost T.3	ex Leeds, 3 FTS. SOC 28/5/76. Nose section, arr 23/7/88.

CHURCH FENTON

Spitfire Vb BM597 'PR-O' left the gate during 7/89 for <u>Fulbourne</u> to become the personal mount of Tim Routsis of Historic Flying Ltd. It was replaced by another 'PR-O', this time a plastic clone. Going back to **W&R10** the hulk of Jet Provost T.5A XW329/8741M left the dump in 1986 and is now reported to have gone to an area near Halifax for an exercise involving the Yorkshire Fire Brigade. Is it still there? The JP T.3A on the dump still lives on.

L1096"	Spitfire replica	on the gate by 10/89.
XM350+	Jet Provost T.3A	ex 7 FTS, 1 FTS, RAFC, A&AEE. Stripped and stored by 2/90.
XN473	8862M Jet Provost T.3A	ex 7 FTS, RAFC. Crashed 15/8/84. Nose section on the dump.

ELVINGTON

(Off the A1079 south east of York) **Yorkshire Air Museum** continues to make great strides with both the establishment of a truly preserved airfield site (the tower is worth a visit alone) and with its ambitious project to create a Halifax where previously there was none. Tony Agar's fabulous Mosquito project has moved here and visitors can see work in progress on a series of restorations. The anonymous Auster frame noted in **W&R11** turned out to be G-ANLU, which moved to <u>Hedge End</u> in 2/88. Terrier 2 G-ASCD arrived at much the same time, and is now on show in the workshop. SE.5A replica F943/G-BKDT had gone by the summer of 1989, in readiness for flight testing. YAM is open from March 31 to Oct 28 inclusive on Saturdays 1400-1700, Sundays and Bank Holidays 1100-1700 and Tuesdays, Wednesdays and Thursdays 1100-1600. Other times by arrangement. Contact : YAM, Elvington, York, YO4 5AT. (0904 85 595).

G-AFFI"+	B'76 HM.14 Pou du Ciel	ex Hemswell, Cleethorpes, Nostell Priory, Rawdon. Arr by 4/89.
HJ711+	Mosquito NF.II	ex Huntington. Composite, under restoration. Arrived 1988.
HR792	Halifax II	ex Isle of Lewis, . Complex composite, under restoration.
TJ704" G-ASCD	Terrier 2	ex Holme-on Spalding Moor, Nympsfield, Blackbushe, PH-SFT, G-ASCD, VW993, 651, 663. CoA exp 26/9/71. See notes above.
WH846+	Canberra T.4	ex Samlesbury, St Athan, Laarbruch SF, 231 OCU. Arr 19/5/88.
WS844"+ WS788	Meteor NF.14	ex Leeming 7967M, Patrington, 1 ANS, 2 ANS, 152.
XD453	7890M Vampire T.11	ex Old Sarum, Salisbury, St Athan, 1 FTS, CNCS, Oldenburg SF, 26. On loan from 58 Squadron, ATC, Harrogate.
XS903+	Lightning F.6	ex Binbrook, 11, 5-11 pool. Flew in 18/5/88.

HUNTINGTON

As can be seen above, Tony Agar moved his Mosquito to <u>Elvington</u> in 1988.

KIRKBYMOORSIDE

At the **Slingsby** plant a Grob Viking has joined the ranks of the fatigue rigs, otherwise things are undisturbed.

G-BECE	AD-500 Skyship	destroyed 9/3/79. Stored.
G-BIUZ	T-67B	static test airframe. 1st allocation of registration, c/n 1998.
c/n 2006	T-67	static test airframe.
ZE686+	Viking TX.1	ex BGA.3099. Static test airframe. First noted 10/87.

LEEMING

Now a fully-fledged Tornado F.3 base, indeed having taken the QRA mantle away from noble Leuchars, the number and shape of **W&R** material here have changed considerably. In **W&R11** Spitfire XVI TE356 continued to hang on to a reference, although of course it had moved to East Midlands Airport and thence to Biggin Hill. Likewise Chipmunk T.10 PAX WG471/8210M managed to get into the listings, despite the narrative above rightly moving it to Stowmarket! Meteor NF.14 'WS844' was put up for tender 3/88 and was acquired by a private individual, but not moved. YAM took it on and it moved to <u>Elvington</u> early in 1990. The Javelin is now the official gate guardian, with two newer fighters arriving for instructional work.

XA634	7641M Javelin FAW.4	ex Shawbury, Colerne, Melksham, makers. Gate guardian.
XR753+	8969M Lightning F.6	ex Binbrook, 11, 5-11 pool, 23, FCTU. Flew in 24/5/88. CR.
XW764+	8981M Harrier GR.3	ex St Athan, 3. Arrived by 10/88 for BDR.

LINTON-ON-OUSE
By 10/88 the dump was cleared out.   It last contained Jet Provost T.3As
XM372/8917M and XN585.   A year later, a Halton Gnat had arrived for crash rescue
training. The Provost still guards the gate.

XF545   7957M Provost T.1   ex Swinderby, Finningley, Shawbury, 6 FTS, 2 FTS. Gate.
XR569+   8560M Gnat T.1   ex Halton, 4 FTS, CFS, 4 FTS, CFS. Arrived by 10/89. Dump.

MARKINGTON
(West of the A61 south of Ripon) The Jodel remains in store at a farm here.

G-AZII   SAN D.117A   ex F-BNDO, F-OBFO. CoA expired 28/6/79. Stored.

SHERBURN-IN-ELMET
Both the Aeronca G-AEVS and Magister G-AKAT left the locality for Breighton during
1988.   At the airfield, F.150J G-WYMP, F.172H G-AVDC"/G-AVKG and Tri-Pacer F-
BHDT/G-BHCW had all gone by 1987. Fates appreciated.

SUTTON BANK
Spares-ship Pawnee G-BENL moved to Old Buckenham by 10/87.

SUTTON-ON-THE-FOREST
(On the B1363 north of York) A yard here was another of those who wished to deal
in bulk Lightnings.   By 7/88 five had appeared here, although by 5/89 it seemed
that they were all being processed for scrap. The owner claims to have bought six,
but this is believed to have included XP761/8438M which was scrapped at Binbrook.
The five are, or were :-

XP749+   8926M Lightning F.3   ex Binbrook, LTF, 11, LTF, 11, LTF, LTF, 5, 111, Wattisham TFF, 111,
                                   CFE. Arrived 18/1/88. See notes above.
XP750+   8927M Lightning F.3   ex Binbrook, LTF, 5, LTF, 23, 111, Wattisham TFF, 111, CFE. Arrived
                                   18/1/88. See notes above.
XP751+   8928M Lightning F.3   ex Binbrook, 5-11 pool, LTF, 5, LTF, 23, 111, 23, 74. Arrived
                                   19/1/88. See above.
XP764+   8929M Lightning F.3   ex Binbrook, LTF, 5, LTF, 5, 29, 23, 56, 74. Arrived 21/1/88. See
                                   notes above.
XR720+   8930M Lightning F.3   ex Binbrook, 11, 29, 56, Wattisham TFF, 56. Arrived 18/1/88. See
                                   notes above.

THIRSK
Last appearing in W&R10, this edition sees the return of Calvert's Scrapyard.
There is a certain uncertainty about this entry on two counts. The first lies with
chunks of a burnt Vulcan still noted in 7/89 - this probably goes back to 1985 when
larger remains of this aircraft were to be seen. This is bound to have come from
Catterick, as were sections of a Sea Vixen present at the same time.   More
substantial, but too vague to put in the listing below is a 'helicopter' that the
owner reckons came from Otterburn. It certainly shows signs of having been shot at
- but as yet has rendered neither its parentage nor serial. The Lightning from
Leuchars is confirmed as having arrived here by 8/89 and confounds the writings
under Glasgow - but the two yards are believed to be connected in some way. This
yard may also have processed the Waddington Victor. The nose of the Lightning is
reported to be bound for Chop Gate. The arrival of two Scimitars from Aberporth by
7/89 filled a couple of potential holes in LOST!.

XD228+   Scimitar F.1   ex Aberporth, Foulness, RAE, A&AEE, 736, Lossiemouth, A&AEE, 803,
                                  700. Arrived by 7/89.
XD231+   Scimitar F.1   ex Aberporth, Foulness, Farnborough, Foulness, Farnborough, RAE,
                                  Brawdy, RAE, NASA, 800B, 800, 736, 800, 803, 700X. Arr by 7/89.
XM169+   8422M Lightning F.1A   ex Leuchars, Leuchars TFF, 23, Binbrook TFF, 111, A&AEE, MoA, EE.
                                   Arrived by 8/89. See notes above.

South Yorkshire

ARMTHORPE
(On the A630 north of Doncaster) **1053 Squadron ATC** still has its Chippax.
WG419   8206M Chipmunk T.10 PAX   ex Finningley, MoA, Laarbruch SF, Gutersloh SF, Ahlhorn SF, Oldenburg SF, CFS, Abn UAS, Bir UAS, 15 RFS, 4 BFTS, 6 RFS.

ECCLESFIELD
(North of Sheffield) **Paul Flynn** continues to work on his former Bingley Vampire NF.10 pod here. See also Firbeck.
WP255   Vampire NF.10   ex Bingley, Church Fenton, 27 MU hack, CNCS, 1 ANS, CNCS, 23. Pod.

FINNINGLEY
As predicted in **W&R11**, Vulcan B.2 XJ782/8766M was scrapped here by 6/88. Sycamore HR.14 XJ380/8628M was offered for tender in 4/88 and had gone by 10/88, finding a new home at <u>Drighlington</u>. A considerable element of doubt has entered into the existence of Jetstream G-ATXH as a cockpit here. The cockpit of T.1 XX477 certainly serves as a procedure trainer with METS, and it is likely that 'XH was confused with this.

WL168	7750M Meteor F.8	ex 'WH456', St Athan, Swinderby, Finningley, APS Sylt, 604, 111. Gate guardian, unveiled 10/6/88.
XJ729	8732M Whirlwind HAR.10	ex 22, 202, 228, MoA, 22. SAREW, instructional.
XP404	8682M Whirlwind HAR.10	ex Benson, 22, SAR Wing, 202, 228. SAREW, instructional.
XS216	Jet Provost T.4	ex 6 FTS, CAW. Fuselage. SAREW, instructional.
XV263	8967M Nimrod AEW.3	ex Waddington, JTU, Woodford, St Mawgan Wing, 203. AES inst.
XX297	8933M Hawk T.1A	ex Red Arrows. Crashed 30/11/86. CR.
XX477	8462M Jetstream T.1	ex Little Rissington, CFS, G-AXXS. Crashed 1/11/74. Cockpit only – see notes above.

FIRBECK
(West of the A60 north of Worksop) Long-term readers of these scribblings will appreciate the almost god-like powers of the compiler. He possesses the amazing ability to move entire locations from one county to another! Firbeck is another victim of these whims, it being more accurately sited in South Yorkshire, although its postal address owes much to Nottinghamshire – where it made a guest appearance in **W&R11**. Home Farm is the base of the **South Yorkshire Aircraft Preservation Society** and the ever-growing and ever-refining museum. SYAPS, to their eternal credit, have taken the role of rescue unit for BAPC member groups, salvaging exhibits and then selflessly letting them move on to deserving locations. Latest example of this policy is Vampire T.11 XK625. SYAPS removed this from the former North Weald Aircraft Restoration Flight on 10/6/89, bringing it to Firbeck. It was picked up in 11/89 and moved further south to <u>Brenzett</u>. The thorough presentation of airframes, support exhibits and the well groomed look of buildings and grounds makes SYAPS a shining example to 'amateur' and some 'professional' museums alike. As can be seen from the listing, there have been many additions, some of which will move on again. The Vampire FB.5 pod is on loan from Paul Flynn (see Ecclesfield) and the CASA fuselage is loaned by Colin Waterworth. The framework of Wellington L7775 moved to <u>Moreton-in-the-Marsh</u> early in 1990. Here it can be given covered accommodation and restoration. Visits to Firbeck can be arranged by prior permission, contact : SYAPS, Home Farm, Firbeck, near Worksop, Notts.   (0709 812168)

G-AEKR"	B'121 HM.14 Pou du Ciel	ex Nostell Priory, Crowle, Finningley.
G-ALYB	Auster 5	ex Bristol, White Waltham, RT520. CoA exp 26/5/63. Restn.
G-AWFH	Cessna F.150H	ex Netherthorpe. Crashed 16/12/79. Fuselage, with tail of G-AWTX.
DJF+	BGA.2146 JSH Scorpion	rebuild of Holmes KH.1 BGA.1666. Acquired by 9/87.
A4850"	B'176 SE.5A scale replica	ex Pontefract. Based on Currie Wot airframe.
WJ880+	8491M Canberra T.4	ex North Weald, Halton, 7, 85, 100, 56, Laarbruch SF, RAE, 16, Laarbruch SF, Gutersloh SF, 104. Arr 30/7/89. Nose section – remainder at Foulness.
WM267+	Meteor NF.11	ex Hemswell, Misson, 151, 256, 11. SOC 30/10/63. Cockpit section. Arrived 7/1/90.

XE864+	Vampire T.11	ex Studley, Chester, Woodford, Chester, St Athan, 8 FTS, 7 FTS, 1 ANS, CFS, 4 FTS. Wings from XD435. Arrived 8/1/89.
XE935	Vampire T.11	ex Sibson, Hitchin, Woodford, Chester, St Athan, 8 FTS.
XM279	Canberra B(I).8	ex Nostell Priory, Cambridge, 16, 3. Nose section.
+	Vampire FB.5	ex Malmesbury. Pod only - see notes above.
E-424 G-9-445	Hunter F.51	ex East Kirkby, Tattershall, Cosford, Dunsfold, Aalborg, Danish AF ESK-724. Arrived by 9/88.
C19/18+ B'118	Albatros replica	ex North Weald, 'Wings'. Arrived 30/7/89.
+	CASA 2-111	ex Eccleston, Henlow, 'Battle of Britain', Spain. Arr by 9/89. See

NETHERTHORPE
This busy airfield makes a re-entry into the realms of **W&R**.

| G-ARFB+ | Caribbean 150 | ex N3625Z. Under rebuild, first noted 11/88. |
| G-ASBB+ | Musketeer 23 | CoA expired 30/3/86. Under rebuild. |

ROSSINGTON
(On the A638 north of Bawtry) With the phase-out of the Lightning at Binbrook, several concerns decided that a potential market existed for the redundant airframes. During June 1988, no less than ten airframes arrived by road from Binbrook and have been since stored in the open at the premises of the Central Bottling Company/Tanks & Vessels Industries. All carried 'codes' based on the serial and the letters 'TVI'. To date, none have left for pastures new.

XR725+	Lightning F.6	ex Binbrook, 11, 5, LTF, 5, 56, 74, 5, 23. Arr 6/88. 'TVI725'.
XR726+	Lightning F.6	ex Binbrook, LTF, 11, LTF, LTF, 11, 5. Arr 6/88. 'TVI726'
XR747+	Lightning F.6	ex Binbrook, 5, 11, 5, 11, 5, 111, 23. Arr 6/88. 'TVI747'.
XR757+	Lightning F.6	ex Binbrook, 5-11 pool, 23, 5. Arr 6/88. 'TVI757'.
XR759+	Lightning F.6	ex Binbrook, 5-11 pool, 56, 74, 5. Arr 6/88. 'TVI759'.
XS416+	Lightning T.5	ex Binbrook, 5, LTF, 11, 74, 226 OCU, MoA. Arr 6/88. 'TVI416'.
XS419+	Lightning T.5	ex Binbrook,LTF, 5, LTF, 5, LTF, 11, 5, 23, 226 OCU.Arr 6/88. 'TVI419'.
XS897+	Lightning F.6	ex Binbrook, 5, 11, 5, 11, 56, 74. Arr 6/88. 'TVI897'.
XS932+	Lightning F.6	ex Binbrook, 5, 11, 56, 11. Arr 24/6/88. 'TVI932'.
XS935+	Lightning F.6	ex Binbrook, 5, 11, 5, 23. Arr 6/88. 'TVI935'.

ROTHERHAM
At the yard of **Cooper's Metals,** the Vulcan nose is thought to live on.

| XH563 | 8744M Vulcan B.2MRR | ex Scampton, 27, 230 OCU, MinTech, 230 OCU, Wadd Wing, 230 OCU, 12, 83. Nose section. |

SHEFFIELD
Work continues on the **Brimpex Metal Treatments** 'Flea'. It is planned to put it on display at a suitable venue when complete.

| BAPC 13 | HM.14 Pou du Ciel | ex Derby, Wigan, Peel Green, Styal. Under restoration. |

West Yorkshire

BATLEY
More precise location for the **Staravia** yard here is in Church Lane, on the Bradford road to the north of the town. The former Dutch Hunter is still stored dismantled.

| N-315 | Hunter T.7 | ex Amsterdam, NLS spares, Dutch AF, XM121. |

BINGLEY
During 5/89 the yard of **Auto Spares (Bingley) Ltd** was undergoing a major sort out and the Vampire NF.10 fuselage pods were reported being broken up. Current status here is therefore unclear and, at least for this edition, the <u>eight</u> pods that remained here are listed again. (Note that WM711 and WM713 - listed in **W&R11** - had long since demised and should be deleted.)

WM705	Vampire NF.10	ex Bradford, Church Fenton, CNCS, 1 ANS, CNCS, 25, 23, 151. Pod.
WM712	Vampire NF.10	ex Bradford, Church Fenton, CNCS, 2 ANS. Pod.
WM714	Vampire NF.10	ex Bradford, Chruch Fenton, CNCS, 1 ANS, CNCS. Pod.
WM727	Vampire NF.10	ex Bradford, Church Fenton, CNCS, 2 ANS, CNCS. Pod.
WM730	Vampire NF.10	ex Bradford, Church Fenton, CNCS, 1 ANS, CNCS, 23. Pod.
WP232	Vampire NF.10	ex Bradford, Church Fenton, CNCS, 1 ANS, CNCS, A&AEE. Pod.
WP239	Vampire NF.10	ex Bradford, Church Fenton, CNCS, 2 ANS, CNCS, 25, CFE. Pod.
WP242	Vampire NF.10	ex Bradford, Church Fenton, CNCS, 2 ANS, CNCS, 25. Pod.

DEWSBURY

Northern Aeroplane Workshops presented their superb Sopwith Triplane replica to the public at the 1988 Finningley Battle of Britain display - in assembled but skeletal form. Work is well advanced and there is ever chance that it will fly this year, from Old Warden as it has been built for the Shuttleworth Collection. Construction continues on the Bristol Monoplane replica. Visits to the workshop are on a prior permission only basis. Contact : Northern Aeroplane Workshops, F W Found, 7 Scoton Drive, Knaresborough, North Yorks.

| N6290" G-BOCK | Sopwith Triplane | c/n NAW.1. 'Dixie' of 8 Squadron. Nearing completion. |
| | Bristol M.1D Mono | c/n NAW.2/PFA 112-10678. Under construction. |

DRIGHLINGTON

(At the junction of the A58 and the A650 east of Bradford) By 10/88 a private collector had acquired two Sycamores and installed them at his home.

| XG540+ 8345M | Sycamore HR.14 | ex Shawbury, XJ385", Ternhill 7899M, MCS, CFS. Arrived by 10/88. |
| XJ380+ 8628M | Sycamore HR.14 | ex Finningley, Catterick, CFS, MoA, HS, 275. Arrived by 10/88. |

ELLAND

(On the A6026 between Halifax and Huddersfield) **Michael Runciman's** Comet nose is still to be found here, as part of his extensive avionics collection.

| XK659 | Comet C.2R | ex Northenden, Pomona Dock, Manchester Airport, 51, 192, G-AMXC. |

LEEDS

There have been two additions to the collection of flying machines held by **Anne Lindsay and Nigel Ponsford**. Their Chipmunk fuselage is still on loan and to be found at Sunderland. The Bristol F.2b components acquired from Guy Black are really too small to merit a mention within the tables and are deleted from this issue. The Ord Hume OH-7 Coupe is quite a find and is, of course, a version of the Luton Minor. Current status is as follows :

G-AEFG BAPC75	HM.14 Pou du Ciel	ex Harrogate, Kirkby Overblow, Wigan. Under restoration.
G-ARIF+	OH-7 Coupe	ex London. Acquired early 1989. Under restoration.
BGA 491	Dagling	ex Great Hucklow. Stored.
BGA 1559+	T.31B	ex XN247. Arrived 1/90.
	Hutter H.17a	ex Accrington. Stored.
	Dickson Primary	ex Harrogate. Under restoration.
RA848	Cadet TX.1	ex Harrogate, Wigan, Handforth. Cockpit section.
BAPC 14	Addyman STG	ex Harrogate, Wigan.
BAPC 16	Addyman Ultra-Light	ex Harrogate, Wigan.
BAPC 18	Killick Gyroplane	ex Harrogate, Irlam.
BAPC 39	Addyman Zephyr	ex Harrogate. Substantial parts, stored.

168 Squadron ATC had their Jet Provost XN600 cockpit tendered during 3/88 and it left by road for Chop Gate on 23/7/88. **Mike Cookman** has held two Typhoon cokpit sections here for some time. One left during 1988 and eventually found its way to Innsworth. Work on the other example continues.

| | Typhoon IB | ex Gloucester, Kemble. Cockpit section - see notes above. |

LEEDS-BRADFORD AIRPORT

(Or Yeadon) The wreck situation here remains remarkably stable. Restoration of the Avian is taking place both locally and within a small workshop on the airfield, and accordingly it is best listed with the other Airport inmates.

G-ACGT	Avian IIIA	ex Linthwaite, EI-AAB. CoA exp 21/7/39. Under restoration.
G-ATND	Cessna F.150F	crashed 9/12/72. Forward fuselage, engine test-rig with YLA.
G-AVGG	Cherokee 140	wfu 16/3/73. Used for spares.
G-AWES	Cessna 150H	ex Blackpool, Glenrothes, N22933. Crashed 2/10/81.
G-AXZJ	Cessna F.172H	crashed 12/12/76. Under rebuild, using parts of T-41 N5162F.

LIVERSEDGE

The Jet Provost T.4 cockpit section here, calling itself 'XM426' with **2490 Squadron ATC** in Bradford Road moved to Lutterworth on 23/7/88.

SIDDAL

(On the A646 south of Halifax) Despite all efforts to the contrary, the scrapyard here continues to live on, with its largely rotary winged decaying inmates.

XG597	Whirlwind HAS.7	ex Warton SAR Flt, CA, makers.
XH587	Victor K.1A	ex St Athan, 57, 15, A&AEE, makers. Nose section.
XL868	A2595 Whirlwind HAS.7	ex Arbroath, 705, HS, 771, 815. Crashed 20/6/69.
XM663	Whirlwind HAS.7	ex Arbroath, 824. Crashed 14/4/59.
XT774	Wessex HU.5	ex 845. Crashed 17/5/69.

WHINMOOR

(On. the A64 north east of Leeds) The former Heli-Leeds base has been wound down and it is thought no more helicopter wrecks remain here.

Part 2

SCOTLAND

Shetland Isles

Orkney Isles

Western Isles

Highlands

Grampian

Tayside

Central

Fife

Lothian

Strathclyde

Borders

Dumfries & Galloway

England

Central

CAUSEWAYHEAD
(North of Stirling) Still to be found within the scrapyard of **William Kerr** is the former Dunblane Sycamore.
XG504	Sycamore HR.14	ex Dunblane, Nostell Priory, Rotherham, 32, MCS, CFS, Khormaksar SF, Aden SF. Poor state.

Dumfries & Galloway

BORGUE
(On the B727 west of Kirkudbright) The **Brighouse Bay Caravan Park** bought the former RAF Carlisle gate guardian. It is displayed within the camp.
WS792+	7965M Meteor NF.14	ex Carlisle, Cosford, Kemble, 1 ANS, 2 ANS. See notes above.

FALGUNZEON
While it is believed that the T.21B is still to be found in the rafters of the Dumfries and Galloway Gliding Club, it has not been physically reported for some time. It may be bound for LOST!
T.21B	Possibly BGA.1315. Stored.	

TINWALD DOWNS
(Off the A701 north west of Dumfries on the former airfield) **Dumfries and Galloway Aviation Group** continue to run their museum here. There have been no changes to the 'fleet', although there is a possibility that the Gannet composite will be disposed of in 1990. Note that the Spitfire is not held on site, viewing possible by prior application. The Museum is open to the public every Sunday April to September from 1000 to 1700. Other times by appointment. Contact : Dumfries & Galloway Aviation Group, 11 Ninian Court, Lochside, Dumfries.
P7540	Spitfire IIA	ex Loch Doon, 312, 266, 609, 66. Crashed 6/7/41. Major sections.
WA576	7900M Sycamore 3	ex East Fortune, Strathallan, Halton, RAE, A&AEE, G-ALSS ntu.
WJ903	Varsity T.1	ex Glasgow Airport, 6 FTS, AE&AEOS, 1 ANS, 2 ANS, 3 ANS. Nose only.
WL375	Meteor T.7(mod)	ex West Freugh, RAE.
XD425	Vampire T.11	ex Stranraer, Woodford, Chester, St Athan, 8 FTS, 5 FTS, 7 FTS, 202 AFS.
	Vampire	pod only. Single seater.
	Venom	ex Silloth. Pod only, single seater. Possibly WK394.
	Gannet AS.	ex Carlisle. Fuselage. Wings from AEW.3 XL471.
FT-36	T-33A-1-LO	ex Sculthorpe, Belgian Air Force, USAF 55-3047.
318	Mystere IVA	ex Sculthorpe, French Air Force.
42163	F-100D-11-NA	ex Sculthorpe, French Air Force.

WEST FREUGH
Previous talking-point at this **Royal Aerospace Establishment** in **W&R11** was the reported Mil Mi-24 'Hind' here. During the summer of 1988 all became much clearer when the said helicopter defected, via Immingham docks for Sweden. It was indeed the cosmetically-treated Whirlwind HAS.7 XN382 previously noted at Thruxton. Once in Sweden, the 'Hind' was blown to bits in a missile trial/promotional film. While a little tattier, the contents of the fire dump have not changed.
VP977	Devon C.2/2	ex Northolt, 207, Baghdad Attache, Rangoon Attache, Bangkok Attache, Djakarta Attache, Saigon Attache, Bangkok Attache, 31, G-ALTS.
XN817	Argosy C.1	ex A&AEE, MinTech, 115, MoA.

Fife

CUPAR
The farm-strip here still holds the Cadet in store.
XE802   Cadet TX.3   Stored.

LEUCHARS
Despite all the hard work in restoring Spitfire F.21 LA198 to immaculate display condition, the base had to give up their gate guardian in the major reshuffle and it left for St Athan on 5/4/89. It was replaced by Britain's first-ever Phantom gate guardian - how time time moves on,. Many **W&R** readers, like the Compiler, must still regard the F-4 as all-that-is-modern! During 1989 tenders went out on four of the Lightnings on base, but as yet only two fates are known : F.1A XM169 was tendered in 5/89 and was broken up by 9/89, the nose at least going to Thirsk [but see Glasgow]; F.2A XN781/8538M was tendered at the same time and moved to Withington. One of the Lightnings (likely XM178) is reported to have been acquired by a French museum. XM178/8418M had gone by 11/89. Not seen for a long time, Sea Prince T.1 WP320 is believed to have perished on the dump by 1989.

XM144	8417M Lightning F.1A	ex Leuchars TFF, 23, Leuchars TFF, Wattisham TFF, 226 OCU, 74. Up for tender 7/89.
XR713	8935M Lightning F.3	ex LTF, 5, 11, 5, LTF, 11, LTF, 5, 111, Wattisham TFF, 111. BDR.
XR749	8934M Lightning F.3	ex 11, LTF, 11, LTF, Binbrook pool, 29, 226 OCU, 56, EE. Overstressed on landing 17/2/87. BDR.
XT857	8913M Phantom FG.1	ex 111, PTF, 767, A&AEE, RAE. Damaged 7/85. ASF airframe.
XT859+	8999M Phantom FG.1	ex 111. BDR
XT864+	8998M Phantom FG.1	ex 111. Mounted on the gate as 'BJ' 111 Squadron by 9/89.
XV588	Phantom FG.1	ex Lee-on-Solent, 892. Wreck, crashed 17/5/77. Minus nose.

Grampian

ABERDEEN
Grampian Fire Service still use the Whirlwind at their base in Anderson Drive.
VR-BBN   Whirlwind Srs 3   ex Redhill, Bristows, G-AOYB.

ABERDEEN AIRPORT
(Or Dyce) The days of long term storage for helicopters have gone, at least for this edition. S-61N G-AWFX was sold in Canada in 5/88 and S-76A G-BJGX was flying again by 10/87. Otherwise, the scene here is much as it ever was.

G-ARPN	Trident 1	ex Heathrow, BA, BEA. Fire service.
N64P	Aztec 250C	ex G-ASTD. Fuselage on dump.
N150JC	Bonanza A35	ex Wick. Crashed 18/6/83. Stored.

ABOYNE
Restoration work on the Stampe continues close to the airfield.
G-BALX   SNCAN SV-4C   ex 'Cheshire', Liverpool, Littleborough, F-BBAN, French military.

BANCHORY
(On the A93 west of Aberdeen) A private collector had acquired an anonymous Vulcan nose here by 2/87.
          Vulcan   Nose section.

CRUDEN BAY

(On the A975 south of Peterhead) **Malcolm Hobson** holds one substantial wreck here
and the remains of another aircraft that will appeal to those who like filling in
'holes'. Malcolm salvaged the tail feathers etc of Beech D.18S N15750 (ex G-ATUM)
from the Balmoral estates. It had been used in a film on the estates in February
1977 when it had been painted as 'CF-RLD'. It played out the highly original plot
of bush-plane down in inhospitable territory - help nowhere in sight. What to do?
Eat your fellow survivors! N15750 last appeared within the pages of this tome at
Lasham in 2/76. It was noted in **W&R6** as having been blown up in a movie, although
we reported the location as deepest Hampshire!

| G-BCIL+ | AA-1B Trainer | ex Auchnagatt, N6168A. Crashed 14/6/86. |

ELGIN

George F Williamson, the company best remembered for the Quarrywood yard, have
established a large scrapyard in Edgar Road. Noted in late 1989 were the smashed
contents of the former Kinloss dump (Shackleton T.4 WB847 and parts from Nimrod
MR.2 XV256). Not yet physically noted here is the latest clear-out from
Lossiemouth's dump - which see.

FORRES

(On the A96 West of Elgin) As explained in **W&R11** the yard of D&S Metals was
cleared by 3/87. The company moved to new premises on the Industrial Estate. They
took with them the smashed remains of Buccaneer S.1 XN973 and an impressively large
pile of aero engines.

KINLOSS

Having not long 'surfaced' after an impressive record of tenacity on the dump, the
hulk of Anson T.21 VV950 was bulldozed away during 1/90.   The single addition is
most likely also the last time ever a Nimrod AEW.3 flew.

XW549	8860M Buccaneer S.2B	ex St Athan, 12, 16. BDR. Sections.
XZ282+	9000M Nimrod AEW.3	ex Abingdon, Waddington, JTU, Woodford. Flew in 14/ 9/89, spares use for Nimrod Main Servicing Unit.
8882M	G-BDIU Comet 4C	ex Woodford, Bitteswell, Dan-Air, XR396, 214. BDR. Centre section.

LOSSIEMOUTH

Having no less that three gate guardians, Lossiemouth was bound to suffer harshly
in the Great Gate Guardian Gadabout. Shackleton MR.2C WL738/8567M and Gannet T.5
XG882/8754M were both put up for tender in 7/89. Both are thought to have gone to
the new Williamson at Eglin. Other than the addition of another 'Brick', status
quo rules here.

With deepest sympathies to colleagues, relatives and friends for the loss of the
crew of Shackleton AEW.2 WL965 on 30/4/90 - 8 Squadron's first flying accident
since reforming on the 'Shack' in January 1972.

WL798	8114M Shackleton MR.2C	ex Cosford, 204, 205, 38. 8 Squadron spares. Minus wings by 2/90 and out on the dump by 3/90.
WR967	8398M Shackleton MR.2C	ex 8, 210, MOTU, 210, 38, 224, 38, 205, 38, 42, JASS. Fuselage only, AEW.2 procedure trainer.
XK532	8867M Buccaneer S.1	ex Manadon, A2581, Lossiemouth, 736. Gate guardian.
XL609	8866M Hunter T.7	ex 12, 216, 237 OCU, 4 FTS, 56. Damaged here 10/85. BDR.
XN929	8051M Buccaneer S.1	ex Honington. Procedure trainer, nose only.
XT281	8705M Buccaneer S.2B	ex 12. WLT.
XV154+	8854M Buccaneer S.2A	ex St Athan, 12, 237 OCU. wfu 7/ 2/86. BDR. (See also Wattisham)

NETHERLEY

Adding to **W&R11**, Terrier G-ASBU moved on from here to Chirk.

QUARRYWOOD

(On the B9012 north west of Elgin) The George F Williamson yard here continues to
hold some long term scrap. A pile of aeronautical scrap noted in late 1989
included the tail of Firefly AS.7 WJ192, Venom wings and Gannet pieces. See also
Elgin for their new yard.

Highlands

EDDERTON
(On the A9 north west of Tain) Both Condors, one donor, one recipient, continue, and the Pup shell lingers on.
G-ASEU	D.62A Condor	CoA expired 29/3/74. Under restoration.
G-AVKM	D.62B Condor	Damaged 3/3/82. Spares for G-ASEU.
c/n 180 Pup		ex Kindeace, Delny, Prestwick, Rearsby. Fuselage only.

INVERNESS AIRPORT
(Or Dalcross) A welcome return to this continually Skeeter-orientated airfield. Not flown since 1984, Skeeter G-BKSC is returning to fitness. The Cessna is a relatively long-term project.
| G-AZZG+ | Cessna 188-230 | ex Southend, OY-AHT, N8029V. CoA expired 1/5/81. Restoration. |
| XN351+ G-BKSC | Skeeter AOP.12 | ex Shobdon, Cardiff-Wales, Higher Blagdon, Old Warden, Wroughton, 3 RTR, 652, 651. CoA expired 8/11/84. Restoration. |

TAIN
Out on the extensive range here, the Sea Venom hulk survives. There may be others out there...
| XG731 | Sea Venom FAW.22 | ex Lossiemouth. Pod and inner wings. Poor state. |

The Islands

ORPHIR
(Near Kirkwall, Orkney) The ditched Jodel is still stored on a farm-strip here.
| G-ASRP | SAN DR.1050 | ex F-BITI. Ditched in Scapa Flow 17/3/86. Stored. |

STORNOWAY AIRPORT
(Isle of Lewis) Surprisingly few reports from here (!), but the Cessna is thought to live on.
| G-GUNN | Cessna F.172H | ex G-AWGC. Damaged 10/11/82. Fire dump. |

SUMBURGH AIRPORT
(Shetland) The firemen still have their Potez 'mini-airliner' to play with.
| F-BMCY | Potez 840 | Wheels-up landing 29/3/81. Fire dump. |

Lothian

EAST FORTUNE
Royal Museum of Scotland – Museum of Flight There has been a further concentration on the buildings at this excellent museum and the many supporting displays have been extended. Hangar IV will be reclad during 1990/1991 and some aircraft will not be available for public view. A new display honouring Sheila Scott has been prepared. The Aeroplane Collection Rapide G-ADAH migrated back to its owners on 7/4/89, going on show at Manchester. Also leaving was the Rolls-Royce TMR XJ314 on

21/2/89, going to join the new VTOL display at Yeovilton.   The Museum is open
1000 to 1600 all week during July and August.   Beyond this period prior application
should be made.   Please note that not all of the airframes listed are on public
view.   Contact : Museum of Flight, East Fortune Airfield, North Berwick, East
Lothian, EH39 5LF.   Telephone 062 088 308.

G-ACYK		Spartan Cruiser	ex Hill of Stake, Largs. Crashed 14/1/38. Fuselage section.
G-AGBN		Cygnet II	ex Strathallan, Biggin Hill, ES915, G-AGBN. CoA expired 28/11/80.
G-ANOV		Dove 6	ex CAFU Stansted, G-5-16. CoA expired 31/5/75.
G-ARCX		Meteor 14	ex Ferranti Flying Unit, Edinburgh, WM261. CoA expired 20/2/69.
G-ASUG		Beech D.18S	ex Loganair, N575C, N555CB, N24R. wfu 12/3/75.
G-ATOY		Comanche 260B	ex Elstree, N8893P. Crashed 6/3/79. The late Sheila Scott's a/c.
G-AXEH		Bulldog 1	ex Prestwick, Shoreham. Prototype. CoA expired 15/1/77.
G-BBVF		Twin Pioneer 2	ex Shobdon, XM961/7978M, SRCU, Odiham SF, 230, 21. dbr 11/3/82.
G-BDFU		Dragonfly II MPA	ex Blackpool Airport, Warton, Prestwick.
G-BDIX		Comet 4C	ex Lasham, Dan-Air, XR399, 216. wfu 29/10/80.
G-BIRW		MS.505 Criquet	ex Duxford, OO-FIS, F-BDQS. CoA exp 3/6/83. Luftwaffe c/s 'FI+S'.
BGA. 852		T.8 Tutor	ex Portmoak, TS291.
BGA. 902		Gull I	ex Newbattle, 'G-ALPHA'. Possibly ex VW912.
BGA.1014		T.21B	ex Feshie Bridge, SE-SHK.
W-2	BAPC.85	Weir W-2	ex Glasgow, East Fortune, Hayes, Cathcart.
VH-SNB		Dragon I	ex Strathallan, VH-ASK, RAAF A34-13.
VH-UQB		Puss Moth	ex Strathallan, G-ABDW.
N9510	G-AOEL	Tiger Moth	ex Strathallan, Dunstable, N9510, 7 FTS, 2 GU, 11 RFS, 1 RFS, 7 RFS, 7 EFTS. CoA expired 18/7/72.
TE462	7243M	Spitfire XVI	ex Ouston, 101 FRS, Finningley SF.
VM360	G-APHV	Anson C.19	ex Strathallan, Kemps Aerial Surveys, TRE, A&AEE.
WF259	A2483	Sea Hawk F.2	ex Lossiemouth SF, 736.
WV493	G-BDYG	Provost T.1	ex Strathallan, Halton 7696M, 6 FTS. CoA expired 28/11/80.
WW145		Sea Venom FAW.22	ex Lossiemouth, 750,891.
XA109		Sea Vampire T.22	ex Lossiemouth, 831, JOAC.
XL762	8017M	Skeeter AOP.12	ex Middle Wallop, 2 RTR, 9 Flt, 651.
XM597		Vulcan B.2	ex Waddington, 50, 35, 101, 9, 50, 35, Wadd Wing, 12.
XN776		Lightning F.2A	ex Leuchars, 92.
591		Rhonlerche II	ex D-0359.
9940		Bolingbroke IVT	ex Strathallan, RCAF 5 B&GS. Under restoration.
191659		Me 163B-1a	ex Cambridge, Cranfield, Brize Norton, II/JG.400.
		WACO CG-4A	ex Aberlady. Nose section only.
BAPC 12		HM.14 Pou du Ciel	ex Chester-le-Street, Newcastle, Wigan. TAC loan.
BAPC 160		Chargus 18/50	hang glider.
BAPC 195		Moonraker 77	hang glider.
BAPC 196		Sigma IIM	hang glider.
BAPC 197		Cirrus 3	hang glider.

As well as working in support of the Museum of Flight, the **Aircraft Preservation
Society of Scotland** also maintain a workshop at East Fortune.   APSS's Auster is
displayed with the main collection, but the other airframes require prior
arrangement for inspection.   Contact : Aircraft Preservation Society of Scotland,
c/o Museum of Flight, East Fortune Airfield, North Berwick, East Lothian, EH39 5LF.

G-AFJU		Miles Monarch	ex York, Strathallan, Lasham, Staverton, X9306, G-AFJU. CoA expired 18/5/64.
G-ARTJ		Bensen B.8M	ex Currie, Cupar. wfu 12/73.
G-ATFG		Brantly B.2B	ex Newport Pagnell. CoA expired 25/3/85.
TJ398"	BAPC.70	Auster AOP.6	ex Inverkeithing, Perth.

EDINBURGH

In Chambers Street, the **Royal Museum of Scotland** has the original Pilcher Hawk on
show.   The Museum is open Monday to Saturday 1000 to 1700 and Sunday 1400 to 1700.
Contact : Royal Museum of Scotland, Chambers Street, Edinburgh, EH1 1JF.   Telephone
031 225 7534.

| BAPC. 49 | Pilcher Hawk | first flown at Eynsham 1896, crashed at Stanford Hall 30/9/1899. |

EDINBURGH AIRPORT
(Or Turnhouse) The Trident continues to serve the local fire crews. In 10/89 the gate guardian Spitfire at RAF Turnhouse was exchanged for a plastic version, including the same 602 Squadron codes - nobody was fooled. RW393 moved to St Athan on 4/10/89.

| G-ARPL | Trident 1C | ex Heathrow, BA, BEA. Fire service. |
| L1070" | Spitfire replica | installed on the gate 10/89. |

Strathclyde

BEARSDEN
(North of Glasgow) It is thought that the wrecked Cessna is still here.

| G-AXBU | Cessna FR.172F | ex Kirknewton, Inverkeithing. Crashed 13/10/74. Wreck. |

CUMBERNAULD AIRFIELD
Our first-ever entry for this pleasant airfield. The Tiger Moth moved from Glasgow for completion.

| G-TCUB+ | J-3C-65 Cub | ex N9039Q, N67666, NC67666, USN 29684, USAAF 45-55204. Under rebuild following accident. |
| N6037+ | G-ANNB Tiger Moth | ex Glasgow Airport, US N6037, D-EGYN, G-ANNB, T6037, 1 RFS, 12 RFS, 23 RFS, 5 RFS, 29 EFTS. Under restoration. |

DUNOON
Is the home of **2296 Squadron ATC**. It is not known if they have 'powered up' their Chippax yet, but it is now known that it was never at Wishaw, so followers of such devices should amend their notes.

| WZ866 | 8217M Chipmunk T.10 PAX | ex Carluke, Cumbernauld, CoAT G-ATEB, Lee UAS, Abn UAS, Bir UAS, Abn UAS, Oxf UAS, Detling SF, Colerne SF. |

GLASGOW
Considerably enlarged and restyled, the new **Museum of Transport** re-opened in 1988. Of principal aviation interest within is the Pilcher Hawk replica. Open weekdays 1000-1700 and Sunday 1400-1700. Contact : Museum of Transport, Kelvin Hall, 1 Bunhouse Road, Glasgow, G3 8DP. Tel 041 357 3929.

| BAPC 48 | Pilcher Hawk rep | Built by 2175 Squadron ATC. |

As **W&R** goes to press, there have been several reports of a scrapyard here operated by two brothers. With no firm location and confusion or duplication with the one at Thirsk [which see], this edition will play safe and mention the yard in a low-key manner, awaiting the input of readers. Reported here are former Lossiemouth gate guardians Shackleton MR.2C WL738/8567M and Gannet T.5 XG882/8754M. From Leuchars Lightning F.1 XM169/8422M was credited with coming here.

GLASGOW AIRPORT
(Or Abbotsinch) Light aircraft in the **W&R** category continue to change here. Of those listed in **W&R11**, Tri-Pacer 160 G-ARFD and Tomahawk 112 G-BKMK were both flying again by 1989. US import Tiger Moth N6037/G-ANNB was here during 1988, but moved to Cumbernauld for completion.

G-ARPP	Trident 1C	ex Heathrow, BA, BEA. Fire service.
G-ATJC	Airtourer 100	CoA expired 30/9/87. Stored off-site.
G-BIUU+	Aztec 250D	ex Lydd, TR-LPZ, 6V-ACB, N13798. CoA expired 10/9/84. Spares use. Arrived 30/12/88.

G-BMDZ	Cessna 310Q	ex OY-BJU, SE-FRB, N7621Q. Spares use.
G-SEAB+	RC-3 Seabee	ex N6210K, NC6210K. Arrived 1988, under restoration.
N9467T+	Tomahawk 112	Arrived 1988, under restoration.
J-1614 G-BLIE	Venom FB.50	ex Dubendorf, Swiss Air Force. Unflown since arrival 27/2/85.

HOLLYBUSH
(On the A713 south east of Ayr) Thought still stored at Skeldon Mill is the Tiger.

| G-ANNN | Tiger Moth | ex Kilkerran, T5968, Wattisham SF, 61 GCF, 3 FTS, 28 EFTS, 57 OTU. |

KILKERRAN
With no evidence to the contrary, the stored items here are thought unchanged.

| G-AIGU | J/1N Alpha | CoA expired 5/9/74. Under restoration. |
| G-AREH | Tiger Moth | ex G-APYV ntu, 6746M, DE241. CoA expired 19/4/66. |

KILMARNOCK
In Aird Avenue, off Dundonald Road, **327 Squadron ATC** can be relied upon for an amendment or two. In the last tome it was the Canberra, this time it is the Hunter nose. This item is now known to be a decided mock-up and should be deleted. The unit is parented by RAF Turnhouse at Edinburgh Airport.

| WB584 | 7706M Chipmunk T.10 PAX | ex Edinburgh Airport, Bri UAS, 12 RFS, 22 RFS. |
| WJ872 | 8492M Canberra T.4 | ex Halton, Wyton SF, 360, 13, Akrotiri SF, 231 OCU. Nose. |

MACHRIHANISH
On the dump the Vulcan survives and the Varsity serves the RAF Police Provost Training School dogs.

| WL635 | Varsity T.1 | ex RAE F'borough, Kemble, 5 FTS, 4 FTS, 1439 Flt, Weston Zoyland SF. |
| XL427 | 8756M Vulcan B.2 | ex 44, Wadd Wing, Scampton Wing, 83. Dump. |

PAISLEY
By 3/88 the aircraft content of the **Alex D Stewart Ltd** scrapyard in Hamilton Street had been 'processed' as the term goes. (They were Aztec 250B G-ASNA, Aztec 250C G-BAHC and F.172G G-OPEL.)

PRESTWICK AIRPORT
There have been no changes of inmates here since **W&R11**. The Fleet Air Arm Historic Aircraft Flight Sea Fury FB.11 TF956 was ditched off the coast on 10/6/89, following a much-publicised undercarriage malfunction. For a short period after the accident, some sections of the aircraft appeared within HMS 'Gannet', but did not stay long. 'Gannet's Gannet, was moved to Yeovilton 23/1/90 by road for a respray before returning to the gate.

G-ATDB	Noralpha	ex F-OTAN-6, French military. CoA expired 22/11/78. Open store.
G-ATXJ	Jetstream	Series 41 mock-up. CoA expired 8/2/71.
G-AWZJ	Trident 3B-101	ex Heathrow, BA, BEA. Flew in 24/2/86.
XL497	Gannet AEW.3	ex Lossiemouth, 849. Gate guardian at HMS 'Gannet'.
XX660	Bulldog T.1	Crashed 25/3/85. Sectioned.

Tayside

ARBROATH
Work continues on the restoration to flying condition of Anson C.19 TX183.

| TX183 | Anson C.19 | ex Duxford, Old Warden, A&AEE, HS, CNCS, 1 ANS, Abingdon SF. |

DUNDEE
During 9/89 Airedale G-ASAI arrived in the area from the Airport for restoration.

| G-ASAI+ | Airedale | ex Dundee Airport, Islay. CoA expired 20/5/77. Arrived for restoration 23/9/89. |

DUNDEE AIRPORT
(Or Riverside) A case of a clear-out here. Airedale G-ASAI left for the locality
of **Dundee** by road 23/9/89. FRA.150M Aerobat hulk G-BDOW has gone, status unknown.

MONTROSE
The Offshore Petroleum Industry Training Board gave up their former Wroughton
Whirlwind to **2288 Squadron ATC** at the TAVR Centre in Broomfield Road in late 1989.

| XJ723 | Whirlwind HAR.10 | ex PITB, Wroughton, 202, 228, 155. See notes above. |

PERTH AIRPORT
(Or Scone) **Scottish Aircraft Collection Trust,** who were set up to 'save' something
from the 'original' collapse of the Strathallan Collection, did not outlast that
Museum by much. Negotiations were underway early in 1990 to try to keep the
aircraft within Scotland. For the moment, the aircraft are still here, but not
available for inspection.

G-AHKY	Miles M.18 Srs 2	ex Strathallan, Blackbushe, HM545, U-0224, U-8.
VS356	G-AOLU Prentice T.1	ex Strathallan, Biggin Hill, EI-ASP, G-AOLU, VS356, CFS, 2 FTS. CoA expired 8/5/76.
VZ728	G-AGOS Desford Trainer	ex Strathallan, Thruxton, Kemps Aerial Surveys. CoA expired 28/11/80.

Operating the airfield is **Air Service Training.** The grounded instructional fleet
has grown by one airframe and seems to have lost none. Visits here are possible
only by prior appointment.

G-ALWS	Tiger Moth	ex N9328, Upwood SF, 6 FTS, 15 EFTS, 17 EFTS, 15 EFTS, 19 EFTS, Duxford SF, Farnborough SF.
G-ARBC	Cessna 310D	ex N6934T. CoA expired 25/6/77.
G-ARPX	Trident 1C	ex Heathrow, BA, BEA.
G-ARTX	Cessna 150B	ex N7377X. Crashed 14/9/72. Fuselage.
G-ARTY	Cessna 150B	ex N7382X. CoA expired 6/10/68.
G-ATNJ	Cessna F.150F	Crashed 24/ 9/74.
G-ATOF	Cessna F.150F	Crashed 25/11/71.
G-ATOG	Cessna F.150F	Crashed 27/ 1/81.
G-AVDB	Cessna 310L	ex N2279F. CoA expired 8/ 7/79.
G-AYBW	Cessna FA.150K	Crashed 8/10/72.
G-AYGB	Cessna 310Q	ex N7611Q. CoA expired 23/10/87.
G-BAIM+	Cessna 310Q	ex N8031Q. CoA expired 15/8/88.
G-BBCF	Cessna FRA.150L	ex Leeds-Bradford. Crashed 8/ 9/84. Fuselage.
G-BEWP	Cessna F.150M	Crashed 4/10/83.
F-BGNR	Viscount 708	ex Air Inter.
WW453	Provost T.1	ex Huntings, 1 FTS, 2 FTS.
XL875	Whirlwind HAR.9	ex Wroughton, Lee SAR Flt, Culdrose SAR Flt, 847, 848, 815.
XT140	Sioux AH.1	ex Middle Wallop.
XX467	Hunter T.73	ex 1 TWU, Jordan AF 836, Saudi AF 70-617, G-9-214, XL605, 66, 92.
	Chipmunk T.10	ex 'G-ASTD', G-AOJZ, WB732, Not UAS, 16 RFS, 11 RFS, Abn UAS, 11 RFS.

Also at the airfield, the restoration of the Alpha continues.

| G-AOFJ | Auster Alpha 5 | CoA expired 20/9/79. Under rebuild. |

STRATHALLAN
The doors of the **Strathallan Aircraft Collection** closed for the last time on
30/9/88. Long anticipated, the event was not announced other than locally, so the
news still came as a quite a shock when it eventually filtered out. At this stage,
there are many question marks relating to what-went-where. As ever, doubtless it
will all be told in technicolour in **W&R13!** Aircraft that had moved on or where
not accounted for at 10/89 were as follows : Replica SE.5A F5447"/G-BKER had moved
elsewhere by early 1989; Kay Gyroplane G-ACVA - returned to Glasgow?; SAAB Safir G-
ANOK; Avro XIX G-AYWA reported as "sold"; SWAIG's Vampire T.11 pod XD547; Sea Hawk
FGA.6 XE340; Whirlwind HAS.7 XG594; Pilcher Hawk replica BAPC.170 and the Fokker
D.VI and D.VII replicas. Sir William Roberts (the Museum and airfield owner) has
retained three airframes and they are within his estate and not for public viewing.

Other airframes have been notified as for sale.

G-BEPV	Fokker S.11-1	ex PH-ANK, Dutch AF E-31. CoA expired 3/12/84. For sale.
R1914	G-AHUJ Magister I	ex Aboyne, Balado, Kemble, 137, 604, Middle Wallop SF, 604. CoA expired 8/5/87. Stored on the Estate.
V9441"	G-AZWT Lysander III	ex RCAF 2355. CoA expired 6/3/87. Stored on the Estate.
W5856	G-BMGC Swordfish II	ex Alabama, RCAF, Wroughton, Manston. Stored on the Estate.
VP293	Shackleton T.4	ex RAE, MOTU, 206, 46, 224. For sale.
XE897"	XD403 Vampire T.11	ex Woodford, Chester, 4 FTS, 1 FTS, 7 FTS, 8 FTS, 5 FTS, 4 FTS. For sale.
XK655	Comet C.2R	ex 51, BOAC, G-AMXA. For sale.

Clwyd

CHESTER AIRPORT

(Or Hawarden or Broughton) The political geography of the area is such that Chester's Airport lies in Wales, much in the same way as West Midlands-based Coventry finds its Airport in Warwickshire! **British Aerospace** completed their restoration of HS.125-1 G-ASSM (ex 9J-SAS) and on 16/3/89 it was delivered by road to the Science Museum at Wroughton. Pending the machinations of the accountants, the BAe 146 is still in store, although it has now aspired to a UK identity. Also, the Nigerian HS.125-1 is thought still stored within the complex.

G-ARYA	HS.125-1	ex Connah's Quay, Chester, Hatfield. Nose section, Apprentices.
G-BRUC	BAe 146-100	ex TZ-ADT, Mali Government. Stored.
5N-AMK	HS.125-1	ex Southampton. Stored. See notes above.
XN685	8173M Sea Vixen FAW.2	ex Cosford, Cranwell, 890, 766, 893, HSA Hatfield. Apprentices.

CHIRK

At the former airstrip here, the Dragon Rapide cache remains unaltered. Inbound, a Terrier moved in from Scotland and damaged SIPA 901 G-BDAO left by road, going to Liverpool Airport by 6/89.

G-AIUL	Dragon Rapide	ex Southend, British Westpoint, NR749, Kemble, 2 RS. CoA expired 29/9/67. Stored.
G-AJBJ	Dragon Rapide	ex Coventry, Blackpool, NF894, 18 MU, HQ TCCF. CoA exp 14/9/61. Stored
G-AKOE	Dragon Rapide	ex British Airways, Booker, X7484, PTS. CoA expired 25/2/82. Stored.
G-ASBU+	Terrier 2	ex Netherley, WE570, LAS, CFS, 2 FTS, CFS. Crashed 12/8/80. Arrived 1988. Stored.
G-BEDB	Norecrin	ex Liverpool, Chirk, F-BEOB. CoA expired 11/6/80. Stored.

CONNAH'S QUAY

(On the A548 west of Chester) At the **North East Wales Institute** a plot that had taken a long, long time to come to fruition was finally achieved in 1/89. After negotiations opened under the aegis of the late Mike Carlton of the Hunter One Collection, a deal was clinched by Adrian Gjertson and Eric Heywood of Jet Heritage Ltd for Swift F.7 XF114. The Swift was moved by road to Bournemouth Airport in 1/89 for restoration to flying condition. Due to arrive in 1990 is Jet Provost T.4 XR658, currently being readied at Bournemouth to act as an instructional airframe. During 1989 the Institute also announced that they would like to exchange the Gannet for a more suitable airframe.

G-APMY	Apache 160	ex Halfpenny Green, EI-AJT. CoA expired 1/11/81.
G-AZMX	Cherokee 140	ex Chester Airport, Halfpenny Green, SE-FLL, LN-LMK. CoA exp 9/1/82.
XA460	Gannet AS.4	ex Brawdy, 849. See notes above.

HAWARDEN

(On the A55 south west of Chester) Not far from Chester Airport, **2247 Squadron ATC**, parented by Sealand, still keep their Vampire in Manor Lane.

XE852	Vampire T.11	ex Chester Airport, Woodford, Chester, Shawbury, 1 FTS, 4 FTS.

SEALAND

The base gave up its locally-related [display airframe with 610 (County of Chester) Squadron] Spitfire XVI TD248/7246M in the real-for-plastic exchange, it moved by road to Earls Colne on 14/10/88. Within a month Cranwell 'donated' their highly relevant former Danish Air Force Hunter to act as a new guardian.

WT720"+	8565M Hunter F.51	ex Cranwell XF979", Brawdy, Dunsfold, G-9-436, Aalborg store, ESK-724, Danish AF E-408. Arrived by 11/88, on gate by 8/89.

Dyfed

ABERPORTH
On the **Royal Aerospace Establishment** airfield, Varsity T.1 WJ893 became elderly and infirm on the dump by 1988 and was put out of its misery with a swift scrapping. **1429 Squadron ATC** still keep their Hunter on the airfield. On the ranges, **W&R11** spoke of a Scimitar hulk. Two such items (XD228 and XD231) were removed by road from the ranges during 1989, bound for the yard at Thirsk.

WT680	7533M Hunter F.1	ex Weeton, DFLS, West Raynham SF.

BRAWDY
The last two stored Hunter FGA.9s (XF419 and XJ683) were despatched to Zimbabwe in autumn 1987. They almost certainly were the cargo on Belfast G-HLFT out of St Athan on 5/10/87, in which case they almost certainly became 8112 and 1813 respectively. A former 1 TWU FGA.9 became a BDR airframe by 1988 and a Wessex retired from range work to join the dump.

XE624	8875M Hunter FGA.9	ex store, 1 TWU, 2 TWU, TWU, 229 OCU, West Raynham SF, 1. Gate.
XF435+	8880M Hunter FGA.9	ex St Athan, 1 TWU, TWU, 229 OCU, 208, 8, 8/43 pool, 8, 43, 247. BDR by 1988.
XL728+	Wessex HAS.1	ex Pendine, Farnborough. On dump by 8/88.

HAVERFORDWEST
(Or Withybush) French F.150L F-BUBA which was suspected as having moved on in **W&R11** left here early in 1986 for the 'South West'. An Auster AOP.9 has taken up the standard here.

XK378+ TAD200 Auster AOP.9	ex Middle Wallop (last noted there 8/75!), 656. First noted 2/89.

LLANELLI
Work is thought to continue on Jeremy Hassel's Proctor V.

G-AHTE	Proctor V	ex Cardiff-Wales, Swansea, Llanelli. CoA expired 10/8/61.

LLANGENNECH
And, Lo!, it came to pass that Maggie's axe did smite the Navy base verily a hard blow and, mighty afeared, Sea Hawk FGA.6 XE327/A2556 did offer up itself for tender and flee to King's Langley.

PENDINE RANGES
(On the A4066 east of Tenby) Foulness-based **Projectile Experimental Establishment** have a ballistics out-station here. Going by the state of the considerable quantity of airframes here, this place has largely eluded **W&R**-sleuths - but recent reports have more than made up for that! By definition, the bulk of the airframes listed below are new - unless noted all were first reported 2/88. Mention should be made of Wessex HAS.1 XL728 which transitted through here from Farnborough, before opting for a quieter life on the dump at Brawdy.

WH844	Canberra T.4	ex Farnbrough, RAE, 231 OCU.
XA938	Victor K.1	ex Foulness, St Athan, RAE, 214, 15, 10. Fuselage only.
XD241+	Scimitar F.1	ex Foulness, Farnborough, FRU, Fleetlands, 803, A&AEE, 736, A&AEE.
XD243+	Scimitar F.1	ex Foulness, Lee-on-Solent, 803, 800B, 800, 807, 803, 807.
XF439+	8712M Hunter F.6A	ex Abingdon, 5 MU, 1 TWU, 229 OCU, 1, 54, 19, 43, 247.
XG158+	8686M Hunter F.6A	ex Farnborough, 5 MU, 4 FTS, TWU, 229 OCU, 4 FTS, 229 OCU, 65, DFLS.
XJ411+	Whirlwind HAR.10	ex Farnborough, Wroughton, 103, 110, CFS, 225, 110, Westlands.
XK536+	Buccaneer S.1	ex Foulness (left there 22/10/85), Boscombe Down.
XM139+	8411M Lightning F.1	ex Wattisham (left there 27/8/86), Wattisham TFF, Leuchars TFF, 226 OCU, 74.
XM147+	8412M Lightning F.1	ex Wattisham (left there 27/8/86), Wattisham TFF, 226 OCU, 74.
XM299+	Wessex HAS.1	ex Farnborough.
XM926+	Wessex HAS.1	ex Farnborough, Bedford.
XN926+	Buccaneer S.1	ex Foulness (left there 17/10/85), Chatham, Honington, Lossiemouth, 736.

XN933+	Buccaneer S.1	ex Foulness (left there 14/10/85), Lossiemouth, 736.
XN965	Buccaneer S.1	ex Farnborough, RAE, Lossiemouth, 736.
XP708	Lightning F.3	ex Foulness Island, Wattisham, 29, 23.
XP735+	Lightning F.3	ex Leconfield (last reported there 12/75, parts also reported at Siddal 1975), 29, Wattisham TFF, 23.
XP748+	8446M Lightning F.3	ex Wembury, Binbrook, 11, 111, 56. First noted 6/89.
XR479+	Whirlwind HAR.10	ex Farnborough, Wroughton, RAE, 103, 110, 103.
XS895+	Lightning F.6	ex Binbrook, 5, 11, LTF, 5-11 pool, 23, 111, 23, 5, 74. Arr 7/88.
XV338+	Buccaneer S.2	ex St Athan (last noted there 3/83), 237 OCU, 12. Minus cockpit, see under Abingdon as 8774M.
XV340	8659M Buccaneer S.2	ex Foulness, Honington, Brough, 15.

TENBY

In the town **1284 Squadron ATC** keep a ¾ Chipmunk fuselage (ie more than a PAX) and may well have done since it was struck off charge.
WD386+   Chipmunk T.10   ex St Athan, 1 FTS, Ox UAS, 22 RFS, 2 BFTS. SOC 29/7/70.

Mid Glamorgan

BRIDGEND

(On the A473 west of Cardiff) Believed still to be found at the TAVR Centre is **1092 Squadron ATC**'s Viscount nose.
G-AOHR   Viscount 802   ex Cardiff-Wales, BA, BEA. wfu 26/8/75. Nose section only.

KENFIG HILL

(North of the B4281 east of Pyle) Off Main Street, in the School grounds, is **2117 Squadron ATC**'s Hunter F.1. 'Parent' is St Athan.
WT569   7491M Hunter F.1   ex St Athan, A&AEE, Hawkers trials.

South Glamorgan

CARDIFF WALES AIRPORT

(Or Rhoose) Major activity of 1989 and doubtless well into 1990 for the **Wales Aircraft Museum** has been moving to a new site within the Airport. Hand-in-hand with this there will be some thinning out of the airframes and the first disposal was one of the Gannets, leaving in late 1989 for a private owner in the Gloucester area. This machine is reported to have had an 'argument' with a motorway bridge during the journey. WAM is open daily June to September from 1000 to 1800. October to May it is open Saturdays 1100 to dusk and Sundays 1400 to dusk. Contact : Gwyn Roberts, 19 Clos Glyndwr, Hendy, Dyfed, SA4 1FW. Telephone 0792 883451.
G-AOJC   Viscount 802   ex British Airways, BEA. Cambrian colours. wfu 9/10/75.
G-ARBY" G-ANRS Viscount 732   ex 'G-WHIZ', British Eagle, Misrair SU-AKY, Hunting G-ANRS, MEA OD-ACH, Hunting Clan G-ANRS. CoA expired 5/5/69. Fuselage.
WB491   Ashton   ex Dunsfold, Farnborough, RAE. Nose section only.
WE925   Meteor F.8   ex Tarrant Rushton, FRL, 229 OCU, 34, 43, 92, 64, 63, 64. Composite, including parts from VZ530.

WG718	A2531 Dragonfly HR.3	ex Yeovilton, SAH Culdrose, Fleetlands.
WH798	8130M Canberra PR.7	ex St Athan, 31, 17, 13, 80, 17, 100, 542. Fuselage, with rear end of WJ581 fitted.
WJ576	Canberra T.17	ex St Athan, 360, MoA, Swifter Flight, 231 OCU.
WJ944	Varsity T.1	ex 6 FTS, 1 ANS, 5 FTS, 1 ANS, 2 ANS, CNCS.
WL332	Meteor T.7	ex Croston, Moston, FRU, Lossiemouth SF, Ford SF.
WM292	Meteor TT.20	ex Yeovilton, FRU, Kemble, 527.
WR539	8399M Venom FB.4	ex 'Midlands', Cosford, Kai Tak, 28, 60.
WT518	8691M Canberra PR.7	ex CTTS St Athan, 8133M, 31, 80, 31. Wings of WJ581.
WV753	8113M Pembroke C.1	ex St Athan, 207, SCS, FCCS, BCCS, MoA, FECS, 81.
WV826	A2532 Sea Hawk FGA.6	ex Swansea, Culdrose SAH-2, Lossiemouth, 738.
WW388	7616M Provost T.1	ex Llanelli, Chinnor, Chertsey, Cuxwold, Chessington, Halton, 2 FTS.
WX788	Venom NF.3	ex Bledow Ridge, Connah's Quay, Makers trials.
WZ425	Vampire T.1 1	ex Woodford, Chester, St Athan, 5 FTS, MoA, RAFC, 229 OCU, CGS.
WZ826"	XD826 Valiant BK.1	ex Abingdon, Stratford, Cosford, 7872M, 543, 232 OCU, 138, 90, 7. Nose section.
XA459	A2608 Gannet AS.4	ex Culdrose SAH-7, Lee-on-Solent, 831. See notes above.
XA903	Vulcan B.1	ex Farnborough, RB.199 test-bed, Olympus test-bed, Blue Steel trials, Avro. Nose section only.
XF383"	E-409 Hunter F.51	ex Dunsfold, G-9-437, Aalborg store, Danish AF, ESK-724.
XG592	Whirlwind HAS.7	ex Wroughton, 705, 846, 705, 700, C(A), HS, Westlands.
XG737	Sea Venom FAW.22	ex Yeovilton, FRU, Sydenham, 894, 893, 891.
XG883	Gannet T.5	ex Yeovilton, 849. See notes above.
XH177	Canberra PR.9	ex Boscombe Down, 13, 58. Nose section only.
XJ409	Whirlwind HAR.10	ex Wroughton, Warton SAR Flight, 1310 Flt, 228, 275, 155, XD779 ntu.
XL449	Gannet AEW.3	ex Lossiemouth, 849. See notes above.
XM300	Wessex HAS.1	ex Farnborough, RAE, Westlands.
XM569	Vulcan B.2	ex 44, Waddington Wing, 27, Cottesmore Wing, 27.
XN650	A2639 Sea Vixen FAW.2	ex A2620/A2612, Culdrose SAH-12, RAE Bedford, 892.
XN928	8179M Buccaneer S.1	ex St Athan.
59	Mystere IVA	ex Sculthorpe, French Air Force.
29963	T-33A-1-LO	ex Sculthorpe, French Air Force.
42160	F-100D-16-NA	ex Sculthorpe, French Air Force.

On the main **Airport** site, both the Viscount on the dump and the Tomahawk cabin trainer live on. AA-1 Yankee G-SEXY got the urge again during 1989 and reflew.

G-AOJE	Viscount 802	ex BA, BEA, G-AOHE ntu. wfu 31/3/81. Fire dump.
G-BGSS	Tomahawk 112	dbr 14/12/81. Cabin section with Cambrian F/C. Identity confirmed.

ST ATHAN

Decisions taken by the RAF's Historic Aircraft Committee brought about the winddown of this superb collection of aircraft with repositioning the airframes to Cosford, Hendon and elsewhere starting from mid 1989. As we close for press, many airframes still remain at the base, including the immaculate Battle restoration which is expected to go directly to Hendon. Doubtless **W&R13** will cover the remaining migrations. Disposals have been as follows : Abingdon Spitfire IX MK356/5690M for assessment for return to flying condition for the BBMF; Cosford Auster C4 WE600/7602M; Me 262A-2a 112372/8482M; Me 410A-1/U2 420430/8483M (having not that long ago come here from there!); Fi 156C-7 475081/7362M; Ki 46 5439/BAPC.84; Ki 100 8476M/BAPC.83; Hendon After a long and painstaking rebuild, Battle I L5353 was rolled out here 6/3/90 and was installed at the RAF Museum by the end of the month; Proctor III Z7197/8380M; Meteor NF.14 WS843/7937M by 4/90; Swift FR.5 WK281/7712M; He 162A-2 120227/8472M; Fw 190F-8/U1 584219/8470M (now made its last-ever ground-run?); Tattershall Thorpe Whirlwind HCC.12 XR486/8727M was offered for tender and moved in mid 1989. Additionally, seven airframes were auctioned by Philips from their Cardiff office on 21/9/89 in the first Ministry of Defence auction for some time (the last being at Colerne on 2/3/76). The silly prices here encouraged them to undertake a similar exercise in 1990. Only one destination is known as we close for press, but high bids were as follows :-

WD935	8440M Canberra B.2	£ 7,200 see notes below.
WL505	7705M Vampire FB.9	£10,200

WV499	7698M Provost T.1	£16,000
XM602	8771M Vulcan B.2A	£33,000 to London property dealer Robert Hughes.
XN341	8022M Skeeter AOP.12	£11,000
XR243	8057M Auster AOP.9	£ 6,500
XS650	8801M Swallow TX.1	£ 2,200

Canberra B.2 WD935/8440M was acquired by Air Support Aviation for its engines and was scrapped on site 11/89. The airframe went to Wing Spares of Burgess Hill from where the nose went on to Kew. That leaves the following :-

G-AEEH	HM.14 Pou du Ciel	ex Colerne.
6232"	BAPC 41 BE.2c replica	ex Halton. Travelling exhibit.
H1968"	BAPC 42 Avro 504K replica	ex Halton. Travelling exhibit.
EE549	7008M Meteor IV Special	ex Abingdon, Hendon, St Athan, Cranwell, CFE, FCCS, RAFHSF.
TJ138	7607M Mosquito TT.35	ex Swinderby, Finningley, Colerne, Bicester, Shawbury, 5 CAACU, 98.
BAPC 47	Watkins CHW	ex Cardiff.
BAPC 92	Fi 103 (V1)	ex Henlow. Likely confusion with Cardington example - which see.

During 1989 RAF sources started to use the hallowed term **4 School of Technical Training** for the unit **W&R and other sources have regarded as the Civilian Technical Training School**. There are four components to 4 SoTT :
Civilian Technical Training School which trains civilian aernautical craft and technician level apprentices.
Electrical Engineering Training Squadron training mechanics and technicians in ground electrics.
Mechanical Engineering Training Squadron specialises in the training of mechanics and technicians from the ground support equipment, workshops, mechanical transport and painter and finisher trades.
Driver Training Squadron trains personnel from all three elements of the armed forces driving skills.
It is CTTS within 4 SoTT that has the airframes, although certainly METS has had finishing airframes before now. With the input of a couple of Jet Provost T.3As and Jaguar GR.1s to the unit (whatever it may be called) there is only one disposal to relate. Devon C.2/2 VP958 was put up for tender in 7/88 and went to an Australian owner. Over at the **St Athan Maintenance Unit** the first Harriers have started to end their lives, and Phantoms have commenced deep storage. Dominating these events has been the arrival of many of the former gate guardian Spitfires. All are to be held here while the MoD uses them for exchange for the benefit of the RAF Museum - time will tell. Disposals from the MU since **W&R11** have been : Canberra PR.7 WH775/8868M went to Cosford as predicted; Hunter FGA.9 XF435/8880M to Brawdy; Hunter FGA.9 XG154/8863M held on behalf of the RAF Museum moved to Hendon by 12/89; Canberra PR.9 XH168 moved out 1/12/87, going initially to Sydenham and then to 1 PRU at Wyton; Jet Provost T.3 XN632/8352M moved to Chivenor 6/12/89; Buccaneer S.2A XV163 was reactivated using a wing from XT272 and the tail of XV157 and flew out to Lossiemouth 6/88. For completeness, several Harrier GR.3s have been processed through here as follows : XV740 ex 1 Sqn '05' on the dump by 4/89 and off to Abingdon 5/89; XV747 (ex 233 OCU 'G', accident 11/11/87) on the dump by 8/88 and to Coltishall by road 29/9/88; XV782 (ex 4 Sqn 'F') arrived 6/5/88 and it left in 1988 for Bruggen; XV793 (ex 4 Sqn 'L') on the dump by 9/88 - both of these were briefly at Swanton Morley - and then to Bruggen; XW764 (ex 3 Sqn 'C') on the dump by 9/88 then to Leeming. All this makes the current situation as follows :

EP120+	8070M Spitfire V	ex Wattisham, Boulmer, Wilmslow, St Athan, 5377M, 53 OTU, 402, 501. Arrived 1/2/89.
LA198+	7118M Spitfire F.21	ex Leuchars, Locking, Worcester, 3 CAACU, 602, 1. Arrived 5/4/89.
PK624+	8072M Spitfire F.24	ex Abingdon, Northolt, Uxbridge, North Weald, 9 MU, 614. Arrived by 9/89.
PK664+	7759M Spitfire F.22	ex Binbrook, Waterbeach, 615. Arrived 11/88.
RW393+	7293M Spitfire XVI	ex Edinburgh Airport/Turnhouse, 602, 3 CAACU, 31, FCCS, 203 AFS. Arrived 4/10/89.

SL542+	8390M	Spitfire XVI	ex Coltishall, Horsham St Faith, Duxford SF, 2 CAACU, 1 CAACU, 695, 595. Arrived 9/12/88.
SL674+	8392M	Spitfire XVI	ex Biggin Hill, Little Rissington, 501, 17 OTU. Arrived mid 1989.
WH780		Canberra T.22	ex FRADU, 81, 82, 527, 58, 542. Stored.
WH797		Canberra T.22	ex FRADU, 81, 58, 542. Stored.
WH801		Canberra T.22	ex FRADU, 17, 31, 13, 58, 540. Stored.
WH803		Canberra T.22	ex FRADU, 7, 17, 540. Stored.
WH984	8101M	Canberra B.15	ex Cosford, HS, 9, Binbrook SF, 9. CTTS/4 SoTT, nose.
WJ574		Canberra TT.18	ex FRADU, 57, 540. Stored.
WJ717+		Canberra TT.18	ex FRADU, 61, 15. Stored.
WJ861+		Canberra T.4	ex 231 OCU, PRU, 39, 7, 100, 85, 231 OCU, 31 Laarbruch SF, Wyton SF, Weston Zoyland SF, Marham SF.
WK144	8689M	Canberra B.2	ex store, 85, 98, 245, 527. Dump. Omitted from W&R11.
WT510		Canberra T.22	ex FRADU, 31, 80, 31. Stored.
WT525		Canberra T.22	ex FRADU, 17, 80. Stored.
WT535		Canberra T.22	ex FRADU, 17. Stored.
WT648	7530M	Hunter F.1	ex 4 SoTT, DFLS. Dump.
XA243	8886M	Grasshopper TX.1	ex Bournemouth School. CTTS/4 SoTT - Glider Ground School.
XE793	8666M	Cadet TX.3	CTTS/4 SoTT - Glider Ground School.
XF526	8679M	Hunter F.6	ex Halton, Laarbruch SF, 4 FTS, 229 OCU, 56, 43, 56, 63, 66. Stored externally for a 4 SoTT instructor.
XH133+		Canberra PR.9	ex 1 PRU, 39, 13, MinTech, 13, MoA. Stored.
XH165+		Canberra PR.9	ex 1 PRU, 39, 13, 58. Stored.
XH168		Canberra PR.9	ex 39, MoD, 39, MoD, 39, 58. Stored.
XL163	8916M	Victor K.2	ex 57, 55, 57, 55, 232 OCU, Witt Wing, 100, 139. BDR.
XL578		Hunter T.7	ex 1 TWU, TWU, 229 OCU. Stored.
XL595		Hunter T.7	ex 1 TWU, TWU, 229 OCU, DFLS, AFDS. Stored.
XM419+	8990M	Jet Provost T.3A	ex 7 FTS, 3 FTS, CFS, RAFC, CFS, 3 FTS, RAFC, 6 FTS, RAFC, 2 FTS. CTTS/4 SoTT - allocated late 1989.
XM468+	8081M	Jet Provost T.3	ex Halton, Shawbury, 6 FTS, RAFC. CTTS/4 SoTT. First noted 3/90.
XN458	8334M	Jet Provost T.3	ex Halton, Shawbury, 1 FTS. CTTS/4 SoTT.
XN551+	8984M	Jet Provost T.3A	ex 7 FTS, RAFC, 1 FTS, 3 FTS, 6 FTS, RAFC. CTTS/4 SoTT. First noted 9/89.
XN632	8352M	Jet Provost T.3	ex Kemble, Shawbury, 3 FTS. CTTS/4 SoTT.
XP502	8576M	Gnat T.1	ex 4 FTS. CTTS/4 SoTT.
XP542	8575M	Gnat T.1	ex 4 FTS. CTTS/4 SoTT.
XP558	8627M	Jet Provost T.4	ex SAH Culdrose A2628, CAW, 3 CAACU, RAFC. CTTS/4 SoTT
XP680	8460M	Jet Provost T.4	ex CAW, 6 FTS. CTTS/4 SoTT.
XR541	8602M	Gnat T.1	ex CFS, 4 FTS. CTTS/4 SoTT.
XT911+		Phantom FGR.2	ex 92, 19, 228 OCU. Stored. First noted 1/88.
XV156	8773M	Buccaneer S.2A	ex store, Honington, 237 OCU, 208. Fuselage on dump.
XV409+		Phantom FGR.2	ex 29, 228 OCU, 56, 111, 56, 111. Stored. First noted 1/88.
XV486+		Phantom FGR.2	ex 29, 228 OCU, 23, 56, 111, 2, 14. Stored. Arrived 7/4/87.
XV495+		Phantom FGR.2	ex 23, 29, 56, 228 OCU, 29, 41, 6. Stored. First noted 1/88.
XV591+		Phantom FG.1	ex 111. On the dump, minus nose, first noted 5/89.
XV759+		Harrier GR.3	ex 233 OCU, 1417F, 233 OCU, 1, 233 OCU, 1, 233 OCU. Arrived 10/1/89, stripped out and on the dump by 8/89.
XV778+		Harrier GR.3	ex 1, 1453F, 1, 1417F, 1. Arrived 27/2/89, stripped and on the dump by 5/89. Allocated to Valley for CR.
XV810+		Harrier GR.3	ex 233 OCU, 4, 20. Arrived 7/2/89, stripped and on dump by 5/89.
XW545	8859M	Buccaneer S.2B	ex store, BAe, 15. BDR.
XW550		Buccaneer S.2B	ex 16, 15. Stored.
XW763+		Harrier GR.3	ex 233 OCU, 1, 1453F, 3, 4, 3. Arrived 22/3/89, stripped and on the dump by 6/89. Allocated to Halton for CR.
XX635	8767M	Bulldog T.1	ex Hms UAS. CTTS/4 SoTT.
XX763+	9009M	Jaguar GR.1	ex Shawbury, 226 OCU. CTTS/4 SoTT. First noted 9/89.
XX764+	9010M	Jaguar GR.1	ex Shawbury, 226 OCU, 14. CTTS/4 SoTT. First noted 9/89.
XZ138+		Harrier GR.3	ex 1, 233 OCU, 1453F, 1, 3, 4, 3. Arr by 1/89, on the dump by 4/89.

West Glamorgan

SWANSEA AIRPORT
(Or Fairwood Common) The withdrawn Pup continues to nestle in the main hangar. The airfield itself is another facing extinction.
G-AWKM   Pup 100   CoA expired 29/6/84. Stored.

Gwent

CAERLEON
(On the A4236 north east of Newport) By 4/89 **1367 Squadron ATC** had taken, on loan, the former Cwmbran Chippax.
WD293   7645M Chipmunk T.10 PAX   ex Cwmbran, QUB UAS, StA UAS, G&S UAS, StA UAS, Chatham Flt, SMR, 1
                                      BFTS. On loan.

CWMBRAN
2308 Squadron ATC loaned their Chippax to the unit at Caerleon by 4/89.

TREDEGAR
A visit to the strip here in 5/89 found that one of the three hulks listed in **W&R11** survives. This means that we can confirm that Tri-Pacer G-APXM and Rally Commodore 150 F-BNBM either demised here or moved on.
G-AXTM   Cherokee 140B   Crashed 21/2/81. Wreck.

Gwynedd

CAERNARFON AIRPORT
(Or Llandwrog) Operators of the airfield, Snowdon Mountain Aviation, succeeded in opening their excellent **Caernarfon Air Museum** on 11/5/89. In a purpose-built building, a goodly variety of airframes have been assembled, with the opportunity to view the on-going restoration of the Anson. Support displays are very imaginative and will appeal to 'buffs' and general tourists alike. Pleasure flying is available, with Dragon Rapide G-AIDL being the prime target of most enthusiasts' interest – availability of pleasure flying and aircraft involved is best checked upon before a visit. The Museum is open March 1 to November 30 0930-1730. Groups at other times can be arranged. Enquiries should be made to :- Snowdon Mountain Aviation, Caernarfon Airport, Llandwrog, Caernarfon, Gwynedd, LL54 5TP. Telephone 0286 830800.

Reg	Type	Notes
G-AIDL	Dragon Rapide 6	ex Biggin Hill, Allied Airways, TX310. Airworthy.
G-ALFT+	Dove 6	ex Higher Blagdon, Stansted, CAFU. CoA expired 13/6/73. Arrived by 11/88.
TX235+	Anson C.19	ex Higher Blagdon, Andover, Shawbury, SCS, FCCS, CTFU, OCTU, 64 GCS, 2 GCS. Arrived by 11/88, under restoration.
WM961+	A2517 Sea Hawk FB.5	ex Higher Blagdon, Culdrose SAH-6, FRU, 802, 811. Arr 1988.
WN499+	Dragonfly HR.3	ex Higher Blagdon, Blackbushe, Culdrose SF. Arrived by 11/88, in playpark.
WV781	7839M Sycamore HR.12	ex Finningley, Odiham, Digby, HDU, CFS, ASWDU, G-ALTD ntu.
XA282	Cadet TX.3	ex Syerston.
XD599	Vampire T.11	ex Bournemouth, Blackbushe, Staverton, Stroud, CATCS, RAFC, 1. Mounted at airfield gate.

XH837	8032M Javelin FAW.7	ex Northolt, Ruislip, 33. Nose section.
XJ726	Whirlwind HAR.10	ex Sibson, Wroughton, 2 FTS, CFS, ME SAR Flt, 22.
XK623	Vampire T.11	ex Bournemouth 'G-VAMP', Moston, Woodford, Chester, St Athan, 5 FTS.
+	Varsity T.1	ex Higher Blagdon. Cockpit section.
BAPC 201+	HM.14 Pou du Ciel	ex Kidlington. Fuselage and tail. Modified undercarriage.

LLANBEDR

Within what was part of the Llanbedr airfield domestic site, an interesting aviation exhibition has been mounted in the **Maes Artro Craft Village**. Centre-piece is the former Llanbedr gate guardian Anson, brought back almost from the dead at Portsmouth. Visitors can view progress on its restoration. Outside, a former 'Piece of Cake' Spitfire replica acts as a gate guardian. The village is open daily. Further details from Artro Enterprises, Reception Building, Maes Artro, Llanbedr, Gwynedd. Telephone : 0341 23 467.

VS562+	8012M Anson T.21	ex Portsmouth, Llanbedr, A&AEE, AST Hamble, CS(A). Arrived 1988. Under restoration.
BAPC 202+	Spitfire V replica	ex 'Piece of Cake'. On the gate by 5/89.

LLANBEDR AIRFIED

Correcting **W&R11**, at the **Royal Aerospace Establishment** Sea Vixen XN657 is not parked next to the dump, but serves as a spares source near the main flight hangar. The Canberra just hangs on to life.

WK145	Canberra B.2	ex RAE, 7, 98, 245, 527. Dump, poor state.
XN657	Sea Vixen D.3	ex RAE, FRL, RAE, ADS, 899, 893. External store.

VALLEY

Where there were three gate guardians, the RAF base now only has one. The Vampire was put up for tender 11/89, but, as yet, we have no fate for it. The Whirlwind was removed over to the care of SARTS by 4/89. The Harrier is an allocation here, not yet having moved from St Athan.

XE874	8582M Vampire T.11	ex Woodford, Chester, Shawbury, 1 FTS, 4 FTS, 8 FTS, 4 FTS, 1 FTS, 4 FTS, 7 FTS. See notes above.
XL392	8745M Vulcan B.2	ex 35, 617, Scampton Wing. Dump.
XP361	8731M Whirlwind HAR.10	ex gate, Boulmer, Chivenor, 202, 22, 103, 110, 225. SARTS.
XR534	8578M Gnat T.1	ex 4 FTS, CFS. Gate guardian.
XT772	8805M Wessex HU.5	ex Wroughton. BDR.
XV778+	9001M Harrier GR.3	Allocation for CR - see St Athan.

Powys

WELSHPOOL

Tiger Moth G-ANJK left the strip here as long ago as 21/6/83 - by road. Destination?

Part 4

CHANNEL ISLES

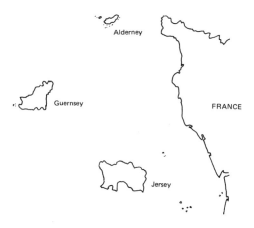

GUERNSEY

Within the island, **Lewis Martin** continues to store his three aircraft at a variety of locations. The status of the Tiger Moth restoration is now doubted, and it may well find itself in LOST!

G-AOAC	Tiger Moth	ex N6978, Upwood CF, 16 EFTS, 22 EFTS. Crashed 22/6/74. See notes above.
G-ASTH	Mooney M.20	ex France, N6906U. Crashed 16/11/66. Stored Sausmarez Park.
G-ATEP	EAA Biplane	CoA expired 18/6/73. Stored at Sausmarez Park.
G-ATHN	Noralpha	ex F-BFUZ, French military. CoA exp 27/6/75. Stored St Peter Port.

GUERNSEY AIRPORT

Apart from an Aztec being donated to the local Air Scouts, the situation is remarkably static.

G-ASHV+	Aztec 250B	ex N5281Y ntu. CoA expired 22/7/85. Donated to Air Scouts 1988.
G-BAZJ	Herald 209	ex Air UK, Alia 4X-AHR, G-8-1. Fire section - non destructive.
G-BCYC	Trislander	ex Glasgow, Loganair, EL-AIB, G-BCYC. Fuselage. Crashed 15/5/79.
TX192	Anson C.19	ex WCS, NCS, 23 GCF, Tech Trng Command CF, Benson Ferry Wing, MCS, 23 GCF, 2 ANS, CFS, Wyton CF. Very poor state.
WJ350	Sea Prince C.2	ex FAAM, Yeovilton, Yeovilton SF, A&AEE, Yeovilton SF, Lossiemouth SF, Yeovilton SF, 781, Yeovilton SF, 781, FOFT, 781, Yeovilton SF. Fire dump.
WL131	7751M Meteor F.8	ex APS Sylt, 601, 111. Nose section, with Air Scouts.

JERSEY

It is believed that the Herald nose is still in use as a plaything at Longueville.

G-APWG	Herald 201	ex Jersey Airport, Air UK, BIA, BUA. Nose section.

JERSEY AIRPORT

Only the addition of a Wassmer Baladou on the fire dump breaks up the entry here.

G-AOJD	Viscount 802	ex British Airways, BEA. Fire service.
G-ASDO	Baron A55	CoA expired 16/4/83. With 2498 Sqn ATC.
G-AVHJ+	Super Baladou IV	Donated to fire service 4/87. CoA expired 9/4/87.
G-BBXJ	Herald 203	ex BIA, I-TIVI. Crashed 24/12/74. Fire service.

Part 5

IRELAND

Northern Ireland

Antrim	Down	Londonderry
Armagh	Fermanagh	

Eire

Carlow	Kilkenny	Offaly
Cavan	Laois	Roscommon
Clare	Leitrim	Sligo
Cork	Limerick	Tipperary
Donegal	Longford	Waterford
Dublin	Louth	Wexford
Galway	Mayo	Wicklow
Kerry	Meath	
Kildare	West Meath	

Northern Ireland

BELFAST
[County Antrim] At **Campbell College** the CCF still look after their Vampire pod.
XD525   7882M Vampire T.11   ex Aldergrove, 1 FTS, 4 FTS, 5 FTS, 7 FTS. Fuselage pod only.

BELFAST AIRPORT
[Or Aldergrove, County Antrim]   It is thought that all remains the same with the
W&R candidates here.   Restoration work on the Meteor was short-lived and it
continues to reside out on the airfield.   The RAF Exhibition Flight continue to
base a 'JP' nose here for touring the Province.

G-AVFE	Trident 2E	ex Heathrow, BA, BEA. Flew in 12/2/85. Fire service.
WS840	7969M Meteor NF.14	ex Bishop's Court, 1 ANS, 64, 264.
WT486	8102M Canberra T.4	ex Wildenrath, 14, 17, 88, Wildenrath SF. Fire dump.
XR700	8589M Jet Provost T.4	ex Abingdon, Shawbury, CATCS, 3 FTS, 1 FTS. Nose section, RAFEF.
XT456	Wessex HU.5	ex Wroughton. BDR.
XT669	8894M Wessex HC.2	ex 72. Damaged 25/10/85. BDR.

BELFAST HARBOUR AIRPORT
[Or Sydenham, County Down]   Shorts' Apprentice School gave up Sea Hawk FB.3 WN108
to the care of the Ulster Aviation Society and it moved to <u>Newtownards</u> on 17/10/89.
The SD.330 prototype continues to be stored on the airfield on behalf of the UAS.
Of note here, was the removal of the last-ever SC.7 Skyvan (the unfinished c/no
SH.1982) which left by road on 13/2/89 for a local scrapman.   It had been stored at
the plant since about 1985.   The former Brazilian Tucano is thought still to be
found here.

G-BSBH	Short SD.330	CoA expired 13/4/81. Stored for Ulster Aviation Society.
1317	T-27 Tucano	ex San Jose dos Campos, Brazil AF. Fuselage, engine test-bed.

BISHOP'S COURT
[County Down]   Ulster Radar still uses the Devon for instructional purposes.

VP957	8822M Devon C.2/2	ex Belfast Airport, Northolt, 207, 21, WCS, SCS, NCS, SCS, WCS, SCS, Andover SF, 38 GCF, AAFCE, 2 TAF CS, BAFO CS.

HOLYWOOD
[Down]   Space restrictions at the **Ulster Folk and Transport Museum** prevent most of
their interesting stock of aircraft going on public display.   The Museum is open
October to April, Monday to Saturday 1100 to 1700, Sunday 1400 to 1700 and May to
September, Monday to Saturday 1100 to 1700, Sunday 1400 to 1700.   Contact : Ulster
Folk and Transport Museum, Cultra Manor, Holywood, Northern Ireland BT18 0EU.
Telephone : 0232 428428.

G-AJOC	Messenger 2A	ex East Fortune, Strathallan, Dunottar. CoA exp 18/5/72. Stored.
G-AKEL	Gemini 1A	ex Kilbrittain Castle. CoA expired 29/4/72. For rebuild into one with G-AKGE.
G-AKGE	Gemini 3C	ex Kilbrittain Castle, EI-ALM, G-AKGE. CoA exp 7/6/74. See G-AKEL.
G-AKLW	Sealand	ex Bradley Air Museum, Windsor Locks, Connecticut, Jeddah, RSaudiAF, SU-AHY, G-AKLW. Stored.
G-AOUR	Tiger Moth	ex Belfast, NL898. Crashed 6/6/65. Stored.
G-ARTZ	McCandless M-2	ex Killough. G-ARTZ No 1.
G-ATXX	McCandless M-4	ex Killough. wfu 9/9/70.
BGA.470	Nimbus I	ex Bishop's Stortford, Duxford. Stored.
VH-UUP	Scion I	ex East Fortune, Strathallan, G-ACUX, VH-UUP, G-ACUX.
XG905	Short SC.1	ex Shorts, Sydenham, Thurleigh, RAE.
IAHC 6	Ferguson Monoplane	ex Dublin.
IAHC 9	Ferguson Monoplane	ex Belfast Airport, Holywood. Stored.

LOUGH FOYLE
[County Londonderry]   Just off shore can be seen the hulk of Corsair II JT693:R, ex
1837 Squadron.

MOVENIS
[Near Garvagh, County Londonderry]   It is thought that the Skylane fuselage can still be found here.

G-AWJA   Cessna 182L   ex N1658C. CoA expired 21/4/85. Fuselage only.

MULLAGHMORE
[County Londonderry]   Another case of status quo.

G-AYTB   Rallye Club   dbr 25/11/80. Wreck.
G-BFPC   AA-5B Tiger   ex Breighton. Crashed 8/5/82. Wreck.

NEWTOWNARDS
[County Down]   The collection of the **Ulster Aviation Society** here has doubled with the acquisition of the Sea Hawk from Belfast Harbour and the much longer-range former Coningsby Vampire T.11. Notes that the prototype Shorts SD.330 is stored for the UAS at Belfast Harbour Airport. The aircraft are not available to public inspection but general enquiries can be made to : Raymond Burrows, 20 Carrowreagh Gardens, Dundonald, Belfast BT16 0TW.

JV482   Wildcat V   ex Castlereagh, Lough Beg. Under restoration.
WN108+   Sea Hawk FB.3   ex Belfast Harbour, Bournemouth, FRU, 806, 895, 897, 800. Arrived
                                 17/10/89.
WZ549+   8118M Vampire T.11   ex Coningsby, Tattershall, Coningsby, CATCS, 1 FTS, 8 FTS, FTU,
                                 C(A). Arrived 1989.
XG736   Sea Venom FAW.22   ex Castlereagh, Sydenham, Yeovilton, ADS. Under restoration.

Concerning the Cessna wrecks on the airfield, nothing new is known.

G-ARFM   Cessna 175B   ex N8176T. CoA expired 23/10/79. Stored.
G-BBIT   Cessna F.150L   Crashed 9/3/75. Fuselage only.

UPPER BALLINDERRY
[Near Crumlin, County Antrim]   Restoration work continues slowly on the Whitney Straight here.

G-AERV   Whitney Straight   ex Newtownards, EM999, Kemble, Abingdon SF, Halton SF, G-AERV.

Eire

ABBEYSHRULE
[West of Mullingar, off the L18, Westmeagh]   Without the benefit of an update at this airfield, the following list, much as it was in **W&R11**, should be regarded even more than usual as a guide only.

EI-ABU   Spartan II   ex Cloughjordan, G-ABYN. Stored.
EI-ANN   Tiger Moth   ex Dublin, Kilcock, G-ANEE, T5418, 63 GCF, 24 EFTS, 19 EFTS,
                                 12 EFTS. Crashed 18/10/64. Spares for EI-AOP.
EI-AOP   Tiger Moth   ex Dublin, G-AIBN, T7967, 18 EFTS, 1667 CU, 1 GCF, 16 PFTS. CoA
                                 expired 12/10/75. Under restoration.
EI-ATL   Champion 7AC   ex 'local', Abbeyshrule, Clondalkin, N1119E. Damaged 26/11/75.
                                 Spares for EI-AVB.
EI-AUP   Rallye Club   ex Coonagh, G-AVVK. Crashed 1/9/83. Wreck.
EI-AVB   Champion 7AC   ex Shannon, 7P-AXK, ZS-AXK. CoA expired 11/11/83. Under rebuild.
EI-BAG   Cessna 172A   ex G-ARAV, N9771T. CoA expired 26/6/79. Stored.
EI-BDB   Rallye Club   ex Weston. Crashed 28/7/78. Fuselage only.
EI-BDH   Rallye Club   ex G-AWOB. CoA expired 2/8/87. Stored.
EI-BGN   Rallye Club   ex TU-TJC, F-OCRU. Cancelled 10/8/83. Fuselage only.
EI-BKE   Super Rallye   ex F-BKUN, F-WKUN. Crashed 5/4/81. Wreck.

CARBURY

[Kildare] Still stored here in Dick Robinson's 1937 'Flea'.
IAHC 3   HM.14 Pou du Ciel   stored, engineless. Never flew.

CASEMENT

[Or Baldonnel, west of Dublin, County Dublin] Instructional and derelict airframes
at the Headquarters of Irish military aviation continue to fascinate. It would
seem that Provosts are made of stronger things than implied in **W&R10** when 181 and
189A were reported as having 'expired' on the dump by 1984. A thorough inspection
in 10/88 found both existing. Indeed 181 left by road for Thatcham 8/3/90, with a
Whirlwind coming in the opposite direction to take its place on the dump. The
other Provost listed as having perished by then, 184, found its way to Waterford.
Returning to **W&R11** the two Vampires noted as 'perished' (187 and 192) again made
the migration to Waterford. Of the Chipmunks listed, 171 had died on the dump by
10/88 and 172 had moved to Gormanston. The instructional SF.260MC 233/I-SYAS was
scrapped, last being noted 2/87. That leaves :-

164	Chipmunk T.20	stored, reported for preservation.
189A	Provost T.51	dump, sectioned. See notes above.
193	Vampire T.55	fuselage pod only, poor state, on the dump.
198	Vampire T.11	ex XE977, 8 FTS, never flew with IAAC. On display Officers' Mess.
221	CM-170 Magister	ex French Air Force No 79 '3-KE', instructional airframe.
XN309+	A2663 Whirlwind HAR.9	ex Thatcham, Lasham, Faygate, Culdrose, Wroughton, Manadon, Culdrose SF, Lee SAR Flight, 'Endurance' Flt, Culdrose SF, 'Endurance' Flt, Culdrose SF, 845, 846, 814.
G-ARLU	Cessna 172B	ex Southend, G-ARLU, N8002X. Damaged 30/10/77. Avionics rig.
c/no 1012	Alouette III	instructional, non-flying, rig.

CASTLEBRIDGE

[North of Wexford, County Wexford] The airstrip hosts two very different Cadets.
EI-ALP   Cadet   ex G-ADIE. Engine seizure 6/77. CoA expired 6/4/78. Stored.
VM659   Cadet TX.2   Stored.

CELBRIDGE

[Kildare] Travel back to **W&R8** (gulp, eight years ago!) when it was noted that the
long-time landmark on the roof of the Crofton Airport Hotel at Whitehall, south of
Dublin Airport, had been salvaged from the roof. Since then it has been confined
to LOST! **Phil Bedford** has it here and under restoration.
G-AHWO+   Proctor V   ex Whitehall, Dublin Airport, EI-ALY ntu. See notes above.

COONAGH

[West of Limerick, off the N18, Limerick] Stored at the airstrip is the French
Auster V.
F-BGOO   Auster V   ex G-AKSY, TJ534. Stored.

CORK AIRPORT

[South of the City, County Cork] Only the removal of Dove 6 G-ASNG to Waterford by
road on 13/5/89 has altered the **W&R** scenery here. The previously removed Dove, VP-
YKF, also went to Waterford.
EI-AUT   F.1A Aircoupe   ex G-ARXS, D-EBSA, N3037G. CoA expired 30/7/76. Under rebuild.
G-ACMA   Leopard Moth   ex BD148, DH, HQ Army Co-Op CCF, 7 AACU, G-ACMA. CoA expired
                              10/7/85. Stored.
N4422P   Geronimo   Stored.

DUBLIN

Still without a permanent home in which to display their airframes the **Irish
Aviation Museum** still holds its stocks at Castlemoate House. Until such time as a
new venue can be found, public inspection is not possible. The 'Flea' here is
owned by the Aviation Society of Ireland.
EI-AOH   Viscount 808   ex Dublin Airport, Aer Lingus. Nose section.

G-AOGA	Aries 1	ex Kilbrittain Castle, EI-ANB, G-AOGA. Damaged 8/8/69.
G-ANPC	Tiger Moth	ex Edinburgh (?), Strathallan, Portmoak, R4950, 2 GS, Kirton in Lindsey SF, Hemswell SF, Oakington SF, 28 EFTS, 25 PEFTS, 17 EFTS, Benson SF. Crashed 2/1/67. Dismantled, stripped airframe.
34	Magister	ex Casement, N5392.
141	Anson XIX	ex Casement. Dismantled.
183	Provost T.51	ex Casement. Dismantled.
191	Vampire T.55	ex Casement. Dismantled.
IAHC 1	HM.14 Pou du Ciel	ex Coonagh.

The airframes listed as being at the **Institute of Technology** (Cherokee 180 G-ATHI and Aztec 250D G-AYWY) were inspected in 10/88 and found to be too small to merit inclusion. Dove 6 176 is thought to have been scrapped at the **Civil Defence Headquarters** near Phoenix Park. It did not go to Waterford as described in **W&R11**, an altogether different '176' turning up there!

DUBLIN AIRPORT
[Or Collinstown, north of the city on the N1, County Dublin] As can be seen from the listing below, this is another Irish location that has changed little. The CASA 352L N9012N is believed to have disappeared, although its final destination is unknown. Most of the wrecked light aircraft inhabit the Iona hangar.

EI-ALU	Cadet	ex G-ACIH. Dismantled.
EI-AMK	J/1 Autocrat	ex G-AGIV. wfu 5/79, CoA expired 28/8/76.
EI-ARY	Cessna F.150H	crashed 14/6/70. Wreck.
EI-AUH	Cessna F.172H	crashed 25/2/72. Fuselage, wings on EI-AVA.
EI-AYJ	Cessna 182P	ex N52229. Crashed 19/9/76. Wreck.
EI-BEO	Cessna 310Q II	ex D-ICEG, N7733Q. Crashed 27/8/85. Stored.
EI-BGO	Canadair CL-44J	ex Aer Turas, TF-LLH, CF-MKP-X. Last flight 3/1/86. Fire service.
EI-BIA	Cessna FA.152	Crashed 28/9/80. Wreck.
G-BHIA	Cessna F.152-II	CoA expired 4/5/86. Stored, poor shape.

GALWAY AIRPORT
[County Galway] Out on the airfield, the Islander hulk lingers.

EI-BBR	BN-2A-26 Islander	ex Aer Arran, F-BVOE ntu, G-BDJS. Crashed 7/8/80.

GORMANSTON
[County Dublin] Good news from here is that the IAAC restored to flying condition Chipmunk T.20 168. It made its first flight on 15/11/89 and will be flown occasionally at displays. To help this restoration along, another of the breed has arrived from Casement.

168	Chipmunk T.20	airworthy - see notes above.
172+	Chipmunk T.20	ex Casement. Arrived by 10/88. Stored.
199	Chipmunk T.20	Spares use.

KILDIMO
[County Limerick] The yard of **Dennehy Commercials** was cleared of all its aeronautical scrap by 11/89. For the record, it is thought to have last held : EI-AOS Cessna 310B; EI-ATH Cessna F.150J; EI-AUD Rallye Club; EI-AUV Aztec 250C; EI-BDM Aztec 250D; EI-BFE Cessna F.150G; EI-BJA Cessna FRA.150L; EI-BML Aztec 250C; G-AZGH Rallye Club; HB-CFI Cessna F.172P; and an unidentified frame, thought to be the MS.230 from Kilbrittain Castle.

KILMOON
[County Meath] The Cubs remain long-termers at the strip here.

EI-AKM	J-3C-65 Cub	ex Weston, N88194, NC88194. CoA expired 30/6/60. Stored.
EI-BCO	J-3C-65 Cub	ex F-BBIV, composite. Stored.

PORTLAOISE
[County Laoise] The pioneering Aldritt Monoplane remains stored in a garage here.

IAHC 2	Aldritt Monoplane	Engineless, stored.

POWERSCOURT

[South of Dublin, County Wicklow] Spares ship EI-AMY has been joined for some time
by EI-AUS in store at the strip here.

EI-AMY	J/1N Alpha	ex Kells, G-AJUW. CoA expired 5/11/69. Spares use.
EI-AUS+	J/5F Aiglet Tnr	ex G-AMRL. CoA expired 2/12/75. Stored.

RATHCOOLE

[County Cork] At the farm strip the contents of the little hangar are unaltered.

EI-AFF	BA Swallow II	ex Coonagh, G-ADMF. Damaged 16/5/66. Stored.
EI-AFN	BA Swallow II	ex Kilkenny, G-AFGV. Stored.
EI-ASU	Terrier 2	ex G-ASRG, WE599, AAC, LAŚ, HCCS. wfu 15/6/77. Stored.

SHANNON AIRPORT

[Clare] With no reports to the contrary another case of condition normal. Both
the Caribou and the 707 are showing their age.

EI-AYW	Aztec 250C	ex N5801Y. Damaged 28/8/80. Stored.
G-AWUP	Cessna F.150H	ex Abbeyshrule. Damaged 1983, stored.
N3760D	Caribou	ex 5H-MRQ. External store.
4R-ALB	Boeing 707-321B	ex Air Lanka, 9V-BBA. Fire service.

Not inspected for some considerable time, the contents of the **Industrial Training
School** on the trading estate side of the airport may or may not remain.

EI-BHU	Skipper	ex Waterford. Crashed 19/7/83.
HB-CCW	Cessna F.172N	wreck.
SP-AFX	Wilga 35	crashed 12/8/85. Wreck.

SLIGO

[County Sligo] Gerry O'Hara's homegrown aircraft are still to be found stored here.

IAHC 7	Sligo Concept	single seat low wing monoplane. Stored, not flown.
IAHC 8	O'Hara Autogyro	on Bensen lines. Unflown. Stored.

WATERFORD AIRPORT

[South east of the town, County Waterford] **South East Aviation Enthusiasts** have
expanded their airframes considerably at their compound at the airfield. With
three items coming from the IAAC at Casement and no less than two Doves from Cork,
they have been busy. Note that the Dove '176' recorded in **W&R11** was not the
Dublin-based airframe, but VP-YKF painted as an IAAC machine.

G-AOIE	Douglas DC-7C	ex Shannon, Autair, Schreiner PH-SAX, G-AOIE Caledonian, BOAC.
G-ASNG+	Dove 6	EI-BJW ntu, ex Cork, Coventry, HB-LFF, G-ASNG, HB-LFF, G-ASNG, PH-IOM. Arrived 1988.
VP-BDF	Boeing 707-321	ex Dublin, Bahamasair. Nose section.
	Gemini	cockpit section. Almost certainly G-ALCS, ex Kilbrittain Castle.
173	Chipmunk T.20	ex Gormanston, IAAC.
176"	VP-YKF Dove 6	ex Cork, 3D-AAI, VQ-ZJC, G-AMDD. Damaged 9/8/82. See notes above.
184+	Provost T.51	ex Casement, IAAC. Arrived· late 1987.
187+	Vampire T.55	ex Casement, IAAC. Arrived late 1987.
192+	Vampire T.55	ex Casement, IAAC. Fuselage pod only. Arrived 1987.

Part 6

RAF OVERSEAS

This is the third time that the 'RAF Overseas' section has appeared within **W&R**, so readers should be well acquainted with what it sets out to cover. Essentially, this is a listing of all British military aircraft to be found in the **W&R** categories on Crown territory or property. It is not the intention to list any foreign aircraft that may be found in such locations (eg the Falklands). Only exception to this is on the Falklands where former Argentine machines are planned to form part of a museum. Please note also that this section does not appear in the Locations Index at the rear.

West Germany

BRUGGEN

With the Harrier GR.3 now becoming an 'elderly' aircraft, there have been several additions to the inmates here and no subtractions. As ever, it is as well to remind readers that the words 'Special Display' is RAF-talk for surface decoy. Two of the Harrier BDR airframes that arrived here did so via the CSDE at Swanton Morley, for reasons as yet uncertain.

XE608	8717M Hunter F.6A	ex 1 TWU, TWU, 229 OCU, CFCS, AFDS, CFE. BDR.
XL566	8891M Hunter T.7	ex Shawbury, Kemble, Laarbruch SF, 4 FTS, 208, 1417F, 43, A&AEE. BDR
XM970	8529M Lightning T.4	ex 19, 92, 60 MU 'hack', 226 OCU, 92, LCS. 'Special display'.
XM973	8528M Lightning T.4	ex 19, 226 OCU, 23, 111, 226 OCU, 74, AFDS. 'Special display'.
XN783	8526M Lightning F.2A	ex 92, 19, 92. 'Special display'.
XN789	8527M Lightning F.2A	ex 19, Handling Squadron, 92. 'Special Display'.
XN792	8525M Lightning F.2A	ex 92. BDR.
XP403	8690M Whirlwind HAR.10	ex 22, SAR Wing, 202, 228. 431 MU for BDR.
XS901+	8965M Lightning F.6	ex Binbrook, 11, 5, 11, 5, 11, 56, 5. Flew in 10/5/88. BDR.
XV358	8658M Buccaneer S.2C	ex 809. BDR, minus wings and tail section.
XV782+	8982M Harrier GR.3	ex Swanton Morley, St Athan, 4, 1453F, 4. Arrived early 1989 for BDR.
XV789+	8966M Harrier GR.3	ex 1, 233 OCU, 1, 1453F, 1, 4. wfu 20/8/87. Arrived early 1989. BDR.
XV793+	8980M Harrier GR.3	ex Swanton Morley, St Athan, 4, 1, 3, 20, 233 OCU. Arrived early 1989. BDR.
XX822"	8563M Jaguar GR.1	complex composite based upon nose and forward fuselage of S.07 XW563. On plinth outside 14 Sqn HQ.
XZ630+	8976M Tornado GR.1	ex BAe Warton, A&AEE. Flew in 24/8/88. WLT.

DETMOLD

Detmold is the Headquarters of 4 Regiment, Army Air Corps. Thankfully not taking any notice of the MoD ruling on RAF 'gates', a former Middle Wallop Sioux is now on show at the base as well as a Skeeter.

XL739	Skeeter AOP.12	ex 15/19 Hussars, 1 Wing, 651, A&AEE, BATUS, A&AEE, C(A). 'Gate'.
XP900+	Scout AH.1	ex Wroughton. BDR. Arrived by 3/87.
XT550+	Sioux AH.1	ex Middle Wallop, Wroughton, 651. Arrived 1989. 'Gate'.
XS571	Wasp HAS.1	ex Wroughton. Boom of XT436. BDR with 71 Workshops.
XV627	Wasp HAS.1	ex Wroughton. BDR airframe for 4 Regiment AAC.
XW615	Scout AH.1	ex Wroughton. Pod only. BDR.

GATOW

[West Berlin] Having become unsafe on the fire dump, Valetta C.1 WJ491 was scrapped here during 1988. Otherwise, no change.

TG503	8555M Hastings T.5	ex SCBS, A&AEE, BCBS, MoA, BCBS, C.1 RRE, RRF, A&AEE, AFEE, A&AEE. Preserved as monument to the Berlin Air Lift.
WF382	8872M Varsity T.1	ex 6 FTS, 1 ANS, 2 ANS, 5 FTS, 1 ANS, 2 ANS, 1 ANS, 3 ANS, CNCS.
A65-69	ZD215 Dakota III	ex RAAF A65-69/VHCUZ, USAAF 43-49866. Monument to Berlin Air Lift.

GUTERSLOH

No known departures to record, but, as elsewhere in RAFG, inbound Harriers join the
list. The new BDR airframe is unconfirmed, but believed to be XZ130.

XF949"	XG152 Hunter F.6A	ex 8843M, 1 TWU, 237 OCU, 1 TWU, TWU, 229 OCU, 19, FCS, FWS, DFLS. Preserved, but technically BDR.
XM244	8202M Canberra B(I).8	ex 16, 3, 16, 3, 16. Fire dump.
XP358	Whirlwind HAR.10	ex Farnborough, RAE, Wroughton, 28, 103, 110, 103, 225. BDR.
XR504"	8922M Wessex HU.5	ex XT467, Wroughton. BDR.
XV278	Harrier GR.1	ex Filton, Farnborough, Filton, Holme-on-Spalding Moor, Bitteswell, HSA. WLT.
XW917+	8975M Harrier GR.3	ex 3, 4, 3. SOC 30/4/88. Display airframe.
XZ989	8849M Harrier GR.3	ex 1, 233 OCU. BDR, fuselage minus cockpit plus wings. Hit by ground fire over Falklands 9/6/82 and written off in crash-landing.
+	Harrier GR.3	noted with BDR by 1/89. See notes above.

HILDESHEIM

Another Army Air Corps base to take on a Middle Wallop Sioux for display purposes.
Hildesheim is home to 1 Regiment AAC.

XP852	Scout AH.1	ex Wroughton. Pod. BDR.
XT438	A2704 Wasp HAS.1	ex Detmold, Wroughton. Pod. BDR.
XT548+	Sioux AH.1	ex Middle Wallop, Arborfield, Middle Wallop, Arborfield, 658. Arrived 1989. For display.

LAARBRUCH

A German museum acquired Canberra B(I).8 XM264/8227M and it left by road 7/2/90.
Otherwise, there have been no changes to the **W&R** airframes here.

XJ673"	8841M Hunter F.6A	ex XE606, 1 TWU, TWU, 229 OCU, 92, 74, 65, 54, CFE. 8737M ntu. Preserved on base.
XN732	8519M Lightning F.2A	ex 92. 'Special display' in convincing 'MiG-21' guise.
XN788	8543M Lightning F.2A	ex Bruggen, 92, 111, 92. BDR.
XN956	8059M Buccaneer S.1	ex Lossiemouth. BDR.
XR758	8964M Lightning F.6	ex Binbrook, 11, LTF, BinWing, 23, 74, 11, 23, Leuchars TFF, 5. BDR.

MINDEN

This entry is getting a little dated now, having had no new input since **W&R11**. 664
Squadron should have :

XP898	Scout AH.1	ex Wroughton. Pod.
XX376	Gazelle AH.1	Crashed 29/9/83. Pod. BDR.

SOEST

The final Sioux from the Middle Wallop trio settled here for display purposes. 3
Regiment AAC have a Scout and a Wasp for BDR.

XP897	Scout AH.1	ex Wroughton. Pod. BDR.
XT190+	Sioux AH.1	ex Middle Wallop, UNFICYP. Arrived early 1989. Display.
XT436	Wasp HAS.1	ex Detmold, Wroughton. Pod. BDR.

WILDENRATH

Having said 'Farewell Pembroke' in **W&R11** there are two of them still serving 60
Squadron! (XF799, XL944) The aircraft were due to be withdrawn on 16/5/90 (eight
days away as this hits the keyboards). Word is that these airworthy lovelies are
not for tender - amazing - but one is destined for crash rescue work within RAFG
and the other for dog training in the UK. (Newton? Syerston?) Another Lightning
has arrived for BDR, otherwise the ground-hugging fleet remains the same here.

WV701+	8936M Pembroke C.1	ex 60, 21, WCS, SCS, Seletar B&TTF, 267, FECS, A&AEE. Inst.
XF418	8842M Hunter F.6A	ex 1 TWU, TWU, 229 OCU, FCS. Displayed, but officially for BDR.
XM995	8542M Lightning T.4	ex 92. 'Special display'.
XN778	8537M Lightning F.2A	ex 92, 19. 'Special display'.
XR727+	8963M Lightning F.6	ex Binbrook, 11, 5, LTF, 23. Flew in 10/5/88. BDR.

Cyprus

AKROTIRI
In April 1989 the station gained a potent gate guardian in the form of former
Binbrook Lightning XS929 bedecked in 56 Squadron colours.   By this time the
Canberra on the dump had given up the ghost.   The Whirlwind listed in **W&R11** under
'Larnaca' is actually here, although its status after the Lightning gaining the
limelight is uncertain.

XD184	8787M Whirlwind HAR.10	ex 84 'A' Flt, 1563F, 228, 155. See notes above.
XJ437	8788M Whirlwind HAR.10	ex 84 'A' Flight, 22, 202, 22, SAR Flt, HAR.4, 228, 225, 155. BDR.
XS929+	Lightning F.6	ex Binbrook, 11, LTF, 11, 56, 11. Flew in 20/5/88. Mounted on the gate 23/4/89.

Falkland Islands

MOUNT PLEASANT AIRPORT
Two former Argentine Armed Forces machines are held in store here for the planned
Falkland Island Museum, which will be located in Port Stanley.

A-529	FMA Pucara	ex Stanley, Pebble Island, FAA. Composite, using A-509 & A-514.
AE-410	Bell UH-1H	ex Stanley, Stanley Racecourse. Stored.

SALVADOR SETTLEMENT
Robin Pitaluga still keeps the hulk of a Whirlwind HAR.9 at his home here.

XM666	Whirlwind HAR.9	ex 'Endurance' Flt, A&AEE, 'Endurance Flt', 'Protector' Flt, 846, 737, 700H. Ditched 17/12/69. Stripped and rotorless.

Gibraltar

NORTH FRONT
As with several places in the UK, the Vulcan is attracting both unfavourable
comments and corrosion.   One or the other will see it off before too long.   A
Hunter was flown in here inside a RAF Hercules on 12/12/89 - yet to be identified.

XM571	8812M Vulcan K.2	ex 50, Wadd Wing, A&AEE, 44, A&AEE, 101, 617, Wadd Wing, 617, 35, Wadd Wing, 35, 27, Akrotiri Wing, Cott Wing, Wadd Wing, Cott Wing, 83. Displayed.
+	Hunter	See notes above.

Hong Kong

SEK KONG
News from here is rare, unlike British passports if you are a prominent member of
the Colony's society!   The Wessex and Scout are believed to live on.

XP906	Scout AH.1	ex 660. Crashed 12/3/85. Dump.
XR500	Wessex HC.2	ex 28, 78, 72, 1 FTU. Ditched off Hong Kong 19/4/79. Derelict.

LOST & FOUND!

This section serves as a way of keeping certain 'chestnuts' from previous pages of W&R in the mind of readers. 'Chestnuts' are aircraft that cannot be accounted for in terms of fate or current status. Via this section a few aircraft held in 'limbo' have been 'found' again and re-entered the main text. It should be pointed out that the over-riding basis for entry in the main text is the <u>physical</u> sighting of an airframe. The book could be swelled considerably in the case of civil aircraft by looking for expired Certificates of Airworthiness and matching these up with the current 'owner' and address. This can be a minefield and serves as good testament to the sterility of some primary sources. The registered 'owner' of a British civil registered aircraft may not be the owner at all, may not operate the aircraft, may even be just a brass plaque somewhere. Registered addresses also provide red herrings in abundance. Sark International Airways (see page 46) are a good example of this. The idyllic island of Sark is all the more idyllic because it has no airfield (heresy, I hear you say!) and their aircraft (a Gnat and a Sea Hawk) can be found at Bournemouth! Hence W&R sticks to physical evidence and the LOST! section is a good way of focussing minds on the real and not 'paperwork' answer to where these airframes have gone.

Listed under LOST! below are a series of airframes that we cannot confirm fates or current existence for. The bracketed reference after each entry gives first the edition number and then the page reference within that edition. With this edition we have included military who-done-its as well. These go back a little further in time, just to keep you on your toes! Needless to say, anyone who can shed light on these please contact the compiler so that the FOUND! section in W&R13 can be much bigger! Over to you!

Compiled by **Tom Poole**

Lost

G-ADKM Hornet Moth Last heard of at Kingsclere, Hants. (11/53)

G-AFIR Luton Minor Stored in the Finmere, Bucks, area for many years. Current status unknown. (10/21)

G-AIUA Hawk Trainer III Roaded out from Benington, Herts, in 1987 along with sister-ship G-ANWO, reportedly for rebuild. (11/62)

G-AKIU Proctor V Removed from North Weald, Essex, and now thought to be in the Leicester area. (11/46)

G-ALTW Tiger Moth Moved from St Albans, Herts, possibly to the Exeter area. Current status unknown. (11/66)

G-AMVS Tiger Moth Supposedly on rebuild at Congleton, Cheshire, until sold. Possibly now in the Cambridge area. (10/32)

G-ANWO Hawk Trainer III See under G-AIUA for details.

G-ANZZ Tiger Moth Last reported stored on the farm at Chessington, London. (11/87)

G-AOEX Thruxton Jackaroo Another of the Kingsclere, Hants, inmates for which a 'forwarding address' is needed. (11/53)

G-ARHX Dove 8 Forward fuselage last known to have been with 85 Squadron ATC at Southgate, London. Fate? (9/93)

G-ARNB J/5G Cirrus Autocar Removed from Bredhurst, Kent, 7/87. Destination unknown. (11/69)

G-ARWH Cessna 172 Sat atop a pizza parlour in Golder's Green, London, until removed in 1988. Scrapped? (11/89)

G-ASJM Twin Comanche Last known to be dismantled at Bournemouth Airport, Dorset. (11/41)

G-ASPA Dove 8 Last reported in use as a spares-ship at Chalgrove, Oxon. Scrapped? (11/107)

G-ASRB Condor Removed from Redhill Aerodrome, Surrey, during 1986. Possibly now on rebuild in the Shoreham area. (11/124)

G-ASUH Cessna 172 Hulk disappeared from Felthorpe, Norfolk, circa 1985. (10/111)

G-ATBF Sabre F.4   Last known to have been in store at Much Hoole, Lancs. Reported to have moved out by 1985. Lincolnshire? Exported?? (11/74)

G-ATDL Cessna 310J   Hulk last reported in a scrapyard at Kenilworth, Warks. (10/149)

G-ATSJ Brantly 305   Hulk removed from display on a garage forecourt at Tyne Dock, Tyne & Wear, by 5/85. (10/147)

G-ATWS Luton Minor Stored dismantled at Hucknall, Notts. Since reported to have been burnt. (11/102)

G-AVMB Condor   Sold off from the Billingshurst, West Sussex, store, circa 1983. Nothing heard of it since. (9/128)

G-AVZY Rallye Club   Roaded out from Chessington, London, 1984. Reportedly bound for the Isle of Wight. (10/96)

G-AWDZ Pup Hulk disappeared from a scrapyard in the Biggin Hill, London, area, 1986. Probably scrapped. (11/86)

G-AXGU Condor   Another of the Billingshurst, West Sussex, inmates for which nothing is known since it moved out in 1983. (9/128)

G-AXRD Campbell Cricket Stored at owner's home at Nelson, Mid Glamorgan, since 1970. Current status unknown. (11/153)

G-AYUE Air & Space 18A   Removed from Biggin Hill, London, in 1987, reportedly bound for Scotland. See also G-BALB. (11/86)

G-AZHO Jodel DR.1050   Stored at Boston Airfield, Lincs, until 1980. Nothing known since. (10/90)

G-AZTM Airtourer 115   Roaded out of Gloucester/Cheltenham Airport, Glos, in 1985. Current status? (11/49)

G-BALB Air & Space 18A   Left Biggin Hill, London, circa 1986. Destination thought to be Scotland. See also G-AYLB. (11/86)

G-BANY Airtourer 115   Hulk had gone from Land's End Airport, Cornwall, by 4/84. (10/36)

G-BDDZ Emeraude   Removed from Tattershall Thorpe, Lincs, circa 1986. Nothing known since. (11/84)

G-BFOY Cessna A.188B   Wreck last known to have been at Bournemouth Airport, Dorset, until 1985. (11/41)

G-BGVM Cassutt Racer   Last reported on rebuild at Hammersmith, London. Possibly moved on. (11/87)

G-BLXK Agusta-Bell 205   Composite on rebuild at Cranfield, Beds. Current status unknown. (11/12)

G-BMFH Dornier Do 27   Stolen from Wycombe Air Park, Bucks, 12/87 - minus wings. (11/19)

G-OFRL Cessna 414A   Wreck last noted with Flight Refuelling at Bournemouth Airport, Dorset. (11/41)

G-PPHC Cessna F.172P   Kept in the Edinburgh area for spares. Current status unknown. (11/147)

D-EMKE Super Cub   Frame was stored at Kingsclere, Hants. (11/53)

EI-AGB Messenger   Wreck was held as spares for G-AGOY at Southill, Beds. Not reported since G-AGOY moved to Hatch, Beds. (10/16)

EI-AHR Chipmunk 22   Last known report stored in shed at Charleville, Eire. (10/180)

EI-BDN Aztec 250   Withdrawn from use and stored at Bournemouth Airport, Dorset. (11/41)

N5246 Nieuport 28   Stored at Watton-at-Stone, Herts, until moving out in 1985. Where to? (11/66)

OO-MEL Piaggio P.149D   At Ludham, Norfolk, until it 'disappeared' in 1985. Lincolnshire? (11/98)

VR-BDX Agusta-Bell 204D   Stored at Redhill Aerodrome, Surrey. Gone by 1986. (11/124)

ZS-HDG Whirlwind Srs 2   Last heard of at Panshanger, Herts. (9/66)

5B-CEQ Bell 47   Stored at Bournemouth Airport, Dorset, along with 5B-CER and 5B-CFA. Nothing known since. (11/41)

5X-UVV Agusta-Bell 206   Stored at Cranfield, Beds. Current status? (11/12)

DE373 Tiger Moth   In store with the Fleet Air Arm Museum at Yeovilton, Somerset. Current status unknown. (11/117)

KF423 Harvard   Cockpit section removed from Sandhurst scrapyard, Bucks.   Fate? (10/20)

RA897 Cadet TX.1   Stored in the Hucknall, Notts, area on behalf of the Newark Air Museum. Current status unknown. (11/102)

WB535 Devon C.2/2 This fuselage, along with those of three other aircraft were used by a JATE team at Sennybridge, Wales,. No reports since 1978. Assumed destroyed. (10/176)

WH854 Canberra T.4   Nose section last heard of a Chalgrove, Oxon. Fate? (11/107)

WK554 Chipmunk T.10   Stored at Shawbury, Salop, until departing 9/86. Destination unknown. (11/112)

WM367 Meteor NF.13   Was under restoration at Powick, Hereford & Worcs, until departing 9/86. Exported? (11/61)

WT333 Canberra B(I).8   Nose section last heard of on the ranges at Bindon, Dorset. Fate? (11/40)

XG573 Whirlwind HAS.3 One of two examples held at Porton Down, Wilts, for the Chemical Defence Establishment (as was). No reports since 1982 - see also XJ445. (11/133)

XJ445 Whirlwind HAR.5   See XG573 above. (11/133)

XM416 Jet Provost T.3   Fuselage was in use by JATE at Sennybridge, Wales, until 1978. See also WB535. (10/176)

XP352 Whirlwind HAR.10   Put up for tender and left Abingdon, Oxon, 1/88. Destination unknown. (11/105)

XP500 Gnat T.1   Another fuselage used at Sennybridge. See WB535. (10/176)

XP537 Gnat T.1   Last of the Sennybridge quartet. See WB535. (10/176)

XR955 Gnat T.1   Sold off and roaded out from Culdrose 10/87. Canada? (10/87)

XT187 Sioux AH.1   In a final attempt (!) to clear up the seemingly never-ending 'Fairoaks saga', this machine, along with XT199, XT567 and XT847, are still unaccounted for. Originally part of a batch purchased by Alan Mann, they were most probably used for spares. Unless you know otherwise. (10/140)

XT838 Sioux AH.1   Possibly the identity of the anonymous example coded 'F' which disappeared without trace from High Melton, South Yorks, in 1984. NB XT847 at Fairoaks was also coded 'F'. (10/157)

XV788 Harrier GR.1   Wreck was removed from Wittering, Cambs, dump by 10/86. Scrapped? (10/31)

XW424 Jet Provost T.5   Last reported in Lew Jackson's yard at Misson, Notts. Fate? (11/102)

XW916 Harrier GR.3   Hulk made a brief appearance on Wittering's, Cambs, dump in 3/87. Scrapped? (11/30)

XX557 Bulldog T.1   No reports to suggest that this is still being used as an instructional airframe at Topcliffe, North Yorks. (11/137)

XZ394 Jaguar GR.1   In store at Shawbury until it was roaded out 17/12/86. Where to? (10/129)

BD+235 T-33 Nose section was at Chalgrove for trials. Fate? (11/107)

41 P-51 Mustang This ex Israeli machine was on long-term restoration at Tees-side Airport, Cleveland, until reports suggested it moved to 'North Yorkshire' in 1987. (11/32)

MM53432 T-6G Texan   Roaded out from Gloucester/Cheltenham Airport, Glos, in 1986. Destination 'South Wales'. (11/49)

BAPC. 46 HM.14 Pou du Ciel   Stored in the Coleford, Glos, area for many years. The current status of this 'Flea' is unknown. (11/48)

BAPC.144 Mercury MPA   Stored at Cranwell North, Lincs. No reports to suggest it is still there. Continued existence now in doubt. (9/81)

BAPC.145 Oliver MPA   Stored at Warton, Lancs, following an accident in 1973. Not recorded for a long time. Possibly scrapped. (11/75)

BAPC.189 Bleriot XI replica   Sold at Christie's London auction 10/86. Current status? (11/203)

Found

Just a few, three of which have Irish connections.

G-AHWO Proctor V Under restoration at Celbridge, Eire.
G-ALCS Gemini Almost certainly to be found at Waterford, Eire.
G-ANLU Auster 5 Under restoration at Hedge End, Hants.
G-ANPC Tiger Moth Unless you know differently. The example 'Lost' in the Edinburgh area is the same machine which was 'Found' in Dublin in 1986.

The BAPC

From February 1990 Britain's representative body co-ordinating the efforts of a large number of organisations united in a desire to ensure the preservation, restoration and exhibition of tangible evidence of the United Kingdom's aviation heritage for the education and interest of present and future generations took on a new name to reflect the wide scope of its concerns - the British **Aviation** Preservation Council (still BAPC).

Member organisations are drawn from the whole spectrum of National, Service, Local Authority, Commercial and Voluntary organisations and range in size from such bodies as the Science Museum to small groups with a few dedicated members. Membership of the Council is by election and is available to any United Kingdom organisation or group with an active interest in aircraft preservation. Associate Membership is available to organisations based in the United Kingdom or elsewhere who wish to support the work of the Council.

Quarterly conferences are staged by the Council, hosted by member organisations. This way the Council acts as a means of communication between aircraft preservation organisations, a channel of information to them, and as a representative body able to speak on their behalf. Close contacts established within the Council serve to reduce misunderstandings, and to prevent rivalries becoming jealousies. While not seeking to own exhibits, the Council is frequently able to place exhibits in the hands of member organisations; and encourage the exchange of material. The Council also makes loans to member organisations for the purchase of exhibits, erection of buildings or other large projects.

Through membership of the Transport Trust and the Association of British Transport Museums, the Council is able to express the needs and interests of the aircraft preservation movement to similar, but broader-based, bodies. Three overseas associations, developed on similar lines to the BAPC - the Canadian Aeronautical Preservation Association, the Federation Francaise des Aeronefs de Collection and the Irish Aviation Historical Council - have been granted Honorary Membership of the Council and, along with Associate Members from overseas, help to spread the word of co-operation and information still further. As a token of its work as 'publisher' for the Council, the Lashenden Air Warfare Museum have also been granted Honorary Membership.

Information is one of the prime aims of the Council and to this end it has developed several specialist services for member organisations. Launched in December 1987 was a quarterly information bulletin, **Update,** supplying a variety of technical topics and acting generally as a 'notice board' to members as well as being a supplement to the quarterly Council Minutes.

Technical information and advice is available from the Technical Registrar, who also acts to funnel queries to those who can answer them. The Project Co-ordinator is tasked with putting square pegs in square holes - monitoring needs and wherever possible finding items to meet them. An extensive Library has been established where member organisations can borrow technical publications and a full catalogue of material available is maintained.

Individual membership of the Council is not possible, but any group working within the aircraft preservation movement is warmly invited to consider the benefits of membership. Enquiries about the Council should be addressed to the Secretary :- David Reader, 151 Marshalswick Lane, St Albans, Hertfordshire AL1 4UX.

BAPC Executive Committee

Chairman   - Michael Hodgson
Vice Chairmen   - David Lee (Imperial War Museum, Duxford)
                                  David Ogilvy (Shuttleworth Collection)
                                  Commander Dennis White
Secretary   - David Reader (Shuttleworth Veteran Aeroplane Society)
Membership Secretary   - Peter Kirk (Derbyshire Historical Aviation Society)
Treasurer   - Jeremy Parkin (Alpha Helicopters)
Press Officer   - Paul Brown (Avon Aviation Museum)
Committee Members   - John Bagley
                                  Steve Thompson (Cotswold Aircraft Restoration Group)
                                  Carl Speddings (South Yorkshire Aviation Society)
                                  Don Storer

Associated Officers

Editor 'Update'   - Trevor Green
Keeper of Aircraft Register   - Ken Ellis ('FlyPast' Magazine)
Librarian   - Peter Felix (Derbyshire Historical Aviation Society)
Project Co-Ordinator   - Tony Southern (Cotswold Aircraft Restoration Group)
Technical Registrar   - Ivor Jenkins (The Aeroplane Collection)

Member Organisations

Current members of the British Aviation Preservation Council are given below. Full members mentioned in the main body of the text do not have their contact address repeated here and a reference guides the reader to the appropriate entry in the book. Where there is no full-blown memntion within the main text, a very brief summary of the activities of the member organisation is given. Name changes since the last edition are also decoded. New members to Council are granted Provisional Membership for one year before being given full status. As **W&R** covers a two-year period no attempt is made here to separate Full from Provisional Members. Enquiries should be accompanied by a stamped addressed envelope to facilitate a reply. Associated Members are given a briefer mention, for completeness, at the end.

Aces High Ltd - see North Weald, Essex.
Aeroplane Collection (The) - see Warmingham, Cheshire.
Aeroplane Restoration Company (The) - see Duxford, Cambs.
Airborne Forces Museum - see Aldershot, Hants.
Aircraft Preservation Society of Scotland - see East Fortune, Lothian, Scotland.
Alpha Helicopters - Jeremy Parkin, 6 Wakefield Close, Byfleet, Surrey, KT14 7NA.
    (09323 52832) Helicopter consultants.
Avon Aviation Museum - see Monkton Farleigh, Wilts.
Air South Ltd, John Pothecary, Shed Eleven, Municipal Airport, Shoreham-by-Sea,
    Sussex BN4 5FF. Well known maintenance, restoration and operating concern.

B-17 Preservation Ltd - see Duxford, Cambs.
Battle of Britain Memorial Flight - see Coningsby, Lincs.
Berkshire Aviation Group - see Woodley, Berks.
Biggin Hill Museum and Friends of Biggin Hill Museum - see Sevenoaks, Kent.
Booker Aircraft Museum - see Wycombe Air Park, Bucks.
Brenzett Aeronautical Collection - see Brenzett, Kent.
Brimpex Metal Treatments, 5, Devonshire Close, Dore, Sheffield, S17 3NX.
    Specialists in the treatment and restoration of metals. And see under
    Sheffield, South Yorks for their 'Flea'.
British Aerial Museum of Flying Military Aircraft - renamed The Aeroplane
  , Restoration Company - qv.
British Aerospace Avro Aircraft Restoration Society - see Woodford, Manchester.
British Balloon Museum and Library - see Newbury, Berks.
British Classic Aircraft Restorations - see Hedge End, Hants.
British Rotorcraft Museum - renamed International Helicopter Museum - qv.
Brooklands Museum - see Brooklands, Surrey

City of Bristol Museum and Art Gallery - see Bristol, Avon.
Charles Church (Spitfires) Ltd - renamed Dick Melton Aviation - qv.
City of Norwich Aviation Museum - see Norwich Airport, Norfolk.
Cornwall Aircraft Park (Helston) Ltd - renamed Flambards Triple Theme Park - qv.
Cotswold Aircraft Restoration Group - see Innsworth, Glos.

Derby Industrial Museum - see Derby, Derbyshire.
Derbyshire Historical Aviation Society, Peter Kirk, 263 Birchover Way, Allestree,
    Derby DE3 2RS. Research and archive association.
Douglas Boston-Havoc Preservation Trust, Richard Nutt, 17 Hinckley Road, Barwell,
    Leicester LE9 8DL. Collecting and restoring Boston and Havoc associated
    material. Forward fuselage as long-term goal - well on the way!
Dumfries and Galloway Aviation Group - see Tinwald Downs, Dumfries and Galloway,
    Scotland.
Duxford Aviation Society - see Duxford, Cambs.

East Anglian Aviation Society - see Bassingbourn, Cambs.
East Midlands Aeropark Volunteers Association - see East Midlands Airport, Leics.
Essex Aviation Group - see Duxford, Cambs.

Fenland Aircraft Preservation Society - see Wisbech, Cambs.
Ken Fern Collection - renamed The Helicopter Collection - qv
Flambards Triple Theme Park - see Helston, Cornwall.
Fleet Air Arm Museum - see Yeovilton, Somerset.
Friends of the DC-3, John and Maureen Woods, 3 Dalcross, Crown Wood, Bracknell,
    Berks RG12 3UJ. Supporters' society.

Grantham Aviation Society, Peter Gibson, 12 Wardour Drive, Grantham, Lincs NG31
    9TY. Research and archive association.
Gloucestershire Aviation Collection, K C Imlah, 71 Christchurch Road, Cheltenham,
    Glos, GL50 2PS. Working to establish a museum in the county.
Greater Manchester Museum of Science and Technology - see Manchester, Greater
    Manchester.

Helicopter Collection (The) - see Stoke-on-Trent, Staffs.
Hemswell Aviation Society - see Hemswell, Lincs.
Historical Radar Archive, S/L Mike Dean, Little Garth, High Street, Scampton, LN1
    2SD. Archive, research and advise on radar and its history.
Humberside Aviation Preservation Society - incorporated into the Hemswell Aviation
    Society - qv.

Imperial War Museum - see page South Lambeth, London and Duxford, Cambs.
International Helicopter Museum - see Weston-super-Mare, Avon.

Lashenden Air Warfare Museum - see page Headcorn, Kent.
Leicestershire Museum of Technology - see Leicester, Leics.
Lightning Preservation Group - see Bruntingthorpe, Leics.
Lincolnshire Aviation Society - see East Kirkby, Lincs.

Macclesfield Historical Aviation Society - see Chelford, Cheshire.
Medway Aircraft Preservation Society Ltd - see Rochester, Kent.
Dick Melton Aviation - see Winchester, Hants.
Midland Air Museum - see Coventry Airport, Warks.
Midland Warplane Museum - see Long Marston, Warks.
Military Aircraft Preservation Group - see Hadfield, Derbyshire.
Mosquito Aircraft Museum - see London Colney, Herts.
Museum of Army Flying - see Middle Wallop, Hants.

National Museums of Scotland - see Edinburgh and East Fortune, both Lothian,
    Scotland.

Nene Valley Aviation Society, K Rookeby, 8 Newtown Road, Raunds, Northants NN9 6LX.
    Enthusiast and historic research society.
Newark Air Museum - see Winthorpe, Notts.
Norfolk and Suffolk Aviation Museum - see Flixton, Suffolk.
North East Aircraft Museum - see Sunderland, Tyne and Wear.
Northern Aeroplane Workshops - see Dewsbury, West Yorkshire.
North Manchester College - Moston Centre, Alan Suffell, Ashley Lane, Moston,
    Manchester M9 1WU. College with aviation department.

Robertsbridge Aviation Society - see Robertsbridge, East Sussex.
Rolls-Royce Heritage Trust (Bristol Branch), J Simpkins, Technical Publications,
    Rolls-Royce plc, PO Box 3, Filton, Bristol BS12 7QE. (0272 791234, ext 94918).
    Research and archive organisation.
Rolls-Royce Heritage Trust (Derby Branch), L Fletcher, 40 Quarn Drive, Allestree,
    Derby. Research and archive organisation.
Rolls-Royce Heritage Trust (Leavesden Branch), D A Valentine, Rolls-Royce plc,
    Leavesden, Watford, Herts WD2 7BZ. (0923 674000 ext 296)   Research and
    archive organisation.
Royal Aeronautical Society, Medway Branch - renamed Medway Aircraft Preservation
    Society - qv.
Royal Air Force Museum - see Hendon, London, Cosford, Salop and Cardington, Beds.
Royal Museum of Scotland - renamed National Museums of Scotland -qv.
Russavia Collection - see Bishop's Stortford, Herts.

Science Museum (The) - see South Kensington, London, and Wroughton, Wilts.
Second World War Aircraft Preservation Society - see Lasham, Hants.
Shuttleworth Collection (The) - see Old Warden, Beds.
Snowdon Mountain Aviation Ltd - see Caernarfon Airport, Gwynedd, Wales.
Solway Aviation Society - see Carlisle Airport, Cumbria.
Southampton Hall of Aviation - see Southampton, Hants.
South Yorkshire Aviation Society - see Firbeck, South Yorks.
Staffordshire Aviation Museum - see Seighford, Staffs.
Stratford Aircraft Collection - see Long Marston, Warks.
Surrey and Sussex Aviation Society, R Hall, Atholl Cottage, Walpole Avenue,
    Chipstead, Surrey. Research and archive association.

Tangmere Military Aviation Museum - see Tangmere West Sussex.
Torbay Aircraft Museum - see Higher Blagdon, Devon.

Ulster Aviation Society - see Newtownards, Down, Northern Ireland.
Ulster Folk and Transport Museum - see Holywood, Down, Northern Ireland.

Viscount Preservation Trust, Paul St John Turner, 'Cades Peak', Old St John Road,
    St Helier, Jersey. Supporting the preservation of G-ALWF at Duxford.

Wales Aircraft Museum - see Cardiff-Wales Airport, South Glamorgan, Wales.
Wellesbourne Aviation Group - see Wellesbourne Mountford, Warks.
Wessex Aviation Society - see Southampton, Hants.
Winbolt Collection (The) - see Bristol, Avon.

Yorkshire Air Museum - see Elvington, North Yorks.

Associate Members
Such members wish to support the work of the Council, but feel that they do not
fill the criteria to be Full Members. As some of the Associate Members of the
Council are preservation groups themselves, or support the work of other
preservation bodies, and therefore may be of interest to readers, greater details
are given here. Other Associate Members are given a brief mention at the end.

Brooklands Society Ltd (The), Peter Dench, Reigate Lodge, Chart Way, Reigate,
    Surrey RH2 0NZ.
Chiltern Aviation Society, Keith Hayward, 52 Pinn Way, Ruislip, Middx HA4 7QF.
Flying Boat Association (The), Brian Lewis, 17 Bramwell Close, Christchurch, Dorset
    BH23 2NP.
International Friends of the DH.89, Graham Simons, 67 Pyhill, Bretton, Peterborough
    PE3 8QQ.
Irish Aviation Museum, J Whorisky, Room 104, Services Annex, Air Lingus Head
    Office, Dublin Airport, Eire.
Lincolnshire Aircraft Recovery Group, D J Stubley, 13 Granville Ave, Wyberton,
    Boston, Lincs PE21 7BY
Lincolnshire's Lancaster Association, D C Richardson, 113 Gordon Fields, Market
    Rasen, Lincs, LN8 3AE.
Manchester Airport Archive, Brian Robinson, Hangar 6 Annex, Manchester Airport,
    Manchester M22 5PA.
Shuttleworth Veteran Aeroplane Society - see Old Warden, Beds.

Also : Air Education and Recreation Organisation (AERO); 'Aeroplane Monthly'; Air-
Britain (Historians) Ltd; 'Aircraft Illustrated'; Air Data Publications; Airfield
Research Group; Argus Specialist Publications Ltd; 'Aviation News'; 'FlyPast
Magazine'; Girls Venture Corps Air Cadets; LAASI International; Macclesfield
College of Further Education; Southern Aviation Research Associates.

And overseas : Australian War Memorial; Fyfield Collection, USA; Gruppo Amici
Velivoli Storici, Italy; Museum of Transport and Technology, New Zealand; Naval
Aviation Museum, Australia; Queensland Museum, Australia; Royal Australian Air
Force Association (WA Division) Aviation Museum; Royal New Zealand Air Force
Museum; United States Air Force Museum; Werftverein Oberschleissheim, West Germany;
Western Canada Aviation Museum; 'World War One Aeroplanes'.

Appendix C   **BAPC REGISTER**

As with **W&R11**, treatment of the British Aviation Preservation Council's Register of
Aircraft is by way of an index pointing the reader to references in the main text.
Some aircraft on the register are not quoted in the main body of the book, and
greater reference is made to those below. The BAPC Register serves as a form of
identity for airframes (generally those held by member groups) that otherwise would
not aspire to another form of registration. (Note : SER = Static External Replica,
outwardly accurate, but using materials and internal structures not as the
original.) None of the SERs placed on RAF base gates have been placed on the BAPC
Register yet, as they _may_ aspire to 'M' Numbers in due course.

BAPC Type No		Other i/d	Status	See under
1	Roe Triplane replica	G-ARSG	Shuttleworth Collection	Old Warden, Beds
2	Bristol Boxkite replica	G-ASPP	Shuttleworth Collection	Old Warden, Beds
3	Bleriot Type XI	G-AANG	Shuttleworth Collection	Old Warden, Beds
4	Deperdussin Monoplane	G-AANH	Shuttleworth Collection	Old Warden, Beds
5	Blackburn Monoplane	G-AANI	Shuttleworth Collection	Old Warden, Beds
6	Roe Triplane static replica	-	The Aeroplane Collection	Manchester, Gtr Man
7	Southampton University MPA	-	Southampton Hall of Aviation	Southampton, Hants
8	Dixon Ornithopter replica	-	Shuttleworth Collection	Old Warden, Beds
9	Humber-Bleriot XI replica	-	Midland Air Museum	Birmingham Airport, W Mids
10	Hafner R-II Revoplane	-	Museum of Army Flying	Middle Wallop, Hants
11	English Electric Wren	No 4	Shuttleworth Collection	Old Warden, Beds
12	Mignet HM.14 Pou du Ciel	-	The Aeroplane Collection	East Fortune, Lothian

13	Mignet HM.14 Pou du Ciel	–	Brimpex Metal Treatments	Sheffield, S Yorks
14	Addyman ST Glider	–	Nigel Ponsford	Leeds, W Yorks
15	Addyman ST Glider	–	The Aeroplane Collection	Warmingham, Ches
16	Addyman Ultra-Light	–	Nigel Ponsford	Leeds, W Yorks
17	Woodhams Sprite	–	The Aeroplane Collection	Wigan, Gtr Man
18	Killick Man Powered Gyro	–	Nigel Ponsford	Leeds, W Yorks
19	Bristol F.2b Fighter	66"	Brussels Military Museum	–
20	Lee-Richards Annular Biplane	–	Newark Air Museum	Winthorpe, Notts
21	Thruxton Jackaroo	–	Last reported in the Stevenage area	–
22	Mignet HM.14 Pou du Ciel	G-AEOF"	Aviodome, Amsterdam	–
23	–	–	Allocated in error	–
24	–	–	Allocated in error	–
25	Nyborg TGN.III glider	–	Eric Rolfe & Paul Williams	Moreton-in-the-Marsh, Glos
26	Auster AOP.9 fuselage frame	–	Scrapped, no longer extant	–
27	Mignet HM.14 Pou du Ciel	–	M J Abbey	Coventry, W Mids
28	Wright Flyer replica	–	Bygone Times Antique Warehouse	Ecclestone, Lancs
29	Mignet HM.14 Pou du Ciel	G-ADRY"	Mike Beach	Brooklands, Surrey
30	DFS Grunau Baby	–	Destroyed by fire, 1969	–
31	Slingsby T.7 Tutor	–	Not extant, believed scrapped	–
32	Crossley Tom Thumb	–	Midland Air Museum	Coventry Airport, Warks
33	DFS 108-49 Grunau Baby IIb	–	Current status unknown	–
34	DFS 108-49 Grunau Baby IIb	–	Current status unknown	–
35	EoN Primary	–	Current status unknown	–
36	Fieseler Fi 103 (V-1) rep	–	Kent Battle of Britain Museum	Hawkinge, Kent
37	Blake Bluetit	–	Shuttleworth Collection	Old Warden, Beds
38	Bristol Scout static replica	A1742"	Last reported at RAF St Mawgan	–
39	Addyman Zephyr	–	Nigel Ponsford	Leeds, W Yorks
40	Bristol Boxkite replica	–	Bristol City Museum & Art Gallery	Bristol, Avon
41	RAF BE.2c static replica	6232	RAF St Athan	St Athan, S Glamorgan
42	Avro 504K static replica	H1968	RAF St Athan	St Athan, S Glamorgan
43	Mignet HM.14 Pou du Ciel	–	Lincolnshire Aviation Society	East Kirkby, Lincs
44	Miles M.14A Magister	L6906"	Berkshire Aviation Group	Brooklands, Surrey
45	Pilcher Hawk replica	–	Percy Pilcher Museum	Stanford, Leics
46	Mignet HM.14 Pou du Ciel	–	–	LOST!
47	Watkins CHW Monoplane	–	RAF St Athan	St Athan, S Glamorgan
48	Pilcher Hawk replica	–	Glasgow Museum of Transport	Glasgow, Strathclyde
49	Pilcher Hawk	–	Royal Museum of Scotland	Edinburgh, Lothian
50	Roe Triplane Type I	–	Science Museum	South Kensington, London
51	Vickers FB.27 Vimy IV	–	Science Museum	South Kensington, London
52	Lilienthal Glider Type XI	–	Science Museum	South Kensington, London
53	Wright Flyer replica	–	Science Museum	South Kensington, London
54	JAP/Harding Monoplane	–	Science Museum	South Kensington, London
55	Antoinette Monoplane	–	Science Museum	South Kensington, London
56	Fokker E.III	210/16	Science Museum	South Kensington, London
57	Pilcher Hawk replica	–	Science Museum	South Kensington, London
58	Yokosuka MXY-7 Ohka II	–	Science Museum	South Kensington, London
59	Sopwith Camel static replica	D3419"	Last reported at RAF St Mawgan	–
60	Murray M.1 Helicopter	–	The Aeroplane Collection	Wigan, Gtr Man
61	Stewart Man Powered Orni	–	Lincolnshire Aviation Society	Tumby Woodside, Lincs
62	Cody Biplane	304	Science Museum	South Kensington, London
63	Hawker Hurricane SER	L1592"	Kent Battle of Britain Museum	Hawkinge, Kent
64	Hawker Hurricane SER	P3059"	Kent Battle of Britain Museum	Hawkinge, Kent
65	Supermarine Spitfire SER	N3289"	Kent Battle of Britain Museum	Hawkinge, Kent
66	Messerschmitt 'Bf 109' SER	1480"	Kent Battle of Britain Museum	Hawkinge, Kent
67	Messerschmitt 'Bf 109' SER	–	Kent Battle of Britain Museum	Hawkinge, Kent
68	Hawker Hurricane SER	H3426"	Midland Air Museum	Coventry Airport, Warks
69	Supermarine Spitfire SER	–	Kent Battle of Britain Museum	Hawkinge, Kent
70	Auster AOP.5	TJ398"	Aircraft Preservation Society of Scotland	East Fortune, Lothian
71	Supermarine Spitfire SER	P8140"	Norfolk & Suffolk Aviation Museum	Flixton, Suffolk

72	Hawker Hurricane SER	V7767"	Brooklands Museum	Brooklands, Surrey
73	Hawker Hurricane SER	–	Current status unknown	–
74	Messerschmitt 'Bf 109' SER	6357+	Kent Battle of Britain Museum	Hawkinge, Kent
75	Mignet HM.14 Pou du Ciel	G-AEFG	Nigel Ponsford	Leeds, W Yorks
				(See BAPC.102)
76	Mignet HM.14 Pou du Ciel	G-AFFI"	Yorkshire Air Museum	Elvington, N Yorks
77	Mignet HM.14 Pou du Ciel	G-ADRG"	Stratford Aviation Collection	Long Marston, Warks
78	Hawker (Afghan) Hind	K5414"	Shuttleworth Collection	Old Warden, Beds
79	Fiat G.46–4b	–	–?–	Lympne, Kent
80	Airspeed Horsa II fuselage	TL659	Museum of Army Flying	Middle Wallop, Hants
81	Hawkridge Nacelle Dagling	BGA 493	Russavia Collection	Eaton Bray, Beds
82	Hawker (Afghan) Hind	–	RAF Museum	Hendon, London
83	Kawasaki Type 5 Model 1b	8476M	Aerospace Museum	Cosford, Salop
84	Mitsubishi Ki 46 III Dinah	5439	Aerospace Museum	Cosford, Salop
85	Weir W-2	W-2	Museum of Flight	East Fortune, Lothian
86	de Havilland Tiger Moth	–	Current status unknown	–
87	Bristol Babe replica	G-EASQ"	Hemswell Aviation Society	Hemswell, Lincs
88	Fokker Dr I scale replica	102/17"	Fleet Air Arm Museum	Yeovilton, Somerset
89	Cayley Glider replica	–	RAF Museum	Hendon, London
90	Colditz Cock replica	–	Imperial War Museum	Duxford, Cambs
91	Fieseler Fi 103R-IV (V-1)	–	Lashenden Air Warfare Museum	Headcorn, Kent
92	Fieseler Fi 103 (V-1)	–	RAF Museum	Hendon, London
93	Fieseler Fi 103 (V-1)	–	Imperial War Museum	Duxford, Cambs
94	Fieseler Fi 103 (V-1)	8583M	Aerospace Museum	Cosford, Salop
95	Gizmer Autogyro	–	Current status unknown	–
96	Brown Helicopter	–	North East Aircraft Museum	Sunderland, Tyne & Wear
97	Luton LA-4 Minor	–	North East Aircraft Museum	Sunderland, Tyne & Wear
98	Yokosuka MXY-7 Ohka II	8485M	RAF Museum	Manchester, Gtr Man
99	Yokosuka MXY-7 Ohka II	8486M	Aerospace Museum	Cosford, Salop
100	Clarke Chanute glider	–	Science Museum	Hendon, London
101	Mignet HM.14 Pou du Ciel	–	Lincolnshire Aviation Society	Tumby Woodside, Lincs
102	Mignet HM.14 Pou du Ciel	–	Not completed, material used in BAPC.75	–
103	Pilcher Hawk replica	–	Personal Plane Services	Wycombe Air Park, Bucks
104	Bleriot Type XI	G-AVXV	Bleriot family	–
105	Bleriot Type XI	–	Goldsmith Trust, Aviodome, Amsterdam	–
106	Bleriot Type XI	No 164	RAF Museum	Hendon, London
107	Bleriot Type XXVII	No 433	RAF Museum	Hendon, London
108	Fairey Swordfish	HS503	Aerospace Museum	Cosford, Salop
109	Slingsby Cadet TX.1	–	Current status unknown	–
110	Fokker D.VIIF static replica	5125/18"	Current status unknown	–
111	Sopwith Triplane static rep	N5492"	Fleet Air Arm Museum	Yeovilton, Somerset
112	de Havilland DH.2 static rep	5964"	Museum of Army Flying	Middle Wallop, Hants
113	RAF SE.5A static replica	B4863"	Current status unknown	–
114	Vickers 60 Viking IV replica	R4"	Brooklands Museum	Brooklands, Surrey
115	Mignet HM.14 Pou du Ciel	–	Rebel Air Museum	Earls Colne, Essex
116	Santos-Dumont Demoiselle XX	–	Flambards Triple Theme Park	Helston, Cornwall
117	RAF BE.2c taxiable replica	1701"	Brooklands Museum	Brooklands, Surrey
118	Albatros D.V static replica	C19/15"	South Yorkshire Aviation Society	Firbeck, S Yorks
119	Bensen B-7 Gyroglider	–	North East Aircraft Museum	Sunderland, Tyne & Wear
120	Mignet HM.14 Pou du Ciel	G-AEJZ	Hemswell Aviation Society	Hemswell, Lincs
121	Mignet HM.14 Pou du Ciel	G-AEKR"	South Yorkshire Aviation Society	Firbeck, S Yorks
122	Avro 504K taxiable replica	1881"	Current status unknown	–
123	Vickers FB.5 Gunbus replica	P641"	Thought reduced to components	–
124	Lilienthal Type XI replica	–	Science Museum	South Kensington, London
125	Clay Cherub ground trainer	G-BDGP"	Current status unknown	–
126	Rollason D.31 Turbulent	–	Midland Air Museum	Coventry Airport, Warks
127	Halton MPA 'Jupiter'	–	Current status unknown	–
128	Watkinson Cyclogyroplane IV	–	International Helicopter Museum	Weston-super-Mare, Avon
129	Blackburn 1911 Monoplane	–	Flambards Triple Theme Park	Helston, Cornwall
130	Blackburn 1912 Monoplane	–	Flambards Triple Theme Park	Helston, Cornwall

131	Pilcher Hawk replica	–	Current status unknown	–
132	Bleriot Type XI	–	Current status unknown	–
133	Fokker Dr.I static replica	425/17"	Torbay Aircraft Museum	Higher Blagdon, Devon
134	Aerotek Pitts S-2A non-flyer	G-CARS"	Current status unknown	–
135	Bristol M.1C Monoplane rep	C4912"	Current status unknown	–
136	Deperdussin 1913 replica	No 19	Exported to the USA 1989	–
137	Sopwith Baby replica	8151"	Current status unknown	–
138	Hansa Brandenburg W.29 rep	2292"	Current status unknown	–
139	Fokker Dr.I static replica	Dr.I/17"	Current status unknown	–
140	Curtiss R3C-2 static replica	No 3	Thought exported to the USA 1989	–
141	Macchi M.39 taxiable replica	–	Exported to the USA 1989	–
142	RAF SE.5A static replica	F5459"	Current status unknown	–
143	Paxton Man Powered Aircraft	–	Current status unknown	–
144	Weybridge MPA 'Mercury'	–	Current status unknown	LOST!
145	Oliver Man Powered Aircraft	–	Current status unkown	LOST!
146	Pedal Aeronauts MPA 'Toucan'	–	Mosquito Aircraft Museum	London Colney, Herts
147	Bensen B-7 Gyroglider	LHS-1	Norfolk & Suffolk Aviation Museum	Flixton, Suffolk
148	Hawker Fury II static rep	K7271"	Aerospace Museum	Cosford, Salop
149	Short S.27 static replica	–	Fleet Air Arm Museum	Yeovilton, Somerset
150	SEPECAT Jaguar GR.1 SER	XX718"	RAF Exhibition Flight	Abingdon, Oxon
151	SEPECAT Jaguar GR.1 SER	XZ363"	RAF Exhibition Flight	Abingdon, Oxon
152	BAe Hawk T.1 SER	XX263"	RAF Exhibition Flight	Abingdon, Oxon
153	Westland WG-33 mock-up	–	International Helicopter Museum	Weston-super-Mare, Avon
154	Druine D.31 Turbulent	–	Lincolnshire Aviation Society	East Kirkby, Lincs
155	Panavia Tornado GR.1 SER	ZA600"	RAF Exhibition Flight	Abingdon, Oxon
156	Supermarine S.6B static rep	S1595"	Exported to the USA 1989	–
157	WACO CG-4A Hadrian fuselage	–	Pennine Aviation Museum	Bacup, Lancs
158	Fieseler Fi 103 (V-1)	–	Defence Explosive Ordnance School	Chattenden, Kent
159	Yokosuka MXY-7 Ohka II	–	Defence Explosive Ordnance School	Chattenden, Kent
160	Chargus 18/50 hang glider	–	Museum of Flight	East Fortune, Lothian
161	Stewart Man Powered Orni	–	Hemswell Aviation Society	Hemswell, Lincs
162	Goodhart 'Newbury Manflier'	–	Science Museum	Wroughton, Wilts
163	AFEE 10/42 Rotachute replica	B-415	Wessex Aviation Society	Middle Wallop, Hants
164	Wight Quadruplane replica	–	Wessex Aviation Society	Southampton, Hants
165	Bristol F.2b Fighter	E2466"	RAF Museum	Hendon, London
166	Bristol F.2b Fighter	G-AANM	Aero Vintage	St Leonards-on-Sea, E Sussex
167	RAF SE.5A static replica	–	Torbay Aircraft Museum	Higher Blagdon, Devon
168	de Havilland Moth replica	G-AAAH"	Gatwick Hilton Hotel	Gatwick Airport, W Sussex
169	SEPECAT Jaguar GR.1 replica	–	1 School of Technical Training	Halton, Bucks
170	Pilcher Hawk replica	–	Current status unknown	Strathallan, Tayside
171	BAe Hawk T.1 SER	XX297"	RAF Exhibition Flight	Abingdon, Oxon
172	Chargus Midas Super E	–	Science Museum	Wroughton, Wilts
173	Birdman Grasshopper	–	Science Museum	Wroughton, Wilts
174	Bensen B-7 Gyroglider	–	Science Museum	Wroughton, Wilts
175	Volmer VJ-23 Swingwing	–	Museum of Science & Technology	Manchester, Gtr Man
176	RAF SE.5A scale replica	A4850"	South Yorkshire Aviation Museum	Firbeck, S Yorks
177	Avro 504K taxiable replica	G-AACA"	Brooklands Museum	Brooklands, Surrey
178	Avro 504K taxiable replica	E373"	Bygone Times Antique Warehouse	Ecclestone, Lancs
179	Sopwith Pup static replica	–	Epping Forest District Council	Waltham Abbey, Essex
180	McCurdy Silver Dart replica	–	RAF Museum	Cardington, Beds
181	RAF BE.2b static replica	687"	RAF Museum	Cardington, Beds
182	Wood Ornithopter	–	Museum of Science & Technology	Manchester, Gtr Man
183	Zurowski ZP.1 helicopter	–	Newark Air Museum	Winthorpe, Notts
184	Supermarine Spitfire IX SER	EN398"	Aces High	North Weald, Essex
185	WACO CG-4A Hadrian fuselage	243809"	Museum of Army Flying	Middle Wallop, Hants
186	de Havilland Queen Bee	K3584"	Mosquito Aircraft Museum	London Colney, Herts
187	Roe Type I Biplane replica	–	Brooklands Museum	Brooklands, Surrey
188	McBroom Cobra 88 hang glider	–	Science Museum	Wroughton, Wilts
189	Bleriot Type XI	–	Current status unknown	LOST!
190	Supermarine Spitfire replica	K5054"	Biggin Hill Museum	Sevenoaks, Kent

191	BAe/McDD Harrier GR.5 SER	ZD472"	RAF Exhibition Flight	Abingdon, Oxon
192	Weedhopper JC-24 microlight	–	The Aeroplane Collection	Warmingham, Cheshire
193	Hovey Whing Ding microlight	–	The Aeroplane Collection	Warmingham, Cheshire
194	Santos Dumont Demoiselle rep	–	Brooklands Museum	Brooklands, Surrey
195	Moonraker 77 hang glider	–	Museum of Flight	East Fortune, Lothian
196	Sigma 2m hang glider	–	Museum of Flight	East Fortune, Lothian
197	Cirrus III hang glider	–	Museum of Flight	East Fortune, Lothian
198	Fieseler Fi 103 (V-1)	–	Imperial War Museum	South Lambeth, London
199	Fieseler Fi 103 (V-1)	442795	Science Museum	South Kensington, London
200	Bensen B-7 Gyroglider	–	The Helicopter Collection	Long Marston, Warks
201	Mignet HM.14 Pou du Ciel	–	Caernarfon Aviation Museum	Caernarfon Airport, Gwynedd
202	Supermarine Spitfire SER	–	Maes Artro Craft Centre	Llanbedr, Gwynedd
203	Chrislea Airguard replica	–	The Aeroplane Collection	Warmingham, Cheshire
204	McBroom hang-glider	–	The Aeroplane Collection	Warmingham, Cheshire

Appendix D   IAHC REGISTER

Run by the Irish Aviation Historical Council, the IAHC register operates on very
similar lines to the BAPC Register. Enquiries about the IAHC should be addressed
to : Joe McDermott, Information Officer, IAHC, 151 Cloncliffe Avenue, Dublin 3,
Eire.

BAPC No	Type	Status	See under
1	Mignet HM.14 Pou du Ciel	Aviation Society of Ireland	Dublin
2	Aldritt Monoplane	Aldritt family	Portlaoise, Laoise
3	Mignet HM.14 Pou du Ciel	R Robinson	Carbury, Kildare
4	Hawker Hector frame	Thought under restoration in Florida, USA	–
5	Morane-Saulnier MS.230 frame	Current status unknown, thought scrapped	–
6	Ferguson Monoplane replica	Ulster Folk & Transport Museum	Holywood, Down
7	Sligo Concept	Gerry O'Hara	Sligo
8	O'Hara Autogyro	Gerry O'Hara	Sligo
9	Ferguson Monoplane replica	Ulster Folk & Transport Museum	Holywood, Down

AUCTIONS

Now a well established part of **W&R**, our review of auctions continues to function as a 'safety net' for aircraft that leave the realms of the book by being 'hammered' out. Major aircraft auctions involving 'our' type of aircraft since the last edition are given below. Major trend to have arisen is the adoption of the auction by the Ministry of Defence as a method of disposing of airframes, with the Cardiff sale attracting bids daft enough to make the men in the pin stripes think they are on to a winner. After their sale of the bulk of the Torbay Aircraft Museum, Sotheby's were the next to take up the auctioneer's hammer on behalf of MoD and the prices there threaten to take every instructional airframe the RAF has out of the SoTTs and off to auction!

Readers are reminded that the figures given below and in the main text represent a 'high bid' and do not necessarily indicate a sale. VAT and buyer's premiums are not included in the bid figures.

Enquiries relating to aircraft auctions can be made to :-
Christie's,   85 Old Brompton Road, London SW7 3LD. 071 581 7611.
Phillips,   Blenstock House, 7 Blenheim Street, New Bond Street, London W1Y
                   OAS. 071 629 6602.
Sotheby's,   34-35 New Bond Street, London W1A 2AA. 071 493 8080.
Wilkins & Wilkins, 31 High Street, Ashwell, Baldock, Herts. 046274 2718 or 2819.

Sotheby's, Billingshurst, 19 October, 1989
With the need to re-site the Torbay Aircraft Museum from Higher Blagdon, Devon, Sotheby's were contracted to sell off much of the collection. The sale was held at their 'Summer Place' at Billingshurst, Sussex, with several days having been put aside for viewing down at Higher Blagdon. Bids and disposals of the Torbay Aircraft Museum can be found listed in full under Higher Blagdon, Devon.

Phillips, Cardiff, 21 September, 1989
Taking place at their Cardiff office, Phillips auctioned ten Ministry of Defence airframes on 21/ 9/89. The largest batch came from the former St Athan Historic Aircraft Collection. All are mentioned under their appropriate location in the main text, but are given here by way of showing the full sweep of the auction.

Hawker Hunter F.1 WT555	at Cosford	£ 10,000
de Havilland Vampire T.11 XD382	Shawbury	£ 6,500
Gloster Meteor NF.14 WS792	Carlisle	£ 4,000
Slingsby Swallow TX.1 XS650	St Athan	£ 2,200
Auster AOP.9 XR243	St Athan	£ 6,500
Saunders Roe Skeeter AOP.12 XN341	St Athan	£ 11,000
Percival Provost T.1 WV499	St Athan	£ 16,000
English Electric Canberra B.2 WD935	St Athan	£ 7,200
Avro Vulcan B.2 XM602	St Athan	£ 33,000
de Havilland Vampire FB.9 WL505	St Athan	£ 10,200

Sotheby's, London 9 March, 1990
Staged in their New Bond Street sales room, Sotheby's were the second auction house to organise a major disposal on behalf of the Ministry of Defence. The Alouettes, Sea Devons and Herons were not in store long enough to be regarded as true **W&R** territory, but are certainly close enough to our hearts to merit inclusion. The unprecedented prices here may well mean a grim long-term outlook for museum acquisitions in the UK. Several museums were present and watched the bidding go way beyond their budget as largely dealers had a field-day. Aircraft were at five locations, with viewing in the days before the sale. Locations and airframe hours are given where known, plus high bids. What destinations are revealed as this work is finalised will be found in the appropriate places in the main text.
de Havilland Sea Devon C.20 XJ319 at Shawbury; total time 11,714 hours £ 15,500

de Havilland Sea Devon C.20	XJ324	at Kemble;	total time	8,993 hours	£	7,500		
de Havilland Sea Devon C.20	XK895	at Shawbury;	total time	8,226 hours	£	19,000	to G-SDEV, based	
								North Weald
de Havilland Sea Heron C.1	XR441	at Shawbury;	total time	21,053 hours	£	7,000		
de Havilland Sea Heron C.1	XR442	at Kemble;	total time	20,896 hours	£	10,000		
de Havilland Sea Heron C.1	XR443	at Shawbury;	total time	17,088 hours	£	5,500		
de Havilland Sea Heron C.1	XR445	at Shawbury;	total time	15,088 hours	£	16,500		
Folland Gnat T.1	XM709	at Halton;	total time	unknown	£	31,000		
Folland Gnat T.1	XP533	at Cosford;	total time	3,652 hours	£	102,000		
Folland Gnat T.1	XP538	at Cosford;	total time	3,183 hours	£	102,000		
Folland Gnat T.1	XR537	at Cosford;	total time	2,935 hours	£	105,000		
Folland Gnat T.1	XR984	at Halton;	total time	unknown	£	34,000		
Folland Gnat T.1	XS102	at Cosford;	total time	3,238 hours	£	88,000		
Folland Gnat T.1	XS105	at Cosford;	total time	3,371 hours	£	84,000		
Folland Gnat T.1	XS107	at Cosford;	total time	2,905 hours	£	122,000		
Folland Gnat T.1	XS110	at Halton;	total time	unknown	£	29,000		
Sud Alouette AH.2	XN132	at Wroughton;	total time	6,661 hours	£	46,000		
Sud Alouette AH.2	XP967	at Wroughton;	total time	8,293 hours	£	40,000		
Sud Alouette AH.2	XR376	at Wroughton;	total time	8,796 hours	£	46,000		
Sud Alouette AH.2	XR378	at Wroughton;	total time	8,067 hours	£	44,000		
Sud Alouette AH.2	XR382	at Wroughton;	total time	7,683 hours	£	24,000		
Sud Alouette AH.2	XR385	at Wroughton;	total time	8,624 hours	£	58,000	to Coventry	
								Helicopters
Sud Alouette AH.2	XR386	at Wroughton;	total time	9,038 hours	£	38,000		

Christie's, Duxford, 28 April, 1990

Making a welcome return to this more than tempting venue, Christie's new Aviation
Department staged this huge auction of airframes and memorabilia just after **W&R12**
went to press! Aircraft lots and high bids are given here with a mention to any
airframes listed in the main text, plus any known transactions. This data is not
given in the main text, so this part of the book is more up to date than the rest!
A lavishly-proportioned sale, it was of particular note in the number of foreign
airframes it attracted. Airframes are listed in Lot order. Several of the Lots
were not on site, they are denoted thus # with a note of location.

Wassmer WA 30 Bijave	F-CDIY	£	4,800	
Sud SO.1221 Djinn	FR145	£	17,000	
Fokker Dr I replica	N5523V	£	13,000	Personal Plane Serives, Wycombe Air Park, Bucks.
Nord 1002 Pingouin	LV-RIE	£	8,500	
Vultee BT-15 Valiant #	N513L	£	32,000	Aces High, on the high seas! Due in at Felixstowe
				7/5/90
NAA T-28C Trojan	G-USAF	£	32,000	See under Wycombe Air Park, Bucks.
EKW C-3605 'Schlepp'	C-558	£	28,000	Personal Plane Services, Wycombe Air Park, Bucks.
MS.733 Alcyon #	F-BLYA	£	3,800	At Aix les Milles, France.
NAA B-25J Mitchell #	G-BKXW	£	45,000	Aces High, at North Weald, Essex. To The Fighter
				Collection, Duxford, Cambs.
CASA 2-111 #	G-AWHB	£	75,000	Aces High, at North Weald, Essex.
Sopwith Triplane replica	G-PENY	£	20,000	
Curtiss Robin C-2	G-HFBM	£	30,000	ex LV-FBM.
Civilian Coupe II #	G-ABNT	£	32,000	At Biggin Hill, London.
Rearwin 8500 Sportster	G-AEOF	£	14,000	
Focke Wulf Fw 44J Stieglitz	D-EFUR	£	40,000	
Boeing PT-13D	G-BRTK	£	32,000	
DH Queen Bee	G-BLUZ	£	30,000	
CASA I-131E Jungmann	D-EHDS	£	32,000	
Eberhart SE.5E	G-BLXT	£ 250,000		Patrick Lindsey Collection, Wycombe Air Park, Bucks.
Bucker Bu 133C Jungmeister	D-EHVP	£	60,000	To The Fighter Collection, Duxford, Cambs.
Piper L-4A Grasshopper	G-BBLH	£	14,000	
Auster J/5F Aiglet Trainer	G-AMTD	£	19,000	
Cassutt 111M	G-RUNT	£	6,500	
Klemm Kl 35D	D-EHKO	£	32,000	

Pitts S-1T Special	G-WILD	£ 38,000	
Beech D.17S	NC582	£ 75,000	
DH Dragon Rapide	G-AIYR	£ 65,000	
Fairchild Argus III	G-BCBL	£ 17,000	
MH 1521M Broussard	G-BJGW	£ 22,000	The Aircraft Restoration Company, Duxford, Cambs.
Sold.			
Cessna 195B	N4461C	£ 45,000	
MS.733 Alcyon	F-BLXV	£ 17,500	
DH Dove 8	G-ARBE	£ 38,000	
Beech 18-3TM Expediter	G-BKGL	£ 60,000	The Aircraft Restoration Company, Duxford, Cambs.
DH Devon C.2/2	G-BLRB	£ 18,500	
Dassault MD.312 Flamant	F-AZEN	£ 29,000	
DH Sea Vixen FAW.2(TT) #	G-VIXN	£ 10,000	At Bournemouth Airport, Dorset. Auctioned on behalf of the BBC TV appeal 'Children in Need'.
DH Venom Mk 54 #	G-BLSD	£ 14,000	Aces High, North Weald, Essex.
DH Sea Vixen FAW.2 #	XN691	£ 14,000	Butane Buzzard Aviation, North Weald, Essex.
NAA TB-25N Mitchell #	N1042B	£ 130,000	Aces High, North Weald, Essex.
Hawker Fury replica	G-BKBB	£ 180,000	Patrick Lindsey Collection, Wycombe Air Park, Bucks. Sold to Belgian collector.
MiG-21PF 'Fishbed' #	G-BRAM	£ 75,000	Aces High, North Weald, Essex.

FURTHER READING

In putting together a book such as **W&R**, many reference sources are dipped into, either to ferret out more news, or to flesh-out histories and confirm identities. Best place to find news on all-things **W&R** is with the enthusiast press and if you are not a member of an aviation society, then any of the ones listed below have always provided the compiler with a consistent flow of information and all dwell on subjects other than **W&R** as well. Following the list of enthusiast magazines there is a bibliography of largely professionally-produced magazines and books.

Enthusiast Magazines

Air-Britain News, Aeromilitaria, and Archive. monthly and quarterly magazines from Air-Britain (Historians) Ltd. Contact : B R Womersley, 19 The Pastures, Westwood, Bradford-on-Avon, Wiltshire.

Air-Strip monthly journal of the Midland Counties Aviation Society. Contact : R Queenborough, 17 Leylan Croft, Birmingham B13 ODB.

British Aviation Review and Roundel monthly and bi-monthly journals of the British Aviation Research Group. Contact : Paul Hewins, 8 Nightingale Road, Woodley, Berkshire RG5 3LP.

Humberside Air Review monthly journal of the Humberside Aviation Society. Contact : 4 Bleach Yard, New Walk, Beverley, Humberside HU17 7HG.

Irish Air Letter monthly journal published by Eamon Power, Karl Hayes and xxxxxx. Contact : 25 Phoenix Avenue, Castleknock, Dublin 15, Eire.

NAG-MAG monthly journal of the Norfolk Aviation Group. Contact : Maurice Baalham, near Village Hall, Witton, North Walsham, Norfolk NR28 9TU.

Osprey monthly journal of the Solent Aviation Society. Contact : Doreen Eaves, 84 Carnation Road, Bassett, Southampton SO2 3JL.

Strobe monthly journal of the East of England Aviation Group. Contact : Alan Warnes, 7 Gayton Court, Westwood, Peterborough, Cambs PE3 7DB.

Winged Words monthly journal of The Aviation Society. Contact : Evan Higson, 14 Brookland Drive, Prestwich, Manchester M25 5GS.

Magazines and Periodicals

Aeroplane Monthly, monthly magazine published by Reed Business Publishing Ltd.

Airfield Review, quarterly journal of the Airfield Research Group.

Air Forces Monthly, monthly magazine published by Key Publishing Ltd.

Aviation News, fortnightly magazine published by Alan W Hall (Publications) Ltd.

FlyPast, monthly magazine published by Key Publishing Ltd.

Pilot, monthly magazine published by Lernhurst Publications Ltd.

Popular Flying, bi-monthly magazine published by the Popular Flying Association.

Propliner, quarterly magazine published by Tony Eastwood.

Update, quarterly bulletin published by the British Aviation Preservation Council.

Warbirds Worldwide, quarterly published by Warbirds Worldwide Ltd.

Books

Air Min, P H Butler, Merseyside Aviation Society, 1977.

Anson File (The), R Sturtivant, Air-Britain, 1988.

Avro Vulcan, R Jackson, Patrick Stephens, 1984.

British Civil Aircraft Registers 1919-1978, J Appleton and I G Cave, Midland
                                          Counties Publications, 1978.

British Gliders, P H Butler, Merseyside Aviation Society, 1980.

British Homebuilt Aircraft since 1920, K Ellis, Merseyside Aviation Society, 1979.

British Military Aircraft Serials 1878-1987, B Robertson, Midland Counties
                                             Publications, 1987.

British Military Aircraft Serials & Markings, M I Draper, M H Pettit, D A Rough,
                                 T E Stone, British Aviation Research Group, 1980.

DH Dove & Heron, C Barber, D Shaw & T Sykes, Air-Britain, 1973.

Douglas DC-3 Survivors, A Pearcy, Aston Publications, Volume 1, 1987; Volume 2, 1988.

English Electric/BAC Lightning, B Philpott, Patrick Stephens, 1984.
European Wrecks & Relics, M Bursell, Midland Counties Publications, 1989.
Falklands - The Air War, M I Draper, M H Pettit, D A Rough, T E Stone, D Wilton,
                                        British Aviation Research Group, 1986.
Harrier, F K Mason, Patrick Stephens, 1983.
Harvard File (The), J F Hamlin, Air-Britain, 1988.
Hawker Hunter : Biography of a Thoroughbred, F K Mason, Patrick Stephens, 1981.
Hawker Siddeley Gnat F.1 & T.1, P A Jackson, Alan W Hall Publications, 1982.
In Uniform, K Ellis, Merseyside Aviation Society, 1983.
Irish Aircraft Register 1987, C F Corcoran, Irish Aviation Press, 1986.
Meteor : Britain's First Jet Fighter, S J Bond, Midland Counties Publications,
                                                                          1985.
Mosquito Survivors, S Howe, Aston Publications, 1986.
Museums and Art Galleries in Great Britain & Ireland, S Alcock (Ed), British
                                            Leisure Publications, 1989.
Mustang Survivors, P A Coggan, Aston Publications, 1987.
RAF Squadrons, W/C C G Jefford, Airlife, 1988.
Royal Air Force Aircraft WA100 to WZ999, J J Halley, Air-Britain, 1983 - and others
                                                               in the series.
Royal Navy Instructional Airframes, BARG Naval Research Group, British Aviation
                                            Research Group, 1978.
Some More of God's Greatest Mistakes, O Colluphid, Megadodo Publications, 2030.
Spitfire : The History, E B Morgan & E Shacklady, Key Publishing, 1987.
Spitfire Survivors Around the World, G Riley & G Trant, Aston Publications, 1986.
Squadrons of the Fleet Air Arm, R Sturtivant, Air-Britain, 1984.
Squadrons of the Royal Air Force, J J Halley, Air-Britain, 1979.
Under B Conditions, D S Revell, Merseyside Aviation Society, 1978.
United Kingdom & Eire Civil Registers, M P Fillmore, Air-Britain, 1989
United States Military Designations & Serials since 1909, J M Andrade, Midland
                                            Counties Publications, 1979.
Vickers Viscount & Vanguard, P W Davis, Air-Britain, 1981.
Viking, Valetta & Varsity, B Martin, Air-Britain, 1975.
Warbirds Worldwide Directory, J Chapman & G Goodall (Ed P A Coggan), Warbirds
                                                    Worldwide, 1989.
Whiskies of Scotland, R J S McDowall, John Murray, 1975.

ABBREVIATIONS

Without the use of abbreviations for the 'potted' histories of the aircraft listed
in **W&R** the book would need wheels! There follows a decode of abbreviations with
extra notes to help readers to wend their way through the individual histories.
Units etc currently in existence are denoted thus *.

A&AEE*	Aeroplane and Armament Experimental Establishment, test and trials facility, based Boscombe Down.
AAC*	Army Air Corps, headquarters at Middle Wallop.
AACU	Anti-Aircraft Co-operation Unit, gunnery facilities unit.
AAIU*	Air Accident Investigation Unit, ground based investigation unit, based at Farnborough.
ACU	Andover Conversion Unit, type conversion unit, based Abingdon.
ADS	Air Director School, FAA school for aircrew training, now part of FRADU.
AE&AEOS	Air Engineers and Air Electronic Operators School, aircrew school.
AEF*	Air Experience Flight, Chipmunk units to give Cadets etc air experience.
AES	Air Engineers School, aircrew school, became part of AE&AEOS.
AES*	Air Engineering School, FAA ground school, based at Lee-on-Solent.
AETW*	Air Engineering Training Wing, AAC ground school, based at Middle Wallop.
AFDS	Air Fighting Development Squadron, tactics and trials unit.
AFEE	Airborne Forces Experimental Establishment, test and trials unit, based at Beaulieu and Ringway.
AFNE*	Air Forces North East, communications unit, based in Norway for NATO
AFS	Advanced Flying School, replaced by the FTSs.
AFWF*	Advanced Fixed Wing Flight, AAC training unit, based at Middle Wallop.
AIU*	Accident Investigation Unit, ground based investigation unit, run by FAA and based at Lee-on-Solent.
ALAT*	Aviation Legere de l'Armee de Terre, French army aviation.
AMARC*	Aerospace Maintenance and Regeneration Centre, new up-market name for the world famous USAF Davis-Monthan AFB 'bone-yard'.
AMS*	Air Movements School, air movements personnel school, based at Brize Norton.
ANG*	Air National Guard, USAF reservist air arm.
ANS	Air Navigation School, flying training unit.
AOTS	Aircrew Officers Training School, continuation training unit.
APS*	Aircraft Preservation Society, standard use suffix.
APS	Armament Practice Station, live firing and bombing facility.
arr	arrived, denotes airframe arrived at location by surface transport.
ARWF	Advanced Rotary Wing Flight, now renamed RCS.
AS	Aggressor Squadron, USAF tactics unit flying from Alconbury, then Bentwaters on F-5Es then F-16Cs. Disbanded in a flush of non-aggression in February 1990.
AS&RU*	Aircraft Salvage and Repair Unit, recovery and transportation unit, based at Abingdon.
ASS	Air Signals School, radio and telegraphy flying training unit.
AST*	Air Service Training, civilian flying and ground school, based Perth.
ASWDU	Air-Sea Warfare Development Unit, based at St Mawgan.
ATA	Air Transport Auxiliary, ferry and communications unit, headquartered at White Waltham.
ATAIU-SEA	Allied Technical Air Intelligence Unit - South East Asia, evaluation unit.
ATC*	Air Training Corps, RAF youth recruitment/training/educational body.
ATDU	Air Torpedo Development Unit, trials unit, based at Gosport.
AuxAF	Auxiliary Air Force, part-time militia air arm.
aw/cn	AWaiting CollectioN, signal from manufacturer to a Service that an aircraft is ready to pick up, either new build, repaired or modified.
AWFCS	All Weather Fighter Combat School, operational training unit.
AWOCU	All Weather Operational Conversion Unit, operational training unit.
AWRE*	Atomic Weapons Research Establishment, based Aldermaston and also at Woomera.
BA	British Airways, mega airline that swallowed BOAC, BEA, British Caledonian et al.
BAAT	British Airways Airtours, tour division of BA.
BAC	British Aircraft Corporation, now British Aerospace plc.
BAe*	British Aerospace, the United Kingdom's national aerospace industry.

BAH	British Airways Helicopters, now British International Helicopters.
BANS	Basic Air Navigation School, aircrew school.
BAOR*	British Army of the Rhine, British Army forces in West Germany.
BAPC*	British Aviation Preservation Council, national council to oversee and promote aircraft preservation.
BATUS*	British Army Training Unit, Suffield, British army cold weather training facility in Canada.
BBMF*	Battle of Britain Memorial Flight, well known airshow attenders, based Coningsby.
BCBS	Bomber Command Bombing School, became SCBS.
BCCF/S	Bomber Command Communications Flight/Squadron, communications unit.
BCDU	Bomber Command Development Unit, trials unit.
BDRF*	Battle Damage Repair Flight, ground school, based at Abingdon.
BDR*	Battle Damage Repair, airframe teaching the art of patching up a shot up aircraft.
BDTF	Bomber Defence Training Flight, air gunner familiarisation and training unit.
BDU	Bomber Development Unit, trials and installations unit.
BEA	British European Airways, now part of BA.
BFTS	Basic Flying Training School, flying school.
BFWF*	Basic Fixed Wing Flight, AAC training unit, based at Middle Wallop.
B&GS	Bombings & Gunnery School (RCAF), flying training unit.
BIH	British Independent Helicopters, ex BAH.
BOAC	British Overseas Airways Corporation, airline, became BA.
BRNC*	Britannia Royal Naval College, ground school, based at Dartmouth - see also FGF.
C(A)	Controller (Aircraft), body that 'owns' trials aircraft, also CS(A) - Controller, Services (Air).
CAA*	Civil Aviation Authority, UK administrative authority.
CAACU	Civilian Anti-Aircraft Co-operation Unit, gunnery facilities unit.
CAFU*	Civil Aviation Flying Unit, calibration and standards unit, now at Stansted.
Cam Flt	Camouflage Flight, flying unit for checking the effectiveness of camouflage.
CATCS	Central Air Traffic Control School, ground and flying unit, based at Shawbury.
CAW	College of Air Warfare, weapons and tactics school, now part of RAFC.
CBE	Central Bombing Establishment, trials unit, based at Marham.
CCAS	Civilian Craft Apprentices School, ground school, became CTTS.
CCF*	Combined Cadet Force, recruitment and education organisation.
CF	Communications Flight, as suffix with other unit, or for an airfield.
CFE	Central Fighter Establishment, trials unit, based West Raynham.
CFS*	Central Flying School, instructor school, headquarters at Scampton with other bases.
CFCCU	Civilian Fighter Control and Co-operation Unit, radar facilities flight.
C&TTS	Communications and Target Towing Squadron, general duties flight.
CGS	Central Gunnery School, gunnery and armament school.
CGS*	Central Gliding School, instructor school, based at Syerston.
CIFAS*	Centre d'Instruction des Forces Aeriennes Strategiques, French conversion unit.
CNCS	Central Navigation and Control School, became CATCS.
CoA*	Certificate (or Permit) of Airworthiness, generally quoted with expiry date.
Cott	Cottesmore, in relation to V-Bomber wings.
CPF	Coastal Patrol Flight, anti-submarine unit, equipped with Hornet Moths and Tiger Moths.
cr	crashed, or other form of accident.
CR	Crash Rescue, training airframe.
CRD	Controller, Research and Development, Government purchasing and research body.
C&RS	Control and Reporting School, procedures school.
CS	Communications Squadron, as a suffix with other units, or for an airfield.
CS(A)*	Controller, Services (Air), Government purchasing body, can also be given as CA.
CSDE*	Central Servicing Development Establishment, trials and administrative body, based at Swanton Morley.
CSE	Central Signals Establishment, electronics and radio trials unit. Also major flying school and fixed-base operator at Oxford Airport.
CSF*	Canberra Servicing Flight, based at Wyton.
CTTS*	Civilian Technical Training School, ground school, based at St Athan.
dbr	damaged beyond repair, to distinguish an aircraft that was written off but did not crash
del	delivered, denotes an airframe that arrived by air.
DFLS	Day Fighter Leader School, tactics and standards unit, based at West Raynham.
ECTT*	Escadre de Chasse Tous Temps, French all weather conversion unit.

EFTS*	Elementary Flying Training School, current example based at Swinderby.
ERS	Empire Radio School, radio and telegraphy flying school.
Esc*	Escadre, French squadron.
ETPS*	Empire Test Pilots School, ground and flight school, now based at Boscombe Down.
ETS*	Engineering Training School, ground school, based at Culdrose.
ETU	Experimental Trials Unit, installations and trials unit.
EWE&TU*	Electronic Warfare Experimental and Training Unit, based at Wyton.
F*	Flight, suffix to four-figure.
FAA*	Fuerza Area Argentina, Argentine Air Force.
FAA*	Fleet Air Arm.
FAAHAF*	Fleet Air Arm Historic Aircraft Flight, well known airshow attenders, based at Yeovilton.
FCCS	Fighter Command Communications Squadron, communications unit.
FC&RS	Fighter Control and Reporting School, procedures school.
FEAF	Far East Air Forces, RAF 'owning' unit for any aircraft in South East Asia.
FECS	Far East Communications Flight, communications unit.
FF&SS*	Fire Fighting and Safety School, ground school, was based at Catterick.
FGF*	Flying Grading Flight, flying school, based at Plymouth Airport.
FLS	Fighter Leader School, an element of DFLS.
FOAC	Flag Officer, Aircraft Carriers, naval officer, with communications aircraft.
FP	Ferry Pool, ferry communications holding unit.
FPP	Ferry Pilots Pool, ferry communications unit.
FRADU*	Fleet Requirements and Development Unit, gunnery and facilities unit, based Yeovilton.
FRL*	Flight Refuelling Ltd, fleet operating and trials company.
FRS	Flying Refresher School, flying standards unit.
FRU	Fleet Requirements Unit, became FRADU.
FSS	Ferry Support Squadron, communications unit.
FSS	Flying Selection Squadron, became EFTS.
FTC	Flying Training Command.
FTS*	Flying Training School, basic or advanced flying school.
FTU	Ferry Training Unit, flying school.
FU	Ferry Unit, communications and ferry unit.
FWS	Fighter Weapons School, armament school.
GE*	Groupement Ecole, French Air Force training unit.
GCF	Group Communications Flight, communications unit.
GTS	Glider Training School, flying school.
GS	Glider School, flying training school.
GSU	Ground Support Unit, army co-operation unit.
GU	Glider Unit, holding both assault gliders and aircraft.
GWDS	Guided Weapons Development Squadron, development unit, based at Valley.
HAB	Hot air balloon.
HCCF/S	Home Command Communications Flight/Squadron, communications unit.
HCEU	Home Command Examining Unit, standards unit.
HCF	Hornet Conversion Flight, type conversion unit.
HDU	Helicopter Development Unit, experimental and trials unit.
HQ	Headquarters.
HS	Handling Squadron, unit tasked with writing pilots' notes for a type.
HTF	Helicopter Training Flight, training unit, based at Middle Wallop.
IAM*	Institute of Aviation Medicine, research unit, based at Farnborough.
IWM	Imperial War Museum, based at South Lambeth and Duxford.
JATE*	Joint Air Transport Establishment, trials unit, based at Brize Norton.
JEHU	Joint Experimental Helicopter Unit, trials unit.
JMU	Joint Maritime Unit, experimental and trials unit.
JASS	Joint Anti-Submarine School, inter-service school.
JCU	Javelin Conversion Unit, type conversion school.
JWE	Joint Warfare Establishment, trials unit, based at Old Sarum.
LAS	Light Aircraft School, flying school using Austers etc.
LTF	Lightning Training Flight, conversion unit.
MCS	Metropolitan Communications Squadron, communications unit.
MEAF	Middle East Air Force, often used in an aircraft's history to denote transfer to that theatre, when specific units are not known.

MECS	Middle East Communications Squadron, communications unit.
MinTech	Ministry of Technology, government operating/research unit, more often than not denoting an aircraft used by RAE or manufacturer.
MoA	Ministry of Aviation, see MinTech entry.
MoS	Ministry of Supply, see MinTech entry.
MOTU	Maritime Operational Training Unit, training unit, flying Shackletons, based St Mawgan.
MPA	Man powered aircraft.
MU*	Maintenance Unit, overhaul, repair and storage facility. The following are mentioned in the main text : 4 Stanmore Park (detachment); 5 Kemble; 6 Brize Norton, 7 Quedgeley; 8 Little Rissington; 9 Cosford; 10 Hullavington; 12 Kirkbride; 14 Carlisle; 15 Wroughton; 16 Stafford; 19 St Athan (also 32); 20 Aston Down; 22 Silloth; 23 Aldergrove; 27 Shawbury; 29 High Ercall; 32 St Athan (also 19); 39 Colerne; 44 Edzell; 46 Lossiemouth; 47 Sealand; 48 Hawarden; 54 Cambridge; 57 Wig Bay; 60 Leconfield; 71 Bicester; 431 Bruggen.
NACDS*	Naval Air Command Driving School, ground school, based at Culdrose.
NASU*	Naval Aircraft Servicing Unit, maintenance and repair units, at Culdrose and Yeovilton.
nea	Non effective airframe, downgrading of an aircraft to non-flying status for long term store.
NCS	Northern Communications Squadron, communications unit, based at Topcliffe.
NIBF	Northern Ireland Beaver Flight, surveillance unit, based at Aldergrove.
NSF	Northern Sector Flight, general duties unit.
OCU*	Operational Conversion Unit, type conversion unit.
OCTU	Officer Cadet Training Unit, experience school, based at Henlow and Jurby.
OTU	Operational Training Unit, front line training unit.
(P)AFU	(Pilot) Advanced Flying Unit, flying school.
PAX	Passenger, as used in Chipmunk PAX trainer, familiarisation trainer.
PCSS	Protectorate Communications and Support Squadron, general duties flight, based Aden.
PEE*	Projectiles Experimental Establishment, research and trials facility, at Foulness Island and out-station at Pendine.
PFS	Primary Flying School, flying training unit.
PP	Pilots' Pool, communications and ferry unit.
PRDU	Photo Reconnaissance Development Unit, development and trials unit.
PTF	Phantom Training Flight, conversion unit, based at Leuchars.
PTS	Primary Training School, flying training unit.
RAAF*	Royal Australian Air Force.
RAE*	Royal Aerospace Establishment (previously Royal Aircraft Establishment), research and development facility, bases at Aberporth, Bedford, Farnborough, Lasham, Llanbedr, West Freugh.
RAeS	Royal Aeronautical Society.
RAF	Royal Air Force.
RAFA*	Royal Air Force Association, benevolent association.
RAFC*	Royal Air Force College, graduate school, based at Cranwell.
RAFEF*	Royal Air Force Exhibition Flight, recruitment display unit, based at Abingdon.
RAFG*	Royal Air Force Germany.
RAFGSA*	Royal Air Force Gliding and Soaring Association, regional gliding clubs.
RAFHSF	Royal Air Force High Speed Flight, record breaking and trials unit.
RAN*	Royal Australian Navy.
RCAF	Royal Canadian Air Force, now Canadian Armed Forces.
RCS*	Rotary Conversion Squadron, Army Air Corps helicopter school, based at Middle Wallop.
Regt	Regiment, Army unit, using Austers and/or helicopters.
RNAY*	Royal Naval Aircraft Yard, naval equivalent of an MU, at Fleetlands and Wroughton.
RNEC*	Royal Naval Engineering College, ground school, based Manadon.
ROC*	Royal Observer Corps, part time observation and monitoring organisation.
RPRE*	Rocket Propulsion Research Establishment, based at Spadeadam and Westcott.
RRE	Royal Radar Establishment, experimental and trials unit, became RSRE.
RRF	Radar Reconnaissance Flight, trials unit.
RS	Radio School, ground and flying school.
RSRE	Radar and Signals Research Establishment, was based at Pershore, absorbed by RAE.
RTR*	Royal Tank Regiment, Auster and helicopters operator.
SAAF*	South African Air Force.
SAC	School of Army Co-operation, flying school, based at Old Sarum.

SAF   School of Aerial Fighting, flying school.
SAH*   School of Aircraft Handling, ground school, based at Culdrose.
SAR*   Search and Rescue.
SAREW*   Search and Rescue Engineering Wing, maintenance unit, based at Finningley.
SARTS*   Search and Rescue Training Squadron, flying school, based at Valley.
Scamp   Scampton, to distinguish a V-Bomber wing.
SCBS   Strike Command Bombing School, became part of the 230 OCU and then disbanded.
SCS   Southern Communications Squadron, communications unit.
SER   Static External Replica, outwardly a replica of the aircraft in question, but using non-
           original construction techniques.
SF*   Station Flight, general duties and communications unit, usual prefixed by an airfield name.
ShF*   Ship's Flight, ship with aircraft detached, usually prefixed with a ship's name.
SFTS   Service Flying Training School, basic flying school.
SLAW   School of Land/Air Warfare, tactics and flying school.
soc   Struck off charge, removed from service inventory, written off.
SoRF   School of Refresher Training, standards unit, absorbed into 3 FTS at Leeming.
SoTT*   School of Technical Training, ground school. The following are mentioned in the main text :
           1 Halton (current); 2 Cosford (current); 4 St Athan (current?); 8 Weeton; 9 Newton; 10
           Kirkham; 12 Melksham.
SRCU   Short Range Conversion Unit, conversion unit, flying Pioneers from Odiham.
SS   Signals Squadron, radio and electronics unit.
SS   Support Squadron, general duties and communications flight.
SU   Support Unit, general duties flight.
TAC   The Aeroplane Collection, based in Manchester.
TAF   Tactical Air Force, NATO component force in Europe.
TAW*   Tactical Airlift Wing, USAF transport unit.
TCCF   Transport Command Communications Flight, communications unit.
TEU   Tactical Exercise Unit, training and co-operation unit.
TFF   Target Facilities Flight, target interception training facility.
TFTAS   Tactical Fighter Training Aggressor Squadron, USAF tactics and training unit, 527th based at
           Alconbury. Later became 527th AS - qv.
TFW*   Tactical Fighter Wing, USAF fighter unit.
Thum Flt   Temperature and HUMidity Flight, weather monitoring flight, based Woodvale.
toc   Taken on charge, date aircraft accepted into service.
TRE   Telecommunications Research Establishment, based at Defford.
TS   Training Squadron, training unit.
TTCCF   Technical Training Command Communications Flight, communications unit.
TWU*   Tactical Weapons Unit, weapons and tactics school, 1 TWU at Brawdy, 2 TWU at Chivenor.
UAS*   University Air Squadron, reservist flying training school. Prefixed with a university name,
           with the following abbreviations : Abn - Aberdeen, Dundee & St Andrews; Bir - Birmingham;
           Bri - Bristol; Cam - Cambridge; Dur - Durham; Edn - Edinburgh; Elo - East Lowlands; Ems -
           East Midlands; G&S - Glasgow & Strathclyde; Lee - Leeds; Liv - Liverpool; Lon - London; Man
           - Manchester & Salford; Nor - Northumbrian; Not - Nottingham; Oxf - Oxford; QUB - Queens
           University Belfast; Stn - Southampton; Wal - Wales; Yor - Yorkshire.
UNFICYP*   United Nations Forces In Cyprus, international peace-keeping force.
USAF*   United States Air Force.
USAAF   United States Army Air Force, became USAF in 1948.
USMC*   United States Marine Corps.
USN*   United States Navy.
Wadd   Waddington, denoting a V-Bomber wing.
WCS   Western Communications Squadron, communications unit.
Witt   Wittering, denoting a V-bomber wing.
WLT*   Weapons Loading Trainer, ground instructional airframe.
WSF   Western Sector Flight, general duties unit.

TYPE INDEX

LOCATIONS INDEX

Other Books from Midland Counties

EUROPEAN WRECKS AND RELICS
by Mike Bursell. For twenty-five years the ever popular 'Wrecks and Relics' has reviewed preserved, instructional and derelict aircraft in the UK and Eire and has become an eagerly awaited 'bible' for enthusiasts. Now the European companion is available, covering Cyprus to Iceland (though excluding Eastern Europe at least for this first edition); nineteen countries are included - not only the current scene in each, but augmented by historical notes covering what has been happening over the last few years, and some aircraft alas now lost forever. The diversity of types and range of locations are full of surprises, and the book contains a great deal of fresh information from the author's correspondents. So not only will this be a well-thumbed reference, it's an absorbing read in its own right. A5 laminated full colour cover hardback, 368 pages, 192 black and white photographs. **£14.95.**

BLACKBURN BEVERLEY
by Bill Overton. This medium-range transport gave sterling service to the Royal Air Force from the mid-50s to the late 60s, with 30, 47 and 53 Squadrons in Transport Command, 84 Squadron in the Middle East and 34 Squadron in the Far East. Its huge capacity and remarkable ability to operate from short and rough fields proved invaluable in so many tasks such as supply flights to British forces in the Yemen, in the Kuwait crisis and in relief work in Kenya. The author is a ex Bev crew member. Well covered are 242 OCU, the Army's extensive involvement, the Brough planemakers and the RAF groundcrews. Individual aircraft histories are included. 186 b/w photos, 9 line illustrations, 12 maps. Hardback 11"x 8" with full colour cover featuring a specially commissioned painting by Keith Woodcock. 160 pages. To quote from *RAF News* 'If there were an annual prize for aircraft histories - their cover, text, illustrations and style of production - then this account . . . . would surely win it for 1990'. And from *Aviation World* 'This is probably one of the best aviation books I have ever read . . . . without doubt the definitive work on the Beverley'. **£17.95.**

LOCKHEED F-117 STEALTH FIGHTER
This 'Aerofax Extra' photo essay is the first book to present detailed and clear photography of what for some years has been a closely veiled secret program and the subject of much speculation - The *Stealth* fighter. The timing is purposefully close on the heels of the Department of Defense's long-delayed decision to release, within the constraints of security as much information as possible on the F-117 and its mission objectives. 85 photographs, including four pages in colour; a 25,000 word narrative tracing the history of the aircraft and technical details concerning construction and systems, radar, principles of operation, weapon options, colour schemes and markings; an accurate 1/100 scale three-view drawing, and provisional drawings of the Lockheed *Have Blue* XST prototype. Softback 8½"x 11" 40 pages. Available now **£6.95**

WARBIRDS WORLDWIDE DIRECTORY
From the 'Warbirds Worldwide' stable comes a comprehensive listing of all known warbirds throughout the world, including those which are no longer active, have been involved in accidents, destroyed or have simply vanished. An indispensible reference listing several thousand aircraft - pistons and jets - of over forty types, each with an introductory narrative. Well illustrated including 16 pages of colour. A5 softback, 320 pages. **£12.95.**

WARBIRDS WORLDWIDE SPECIAL - THE B-17
Following the success of earlier WW Specials on the Mustang and Jets, a treat for big bomber fans. Features include - Flying the B-17 by Jeff Ethell; Black Jack's Last Mission by Steve Birdsall; Baby Comes Home - story of the donation of a B-17 to the USAFM at Wright-Patterson and its restoration; Memphis Belle - illustrated story of the recent filming, and then the story of the return flight to the USA of David Tallichet's B-17; Sentimental Journey - restoration and operation of the Confederate AF B-17, and IGN B-17s. Softback A4 48 pages incl colour photos. **£4.50.**

Aviation & Military Books by Post

We stock many thousands of books from all over the world for world-wide mail order. Our quick turn-round and superb packing is unrivalled. Free informative and illustrated catalogue on request - write or 'phone —

Midland Counties Publications
24 The Hollow
Earl Shilton
Leicester
LE9 7NA

Telephone: 0455 - 847091/847256